WAR

American soldier in Vietnam; © Al Rockoff

WAR

by Gwynne Dyer

CROWN PUBLISHERS, INC.
NEW YORK

Published by Crown Publishers, Inc., One Park Avenue, New York, New York 10016

CROWN is a trademark of Crown Publishers, Inc.

Manufactured in the United States of America

Library of Congress Cataloging in Publication Data
Dyer, Gwynne.
    War—past, present, and future.
    Based on the PBS television series.
    1. War. I. Title.
U21.2.D93   1985   355'.02   85-5704
ISBN 0-517-55615-4

10 9 8 7 6 5 4 3 2 1

First Edition

Many of the quotes within the book which are unfootnoted are from personal interviews with the author. Portions of this work are reprinted from: *Men Against Fire* by S. L. A. Marshall whose collection is now with the University of Texas at El Paso's S. L. A. Marshall Military History Collection; *Wizards of Armageddon* by Fred Kaplan by permission of Simon & Schuster, © 1983 by Simon & Schuster; *Counsels of War* by Gregg Herken by permission of Knopf, © 1985 by Knopf; *Iliad* by Homer by permission of the University of Chicago Press; © 1951 by the University of Chicago Press; and *History of the Peloponnesian War* by Thucydides by permission of Penquin, © 1954 by Penquin.

Typeset in 10 point ITC Bookman by Walker Graphics, San Francisco.

Credits

Photo Research and Captions: Holly Dressel

Consulting Editor: Michael Bryans
Production Editors: Jack Jennings and Andrea Connolly, BMR,
    San Francisco
Book Design and Photo Layout: David Crossman, BMR,
    San Francisco
Cartography: QR, Inc., San Francisco
Copyeditor: Mary Roach

to the Old Firm

Contents

Acknowledgments

This book grew out of the making of a television series, which is not generally thought to be the most hospitable environment for ideas. Nor is it, I suppose, but they flourished nevertheless. Some of them were mine, but many were not.

Two people should have their names on this book as co-authors, because so much of it comes from them: Michael Bryans and Tina Viljoen. From the very beginning (the series was originally Michael's idea) to the end (Michael and Tina were the only people who read and criticized each chapter of the book as I churned it out), their share in what is here is as great as mine. (They also made two fine films.) Tradition requires that I take personal blame for the errors, omissions and bad bits in this book—which is only fair, since my name is on the cover—but our collaboration was so close that even this is only a formality.

For most of a decade before I became involved in the *War* film series I had worked entirely alone as a free-lance journalist, and I had forgotten—or maybe never knew—just how much could be accomplished by a group of talented and intelligent people working on the same subject every day (and many nights) for a couple of years. It was chaotic much of the time, and sometimes downright paranoid, but what emerged at the end was a perspective that none of us had when we started.

Obviously I can't mention all the people on such a large production who had some influence on the shaping of that perspective, but these people had a particularly large share: Donna Dudinsky, who knew that there should be a seventh film when nobody else did; Hannele Halm, who finally made sense of a film that was in danger of becoming a history lecture, and gave good counsel in a crazy time; Paul Cowan, who shot two superb documentary films that made emotional sense of intellectual propositions; Doug Kiefer, who nearly bit my head off a couple of times (but then he had a lot to put up with); Judith Merritt, who was in the worst trenches for a long time, but never gave up; and Barbara Sears, who certainly had a major effect on the series.

Many of the people who worked on location also had a significant influence on the thought and the tone of the series: especially Hans Oomes, Bev Davidson, Mike Mahoney, Kent Nason and Liudmila Peresvetova. Paul Wright of the CBC was the most intelligent, patient and kind network producer anybody ever had. Above all there was Barry Howells, the executive producer of the series, without whose insight and courage we would never have made it.

This is all about the people who worked on the series, not the book, but that is as it should be: the book is mostly what we thought, expressed in a rather large number of words. I am very fortunate to have such people as friends.

As for the book more narrowly defined, almost all the quotes in the text, if no other reference is given, are taken from personal interviews, mostly conducted while filming the *War* series. I must make a special acknowledgment of the great use I have made of the recent and excellent books by Gregg Herken and Fred Kaplan in writing the tenth chapter. I owe a large debt of gratitude to Ian Cowman, who did excellent research work (and to my sons Evan and Owen, who also did good research when they were free); to Holly Dressel, who not only did a fine job with the illustrations but also with the research; to Jack Jennings, Andrea Connolly and David Crossman at BMR and Jim Wade at Crown, who coped superbly and (mostly) uncomplainingly with the delays that I wasn't well organized enough to avoid; to Knox Burger, my agent, who isn't speaking to me at the moment for the same reason; and of course to the Glenmorangie whisky distillery, various cigarette manufacturers and CHOM-FM, without whose moral support I would probably have given up during the final lunatic drive to get this thing finished.

London, New York and Montreal, 1984–85.

Introduction

To begin quite close to the end: we may inhabit the Indian summer of human history, with nothing to look forward to but the "nuclear winter" that closes the account. The war for which the great powers hold themselves in readiness every day may come, as hundreds of others have in the past. The megatons will fall, the dust will rise, the sun's light will fail, and the race may perish.

Nothing is inevitable until it has actually happened, but the final war is undeniably a possibility, and there is one statistical certainty. Any event that has a definite probability, however small, that does not decrease with time will eventually occur—next year, next decade, next century, but it will come. Including nuclear war.

It is therefore the dilemma and the duty of our generation, and as many more as have time to be born, to learn how to make the probability of nuclear war shrink and eventually vanish. Since the scientific and organizational abilities that have swollen war to this monstrous scale cannot be forgotten, the task is even larger: to discover how to dispense with war altogether. The starting point must be to see the institution of war as a whole and to understand how it works.

Wars are not an interminable series of historical accidents, nor the product of the machinations of evil men, nor yet the result of some simple single cause like capitalism or overpopulation. Neither is warfare merely the heritage of our evolutionary past, an outlet for our "natural aggressiveness." War is a central institution in human civilization, and it has a history precisely as long as civilization.

For most of that history, war has been a more or less functional institution, providing benefits for those societies that were good at it, although the cost in money, in lives, and in suffering has always been great. In recent centuries it has begun to trouble our consciences occasionally, since the essence of war is killing other people in order to force the community they represent to do our bidding. But most people all down through history have accepted killing in war as legitimate, partly because it is hallowed by tradition, but also because those who do the killing are themselves willing to sacrifice their lives. There is a heightened humanity, both good and bad, about the way soldiers behave in battle which seems to transcend ordinary morality and place them in a special category.

Only in this century have large numbers of people begun to question the basic assumptions of civilized societies about the usefulness and inevitability of war, as two mutually reinforcing trends have gained strength. One is moral: for all the atrocities we still practice on each other, the people of the twentieth century are nevertheless more able than their ancestors to imagine that war—that is, killing foreigners for political reasons—may be simply wrong. The same great changes in society that have made war so lethal have also enabled us to see broader categories of people—even those on the far side of the nuclear palisade—as being essentially human beings like ourselves. And even if morality is no more than the rules we have made up for ourselves as we go along, one of those rules has always been that killing people is wrong.

The other factor is severely practical: we will almost all die, and our civilization with us, if we continue to practice war. A civilization confronted with the prospect of a "nuclear winter" does not need moral incentives to reconsider the value of the institution of war; it must change or perish.

This does not mean, of course, that we will change or that we will survive. The universe does not issue guarantees. But the time is certainly ripe for change, and change is certainly possible, so long as we understand the nature of the institution we are trying to change and are willing to accept the consequences of changing it.

1: The Roots of War

You know, I turn back to your ancient prophets in the Old Testament and the signs foretelling Armageddon, and I find myself wondering if—if we're the generation that's going to see that come about. . . . There have been times in the past when we thought the world was coming to an end, but never anything like this.
—Ronald Reagan[1]

There is reason to believe that those who organised this provocation deliberately desired a further aggravation of the international situation by striving to smear the Soviet Union, sow hostility towards it, and cast aspersions on Soviet peace-loving policies.
—TASS (Soviet news agency)[2]

The game goes on as if we had all the time in the world, even though we know perfectly well that time has run out. A Korean airliner on a flight from New York to Seoul strays over Soviet territory in northeastern Asia (or is deliberately diverted there by Western intelligence services to gather electronic information). A Soviet fighter shoots it down in accordance with squadron standing orders (or as the result of a deliberate political decision in Moscow). Two hundred sixty-nine people drown in the icy waters of the Sea of Okhotsk, and the great powers ritually accuse each other of being the enemies of all mankind.

It was a minor incident—no more important than the assassination of the Archduke Franz Ferdinand of Austria in the obscure Bosnian town of Sarajevo in July 1914—and in the end nothing much came of it. Some of the passengers' belongings were washed up on the beaches of Japan; the Soviet and the U.S. navies spent a few futile weeks grappling for the "black box" flight recorder which would determine whether the airliner was on a spy mission, and the world moved on.

Every year or so brings some incident like this between the superpowers and dozens of similar armed brushes between the multitude of other powers, great and little, that clutter the world. Not many of them end in war, for most states are ruled by people who realize more or less clearly that modern wars almost always cost more than is justified by the stakes they are fought for; few countries will fight at the drop of a hat. And no clash between great powers has ended in war since the introduction of nuclear weapons (only once, in Cuba in 1962, have they even come close), because their leaders are utterly terrified of what nuclear war would mean.

Yet the enormous inertia of modern states makes it very hard for them to stop or change direction quickly if they find themselves on a collision course, and every year one or two wars break out somewhere in the world. None of these wars has yet involved the nuclear powers in a direct confrontation, because they behave with even more caution than the others. But all that means is that you have to drop more hats (or the right hat) before they will fight. If governments really believed that nuclear war was impossible, they would not devote huge sums of money each year to perfecting new nuclear delivery systems that go beyond simple deterrence to a "nuclear war fighting capability," and new defenses against them. If you really think you are immortal, you do not buy life insurance.

We know, as surely as we know that we are alive, that the whole human race is dancing on the edge of the grave. Yet most of us believe in our hearts that it can never really happen—just as we do not really believe we are going to die. We use the soothing, anesthetic formulas of deterrence theory to smother our doubts. We hold these mutually opposed beliefs in separate compartments of our minds and only rarely look in the compartment containing the darker conclusions, because to act on them would be too difficult and too painful.

I can't understand war in the first place. In fact, it makes me want to cry, because you know when the thing with Iran happened and everybody said we should just go bomb 'em, they didn't understand that those people, even though they were Iranians, had little two-year-olds just like we do. And I thought if somebody did that to us, it's just such a horrible waste, you know, and I don't really like the idea that that's what Scott would have to do.

But I know that he would only have to do it if it became necessary and something that we loved was threatened. But I try not . . . really, honestly, I try not to think about that because it's not a pleasant thought.

Rhonda Martin, wife of a B-52 bomber pilot

It is not a pleasant thought, but it cannot be ignored: the game of war is up, and we are going to have to change the rules if we are to survive. During the last two years of World War II, over one million people were being killed *each month*. If the great powers go to war with each other just once more, using all the weapons they now have, a million people will be killed each minute. Technology has invalidated all our assumptions about the way we run our world.

Yet the easiest and worst mistake we could make would be to blame our present dilemma on the mere technology of war. Napalm, nerve gas, and nuclear weapons were not dropped into our laps by some malevolent god; we put a great deal of effort into inventing and producing them because we intended to fight wars with them. It is our attitudes toward war and our uses for it that really demand our attention.

Those are the things that have remained unchanged, that provide the permanent framework within which our present technology, organization, and resources have inflated war to the point where it threatens to destroy us all. War is an institution as old, as complicated, and as pervasive as religion or property, and to understand why the unchanging things about it have not changed—why every state in the world constantly prepares for war, no matter what its propaganda says—we have to go back to the beginning of civilization.

A lot of people know that seventy thousand died at Hiroshima, but few people know that two hundred twenty-five thousand died in Tokyo, as a result of only two raids with conventional bombs. I was a bomber pilot a long time ago. I bombed Hamburg. Seventy thousand people died there when the air caught fire. Eighty thousand or so died at Dresden. And if you want to talk about numbers, one hundred twenty-three thousand died at Iwo Jima—and they died in Lebanon, as you know, very recently. And so the problem is war, not nuclear war. —Man in the street in Washington, D.C.

The essential soldier remains the same. Whether he was handling a sling-shot weapon on Hadrian's Wall or whether he's in a main battle tank today, he is essentially the same. —Gen. Sir John Hackett

The soldier was one of the first inventions of civilization, and he has changed remarkably little over the ten thousand years or so that armies have existed. The teenage Iranian volunteers stumbling across minefields east of Basra in 1984 or the doomed British battalions going over the top in the July Drive on the Somme in 1916 were taking part in the same act of sacrifice and slaughter that destroyed the young men of Rome at Cannae in 216 B.C.; the emotions, the odds, and the outcome were fundamentally the same. Battle, the central act of warfare, is a unique event in which ordinary men willingly kill and die as though those extraordinary actions were normal and acceptable, and changing weapons and tactics have not altered those essential elements of its character.

However, the *consequences* of war can and do change. In our time, the likely consequences of war have grown drastically and irreversibly, so that they potentially include the destruction of the entire human habitat: war and civilization, which were born as Siamese twins, may also end together. But the drastic change in the scale of war in our time has been caused by the application of modern science, industry, and organizational skills to an ancient institution that still obeys its ancient rules.

Moreover, war has always had an innate tendency to expand to the absolute limit of the resources available to the societies waging it, and sometimes far beyond their capacity to accept punishment. Force is the ultimate argument, and once it has been invoked, the only effective reply is superior force; the internal logic of war has frequently caused it to grow far bigger in scale than the importance of the issue originally in dispute would justify. World War I is a striking example; the third world war will be even more convincing, if there is anyone left to convince.

Yet modern soldiers do not behave any more ruthlessly than their ancestors. The residents of Dresden and Hiroshima in 1945 suffered no worse fate than the citizens of Babylon in 680 B.C., when the city fell to Sennacherib of Assyria, who boasted: "I levelled the city and its houses from the foundations to the top, I destroyed them and consumed them with fire. I tore down and removed the outer and inner walls, the temples and the ziggurats built of brick, and dumped the rubble in the Arahtu canal. And after I had destroyed Babylon, smashed its gods and massacred its population, I tore up its soil and threw it into the Euphrates so that it was carried by the river down to the sea."[3] It was a more labor-intensive method of destruction than nuclear weapons, but the effect (at least for an individual city) was about the same.

Most of the major cities of antiquity sooner or later met a fate similar to Babylon's—some of them many times, over the centuries—when the fortunes of war eventually left them exposed to their enemies. The difference between the destruction ancient military commanders wrought in war and what the commanders of today's strategic nuclear forces could do in war is determined mainly by their respective technologies and resources, not by a different mentality. And that "military mentality," despite the idealism and sentimentality in which it has traditionally indulged to soften the realities of the trade, has always had a cold and steady awareness at the professional level that the key to military success is efficient killing. Today it's better cluster bombs or heat-seeking missiles, but the search for efficiency was the same when the only means of introducing lethal bits of metal into an enemy's body was by muscle-power. The following, for example, are instructions on the use of the sword in a Roman army training manual:

> A slash cut rarely kills, however powerfully delivered, because the vitals are protected by the enemy's weapons, and also by his bones. A thrust going in two inches, however, can be mortal. You must penetrate the vitals to kill a man. Moreover, when a man is slashing, the right arm and side are left exposed. When thrusting, however, the body is covered, and the enemy is wounded before he realises what has happened. So this method of fighting is especially favoured by the Romans.[4]

But if the willingness of soldiers to kill and the tendency of war to become as destructive as the existing technology and resources will permit have both been relatively constant throughout human history, then we must consider an unwelcome possibility: that war is the inevitable accompaniment of *any* human civilization, and that a technologically advanced culture like our own will sooner or later become involved in a war in which all the available technology and resources are committed to the task of destruction. There is a daunting amount of evidence to support this belief, but there is also a fundamentally important fact that offers some kind of hope. War is part of our history, but it is not in at all the same sense part of our prehistory. It is one of the innovations that occurred between nine and eleven thousand years ago when the first civilized societies were coming into being. What has been invented can be changed; war is not in our genes.

> Walbiri society did not emphasise militarism—there was no class of permanent or professional warriors; there was no hierarchy of military command; and groups rarely engaged in wars of conquest. . . . There was in

any case little reason for all-out warfare between communities. Slavery was unknown; portable goods were few; and the territory seized in a battle was virtually an embarrassment to the victors, whose spiritual ties were with other localities.[5]

Only a generation ago the Walbiri aborigines of Australia still lived in small bands in a hunting-and-gathering economy, as the entire human race did for at least 98 percent of its history, and although every male Walbiri was a warrior, their way of fighting did not resemble what we call "war." Very few people got killed; there were no leaders, no strategy, and no tactics; and only the kinship group affected by the issue at stake—most often revenge for a killing or a ritual offense committed by another group, and hardly ever territory—would take part in the fighting.

We cannot directly examine the primitive societies from which the first civilizations arose (for they disappeared in the process), but hundreds of Old Stone Age societies have survived into the recent past or present in the Western Hemisphere and Oceania, in most parts of which "civilization" arrived with the Europeans over the past few hundred years. There is no reason to believe that these modern examples of hunting-and-gathering cultures are significantly different from those that inhabited the Middle East ten or fifteen thousand years ago, and almost all of them have the same attitude toward "war": it is an important ritual, an exciting and dangerous game, and perhaps even an opportunity for self-expression, but it is not about power in any recognizable modern sense of the word, and it most certainly is not about slaughter.

It is no surprise that a race that lived largely by hunting and that knew effective techniques for killing animals would have the same techniques available for killing its own members. Since conflict is inevitable, it is also not surprising that people sometimes kill people. Some moralists suggest that this is the human race's original sin, pointing out that few other higher species deliberately kill their own members, but the reason for our relative distinction in this area seems to be simply that man is an evolutionary latecomer to killing, sprung from a long line of nonpredators. That means the weapons our ancestors learned to use in hunting over the past few million years were not accompanied by the inhibitions against using them on our own species that hereditary predators generally have. No doubt this lack could prove to be the fatal flaw in human nature, but the important point about precivilized societies is that people did not kill people *much.*

The dominant trend in the history (and prehistory) of human culture has been the creation of larger and larger groups within which each member is defined as "one of us": a kinsman, a fellow tribesman, a fellow citizen. Ten thousand years ago the average human being's social horizon was the fifty to two hundred members of his own band of hunter-gatherers, all of whom knew each other personally; there are ten states in the world today in which over one hundred million people are considered "one of us." The advantages of living in societies where large numbers of people can cooperate with each other in innumerable ways and contribute all their individual and collective achievements to an ever-growing pool of wealth and knowledge are beyond dispute; we owe almost everything we have of value to this accumulated heritage. But there is also a dark side to living in large groups.

Within each group, it has meant the creation of impersonal and often harsh controls to enforce cooperation and to keep the social peace. Most of the large-scale societies of history (and of the present) are to a greater or lesser extent tyrannies. And as the societies we live in have grown larger, so have the conflicts between them; indeed they have changed radically and have become the modern phenomenon of war. The logical end point of living in ever larger groups is the evolution of a politically united world society in which every human being is regarded as "one of us," but the penultimate stage in which we live, with the world divided into about three dozen powerful states and over a hundred weak ones, is probably the most violent, and certainly the most dangerous, phase of human history.

At the outset, there was little violence against individuals and no danger to humanity. All of humankind lived in small groups that made their living by hunting and gathering, each moving around within a relatively vast territory and having little contact with any other band. The Bushman population of South Africa before the arrival of the blacks and the whites, for example, is estimated to have been ten or twenty thousand people living in one or two hundred bands, occupying a territory of some 350,000 square miles—around two or three thousand square miles per band.

Within each Bushman band, which was made up of a dozen or so related families, there was no center of authority and little specialization of role beyond the fact that the men hunted and the women gathered plant food and cared for the children. There was some cooperation between hunters in larger projects, like building fences to trap game, but each family was mainly dependent on its own efforts for food. The extreme isolation of each band is shown by the great diversity in the Bushman languages; in some cases even neighboring bands were unable to understand each other.[6]

Since every family was essentially autonomous, there was little cause for violent conflict between members of the same band. Each band had a strong sense of its own territory and reacted strongly to infringements of its boundaries, but the fact that the Bushman's principal weapon was the poisoned arrow, slow-acting but inevitably fatal, imposed great restraint even on clashes between different bands.

Within Bushman bands to this day, everything possible is done to defuse situations that could lead to clashes between individuals in which poisoned arrows might eventually be exchanged. If it reaches this stage, both belligerents are likely to die in lingering agony. . . . In their relations with other bands . . . the poisoned arrow was the Stone Age equivalent of a nuclear deterrent. . . . The slow action of the poison left a stricken adversary ample time in which to avenge the suffering that lay ahead of him.[7]

There was some violence, but no such thing as war in the Bushman's world before more complex cultures arrived in South Africa, and the same was true of other hunter-gatherers living in societies essentially confined to a single band. They were rarely capable of imagining a degree of coordination that would make it possible to conquer another band and hold its territory, nor indeed would there have been much point. Other bands had few material possessions worth seizing, slaves were practically valueless in that sort of subsistence economy (where they could do little more than feed themselves), and additional territory was generally of only marginal use to migratory hunters. But there must have been enough population pressure on food resources, here and there in the distant past, to drive some bands of hunter-gatherers into serious conflict, for even the first increase in the scale of human groups was almost certainly driven by military considerations.

There is no way we can ever know when the first bands linked together into tribes incorporating some thousands of individuals, for it involved no change in the economic basis of society that would have left physical evidence behind. It must have been at least ten thousand years ago, for the tribe is a necessary intermediate step between the tiny hunting band and the first civilized states, but it could have been fifty thousand years ago or more in some areas. The essence of the change was that various hunting bands created a broader common identity, mainly by establishing complex ties of kinship among themselves (there was not necessarily any chief or central authority), in order to increase their fighting strength. And the consequence was that the hunters redefined themselves as warriors, whose main source of pride and self-respect came from their prowess in killing not animals, but other men.

Many modern tribal societies own herds of animals or practice primitive agriculture, which gives them some material incentive to raid each other, but all the early tribes were still hunter-gatherers, so the only possible source of serious conflict between them was over scarce hunting grounds. This was probably not a frequent occurrence, but once the new form of social organization had been created, it tended to persist. Its most striking features were the dominance of a warrior class—and the depoliticization of women.

Within the traditional small hunting band, where men and women both provided food and the center of power was the individual family, the effective political power of women was probably not much less than that of men. But in the new tribal societies, where military considerations were paramount and warriors made the important decisions collectively, women were automatically excluded from power, for men could be warriors, and women—at least at that time—could not.

> Because the men fought the wars, it was they who reaffirmed the right to decide between war and peace. Such decisions required high political authority. In a sense, men became politically preeminent because they were militarily preeminent. And they became militarily preeminent because . . . primordial kinship culture . . . gave the club or the spear to the spouse with greater muscular throwing power. . . . Men are above women

in politics because men are warriors and not because men were in some
societies the breadwinners.
—Ali A. Mazrui[8]

It all seems perfectly logical, and there certainly must have been occasions in the past when small bands were genuinely driven to amalgamate into larger tribal societies dominated by the warrior ethic through stark military and economic necessity. (Otherwise, why would they have bothered?) And yet one is left with the sneaking suspicion that this was mainly a vast prehistorical con game, for the fact is that there was still not much to fight about most of the time for the overwhelming majority of tribal societies living in a hunting-and-gathering economy.

Of all the hundreds of societies of this type encountered during the great phase of European maritime expansion into the Stone Age world of the Western Hemisphere, Oceania, and parts of Africa, there is scarely one recorded example of a tribe being locked into a death struggle with its neighbors because of population pressure and economic scarcity. They were almost all continuously involved in low-level warfare against their neighbors in their spare time, but nobody thought "winning" was sufficiently important to put much thought into organizing warfare efficiently; rather, it provided justification for the fact that the warriors ran everything, and gave meaning to their lives.

This sort of tribal warfare is almost always very limited and bound by ritual. "Battles" are often prearranged, but once they begin, they are not much more than the sum of the individual actions of many warriors acting on their own without direction or coordination. The fighting often stops for the day after one side has exacted a death, with the losers mourning their loss and the other side celebrating its victory within sight of each other. There are often deliberate steps taken to ensure that the killing does not get too efficient. There is a New Guinea tribe, for instance, that is well aware that arrows with flights are more accurate and always fits feathers to its hunting arrows—but leaves them off its war arrows.

Similarly, the Piegan and Shoshoni Indians, who engaged in large-scale battles on foot before the use of horses spread to the American plains, used to form lines facing each other that were just barely within arrow range and shoot at their opponents while taking cover behind shields three feet in diameter. Though they also had more lethal weapons—lances and battle-axes—they never closed in to use them unless they had overwhelming numerical superiority.[9]

There are no figures for the number of people this kind of warfare has killed, although down the trackless millennia of our prehistory it must amount to tens of millions. Among the Eskimos, whose prehistory ended in this century, it killed practically nobody, but among more warlike cultures it may have been the eventual cause of death for quite a large proportion of the adult men. But there is still a vital distinction: primitive warfare is not lethal, nor even very destructive, to the societies that indulge in it. Individuals get killed, a few at a time—mostly young males, who are both biologically and economically the most dispensable members of the tribe—but the society survives intact.

Even the most warlike of Old Stone Age people, like the Indians of North America, regarded warfare much more as a ritual activity—part art form, part healthy outdoor exercise—than as a practical instrument for achieving economic and political aims, and therefore it never became the object of human ingenuity seeking to make it more efficient. "The idea of conquest never arose in aboriginal North America, and this made it possible for almost all these Indian tribes to do a very extreme thing: to separate war from the state," wrote anthropologist Ruth Benedict in 1959. But it was not an extreme thing; it was normal and natural in primitive peoples.

> "The state was personified in the Peace Chief . . . but he had nothing to do with war. . . . Any man who could attract a following led a war party when and where he could, and in some tribes he was in complete control for the duration of the expedition. But this lasted only until the return of the war party. The state . . . had no conceivable interest in these ventures, which were only highly desirable demonstrations of rugged individualism."[10]

In fact, the highest honor a warrior could gain among the Indians of the Great Plains was not to kill the enemy, but to "count coup"—to approach the enemy without weapons and touch him with a stick or his hand. The point of intertribal warfare was to give the warriors an opportunity to demonstrate their courage. The most famous and respected Comanche warrior of his time was a man who acquired a blanket made by the Utes, his tribal enemies, and used it to walk in among them unarmed.

> "After dark, he drew his blanket over his head and sauntered into the Ute encampment. From within one of the lodges he heard the songs of a hand game in progress. Protected by his disguise, he walked right through the door to join the spectators. Nobody paid any attention to him. Casually and slowly moving about he touched one after another all the Utes in the lodge. When he had touched them all, he strolled out and rejoined his friend. He had counted coup on twenty enemies at once. It was a great deed."[11]

Though precivilized warfare served various ritual and magical purposes and may have had broader social functions, it was predominantly a rough male sport for underemployed hunters, with the kinds of damage-limiting rules that all competitive sports have. This is borne out by the fact that war tends to bulk larger and get more destructive among the more sophisticated aboriginal peoples, who have moved on to primitive agriculture or herding; the warriors have even more free time, and they are beginning to acquire material interests to defend. Quincy Wright, who studied data from 633 primitive cultures, concluded that "the collectors, lower hunters and lower agriculturalists, are the least warlike. The higher hunters and higher agriculturalists are more warlike, while the highest agriculturalists and the [pastoral peoples] are the most warlike of all."[12]

It seems almost as if we were gradually working up to the kind of war that civilization would bring with it, and perhaps we were. But the gulf between primitive and civilized societies is as vast in warfare as it is in other respects. The essence of the Neolithic revolution was not the discovery, between 9000 and 7000 B.C. in various parts of the Fertile Crescent, that food could be obtained more reliably and in far greater abundance by planting and harvesting crops and taming and breeding animals, nor even the huge increase in population density that these discoveries made possible. It was the insight that human will and organization could exercise control over the natural world—and over large numbers of human beings.

"To exert power in every form was the essence of civilisation; the city found a score of ways of expressing struggle, aggression, domination, conquest—and servitude," wrote Lewis Mumford about the first civilizations of mankind.[13] The roots of human civilization lie in states so absolutist and so awesomely cruel that even the death camps of Nazi Germany would have been regarded as a moral commonplace. Civilization, first and foremost, was the discovery of how to achieve power over both nature and people, and it cannot be denied that it went to our heads: on the one hand, pyramids and irrigation canals; on the other hand, wars of extermination.

That is not to say that civilization is therefore a Bad Thing or that it is necessarily doomed to destroy itself. It is civilization that gives the human experiment its meaning, and it is possible to overcome an unfortunate early upbringing. There was probably never any choice in the matter anyway; it is difficult to imagine any basis for the first civilizations other than the brutal exercise of absolute power. But we do carry our history within us, and ten thousand years later our civilization faces the prospect of an abrupt end because of the enduring institution that was the key invention of the first civilized men: military power.

I am afeard there are few die well that die in battle. —Shakespeare, Henry V

To avoid death he shrank back into the host of his companions; but as he went back Meriones, dogging him, threw the spear and struck between navel and genitals where beyond all places death in battle comes painfully to pitiful mortals. There the spear struck fast driven and he, writhing about it . . . gasped for a little while, but not long, until fighting Meriones came close and wrenched the spear out from his body. —Homer, Iliad

It can never be proved, but it is a safe assumption that the first time five thousand male human beings were ever gathered together in one place, they belonged to an army. That event probably occurred around 7000 B.C.—give or take a thousand years—and it is an equally safe bet that the first truly large-scale slaughter of people in human history happened very soon afterward.

The first army almost certainly carried weapons no different from those that hunters had been using on animals and on each other for thousands of years previously—spears, knives, axes, perhaps bows and arrows. Its strength did not lie in mere numbers; what made it an army was discipline and organization. This multitude of men obeyed a single commander and killed his enemies to achieve his goals. It was the most awesome concentration of power the human world had every seen, and nothing except another army could hope to resist it.

The battle that occurred when two such armies fought has little in common with the clashes of primitive warfare. Thousands of men were crowded together in tight formations that moved on command and marched in step. Drill, practiced over many days and months until it became automatic, is what transformed these men from a mob of individual fighters into an army. (The basic forms of military drill are among the most pervasive and unchanging elements of human civilization. The Twelfth Dynasty Egyptian armies of 1900 B.C. stepped off "by the left," and so has every army down to the present day.)

And when the packed formations of well-drilled men collided on the forgotten battlefields of the earliest kingdoms, what happened was quite impersonal, though every man died his own death. It was not the traditional combat between individual warriors. The soldiers were pressed forward by the ranks behind them against the anonymous strangers in that part of the enemy line facing them, and though in the end it was pairs of individuals who thrust at each other with spears for a few moments before one went down, there was nothing personal in the exchange. "Their shields locked, they pushed, fought, killed and died. There was no shouting, and yet not silence either, but rather such a noise as might be made by the angry clash of armed men."

The result of such a merciless struggle in a confined space is killing on an unprecedented scale. Hundreds or thousands of men would die in half an hour, in an area no bigger than a couple of football fields. "The battle over, one could see on the site of the struggle the ground covered with blood, friend and foe lying dead on one another, shields broken, spears shattered and unsheathed swords, some on the ground, some fixed in corpses, some still held in the hands of the dead. It was now getting late, so they dragged the enemy corpses inside their lines, had a meal and went to rest."[14]

And the question we rarely ask, because our history is replete with such scenes, is, How could men do this? After all, in the tribal cultures from which we all come originally, they could not have done it. Being a warrior and taking part in a ritual "battle" with a small but invigorating element of risk is one thing; the mechanistic and anonymous mass slaughter of civilized warfare is quite another, and any traditional warrior would do the sensible thing and leave instantly. Yet civilized men, from 5000 B.C. or from today, will stay at such scenes of horror even in the knowledge that they will probably die within the next few minutes. The invention of armies required more than just working out ways of drilling large numbers of people to act together, although that was certainly part of the formula. A formation of drilled men has a different psychology—a controlled form of mob psychology—that tends to overpower the personal identity and fears of the individuals who make it up.

> *You're dealing here with complicated psychological states. No man in battle is really sane. The mind set of the soldier on the battlefield is a highly disturbed mind, and this is an epidemic of insanity which affects everybody there, and those not afflicted by it die very quickly.*
>
> William Manchester, World War II veteran

> *People say, well, I could never kill a man. That's bullshit. They can. Anybody can kill. It takes more to make one man kill than it does the next. The training helps a lot; it gets you there. But combat—you know, once they start shooting at you, if you don't shoot back, you're a damned fool.*
>
> U.S. veteran, Vietnam

By the time it has become clear to the individual soldier seeing civilized war for the first time that a battle is no place for a sane man to be, there is often physically no way to leave—and in all armies the penalty for trying to leave is death at the hands of your own side. But even experienced soldiers who know what to expect submit themselves to the ordeal of battle again and again, more or less willingly, because to do otherwise is to disgrace themselves in front of the people whose respect is the foundation of their own self-respect: their fellow soldiers. Men will kill and die rather than lose face, but the face that is being saved, the image that is being preserved, is that of the tribal warrior of the precivilized past, who fought for personal glory and stood a very good chance of surviving the fight.

Aggression is certainly part of our genetic makeup, and necessarily so, but the normal human being's quota of aggression will not even cause him to kill acquaintances, let alone wage war against strangers from a different country. We live among millions of people who have killed fellow human beings with pitiless efficiency—machine-gunning them, using flame throwers on them, dropping explosive bombs on them from twenty thousand feet up—yet we do not fear these people. The overwhelming majority of those who have killed, now or at any time in the past, have done so as soldiers in war, and we recognize that that has practically nothing to do with the kind of personal aggression that would endanger us as their fellow citizens.

We assume that people will kill if they find themselves in a situation where their own survival is threatened, and nobody needs lessons to learn how to die. What is less obvious is that practically anybody can be persuaded and manipulated in such a way that he will more or less voluntarily enter a situation wherein he must kill and perhaps die. Yet if that were not true, battles would be impossible, and civilization would have taken a very different course (if indeed it arose at all).

> *Man, supposing you and I, escaping this battle, would be able to live on forever, ageless, immortal, so neither would I myself go on fighting in the*

foremost nor would I urge you into the fighting where men win glory. But now, seeing that the spirits of death stand close around us in their thousands, no man can turn aside or escape them, let us go on and win glory for ourselves, or yield it to others. —*Sarpedon of the Lykians*[15]

Come on, you sons of bitches! Do you want to live forever?

Gunnery Sgt. Dan Daly, USMC, Belleau Wood, 6 June 1918

Patriotism, religion, the belief that you are defending your home and family, are powerful reasons for men to fight, but mercenary troops with none of those motives to sustain them have often fought to the death too. The most important single factor that makes it possible for civilized men to fight the wars of civilization is that all armies everywhere have always exploited and manipulated the ingrained warrior ethic that is the heritage of every young human male.

It is not that soldiers delude themselves about the possibility of dying in battle or about the terrible things that weapons do to living flesh; on the contrary, they are all too aware of it. Even the earliest surviving accounts of battle dwell in almost obsessive anatomical detail on how death comes to soldiers: "Ideomeneus stabbed Erymas in the mouth with the pitiless bronze, so that the brazen spear smashed its way clean through below the brain in an upward stroke, and the white bones splintered, and the teeth were shaken out with the stroke and both eyes filled up with blood, and gaping he blew a spray of blood through the nostrils and through his mouth, and death in a dark mist closed over him."[16]

Soldiers know about violent death in all its forms, and though they have their preferences among the forms—there was, for example, an irrational but understandable preference in the trenches of World War I for death by bullets rather than by artillery fire, because a close shell explosion would distort and rend the victim's body into scarcely human fragments—nevertheless they accept the chance of death. But what they require in return is the assurance (or the illusion) that their death will not be wasted or unnoticed or meaningless. Yet most soldiers' deaths in civilized warfare are all of those things. The tribe will not mourn the fallen warrior's death or sing songs about his prowess, and the purposes of the war have little to do with his personal life, even in the unlikely event that his death affects its outcome. So to make the bleak realities of civilized war more acceptable to the regimented soldiers of civilization there is a universal conspiracy to pretend that they still dwell in a moral and psychological landscape of a more bearably human scale: that of the distant tribal past.

From the earliest recorded history, the language that civilized armies consistently use to describe their slaughterhouse battles employs the old vocabulary of the primitive warrior. Soldiers are heroes doing deeds of valor, not number fifty-four in the second rank of the fifth cohort. Battles are decided by such deeds of valor, not by numbers or better weapons or sheer chance; every man counts. And of course the victims of these falsehoods generally collaborate in the deceit, even if they are veterans who have seen battle before, because to question them would be to undermine the value of their own courage and professionalism.

It is doubtful that some single cynical genius of the distant past invented this doublethink, whereby the soldier's trade is always described in warrior's terms. More likely it evolved over many generations out of necessity, but it is nevertheless true of the great majority of descriptions of battle from the time of Sargon of Akkad to John Wayne's war movies. Even now the old vocabulary and the old perspective predominate, especially in the military. They have to, or soldiers would not do their jobs. But the reality is different, and always has been.

> *Aramu the Urartian, being struck with fear by the terror of my mighty army . . . withdrew from his city and went up into the mountains of Adduri. Then I went up after him and fought a mighty battle in the mountains. With my army I overthrew 3,400 warriors; like Adad I brought a great raincloud down upon them; with the blood of the enemy I dyed the mountain as if it had been wool, and I captured their camp. Then Aramu, to save his life, fled to an inaccessible mountain. In my mighty strength I trampled on his land like a wild bull, and his cities I reduced to ruins and consumed with fire.* —Shalmaneser III of Assyria, on the campaign against Urartu[17]

When Shalmaneser took Arzashku, the royal capital of Urartu (near Lake Van in eastern Turkey), he impaled the defenders on sharpened stakes and then piled their severed heads against the city's walls. We know this because he boasted of his deed on bronze gates he had erected in the city of Imgur-Enlil, near his capital of Nineveh. The Assyrians had the reputation of being particularly ruthless even in the ancient world, but Shalmaneser's behavior was by no means unusual.

One of the very earliest records of Egypt, dating from around 3200 B.C., shows the Pharaoh Narmer (who may have been the man who united the entire kingdom for the first time) with the headless bodies of slain enemies. The oldest inscription that has survived from Mesopotamia is the Stele of the Vultures, which shows carrion birds fighting over the entrails of soldiers killed in the battle in which Eannatum of Lagash defeated the rival city-state of Umma. War has been the constant companion of civilization, and most of the time it has been waged with savage cruelty toward the defeated—far more remorseless and efficient cruelty than most of the world's "savages" have ever displayed. And the reason for this is contained in the way that civilization was born.

There is practically no direct evidence regarding the political and military structure of the earliest civilizations, when various tribes in the Middle East were first learning how to grow crops and domesticate animals, and when the first villages began to grow into towns. But war must already have been changing into a disciplined business with political and economic purposes that we would understand, for as early at 7000 B.C. there was at least one fortified town: Jericho. The population was probably no more than two thousand, crammed into a space of about ten acres, but Jericho was surrounded by a massive wall twelve feet high and six and a half feet thick, flanked by a circular stone tower and encircled by a deep ditch. The citizens of Jericho felt they had wealth worth defending, and they lived in a world where others would try to take it from them by force and could not be stopped by lesser defenses.

It was in this earliest period, and over the next four thousand years—half of the history of civilization—that armies and states must have evolved into more or less the forms in which we know them today, but we know nothing about the details of the process, for writing had not been invented. By the time written records started about five thousand years ago, the state and the army were already fully formed institutions of great antiquity. Nevertheless, it is possible to deduce how these twin institutions emerged and grew steadily in scale and power until they towered above the mortal men who supported them.

The basis of civilization is agriculture, which transforms the land into a valuable possession requiring protection. In many parts of the ancient Middle East this protection was probably provided at first simply by transforming the tribal warriors into a loosely organized militia. This is already a momentous change. Warfare had become a purposeful activity with serious consequences for the whole community in the case of defeat, and so there was every incentive to apply human ingenuity to improving the organization and tactics of the tribal militia. But in the most fertile lands of all, in the great river valleys of the Nile and Euphrates, organization was needed on a far wider scale.

Both these regions are flood plains where the rivers, left to their own devices, will inundate the land for a few months of the year and leave it relatively parched for the rest. To farm these areas effectively, men must raise levees to keep the river within bounds and then build elaborate networks of irrigation canals and dikes to lead the water into the fields and retain it. Given the unreliability of the flood (seven years out of ten the Nile delivered either too much water or too little), the farmers must also lay up reserves of grain in the good years to share out in the bad. All this requires a central authority able to plan and coordinate the work of large numbers of people over wide areas—and the human race has never been short of people willing to volunteer for the job of running things.

> Ashurbanipal, the Great King, the Mighty King, King of the Universe . . . who from beyond the Tigris even to Mount Lebanon and the Great Sea has brought into submission at his feet the whole of the land of Lake, the land of Suhi as far as the city of Rapiku. . . .
>
> Inscription on boundary stone, Assyrian Empire[18]

Doubtless self-interest provided some degree of voluntary cooperation among the small peasant communities living side by side in the river valleys (in many cases they would have been of the same or related tribes), but it is equally certain that a significant degree of compulsion was necessary to unite their efforts. We know that the compulsion was supplied by military force, because that was the dominant means of enforcing obedience at the time the historical record begins. It also makes logical sense. The successful users of military force would gain control over a large area, which would prosper from better coordination of its efforts in farming the flood plain. The rulers of the area would then gain further power from having control over these increased resources, and so the system becomes self-sustaining and self-perpetuating. The state and the army were indeed Siamese twins.

Precisely who invented the first real armies, and how, we can never know. It may even have come about in different ways in different places. In one case a village militia may have discovered the rudiments of discipline and gained experience in a series of intervillage squabbles, and then been taken in hand by a prehistoric Napoleon who saw the possibilities in a systematic program of conquest. (He may have been more interested in loot, slaves, and rape than in creating the basis for a complex and productive farming economy, but his conquests would nevertheless produce the latter effect.)

In another case, an agricultural area may have been conquered by warriors from a tribe of hungry nonfarmers who then turned themselves into a military ruling caste. It is even conceivable that in some cases the initial work of political and economic unification over quite large areas proceeded without violence, but in a world where armies have come into being, even such a pacific society will survive only if it rapidly develops an army of its own.

> *Shalmaneser, the Mighty King, King of the Universe, a King without rival, the Autocrat, the Powerful One of the Four Regions who shatters the princes of the whole world, who has smashed all his foes like pots. . . . Conqueror from the Upper Sea to the Lower Sea—the lands of Hatti, Luhute, Adri, Labnana, Kue, Tabali, Melidi. Discoverer of the sources of the Tigris and the Euphrates.* —Another case of false modesty[19]

There was more to these earliest states than just an army, of course. They had to have an administration that organized the work of irrigation and collected the tithes of grain (the universal form of taxation) that fed the ruler's courts, the soldiers, and the bureaucrats themselves. The centers of administration became the first cities, where a nonfarming population pursued not just the tasks of government but a rapidly diversifying variety of trades and services. And since the exercise of authority is both cheaper and easier if it rests on something beyond the mere threat of naked force (though that remains the final sanction), the old tribal religions were modified into state religions in which the gods underwrite the rulers' authority. Frequently the rulers themselves were declared minor gods, and more often than not the priesthood and the state bureaucracy were the same thing.

There was also, in the ancient kingdoms, a persistent phenomenon that is all too familiar to the citizens of modern states: the intoxication of power. Though no man can have absolute power, the illusion of it is engendered at all levels in a state administration that is backed by the right and ability to punish or even kill those who disobey. The practical basis for ordinary moral behavior is the recognition of shared humanity and mutual vulnerability, which is precisely what is destroyed by the illusion of absolute power. Thus those who controlled the first civilized states—which were all, without exception, totalitarian tyrannies—felt entitled to torture and kill their own subjects for any act of defiance and to massacre entire populations of foreigners who threatened their power. The former assumption is still very common, and the latter universal, in the states of today.

> *Tell me one operation of war which is moral. . . . Sticking a bayonet into a man's belly, is that moral? Then they say, well, of course strategic bombing involved civilians. Civilians are always involved in major wars.*
>
> *After all, previous wars ended up in the besieging of major cities, and in besieging a city what was the idea? To cut off all supplies, and the city held out if it could until they'd eaten the last dog, cat, and sewer rat and were all starving, and meanwhile the besieging forces lobbed every missile they could lay their hands on into the city, more or less regardless of where those missiles landed, as an added incentive to surrender. . . .*
>
> Sir Arthur Harris, head of RAF Bomber Command, 1942–45

There is no significant difference between what Shalmaneser III did to Arzashku in 858 B.C. and what British Bomber Command and the United States Eighth Air Force did to Dresden in 1945. Shalmaneser, being Assyrian, unquestionably took more pleasure in it, and the means of execution seem rather more exotic to us, but the ultimate consequences for the victims were identical. So was the moral basis for both acts. According to the conventional morality of every civilized society, it is justifiable and indeed praiseworthy to inflict death and suffering on the enemy when states are at war with each other. From time to time there have been quibbles about including noncombatants in the category of "enemy," but they are not to be taken seriously in a world of nuclear weapons.

No human beings can escape the category of potential enemy, for the rules of the international system decree that all states are always potentially at war with each other. Within the past two hundred years Britain and France, France and the United States, the United States and Britain, have all been both enemies and allies; Italy has gone from alliance to enmity with Germany and back again five times since 1914. Some things have changed since ancient times: the rules for the behavior of the rulers toward the ruled have been modified considerably within some states, particularly in the past few centuries. But other things have not changed at all: the international environment of armed and perilous anarchy in which all states live had already taken on its present form five thousand years ago.

Each state is solely responsible for its own survival and can only ensure it by having sufficient military force, either on its own or in alliance with others, to resist the armies of those who are in a position to threaten it. The threat is real: over 90 percent of all the states that have ever existed have been destroyed—and often their people with them—because they failed to have enough military power available at the critical moment. It is a lesson that is indelibly engraved in the consciousness of every government from Pharaoh Narmer's to Premier Gorbachev's.

Nobody now alive, nor anybody on this side of the historical horizon, has "chosen" war instead of peace; that would be like saying that someone has chosen to breathe air instead of water. Individual leaders and even whole nations may decide from time to time that they want a particular war (though far more wars begin as a result of miscalculation), and other leaders and countries may strive desperately to stay at peace, but it all takes place in a political context wherein war is always an option. That context has been the same since the beginning of recorded history. Indeed, it is almost certainly a good deal older than history.

Far beneath the waters of Lake Nasser, which now stretch a hundred miles southwards from the Aswan High Dam, twenty giant mud-brick fortresses are gradually dissolving along the submerged banks of what used to be the Second Cataract of the Nile. They were built to guard the southern approaches of Egypt between five thousand and four thousand years ago, but they were far from primitive. It is easy enough to build simple walled enclosures, even ones with walls fifteen to twenty feet thick and over thirty feet high, but the elaborate defenses of these frontier forts, from Buhen in the north to Semna and Kumma in the south, were designed by people who had had many generations of experience in siege warfare.

> The defending archers could direct their arrows from three different angles downwards on to the attackers in the ditch, and level onto targets coming over the counterscarp. Some conception of the immense strength of these defenses is apparent when, standing at the bottom of the ditch, we realize that an attacking force must first storm the glacis, destroying any outposts concealed in the covered way, while under fire from sling-shots and arrows from the main wall above. They would then have to descend the steep counterscarp to the bottom of the ditch, under an intense cross-fire from the loopholed ramparts and bastions, behind which the defenders would be completely concealed. Should they survive this ordeal, they would then have to storm the scarp and rampart above it, only to find themselves in a narrow corridor at the foot of the main walls, from the top of which would come a shower of stones and other missiles.[20]

People do not build fortifications of this complexity and sophistication (they compare favorably with the medieval castles of only eight centuries ago) unless they inhabit a world full of highly competent armies. The military engineers who built Buhen and the other forts already lived in that kind of world, and their sophisticated knowledge of military architecture, like the technical skills and discipline of the potential attackers that made it necessary, must have evolved over many centuries. It suggests that there were already highly professional armies in existence long before we had enough scraps of evidence to start piecing together anything resembling a coherent history of civilization.

In the end the forts, each garrisoned by up to three thousand soldiers, were taken by some determined attacker; there was much evidence of fire and deliberate destruction in the ruins. But while they stood, for almost a thousand years, they protected Egypt from invasion from the south, and the deserts on either side of the Nile provided equal protection to the east and west. This isolation made Egypt a relatively stable and unmilitary society, once the long process by which the little local states of the Nile Valley were consolidated into large units culminated, around 3200 B.C. in the conquest of the northern kingdom by the southern. For the next millennium and more, Egypt was unique in the world: a single state almost six hundred miles long (though only a dozen miles wide for most of its length), with a population of up to two million people sharing a common language, religion, and national identity, whose only serious conflicts were occasional civil wars.

But elsewhere the patterns of war were starting to assume a more familiar shape. Most people in the world still lived in tribal bands of a hundred or so, but in Asia Minor and in the Indus and Yangtze valleys most early civilizations took the form of little city-states with a population of one or two hundred thousand people, each controlling a substantial surrounding area of rich agricultural land. And they were almost constantly at war with each other, or recovering from war, or preparing for another war.

How, O Sumer, are thy mighty fallen!
The holy king is banished from his temple.
The temple itself is destroyed, the city demolished.
The leaders of the nation have been carried off into captivity.
A whole empire has been overthrown by the will of the gods.

Lamentation over the destruction of Ur, 2000 B.C.[21]

In Mesopotamia (present-day Iraq) there were some twenty rival city-states in the valleys of the Tigris and Euphrates by early in the third millennium, and the scale and ruthlessness of their wars were increasing rapidly; around 2700 B.C., all the Mesopotamian cities began surrounding themselves with fortifications. We know very little detail about the history of these wars—nor would we much care to, any more than the citizens of A.D. 6625 (assuming there are any) will be eager to learn the details of World War II—but they must have mattered a great deal to the people who lived through them.

There was, for example, a conflict between the cities of Umma and Lagash over the line of their common border on the river, the exploitation of the river's waters, and the possession of grazing lands beyond the irrigated areas, which lasted for about two centuries (ca. 2550–2350 B.C.). It must have dominated the lives of everybody in both cities, for the disputes erupted into open war several times in each generation without ever bringing about a final settlement, until at last the army of Umma under King Lugalzagesi won a decisive victory, sacked the city of Lagash, and looted its temple. And even then the enfeebled survivors of Lagash continued to wage what amounted to guerrilla warfare until both cities were ultimately subjugated by a new phenomenon: the world's first military empire.

Sargon of Akkad was the prototype of Alexander, Napoleon, and Hitler: a man who set out to conquer the world (or at least those parts of it that he knew). In his fifty-five years on the throne, beginning 2302 B.C., he waged thirty-four wars and overran not just all the cities of Mesopotamia, but much of what is now northern Syria and southeastern Turkey. Akkad was an empire that recognized no boundaries of language, religion, or natural geographical zones, only those set by the limits of its military power. The chronicles boasted that Sargon's dominion ran "from the Lower Sea to the Upper Sea" (from the Gulf to the Mediterranean), and his instrument for controlling this empire of many different peoples was a large standing army: in one inscription he states that fifty-four thousand men daily took their meals in his presence.

However, Sargon's empire also suffered from the classic defect of this kind of state: it rested on nothing except military power, and his army could not be everywhere at once. Sargon and his successors spent their entire reigns dealing with the endless revolts that broke out in all quarters as soon as any sign of Akkadian weakness was detected. At the beginning of his grandson Naram Sin's reign in 2260 B.C., he faced simultaneous revolts in the Mesopotamian cities of Kish, Kutha, Kazallu, Marad, Umma, Nippur, Uruk, and Sippar, and in eight other provinces of his empire. In spite of all the cities shorn of their walls or destroyed outright for daring to rebel, the Akkadians were eventually worn down by the ceaseless effort to control the empire they had inherited from Sargon. By 2159 B.C. the empire was gone and the city of Akkad itself had been destroyed.

The pattern will be repeated hundreds of times as other empires rise and fall. Indeed, it is the predominant theme in the political history of civilization, from Akkad and Assyria to the Third Reich and the Greater East Asian Co-Prosperity Sphere of the day before yesterday. And yet the temptation to build an empire has proved almost irresistible to any state that has possessed the military power to do so, not just because of the wealth and glory that accrue to the empire-builders, but also because becoming bigger and more powerful has the apparent advantage of making a state safer from its potential enemies. It does not make things safer, however. Since a potential enemy may be defined as any state with the power to hurt you, becoming a more powerful state simply attracts the hostile attention of bigger potential enemies. (This is precisely the process by which the United States and the Soviet Union identified each other as mortal enemies when they emerged from World War II as the world's strongest powers.)

Rival superpowers contributed nothing to the downfall of Akkad, which was largely nibbled to death by the revolts of its own subject peoples, for the world was still a fairly empty place and Akkad was not in direct contact with any other comparable empire. Although there was considerable trade and travel across the ancient world, Egypt was still effectively isolated within the valley of the Nile, and a thousand miles of mountains and deserts separated the Fertile Crescent from the civilization of the Indus Valley. As for China, it still lived in its own utterly enclosed world.

And at this point the history of civilization more or less stopped for a while. The early centuries of the second millennium B.C. are a dark age of sorts; it was the first time we know of (though probably not really the first and certainly not the last) when the barbarians got the upper hand over civilization.

In the few generations before 2000 B.C., nomadic herdsmen from southern Russia, who had discovered the use of horse-drawn chariots, began expanding in every direction. Within a couple of hundred years these "Indo-European" peoples had spread over most of Europe and spilled over the mountain wall separating the great Eurasian plain from Asia Minor and northern India. Eventually they overran most of northern Asia Minor (and Semitic refugees fleeing before them conquered Egypt for the first time in its history). Further east, the Aryan branch of the Indo-Europeans extinguished the urban civilization of the Indus Valley so thoroughly that not even its language is known.

By about 1500 B.C., however, the worst of the upheavals was long past. Egypt had thrown off foreign rule, and the Indo-European conquests to the north, like the domains of the Hittites and the Mitanni, had become civilized kingdoms themselves. The Middle Eastern and Mediterranean world had never been so prosperous or so intimately interconnected by trade and travel; it was almost a golden age. And it was in this period, when historical records are relatively plentiful, that an Egyptian army marched north to a place called Armageddon and left us the first detailed account of a battle.

How can we take this pass which is so narrow? It is reported that the enemy are at the exit in great numbers. Will not the horses have to go single file; and the soldiers likewise? Won't our vanguard already be fighting (at the far end of the pass) while the rear stands here at Aruna and does not fight?

Advice of Tuthmose III's officers on the eve of the battle of Armageddon[22]

You determine to go forward, though you don't know the way. Shuddering seizes you, the hair of your head stands on end, your soul lies in your hand. Your path is full of boulders and shingle, there is no passable track, for it is all overgrown with thorns, neh-plants and wolf's-pad. The ravine is on one side of you, the mountain rises on the other. On you go and guide your chariot beside you, and fear that the horse will fall. . . . The sky is open, and you imagine that the enemy is behind you.

Letter from Hori, an Egyptian scribe and veteran, to a young officer[23]

For several generations past, the cities of Palestine and Syria had been vassals to Egypt, but in 1480 B.C. the king of Kadesh, a rich and strategically important city at the northern end of the Bekáa valley in Lebanon, declared his independence. Most of the other cities in the region promptly acknowledged his rule, for the Egyptian army had not left the valley of the Nile in twenty-two years. But by early the following spring there was a new pharaoh on the throne, and the army moved north.

The Egyptian army that the young Pharaoh Tuthmose III led into his first campaign at the age of twenty-two was noticeably different from the armies of five centuries (or five millennia) before. Some twenty thousand strong, it still consisted mostly of infantrymen carrying spears, swords, and axes, but it also included archers with the relatively new and far more powerful composite bow. It was divided into divisions of about five thousand men (which were given the names of the gods—the division of Re, the division of Amun, etc.) and so had the ability to perform at least some modestly complicated maneuvers on the battlefield.

Tuthmose's army also had horses, which had arrived in the Middle East with the Indo-European invaders about five hundred years before. They were not used as cavalry chargers—partly because most of the horses of this period were still too light and too weak in the back to be ridden for long by a man in armor and partly because before the invention of stirrups the back of a horse was not a stable fighting platform. But yoked in pairs the horses would pull light two-wheeled chariots carrying a driver and a warrior armed with a bow and throwing spears. The Egyptian army, like others of this period, had hundreds of chariots which could maneuver in mass formations. Chariots were attached to each division and were very useful to harass unbroken formations of enemy infantry from a distance, darting in, launching weapons, and swiftly withdrawing again. They only tried to charge home, however, against troops already showing signs of flight; the best way to take or hold ground was still, as always, to mass infantrymen on it shoulder to shoulder.

Tuthmose's army took three weeks to march from the Egyptian frontier fortress at Tjel (approximately on the present Suez Canal) to a place called Yehem in northern Palestine, just the other side of the mountains from the city of Megiddo, also known as Armageddon, where the army of Kadesh was drawn up to meet him. There were three passes through the mountains, two of them long and circuitous but wide enough for an army to preserve some sort of formation while passing through; the other, through the village of Aruna, shorter but dangerously narrow.

Emerging from any of the passes into the plain of Armageddon would be a risky business, for the enemy army might be waiting at the exits and attack Tuthmose before his forces had time to deploy into battle formation. At the staff conference on the evening before the final advance, the pharaoh rejected the advice of his officers (quoted above), and decided to chance taking the Aruna road. He might have had up-to-date intelligence of the enemy's positions on the other side of the mountains, but he was probably just gambling that the Kadesh forces, unwilling to spread themselves too thin by covering all three passes, would reckon that nobody in his right mind would take the Aruna road, and so would leave that pass unguarded.

The Egyptian army began marching up the narrow pass soon after dawn with great trepidation, for this was enemy territory, and even a small force in the hills could cause great difficulty for the strung-out Egyptians. But the head of the Egyptian column emerged from the defile to discover that the pharaoh's gamble had been correct; the forces of Kadesh had been divided between the exits from the other two passes, and the Egyptian vanguard began to deploy on the plain unhindered.

There is a hint in the account on the temple walls at Karnak that the young commander may have rashly proposed to push his luck by attacking the nearer fraction of the divided Kadesh army before all his own troops had gotten clear of the pass, for at this time his officers addressed him again: "Behold, His Majesty has come forth together with his victorious army and they have filled the valley; let our victorious lord hearken to us this once, and let our lord await the rear of his army. When the rear of the army has come right out to us, then we shall fight against these Asiatics [as the Egyptians contemptuously called all the Levantine peoples]." This time the pharaoh heeded his officers, and waited until all of his army was through the pass, around noon, before advancing toward Megiddo. There was no contact with the enemy that day, and around seven in the evening the Egyptian army camped south of Megiddo by the side of the stream.

The mood of an army on the eve of a great battle is always the same: the veterans tense because they know what will happen, the younger soldiers nervous because they don't know, and all of them talking confidently to smother their fear or busying themselves with their equipment to hide it. "Command was given to the whole army, saying 'Equip yourselves! Prepare your weapons! For we shall advance to fight the wretched foe in the morning!' Therefore the pharaoh rested in the royal tent . . . and the watch of the army went about saying 'Steady of heart! Steady of heart! Watchful! Watchful!' . . . One came to say to His Majesty 'The land is well, and the infantry of the South and the North [of Egypt] likewise. . . . ' "

And in the morning the army marched out with all the panoply and splendor it could muster: "His Majesty went forward in a chariot of electrum [an alloy of gold and silver] arrayed in his weapons of war, like Horus, the Smiter, lord of power; like Montu of Thebes, while his father, Amun, strengthened his arms." And there, unfortunately, the account lapses, for the chronicler simply says that the pharaoh "prevailed against" his enemy. There is no account of the tactics of the actual fighting.[24] But there is a reason for this: the story was engraved on the walls of Karnak in order to glorify the role of Tuthmose in achieving the victory, but once battle has been joined, in armies like this, there is little for a leader to do. A commander's role is to train his troops beforehand and position them as advantageously as possible before the battle begins, but the key phase is the head-on clash of massed formations of heavy infantry who can neither hear a commander's orders over the noise, nor obey them if they could hear them.

What really matters is what happens at the line of contact where the two disciplined mobs of soldiery crunch together. And there it is push and stab and shove and stumble in a sweating frenzy, with the leading edge of the two formations eroding moment by moment as men go down, until one side starts to panic and tries to break contact. But it cannot break contact, of course, for there are other lines of men behind who have not yet caught the panic and who continue to press forward. So the cohesion of the losing formation breaks, and once that happens it is doomed. The men seeking to flee find themselves trapped in their own crowd and are cut down from behind.

The Egyptian account of Megiddo contains no description of what happened at this crucial moment, when the forces of Kadesh lost their nerve and so were lost, but the same moment comes in almost every battle. Four or five centuries later, in one of the battles on the plain below Troy, a thousand miles to the northwest, a similar moment came and was remembered centuries afterward in Homer's *Iliad*. Despite the typical emphasis on the deeds of individual heroes and the absence of any explicit discussion of tactics, it is quite clear what happened when the losers turned to flee.

> *Meriones pursued and overtaking [Pheraklos]*
> *struck in the right buttock, and the spearhead drove straight*
> *on and passing under the bone went into the bladder.*
> *He dropped, screaming, to his knees, and death was a mist about him.*
>
> *Meges . . . killed Pedaios . . .*
> *struck him the sharp spear behind the head at the tendon*
> *and straight on through the teeth and under the tongue cut the bronze blade*
> *and he dropped in the dust gripping in his teeth the cold bronze.*
>
> *Eurypylos . . . killed brilliant Hypsenor . . .*
> *running in chase as he fled before him struck in the shoulder*
> *with a blow swept from the sword and cut the arm's weight from him,*
> *so that the arm dropped bleeding to the ground, and the red death*
> *and destiny the powerful took hold of both eyes.*
>
> *So they went at their work all about the mighty encounter.*[25]

Unless two armies were grossly dissimilar in numbers or weaponry, what decided most ancient battles was principally the morale and discipline of the troops—which side could hold its formation one minute longer—plus, as always in military affairs, a substantial element of chance. On the plain of Armageddon, it was the army of Kadesh that panicked. "They fled headlong to Megiddo in fear, abandoning their horses and their chariots of gold and silver."[26] The people of the doomed city slammed the gates shut against the fugitives for fear that the Egyptians would follow them in, but it was an unnecessary precaution. At that point greed overcame discipline in the Egyptian ranks, and the troops stopped to loot the fallen, leaving time for most of the Kadesh army's survivors to be hauled up inside the walls on ropes fashioned from their own clothing.

Megiddo's garrison, thus reinforced, withstood a long siege, in which Tuthmose built a great wooden wall around the city to prevent any movement in or out. The city was eventually starved into surrender, and many of the citizens enslaved. The pharaoh then went on to capture and plunder a number of other cities in the Lebanon, and the rich loot that he gathered from them (carefully itemized in the inscription) was more than enough to repay the costs of the expedition. Tuthmose was so favorably impressed by this return on investment that he waged fifteen more campaigns in Lebanon and Syria during his reign, all of them successful.

The battle of Megiddo can stand as the model for almost all the battles fought in the world from 5000 B.C. to at least four thousand years later. The weapons became somewhat more effective with time, as stone spearheads gave way to bronze and then to iron, and the average numbers involved in a big battle probably rose gradually as empires grew bigger and richer. However, even at the end of the period, armies rarely exceeded twenty thousand men, and probably never got much bigger than fifty thousand, partly because these were all still subsistence agricultural societies which simply couldn't afford to support large numbers of nonproductive members like soldiers, but more importantly because of the practical difficulties in supplying larger numbers of troops in the field or controlling them in battle.

There must have been at least several thousand battles like Megiddo over the millennia before 1479 B.C., and there have certainly been many thousands like it since. For those who were there, each battle was a matter of life and death, with the whole future seeming to hang in the balance. And they were not entirely wrong in their perceptions, if the future is defined simply as the rest of their lives. From the historian's point of view empires rise and fall, whole peoples appear and disappear, and borders fluctuate like droplets of rain running down the windowpane as the centuries flicker past, but ordinary mortals do not enjoy such a godlike perspective.

For ordinary men born in Egypt in 1500 B.C., the wars in Syria that began when they were twenty were still the dominant foreign event in their lives in 1450 B.C., when they had probably become grandfathers—unless, of course, they died at Megiddo when they were twenty. And the outcome of battles like that really mattered at the time, for although most were not decisive, a single catastrophic defeat, happening between dawn and sunset on a single day, could leave a whole empire exposed to invasion, plunder, and massacre.

It is little wonder that most of the history of those times that has come down to us is military history, for how an army of twenty or thirty thousand men fared on a single day of battle could determine the future of vast areas for generations or centuries. Military power had become not just the symbol but the real basis of political power across the whole civilized world, and war was the most important task a ruler had. And although the language we use to describe what we do today disguises the similarities, war is still our rulers' most important task.

Yet all the effort and sacrifice entailed in fighting wars—each of which seems so important at the time—doesn't actually lead anywhere; in the end, it is virtually canceled out. The only thing that makes the battle of Megiddo important to us is the fact that we know about it. It is hard to feel any real sense of regret about the men who lost the rest of their lives on that day, because they would have been dead for over 3,400 years now anyway. It is impossible to care much about who won the battle, because both sides lived long ago and far away, and most of what they cared for—their family and friends, their language, their religion, their personal and political hopes and fears—has vanished utterly. This is not at all the way we feel about the Normandy invasion of 1944, but if history goes on long enough, the day will come when Megiddo and Normandy will seem on a par: equally futile and equally meaningless.

Naturally, we resist and resent that conclusion with all our strength. That war of 3,400 years ago was obviously a mere power struggle with no moral justification, whereas any war our own nation becomes involved in today will be just and necessary. The soldiers who were killed on the battlefield of Megiddo died in vain, but if today's generation of young men have to die on the Central Front in Europe, it will decide the moral fate of mankind forever. The man in the ranks of Tuthmose III's army of Armageddon was deluded about the importance of his death, but the man in a Chieftain tank (or a T-62) in Germany today is not. And I am the Queen of Sheba.

NOTES

1. Conversation with Thomas Dine, executive director of the American-Israeli Public Affairs Committee, 18 October 1983, and an interview with *People Magazine*, 6 December 1983.

2. Wire service of 3 September 1983.

3. James Wellard, *By the Waters of Babylon*, London: Hutchinson, 1982, p. 147.

4. Leonard Cottrell, *The Great Invasion*, London: Pan, 1961, p. 83.

5. M. J. Meggitt, *Desert People*, Chicago: University of Chicago Press, 1960, p. 245

6. John B. Wright, *Bushman Raiders of the Drakarsberg, 1840–1870*, Pietermaritzburg, South Africa: University of Natal Press, 1971, pp. 3–4.

7. A. Warnerburg, *The Bushman*, New York: Mayflower, 1979, p. 39.

8. Ali A. Mazrui, "Armed Kinsmen and the Origins of the State," pp. 10–11.

9. Edward E. Walker, Jr., *The Emergent Native Americans*, Boston: Little, Brown, 1972, p. 261.

10. Margaret Mead (ed.), *Ruth Benedict: An American Anthropologist at Work*, Boston: Houghton Mifflin, 1959, p. 374.

11. Ernest Wallace and E. Adamson Hoebel, *The Comanches*, Norman, Okla.: University of Oklahoma Press, 1952, p. 247. The story was told to the authors in the 1930s by Post Oak Jim, an old Comanche who as a youth had been the friend waiting outside the Ute encampment.

12. Quincy Wright, *A Study of War*, Chicago: University of Chicago Press, 1965, p. 63.

13. Lewis Mumford, *The City in History*, New York: Harcourt Brace, 1961, p. 44

14. Xenophon *Agesiluas* ii, 9. The Battle of Coronea (394 B.C.) is far closer in time to us than to the earliest kingdoms, but the nature of battles between infantry phalanxes remained essentially the same for at least 5000 years.

15. Homer *Iliad* 15. 322–28 tr. Richard Lattimore, Chicago: University of Chicago Press, 1951.

16. Ibid, 16, 345–50.

17. Boris Piotrovsky, *The Ancient Civilisation of Urartu*, London: Barrie and Rockliff: The Cresset Press, 1969. p. 47.

18. Daniel David Luckenbill, *Ancient Records of Assyria and Babylonia*, Chicago: University of Chicago Press, 1926. p. 110.

19. Ibid, p. 244.

20. W. B. Emery, *Egypt in Nubia*, London: Hutchinson, 1965.

21. Wellard, op cit., p. 101.

22. Leonard Cottrell, *The Warrior Pharaohs*, London: Evans Brothers, 1968, p. 80.

23. Ibid, p. 99.

24. The account of Megiddo is mainly taken from Ibid., pp. 79–83.

25. Homer, op. cit., Book 5, 65–84.

26. Cottrell, op. cit.

"I levelled the city and its houses. . . . I consumed them with fire . . . after I had destroyed Babylon . . . and massacred its population; I tore up its soil and threw it into the Euphrates." *Assyrians looting and destroying an Egyptian city; bas-relief from Nineveh, Palace of Ashurbanipal (118912), Courtesy of The British Museum*

"A slash-cut rarely kills," the Roman army manual says, but it makes for great artistic drama. A Greek and a Galatian slashing at each other in a Roman version of the Battle of the Galatians. *The Ammendola Sarcophagus. Courtesy of the Capitoline Museum, Rome/ Photo by Barbara Malter*

Although every male in the hunting-and-gathering economy of the Yano-mamo of South America is a warrior, their brand of fighting is a far cry from what we would call "war." Here the headman, on the left, his arm out-stretched, is stopping a ritual club fight from escalating to bows and arrows. *From Yanomamo: The Fierce People, Second Edition by Napoleon Chagnon. Copyright © 1977 by Holt, Rinehart & Winston. Reprinted by permission of CBS College Publishing*

A

B

For American Indians, the State was personified in the Peace Chief. War Chiefs were temporary leaders, for the duration of an expedition. The Navaho Peace Chief Barboncito and War Chief Manuelito. *(A) Courtesy of the City Art Museum, St. Louis, (B) Courtesy of the Museum of New Mexico/Photo by Charles M. Bell*

The point of inter-tribal warfare was to give the warriors an opportunity to demonstrate their courage, not to wipe out hundreds of people or seize territory. This glorious battle between a Mandan and a Cheyenne chief followed strict rules akin to a European duel. Although wounded by a knife, the Mandan inflicted more serious damage with his tomahawk and then permitted the Cheyenne to escape. *The Library of Congress*

The Vulture Stele of King Eannatum of Lagash, from around 3,000 B.C., the oldest Mesopotamian record to survive. It shows both the basic forms of military drill (note the shields held in front of the soldiers in rank) and, elsewhere, the gruesome fate of combatants. *Louvre Museum*

Blackfoot stick for "counting coup," that is touching the enemy to humiliate him, considered a far braver deed than wounding or killing. *Courtesy of The British Museum (PS 031321)*

This Predynastic Egyptian knife is decorated with the two preoccupations of the primitive artist, animals and fighting. This side shows one of the relatively disorganized skirmishes with knives and clubs that eventually gave rise to a united kingdom and a real army, interested in conquest. *The Ivory Knife Handle from Jebel El Arnak, Louvre Museum*

The Assyrians had a reputation for enjoying nastiness. Here the rebel captive Dananu, wearing his ally's severed head slung around his neck, is being spat upon by a conquering Assyrian to the amusement of the other nobles. This scene was carved on the palace wall at Nineveh. *Nineveh, South West Palace, British Museum (124801), detail*

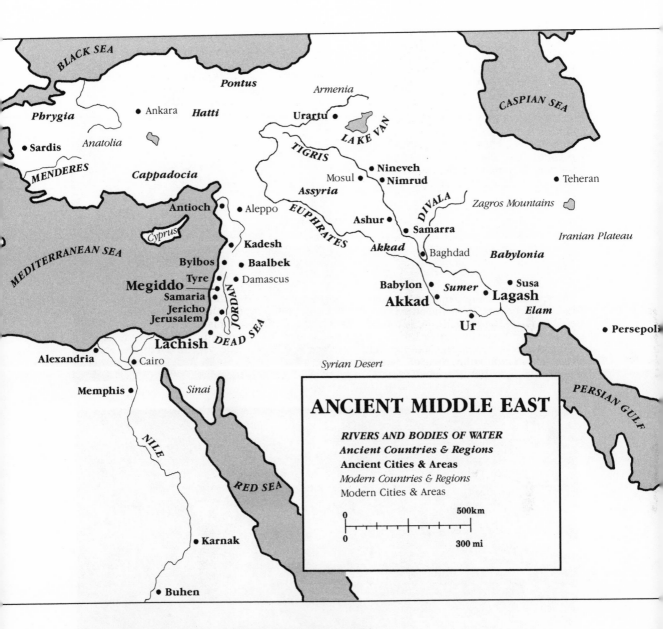

ANCIENT MIDDLE EAST

RIVERS AND BODIES OF WATER
Ancient Countries & Regions
Ancient Cities & Areas
Modern Countries & Regions
Modern Cities & Areas

0   500km

0   300 mi

BLACK SEA

Pontus

Armenia

CASPIAN SEA

Phrygia

• Ankara   *Hatti*

Urartu •

• Sardis   *Anatolia*

MENDERES

Cappadocia

LAKE VAN

TIGRIS

Mosul •   • Nineveh
      • Nimrud

• Teheran

Assyria

DIVALA

Zagros Mountains

Antioch •

    • Aleppo

EUPHRATES

Ashur •

Iranian Plateau

Cyprus

• Kadesh

Samarra •

Bylbos •

   • Baalbek

Akkad

• Baghdad

Babylonia

Tyre •

   • Damascus

MEDITERRANEAN SEA

Megiddo

Samaria •

JORDAN

Babylon •   *Sumer*

• Susa

Jericho •

Akkad

• Lagash

Jerusalem •

Elam

Lachish   *DEAD SEA*

Ur

• Persepoli

Alexandria •   • Cairo

Syrian Desert

Memphis •

Sinai

PERSIAN GULF

NILE

RED SEA

• Karnak

• Buhen

Some of the earliest cities and civilizations interested in power and the acquisition of territory. All these states had real armies, and a few had their own Neolithic versions of Napoleon.

Pharaoh Tuthmose III's army was different from those that came before; it combined the basic spear-and-shield infantrymen with well-equipped archers and two-horse chariots, and was organized into divisions for relatively complicated maneuvers. His first great victory was at Megiddo—or Armageddon. *Tuthmose III, a limestone relief from Thebes, 1501–1447 B.C./The Metropolitan Museum of Art, Gift of Edward S. Harkness, 1926, Carnarvon Collection. All rights reserved.*

The aftermath of any war of conquest: itemizing the loot. Here, the curly, severed heads of Babylonians are carefully recorded by Assyrian scribes, to the left. *Scribes recording the booty of the Babylonian campaign; Nineveh, South West Palace, British Museum (124825)*

The five-thousand-year-old fortress of Buhen, now dissolving under the waters of Lake Nasser, is witness to the antiquity of true warfare. Nobody builds fortifications like this unless they live in a world of highly competent armies. *Royal Ontario Museum/Masterfile*

The empire of the first World Conquerer, Sargon of Akkad, was based on military force alone and didn't last too long. Here his grandson, Naram-Sin, is putting down one of many simultaneous revolts by having the captives commit suicide in his presence. A hundred years later, even the Akkadian capital was a memory. *The Stele of Naram-sin, King of Akkad, 2,000* B.C.; Louvre Museum

One of the horse-drawn chariots used by nomadic Indo-European herdsmen from Southern Russia to invade Europe and Asia Minor around 2000 B.C. *Model of battle wagon in gold, Scythian/British Museum*

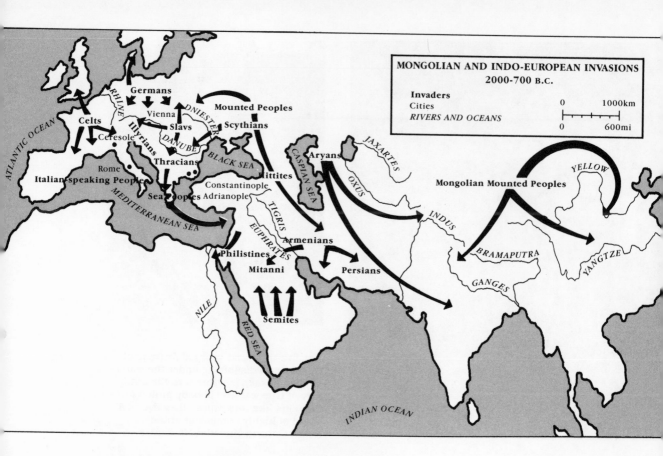

MONGOLIAN AND INDO-EUROPEAN INVASIONS
2000-700 B.C.

Invaders
Cities
RIVERS AND OCEANS

0   1000km
0   600mi

The first of the great barbarian waves; the Thracians
became Greeks, the Hittites and Philistines got
mixed up with the Semites, the Celts and Germans
became the dominant races of Western Europe. As for
the peoples whom they invaded, their cultures and even
languages were almost completely eradicated.

2: *The Middle Passage*

The first modern army that could not have been defeated by the army of Alexander the Great [330 B.C.] was probably the army of Gustavus Adolphus [A.D. 1620].
                                        —Col. T. N. Dupuy, U.S. Army, ret'd.

Most of human history seems to be just one damn thing after another, and this is especially true of the long middle passage between about 1500 B.C. and A.D. 1500. During those three thousand years, for which historical records are far more ample than for previous years—and most of the history recorded is military—there was scarcely any change in the pattern of warfare that would seem important to any but those dedicated to the minutiae of military history. There were incessant wars, of course, but it was mainly the same old things happening over and over again.

Most military historians would readily agree that competent professional armies chosen at random from anywhere between 500 B.C. and A.D. 1500 would stand a roughly equal chance in battle against each other—and that span of years could probably be pushed all the way back to around 1500 B.C. (the time of Megiddo) if the earlier armies were allowed to exchange their bronze weapons for iron ones. An understanding of the institution of warfare does not require a chronological trudge through three millennia of forgotten wars. During the middle passage of the history of civilization, warfare was more or less a "steady state" phenomenon.

> *An ancient city was falling and the long years of her empire were at an end. Everywhere the dead lay motionless about the streets, in the houses, and on these temple stairs which our tread had reverenced so long. . . . The Greeks were dashing to the [palace], and thronging round the entrance with their shields locked together over their backs; ladders were already firmly in place against the walls, and the attackers even now putting their weight on the rungs near the door-lintels. Holding shields on their left arms thrust forward for protection, with their right hands they grasped the roof. To oppose them the Trojans, on the brink of death and knowing their plight was desperate, sought to defend themselves by tearing up tiles from the roof-tops of houses . . . to use as missiles. . . . Inside the palace there was sobbing and a confused and pitiful uproar. The building rang from end to end with the anguished cries of women.*[1]

Troy actually fell some time in the twelfth century B.C.—the traditional date is 1183 B.C.—at a time when history was rapidly transformed into legend. The story of the Trojan Horse, for example, may well be a garbled account of the siege machinery with which the city's walls were finally breached. The semibarbaric Achaean Greeks besieging Troy lacked such advanced technology, but they could easily have hired military engineers from one of the more civilized countries to the east: around this time the fall of the Hittite empire (under the onslaught of a new wave of nomadic invasion) would have left a lot of unemployed professional soldiers on the loose in Asia Minor. If Hittite mercenaries had built a proper siege tower for the attackers— a wooden structure several stories high, mounted on wheels, with a hide-covered roof to protect the men inside and a metal-tipped battering ram slung in the interior—the Achaeans might well have dubbed it a wooden horse, leaving subsequent generations to embellish the story. (A siege tower pictured in a roughly contemporary Assyrian bas-relief does look somewhat like a giant horse.)

Actually, Troy was destroyed after a long siege—the excavated ruins show evidence of huge fires and destruction among the great stone buildings of the city and refugee hovels packed tightly between them—but Homer did not write his account of the siege until four centuries later. It was about eight centuries after that when Virgil wrote his vivid account of the sack of Troy, in a personalized style that would never have been used by those who lived through the event. What he writes is almost all fiction, but it is also as true to the essence of the disaster as if he had been there himself. He lived in a world where some unfortunate city met its end like this every few years for as long as memory ran, and he had no more freedom to distort the events and emotions of such a siege than a modern European writer would have to misrepresent the experience of an air raid: too many people knew what it was really like.

Carthage, for example, was stormed by Roman troops in 146 B.C. after a three-year siege at the end of the Third Punic War, and there is an eyewitness account of how the despairing, half-starved Carthaginians held out inside the city through six more days of street fighting: "Three streets leading from the market place to the citadel were lined on both sides with six-storey houses, from which the Romans were pelted. They seized the first houses and from their roofs they made bridges of planks and beams to cross over to the next. While one battle was in progress on the roofs, another was fought, against all comers, in the street below. Everywhere there was groaning and wailing and shouting and agony of every description. Some were killed out of hand, some flung down alive from the roofs to the pavement, and of those some were caught on upright spears. . . . "[2]

And when the tangle of debris and civilian bodies in the streets threatened to impede the advance of solid ranks of Roman infantry, auxiliary troops were sent forward to clear it: "Those told to remove the debris . . . shoved the dead and those still living in pits in the ground, using their axes and crow-bars and shoving and turning them with their tools like blocks of wood or stone. Human beings filled up the gullies. Some were thrown in head down, and their legs protruding from the ground writhed for a considerable while. Some fell feet down and their heads were above the surface. Their faces and skulls were trampled by the galloping horses. . . . "[3]

Those familiar with the activities of SS *Sonderkommandos* in Russia in 1941 at places like Babi Yar will recognize the scene. And the final solution enforced at Carthage (and at Troy) was in no way less ambitious than Hitler's: the relatively few Carthaginians who survived the siege and sack of their city (out of a population of about three hundred thousand) were sold into slavery, and the devastated site was formally cursed and sprinkled with salt by the victorious Roman general. It remained uninhabited until a Roman colony was founded on the ruins over a century later. And if the numbing frequency with which this sort of thing happens throughout history gives rise to some speculation about exactly what kind of a change civilization brought about in our behavior—well, so it should.

It is tempting to see the whole of history, from the end of the first known dark age around the middle of the second millennium B.C. to the beginning of the present era four or five centuries ago, as a sort of middle passage in a long ocean voyage. The shores of the tribal past, on which we built the ship of civilization, have long since dropped astern, and the opposite shore, the new world of rapid change and expanding possibilities, is not yet in sight; the crew is turbulent, but the ship and the horizons do not seem to change.

This view involves an optical illusion, in the sense that the more distant past is not so much different as largely unknown. So little information has survived about the world of 3000 B.C. or 5000 B.C. that the history of those times seems to move quite quickly. If archaeologists know only a dozen facts about a whole century in the history of an ancient empire, then the centuries of its life flash by so rapidly that the pace of change seems fast. Once we reach the period when facts become more plentiful and the years are crowded with incident, centuries take on something closer to their real length (in our view), and the actual slowness of change becomes more evident to us.

In fact the pace of change was generally even slower in the five or six thousand years before the period I have arbitrarily called the "middle passage." That was, however, the era in which the very idea of civilization, and all of its main institutions and patterns of behavior, were invented, and as such it has a fundamental importance which can never fade. But the basic edifice of civilization, and indeed of civilized warfare, was more or less complete by 1500 B.C.

Perhaps, to be fair to the hundreds of later generations caught on the apparent treadmill of the middle passage, we should acknowledge that this was when people's minds, if not their behavior, were gradually evolving the new ideas and perspectives that would eventually allow civilization to break out into the vast and terrifying possibilities of the present. But that was certainly not how it appeared to people at the time.

What they saw—and what we see, looking back—was an endless series of triumphs and tragedies that dwindled into meaninglessness with the passage of a few generations: battles and sieges, the rise and fall of empires, and the constant oppression of violence and cruelty, both organized and random. Things might get better for a time—they might even stay that way for whole generations, in some fortunate intervals of peace and prosperity—but there was no apparent progress toward real security and stability. In the long run, it was three steps forward, three steps back. It is hardly surprising that the world view of most civilized peoples until modern times saw the basic trend of history not as progress toward a better future but as decline from a lost golden age—the feeling that surely things couldn't always have been this bad.

But they always were, because all the wars and the massacres, the ruthless application of power and the unrestrained cruelty of the victors, were implicit in the invention of civilization. Only hopeless romantics idealize the cultures of precivilized peoples; their lives were indeed mostly nasty, brutish, and short, and they lived them out in subservience to the caprices of the natural environment and the bonds of custom and tradition. Civilization liberated people from much of that and allowed them to lead broader, longer, more interesting lives—but it also set something else free in the world: untrammeled, boundless violence.

The logic of power, unlimited by the physical and traditional restraints of the tribal past, found its highest expression in the armies that emerged simultaneously with the first civilized states. The ability to compel people to obey seemed to confer the right to do so, and there were no longer any real restrictions on the degree of violence employed in the process. The shattering of the bonds of customary law in the new mass societies, thousands or even millions strong, that now inherited the earth meant that by the time we begin to have a clear picture of the civilized world as a whole, around three thousand years ago, armed force dominates everything. From piracy on the seas and organized banditry in the hills, to enslavement, looting, and wholesale destruction as the natural fate of captured cities and their inhabitants, organized violence wrote its own rules as it never did in primitive societies. It was the only way to survive—and it was the quickest way to get rich:

> As the light faded, the Flavian army arrived in full strength [outside the city of Cremona]. Once they began to march over the heaps of dead and the fresh traces of bloodshed, they thought that the fighting was over and clamoured to press on towards Cremona to receive, or enforce, the surrender of the beaten enemy. This at any rate was what they said openly, and it sounded well. But what each man thought in his heart was something different. A city on flat ground could be rushed, and an army which forced an entry during the hours of darkness would . . . enjoy greater licence to plunder. But if they waited for dawn, it would be too late; there would be peace-terms, and appeals for mercy. . . . When a city was stormed, its booty fell to the troops, when surrendered, to the commanders.[4]

The city did in fact surrender, but this did not prevent the Roman troops from sacking it. Neither did the fact that this was a civil war and the citizens of Cremona were fellow countrymen.

> *Forty thousand armed men forced their way in to the city. . . . Neither rank nor years saved the victims from an indiscriminate orgy in which rape alternated with murder and murder with rape. Greybeards and frail old women, who had no value as loot, were dragged off to raise a laugh, but any full-grown girl or good-looking lad who crossed their path was pulled this way and that in a violent tug-of-war between the would-be captors. . . . A single looter trailing a hoard of money or temple-offerings of massive gold was often cut to pieces by others who were stronger. . . . In their hands they held firebrands, which, once they had got their spoil away, they wantonly flung into empty houses and rifled temples. . . . There was a diversity of wild desires, differing conceptions of what was lawful, and nothing barred. Cremona lasted them four days.[5]*

The destruction of Cremona in A.D. 69 caused a scandal throughout Italy—an undefended Roman city sacked by Roman legions—and the soldiers who had done it found their captives valueless because of a concerted refusal to buy them as slaves. Although many were then murdered by their captors, some were ransomed by relatives, and other Italian cities contributed to the rebuilding of Cremona. In the vast majority of cases, there was no such outside help for a slaughtered city or a devastated province. Yet, provided there was a generation or two of relative peace, the city would usually be restored, the fields repopulated—in time for the same thing to happen again. Civilization was very resilient; it had to be.

Things went on like this, essentially unchanged, for another fifty generations after the sack of Cremona. Languages and religions changed, borders fluctuated or vanished, the population of areas grew or fell drastically as periods of relative order were succeeded by eras of chaos (though there was a slow long-term increase in the world's population). The problem with history is that there is too much of it, and this is nowhere truer than in military history. Almost fifteen hundred years after Cremona fell, practically the identical scene was being reenacted a few hundred miles to the south, in Rome. Sebastian Schertlin, commander of the Spanish Imperial troops, recalled: "In the year 1527, on 6 May, we took Rome by storm, put over 6,000 men to the sword, seized all that we could find in the churches and elsewhere, burned down a great part of the city, tearing and destroying all copyists' work, all registers, letters and documents."[6]

After leading a charmed life in the first thousand years of its history, Rome had been sacked half a dozen times in its second millennium and had shrunk to a tenth of its former population, but the events of A.D. 1527 were probably the most brutal since the Visigoths under Alaric had ravaged the city for the first time in A.D. 410. The conquerors were greedy, they were imaginative, and they had plenty of time to deal with the citizens at leisure. According to Luigi Guicciardini, "many were suspended for hours by the arms; many were cruelly bound by the private parts; many were suspended by the feet high above the road, or over water, while their tormenters threatened to cut the cord. Some were half buried in the cellars, others nailed up in casks, while many were villainously beaten and wounded; not few were cut all over their persons by red-hot irons. Some were tortured by extreme thirst, others by insupportable noise and many were cruelly tortured by having their own good teeth drawn. Others again were forced to eat their own ears, or nose or their roasted testicles. . . . "[7]

> *I am a prisoner of the Spaniards. They have fixed my ransom at 1,000 ducats on the pretext I am an official. They have tortured me twice, and finished by lighting a fire under the soles of my feet. . . . Dear brother, do not let me perish thus miserably. . . . For the love of God and the Blessed Virgin, help me.*
> —Giovanni Barozzi[8]

In essence it was no different from the aftermath of thousands of other sieges; it was the way a victorious army usually collected its reward, and the price losers generally paid for defeat, in a world where battles were the main way of deciding practically everything.

> *In the battle line each man requires a lateral space of three feet, while the distance between ranks is six feet. Thus, 10,000 men can be placed in a rectangle about 1,500 yards by twelve yards.* —Vegetius on Roman tactics[9]

Battles determined the course of our ancestors' lives. They were no less clever than we; if they could think of no better way to fight than the traditional way for several thousand years, there had to be a very good reason. Soldiers are notoriously conservative about experimenting with new weapons and tactics—often with very good reason, for if the innovations fail to perform as advertised, then soldiers will die—but there have been, on the countless battlefields of the past, enough desperate men with nothing left to lose that practically everything got tried sooner or later. And nothing, until well after the introduction of firearms, worked better than the organization and tactics that were already more or less standard before Alexander's time.

In a world that possesses no force superior to that of arms, a body of armed men that attacks an enemy's territory can do pretty much what it wants—rob and kill anybody it meets, destroy the crops, burn the houses—unless the enemy produces a similar body of armed men. At that point, in precivilized times, the attackers would probably go home, with or without a token skirmish. But civilized armies are far more determined and generally have broader political purposes in view, which are utterly unacceptable to the defenders. The latter cannot just sit behind their walls (they'd eventually starve to death), so in civilized times they usually come out to fight; war almost always involves a real battle.

A battle, for almost all of human history, has been an event as stylized and limited in its movements as a classical ballet, and for much the same reasons: the inherent capabilities and limitations of the human body. When two large groups of men fight, using hand-held weapons or missiles that can be hurled at most a hundred yards or so, the possibilities are very restricted. This is all the more true because the highest priority for both sides is to keep their men disciplined and organized. A few hundred armed men acting in concert, moving in the same direction and with a common purpose, will always be more powerful than a mob ten times their number. In the battle of Mantinea, in 418 B.C., "the Spartans came on slowly and to the music of many flute-players in their ranks. This custom of theirs has nothing to do with religion; it is designed to make them keep in step and move forward steadily without breaking their ranks, as large armies often do when they are just about to join battle."[10]

Modern armies talk of winning or losing ground, and for them it has some relevance, but for all the armies of earlier times the ground is merely the stage across which the formations move. It is the formations themselves that count, and the ground matters only if it includes obstacles that disrupt those carefully aligned and articulated ranks of thousands of well-drilled troops. The strength of the formation vanishes if gaps open up in the line, for the army can only face and fight to its front and will meet disaster if the enemy can attack it from the side or the rear. It will also be helpless if the terrain (or panic) causes the men in the formation to crowd together so closely that they do not have the space necessary to swing or hurl or jab with their weapons: a great deal of the endless drill goes into training the soldiers to maintain that vital three-foot interval at all costs.

But if they are well trained, these soldiers are a formidable fighting machine. A Greek phalanx of the fifth century B.C., for example, consisted of thousands of hoplites (heavy infantry) in serried ranks, almost fully protected in front by large shields and bronze greaves on their shins, with the glittering points of sixteen-foot spears extending forward beyond the shield wall. It took a great deal of time and effort to array such huge formations on a battlefield facing the enemy; it would be better to line up facing the enemy's flank or rear, of course, but the difficulties of complicated movements with these unwieldy masses of men meant that that almost never happened—and besides, there was little time to decide the issue once the two phalanxes met head on.

The men in the front ranks fought each other for a time, being replaced from behind as they fell, until one side or the other thought it was getting the upper hand. At that point all the ranks united their efforts in a gigantic shove to break the enemy's line decisively, and if they succeeded, they had won. The enemy's formation would crumble, men would turn to flee, and the massacre would begin. The losers would typically suffer casualties of half their force or more—almost all of them killed, for no quarter was given—while the winners lost no more than 5 to 10 percent of their men.

After the phalanxes joined battle, there was practically nothing for a general to do except wait. Even beforehand the main tactical decision to be made was whether to make the phalanx as deep as possible to avoid being broken through (at Leuctra in 371 B.C. the Thebans used a formation 50 men deep) or to make it shallower but longer so as to outflank the enemy's phalanx. Even this tactic would often prove irrelevant, for when phalanxes advanced they would tend to drift to the right (the shields were carried in the left hand and each man tried to protect his exposed right side by tucking in behind the shield of the man to his right) so that, despite the hundreds of hours spent on the parade ground, the two opposing lines would overlap each other on the right by the time they collided.

> The Athenian troops weakened their centre by the effort to extend the line sufficiently to cover the whole Persian front; the two wings were strong, but the line in the centre was only a few ranks deep. . . . The word was given to move, and the Athenians advanced at a run towards the enemy, not less than a mile away . . . the first Greeks, so far as I know, to charge at a run. . . . In the centre . . . the foreigners breached the Greek line . . . but the Athenians on one wing and the Plataeans on the other were both victorious. . . . Then . . . they turned their attention to the Persians who had broken through in the centre. Here again they were triumphant, chasing the routed enemy, and cutting them down until they came to the sea, and men were calling for fire and taking hold of the [Persian] ships. . . . Cynegirus [the brother of Aeschylus the playwright] had his hand cut off with an axe as he was getting hold of a ship's stern, and so lost his life. . . . The Athenians secured in this way seven ships, but the rest got off. . . . [11]

The only real formula for success was "more hoplites, or better hoplites, or more and better hoplites,"[12] and these clumsy and bloody shoving matches like gigantic, regimented caricatures of an American football game or a rugby scrum, fought over a couple of hours on a rectangular patch of ground perhaps a hundred acres in area, could determine the future of whole peoples.

There were also lightly armed infantry on the typical Greek battlefield who would advance in skirmish line ahead of the main formations and attack the other side with missile weapons, but they were rarely decisive. "First the stone-throwers, slingers and archers on both sides engaged each other in front of the main lines of battle, with now one party and now another having the advantage, as is normal with these light troops," said Thucydides dismissively about their role in one battle. They could be an infernal nuisance to a phalanx of heavy infantry, which could not deal with them even by charging them—"In a short distance no infantryman, however fast he runs, can catch up with another who has a bow-shot's start of him," Xenophon sourly remarked—but they could not hope to defeat the phalanx unless it ventured onto ground so broken that its formation dissolved.

And there were cavalry (for mounted horsemen had now replaced chariots on the battlefield), who could move rapidly around to the flank or rear of the other side's phalanx and cause considerable disruption by throwing spears and arrows, if they were not first intercepted by that side's own cavalry. They might even charge the infantry if they caught them off guard, but they would almost never try to charge well-trained infantry who were prepared to receive them. A mass of horsemen thundering down on a formation of mere pedestrians looks irresistible, but horses, whatever their riders' views on the matter may be, are usually much too sensible to run straight into an unwavering line of spear-points. They will stop or turn aside at the last moment, and so long as the infantry could keep that thought firmly in mind and hold their formation, they were relatively safe from charges. The cavalry's main purposes were scouting, skirmishing, and above all, riding down the refugees of the defeated side once they had turned to flee.

Heavy infantry dominated the battlefield, as they had since the earliest known battles, and within fairly wide limits even their numbers were less important than their discipline and morale. When Alexander the Great fought the Persian army of Darius at Issus in 333 B.C. he had only forty thousand men (including light infantry and cavalry) against one hundred thousand; Alexander's army fully deployed extended for considerably less than a mile, while the Persian army's front was about two miles. But once the preliminaries to the battle were past, his veteran hoplites charged straight across the field at the Persian center. The effect can best be understood in terms of sheer physics: a disciplined mass of, say, thirty thousand heavily armed and armored men running in tight formation would have hit the Persian line with a force equivalent to twenty-five hundred tons moving at six or seven miles an hour, building up over just a few seconds—and at its leading edge was a hedge of spear-points. There were probably not many men in the first two ranks of Alexander's phalanx who survived the impact (which is why the more experienced veterans would find themselves places a little further back in the phalanx), but the sheer momentum of this force smashed through the center of Darius's army in only a few minutes, long before the troops on either end of the longer Persian line could curl around to take Alexander's men in the flank and rear. With its cohesion gone, the Persian army was efficiently exterminated by Alexander's troops; probably half the Persian force was killed within two hours.

As time went on, various military leaders tinkered with this basic formula for military success in order to make it more flexible. The Romans were best at it. In over two centuries of almost constant war in which they first subjugated all the other city-states of Italy and then conquered the other great power of the time, Carthage, they evolved a far more sophisticated version of the phalanx. The unwieldy mass of the phalanx gave way to the more open battle formation of the legion, in which the troops were broken up into mini-phalanxes ("maniples") of about 150 men in three ranks, the maniples being distributed checkerboard fashion in three overlapping lines. It gave them far more maneuverability, especially on broken ground. At the battle of Zama (202 B.C.)during the Second Punic War, when the Carthaginians tried to rout the Roman legions by a massive elephant charge, Scipio Africanus was even able to move the maniples of his middle line sideways in order to create straight corridors through all three lines of his formation, down which Hannibal's elephants were herded quite harmlessly.

The weapons grew more sophisticated too. In the Roman legions the sixteen-foot spear gave way to two shorter throwing spears, one lighter and of longer range than the other, which the legionaries threw in succession as they advanced, plus a short sword for close-in work when they had made physical contact with the enemy. Battles became less of a mere shoving match, and all manner of tactical stratagems flourished. But the basic logic of the battlefield remained: masses of armed men in highly disciplined formations, equipped only with edged weapons powered by their own muscles, have very limited alternatives for effective fighting, and infantry ruled the battlefields of the third century A.D. as confidently as it had the battlefields of the thirty-third century B.C.

Straightway ship struck ship with brazen beak. The attack was started by a Greek ship which sheared off the whole prow of her Phoenician foe, and others aimed their onslaught on different opponents. At first the flood-tide of the Persian fleet held its own. But when the ships became jammed and crushed in one place, they could bring no help to each other. Ships began to strike their own friends with their bronze-jawed rams, and to shatter the whole bank of oars. The Greek ships, in careful plan, began to press round us in a circle, and ships' hulls gave in. You could no longer see the water, so full was it of wrecked vessels and dead men, while the beaches and rocks were thick with corpses.

Aeschylus, describing the battle of Salamis, 480 B.C.[13]

Navies have always been far more dependent on technology than armies: a ship is a kind of machine, even if it is a galley whose oars are powered by human muscles. The sea is an alien environment for human beings, and it was never possible for them to survive there without technology. Nor did significant numbers of people have any need to be able to operate in this environment until civilization was well established.

Armies were centrally important to the creation of civilized societies, but navies became possible and necessary only after those societies already existed. Precivilized peoples used small boats for fishing and for crossing narrow waters, but the extensive use of the sea for trade had to await the emergence of civilizations that produced a variety of specialized goods, such as grain, minerals, and manufactured products, worth trading in bulk. Once trade of this sort did become desirable, however, it was inevitable that most of it would be conducted by sea. Ships are by far the most economical means of transporting large volumes of goods over long distances even today, and were virtually the only means until the invention of railways only 150 years ago.

Attacking the maritime commerce of states that derived much of their wealth from trade was an obvious (and highly profitable) tactic in war, and undoubtedly the first specialized warships were developed for this purpose. Moreover, the transport by ships of whole armies was an especially attractive military option in the Mediterranean, where the sea was more often than not the quickest route between any two points. Given such valuable targets, naval warfare in the Mediterranean soon grew into an affair of large fleets of warships whose first purpose was to destroy the other side's navy, after which the enemy's merchant shipping could be destroyed with impunity. The most striking fact, however, is that through the whole of the middle passage, maritime technology, complex though it was by the standards of the time, scarcely changed at all.

There was extensive maritime commerce more than four thousand years ago on the inland seas like the Mediterranean, and it was already beginning to expand outward along the coasts and rivers to northern Europe at one extreme and India at the other. Then, and for three and a half millennia afterward, the merchant ships employed a combination of sail and oars, but the warships, which needed to move rapidly in any direction regardless of wind, depended mainly on muscle-power: three, four, or even five banks of rowers to pull the naval vessels through the water at high speed. The need for discipline and coordination was as great as in the phalanx, whether the crews were free or slaves.

Moreover, large-scale naval warfare has always called for techniques of organization and production that resemble those of industrial societies. When Greece was faced with the great Persian invasion early in the fifth century B.C., the Athenian shipyards adopted mass production methods and produced between six and eight triremes (galleys with three banks of oars) each month for over two years, paying for them with the accumulated silver reserves of the state. By 480 B.C. some 250 galleys had been built, requiring over forty thousand men to man them. All the military manpower of Athens went into the fleet, leaving the other Greek city-states to provide the land forces for the peninsula's defense. But this diversion of effort proved its worth when the Greek fleet, predominantly Athenian, destroyed the Persian fleet at Salamis and forced Xerxes to retreat from Greece.

> Now, as for the battle, if I can help it, I shall not fight it in the gulf, nor shall I sail into the gulf. I fully realise that a lack of sea room is a disadvantage for a small, experienced and fast squadron [like ours] fighting against a lot of badly managed ships. One cannot sail up in the proper way to make an attack by ramming, unless one has a good long view of the enemy ahead, nor can one back away at the right moment if one is hard pressed oneself; it is impossible also to sail through the enemy's line and then wheel back on him—which are the right tactics for the fleet which has the superior seamanship. Instead of all this, one would be compelled to fight a naval action as though it were a battle on land, and under those circumstances

the side with the greater number of ships has the advantage. So you can be sure that I shall be watching out for all this as far as I can.[14]

Naval warfare in classical times was a simple affair, sometimes virtually the aquatic version of a land battle. The two opposing forces of galleys, often numbering in the hundreds, would line up facing each other off some stretch of coastline (for galleys hugged the coasts whenever possible; such ships were not very seaworthy nor were their captains capable of accurate navigation out of sight of land), and charge at each other. The ships would endeavor to hole each other headon with their bronze rams or at least shear off the oars on one side of the opposing ship (crushing most of the rowers on that side in the process) and then turn back and ram the disabled enemy from astern. More often than not, however, they would end up lying alongside each other, with the soldiers each galley carried fighting it out along the decks of one or the other ship, as in the battle in Syracuse harbor, 413 B.C.:

> *Many ships crowded in upon each other in a small area [indeed, never before had so many ships fought together in so narrow a space. There were almost two hundred of them on the two sides]. Consequently there were not many attacks made with the ram amidships. . . . Once the ships met, the soldiers fought hand to hand, each trying to board the enemy. Because of the narrowness of the space, it often happened that . . . two, or sometimes more, ships found themselves jammed together, so that the steersmen had to think of defence on one side and attack on the other . . . and the great din of all these ships crashing together was not only frightening in itself, but also made it impossible to hear the orders given by the boat swains.*[15]

The greatest naval battles of classical times were fought between Rome, essentially a land power at the beginning of the Punic wars in 264 B.C., and Carthage, a maritime power with possessions or allies in Spain, Sardinia, Sicily, and southern Italy. The naval harbor of Carthage (near modern Tunis) was an entirely man-made construction approached through the commercial port, which was itself protected by a series of heavy iron chains across the entrance. Inside the naval harbor, a circular space over a thousand yards across with a central island, there were sheds for working on two hundred galleys at once—and a standard Carthaginian quinquireme (five-banked galley) bore a crew of 270 rowers, 30 officers, and 120 marines for fighting. Carthage's shipyards were able to build as many as sixty galleys in a month.

In the generations of war from 264 to 146 B.C. that convulsed the western Mediterranean before Rome finally defeated Carthage, the Romans learned to build a navy too. Once again, the rate of production was remarkable: soon after the outbreak of the war, realizing they would need a navy, the Romans adapted a Carthaginian design and produced a fleet of a hundred quinquiremes and twenty triremes in less than two months. In the naval battles that followed, and even more so in the sudden storms that sometimes overtook the fleets of flimsy galleys in open waters, the losses were tremendously heavy.

At Ecnomus off the coast of North Africa in 256 B.C., a Roman fleet of 330 galleys routed a Carthaginian fleet of equal size, sinking 30 and capturing 64, a loss to the Carthaginians of between thirty and forty thousand men. And on its return to Italy the Roman fleet was caught in a great storm off the west coast of Sicily and 270 of its ships were sunk or driven ashore, drowning about a hundred thousand men. There has not been a comparable loss in naval warfare since the beginning of the modern era.

The nature and scale of naval warfare two thousand years ago compel two observations. One is the obvious, by now repetitive remark about the "steady state" of warfare during the middle passage. Eighteen hundred years after Ecnomus, in A.D. 1571, the allied naval forces of Western Christendom fought the Turkish navy at Lepanto. There were over two hundred galleys on each side, built from designs that would not have caused any surprise in the shipyards of ancient Carthage, and the tactics would not have surprised them either: ram if you can, board if you can't. And close to thirty thousand men drowned in an afternoon.

The other observation is that the conflict between Rome and Carthage was as close as classical civilization ever got to the concept of total war.

Carthage must be destroyed. —Cato the Elder

Although they never got the technology side of things going, the Romans did know about total war. For over sixty years, with a break of two decades in the middle, the Romans fought a life-and-death struggle with Carthage wherein the degree to which they mobilized their resources of manpower and production compares with the world wars of this century. And the reason their conflict grew to such monstrous proportions was also essentially the same.

The Mediterranean was big enough for both Carthage and Rome, just as it is big enough to contain both Tunisia and Italy today. There was no deep-rooted historical or racial hatred between the two peoples before the Punic wars began (though there certainly was by the end, over a century later). The basic cause of the wars was no more (and no less) than the anxiety of two rising imperial powers over the existence of a rival that possessed enough power to pose a serious threat. The potential for war became the reason for war, and once begun, the conflict escalated rapidly to a war of annihilation, because neither side was willing to back down.

The classical civilizations of the second century B.C. were capable of feats of organization and production at least equal to those of sixteenth-century Europe: a society that can send over a hundred thousand men to sea would be a formidable contender in the great-power stakes even today. Moreover, the classical Mediterranean world seems in almost every respect, not just the naval, to be as competent in the tasks and trades of civilization as was the world of the sixteenth century.

Rome and Carthage were not just building huge fleets of warships to fight each other; at times they were also maintaining armies on three or four fronts simultaneously, spread all over the western Mediterranean. The drain on manpower was huge: it has been calculated that at the height of the Second Punic War in 213 B.C., 29 percent of Rome's male citizens were serving in the army,[16] a level that has rarely been exceeded even in this century's wars. Although Rome was ultimately victorious, 10 percent of its entire male population was killed in battle during the final two decades of the war.[17] As for the Carthaginians, their casualties were virtually total: by the end of the Third Punic War in 146 B.C., not only was their empire gone, but Carthage itself was razed, and those Carthaginians left alive were sold into slavery—not even their language survived. A nuclear strike on Carthage would have ended their agony more quickly, but the result would not have differed much.

The Punic wars are the outstanding case—or at least the best-documented case—of an approach to total war between civilized states before modern times. In terms of the three elements that make our kind of total war possible today—the ability to mobilize the entire population for war, the resources that make that degree of mobilization possible, and the technology—only the technology was obviously missing in the Punic wars. All that meant, in the end, was that it took longer to utterly destroy Carthage than total destruction would take these days. (And, of course, it only happened to one side.)

But although the example is apt enough in terms of how wars have always tended to escalate to the furthest extremes that the available resources will permit, regardless of the original cause, the Punic wars were not really comparable in scale to the wars of the past two centuries.

Rome was a complex and sophisticated civilization, but it was fundamentally different in certain key respects from our own. Its organizational ability was great, as was its aptitude for large-scale civil engineering projects, but its interest in technological innovation was very low. The tradition of rational and dispassionate analysis that the Romans inherited from Greece was consistently applied to political, legal, military, and cultural topics but very rarely to the economic or scientific subjects that were the key to changing the age-old terms of the argument and setting rapid technological change loose in the world. Throughout its history the Roman empire remained a mostly illiterate peasant society in which the availability of a huge and growing slave population made any departures from existing political and economic arrangements unattractive to the few million people who had a say in things. Rome lived—and died— in the mold of classical civilization, without ever showing any sign of being able to get off the treadmill: it was a fully adapted inhabitant of the middle passage.

Classical civilization also lacked the wealth necessary for total war. The city-states of Rome and Carthage, each containing fewer than a million full citizens, both controlled large empires whose resources they could draw upon—three quarters of the Roman state's revenues came from abroad by 200 B.C.—and so they were able to mobilize a high proportion of their citizens for war. Both sides also used allied troops in large numbers, but the basic military equation of premodern times held true: societies whose economic basis is subsistence agriculture cannot afford to withdraw more than a very small fraction of their population from production to be sent off to war.

Rome and Carthage were able to draw on the resources of the entire western Mediterranean in their war, and yet the total number of men they had under arms probably never exceeded three quarters of a million—around 3 percent of the total population of the region. That was probably close to the upper limit that any pre-modern civilized society could afford to devote to war, even though the armed forces did not then make further huge demands on the civilian economy for supplies. The soldiers had to be fed, but the only other major calls the war made on scarce resources were in terms of iron for weapons—a few hundred tons a year—and wood and labor for ship-building. The Punic wars were total for the cities of Rome and Carthage in a quite modern sense, but for the western Mediterranean as a whole they were nothing of the sort.

The actual size of the Roman army in later times, when Rome ruled the entire Mediterranean and had legions guarding borders as far away as Scotland and Sudan, is a more accurate measure of the size of military forces a premodern agrarian society—even one with a highly developed commerce—could sustain over the long run. At the turn of the millennium, A.D. 1 or thereabouts, the population of the Mediterranean region was around sixty million, and the total size of the army, including not only legionary troops but all the cavalry and auxiliary forces, was not much above three hundred thousand. Even in the late third century A.D., when the population had risen to one hundred million and the pressure of the barbarians on the frontiers was becoming acute, the Roman army never exceeded three quarters of a million.[18] And in the end, the empire, and most of Europe's civilization, went under. It was almost a thousand years before it reached the same level.

In A.D. 378 the combined forces of the Visigoths and the Ostrogoths, having spent decades wandering along the Vistula and Dniester rivers, crossed the frontier into the Roman empire with over a hundred thousand men. As usual they were accompanied by their families, and the wagons formed a vast encampment eight miles from the city of Adrianople while the bulk of the riders raided through central Thrace. The Roman Emperor Valens marched out from Constantinople with sixty thousand soldiers, two thirds of them infantry, and reached Adrianople on 9 August.

Just as the Roman army began to rush the camp, tens of thousands of Visigothic horsemen swept down from the flank, swamped the Roman cavalry, and swarmed around the unprotected sides and rear of the Roman legions. Forty thousand of them were slaughtered in a couple of hours, including the emperor himself.

The barbarians had destroyed a Roman army for the first time since Varus had led three legions too far into the forests of Germany over three and a half centuries previously—and this time it was not an isolated incident; it was the turning point. The first sack of Rome came only thirty-two years later.

The classical world took a long time dying: western and southern Europe went down with the barbarian invasions in the fourth and fifth centuries, but most of North Africa and the Fertile Crescent kept a version of the old civilization alive until they were overrun by Arab nomads fired by the new faith of Islam in the seventh and eighth centuries. The Eastern Roman (Byzantine) Empire preserved a Christian and Greek-speaking version of Roman civilization in the Balkans and Asia Minor until the destruction of the main Byzantine army by Turkish nomads at Manzikert in A.D. 1071, after which it was reduced to a small area around Constantinople (now Istanbul) in little more than a century. The Dark Ages—or rather the latest dark age—had arrived.

The history of civilization cannot be explained only in terms of war, any more than it can be seen solely in terms of climatic change or monetary policy or even the spread of infectious diseases (though all of these have been attempted). But we, who live amid constant change, feel the need for an explanation of why change was so slow until the recent past—why the middle passage took so long—and what we overlook is how vulnerable earlier civilizations were. They did quite enough damage to themselves with their incessant wars, but they faced a greater peril from outside.

Happiness lies in conquering one's enemies, in driving them in front of oneself, in taking their property, in savoring their despair, in outraging their wives and daughters. —Genghis Khan[19]

By now we have forgotten the terror, and nomads are picturesque, dying cultures to be preserved and patronized. But for most of recorded history the civilized societies of the world were relatively small areas—in China, northern India, the Middle East, and Europe—fringing the vast five-thousand-mile sweep of open grasslands from Southern Russia to Mongolia that nurtured the nomad peoples. And periodically the nomads erupted outwards from the Eurasian heartland to smash those civilizations or drive them back to a lower level. They also guaranteed that all the survivors would be thoroughly militarized states.

The nomads (more properly, the pastoral peoples, for they did not normally migrate voluntarily over vast distances) were as different from the tiny hunting-and-gathering tribes of ten thousand years ago as the civilized peoples were, but they had taken a different route. Their economy was not based on agriculture but on herds of animals, and they were inevitably the envious enemies of peoples who had learned to farm more fertile lands, built cities, and grown comparatively rich.

What made the nomads so dangerous was that they were not savages. The weapons technology of civilized societies was so simple and slow to change that all but the heaviest siege weapons soon diffused into the nomad lands by trade and example—and something else was transmitted as well. Even when the first recorded mass movement of pastoral peoples, that of the Indo-Europeans, inundated much of the civilized world four thousand years ago, they had already learned to combine into super-tribes so numerous that they were comparable in some ways to whole states on the move, complete with a rudimentary army patterned loosely on those of the settled peoples.

It is still not entirely clear what periodically set the pastoral peoples into motion en masse toward the borders of civilization. The leading edge of the migrations that actually hit the frontiers was often made up of tribes in flight from other, more powerful peoples behind them, who were in turn refugees from some other group back in the Central Asian heartland of the nomads' territory. Population pressure and periodic decreases in rainfall over the finely balanced ecology of the grasslands probably provided the initial push as a rule, but there was also the attraction of the rich plunder to be had in the settled lands. And when the nomads came up against civilized armies, they had considerable advantages.

They were poorer, less well organized, and less heavily armed, but they were enormously mobile, being mostly mounted on horses. Moreover, they could put practically their entire male population of military age into battle. There were no "nomadic hordes": the civilized peoples greatly outnumbered the nomads even several thousand years ago, because farming feeds far more people from the same area of land than herding. But a pastoral nation that can put 100 percent of its young men into highly mobile raiding parties can take on a peasant society of ten times its population with a good prospect of success, if its weapons are comparable—and very often the nomads did succeed.

The dark age that Europe remembers, when successive waves of nomadic invaders—Goths, Vandals, Huns, and Magyars—overran the Western Roman world in the fourth century and kept coming until the ninth, was at least the third such upheaval to devastate and disrupt the civilizations based around the Mediterranean since 2000 B.C. Each time it took centuries to put the pieces back together—especially since it was often the victorious nomads who had to do the job of reconstructing civilization. Of all the areas where civilizations emerged in the Old World, only China still speaks the language it started out with; elsewhere, the Indo-European, Turkish, and Arab languages of various waves of nomadic conquerors have blotted out the old tongues.

Although China's language and culture survived the nomads, its people often didn't: the Great Wall was not a lasting military success. The Huns overran northern China in A.D. 304 (some seventy years before Fritigern destroyed the Roman legions at Adrianople), initiating an era of complete chaos that lasted four centuries. The Mongols in the thirteenth century were even worse. Though they were eventually absorbed by Chinese culture, it was not before they had carried out the greatest genocide in history: an estimated forty million Chinese were systematically slaughtered by Genghis Khan's soldiers to depopulate the northern areas of the country and free them for nomadic herding. And Iraq, which was visited by the Mongols for only two years, in 1258–60, was so thoroughly devastated that its population did not recover to the pre-Mongol level until this century.

The delays, setbacks, and lost chances suffered by civilization through most of its history because of these sporadic but overwhelming catastrophes cannot be calculated precisely, but they must go a long way toward explaining why "progress" is a relatively recent concept. It is, after all, only seven centuries since Mongol troops were operating a day's ride from Vienna—and if they had overrun Western Europe at that time, it is hard to believe that the process of cumulative and accelerating change that arose in that region over the following centuries to produce the modern world would ever have begun at all. But when Hungary and Poland were already in the Mongols' grasp, Genghis Khan died, and they turned back to deal with the succession struggle within the Mongol Empire. Europe got its chance, and the style of civilization it produced has now pushed the nomads to the utmost borders of irrelevance. It has also delivered us to the brink of the abyss.

The history of warfare is inevitably Eurocentric, because it was, after all, the Europeans who eventually conquered most of the world, and the weapons and modes of warfare devised by European civilization still dominate the planet. But the emphasis on European military history can be a considerable obstacle to a clear view of the relatively straightforward way in which warfare actually developed over time. For during a period of almost a thousand years, in the latter part of the middle passage, Europe fell out of the military mainstream and adopted a rather eccentric style of warfare. The barbarians had taken over, and they brought their military customs with them.

The Dark Ages were never so dark as Europeans tend to think, especially in those areas that were overrun by the Islamic cultures. In the Muslim states, after an initial period of chaos and slaughter, what eventually emerged was essentially a politically fragmented variant of the old classical civilizations in an Islamic idiom. In Western Europe the invaders were genuine barbarians, sharing none of the assumptions and values of civilized societies, and the destruction was far greater. There were several centuries of almost total breakdown, and when a stable social structure reemerged, it was based on an extreme dispersal of political and military power: the real power base in feudal times was not the state (which scarcely existed) but the few dozen or hundreds of square miles that had been nailed down by some local warrior.

Everywhere in the European/Mediterranean region, moreover, the nomad conquests meant that cavalry came to dominate the battlefield and continued to do so even many centuries after the new order was thoroughly established. In the East, it remained largely in the original nomad tradition of fast, lightly armed, and armored clouds of horsemen whose main weapons were the bow and arrow for harassing attacks from a safe distance, and the sword and light lance for the much rarer occassions when they closed with their opponents. In the West, cavalry warfare eventually evolved into the unique forms of riders wearing armor covering their entire bodies, astride great, lumbering horses bred for their ability to carry weight, depending for their effect on the sheer impact of their charge— sort of a mounted (and distinctly less organized) version of the phalanx.

Horses were practically a way of life for the nomads when they first burst through the borders of civilization, and horses had played a key role in their original conquests. However valuable infantry may be on the battlefield, they are of no use if they can't be there when you need them— and men on foot move more slowly than men on horseback. Once the classical world began to be faced with constant incursions by mounted bands of nomadic peoples, it had to respond with equally fast-moving forces of its own: the proportion of cavalry to infantry rose steadily in late Roman armies. But the total dominance that cavalry enjoyed in the centuries after the nomads had won can't be explained simply in terms of military logic.

The continuing preference for cavalry, long after the conquerors were the established rulers of large settled populations able to provide trained and disciplined infantry armies in the old pattern, was in some measure simply a question of cultural style. Horses, as the upper class everywhere in Europe remembers to this day (and as every former infantryman would readily agree), are much more fun. They also offered far more scope for the individual feats of glory that were the whole reason-for-being of the nomadic warriors and their heirs, the European nobility, than being stuck somewhere in the middle rank of a phalanx—and if nobody spoiled the game by raising a serious force of infantry, then cavalry would settle all the battles.

Warfare is a serious business, and it may seem incredible that anything so frivolous as one kind of fighting being more fun and more "honorable" than another could influence the dominant military style of an entire era, but there may be a precedent. Generations of military historians have tried to explain the prominence of the chariot in the warfare of the early second millennium B.C. in strictly military terms (without great success), overlooking the fact that the chariot was the hereditary fighting vehicle of the Indo-European nomads who seized much of the civilized world in that earlier dark age—and the fact that it was much more exciting (and probably safer) to dash glamorously around the battlefield in a chariot than to be an infantryman. The chariots were the fighter planes of their day, and every red-blooded young noble wanted to be in one. The suspicion lingers that the dominance of cavalry in the centuries between the fall of Rome and late medieval times owes much to a similar sentiment.

The other factor militating against a revival of infantry was practical: it would have meant handing over military power from the rulers to the ruled. The average subject in a medieval peasant society could not take part in cavalry warfare because only wealthy feudal landowners could afford the horses and armor required, but given proper training he could certainly have been turned into an effective infantry-man. However, infantry means large numbers, and so necessarily implies placing military power in the hands of ordinary citizens. This did not pose a serious problem for classical civilization, which began as homogeneous city-states and ended up as mass societies in an almost modern sense—the widening of the recruiting base of the Roman army and the gradual extension of Roman citizenship to embrace the entire empire proceeded more or less in step— but it would have had (and eventually did have) revolutionary implications for the rigidly stratified societies that grew out of the nomadic conquests.

In every society the nomad invaders conquered, they were never more than a minority of the population. The Franks in France, the Arabs in Spain, the Turks in Anatolia, each constituted a warrior ruling caste that naturally monopolized military power and equally naturally favored the form of military power they knew best, cavalry. Quite apart from the fact that, in Western Europe at least, society had taken such a battering that it probably lacked the social discipline and organizational skills to produce highly trained and highly motivated formations of infantry in the first centuries after the barbarian conquests, it was nowhere in the conquerors' interests to call back into existence a form of warfare that would undermine the primacy of their cavalry formations.

Even though within a few centuries the cultural and linguistic gulf between conquerors and conquered was usually erased by assimilation in one direction or the other—in France, for example, the Franks became Christian and took to speaking Old French, while in Anatolia the formerly Christian and Greek-speaking peasantry became Islamized and Turkish-speaking—the descendants of the conquerors remained the ruling class, though they increasingly recruited among the conquered population to replenish their ranks, and their understandable preference for cavalry warfare survived for a very long time.

This admittedly begs the question of why, in that case, the infantry-based armies of classical civilization were ever overwhelmed by the nomads in the first place. There is no truly satisfactory military answer, and generations of historians have built successful careers on searching for equally elusive answers in the economic, political, and social fields. (The real answer is "insufficient data": we have fewer hard facts about ten centuries of Roman history than about the last ten years in Rwanda.) Nevertheless, by the late Middle Ages, when the population, prosperity, and organizational competence of Western Europe were again approaching the level of Roman times, infantry reemerged as the dominant force on the battlefield, even though there had been no significant change in the technology of weapons.

The first signs of the shift back to infantry came during the Hundred Years' War (fourteenth to fifteenth centuries), in which English longbowmen protected themselves from cavalry charges by patterns of holes dug in front of their lines to break the legs of charging horses or by pointed stakes dug into the ground (the equivalent of the phalanx's hedge of spears), and repeatedly decimated French formations of heavily armored cavalry. (It is probably significant that this development came at a time when the English monarchy had at last begun to break the dispersed power of the feudal nobility, and a truly national English society with a real central government was beginning to emerge.)

In an attempt to deal with the threat posed by longbows (and crossbows), which propelled an arrow with enough force to penetrate chain mail at a considerable distance, the mounted knights were first driven to the use of plate armor: the classic iron pajamas worn by the last few generations of European chivalry. Their plate armor was carefully designed with ridges and oblique facets that would deflect arrows—to pierce plate armor effectively, an arrow had to strike it at an angle of nearly ninety degrees within a distance of two hundred yards—but they could not protect their horses all over with similar armor; the weight was simply too great. The last battles of the Hundred Years' War, like Agincourt in 1415, saw the pathetic spectacle of dismounted knights, wearing about sixty pounds of plate armor each, attempting to charge on foot like infantry. Chivalry, in the most literal sense, was dead.

The lesson was taken: if infantry is really the most effective element on the battlefield, then it ought to be really infantry, and not dismounted horsemen in metal clothing. By the sixteenth century, despite the advent of gunpowder weapons on the battlefields of Western Europe, combat once again centered on clashes of heavy infantry fighting in a style that would have been entirely familiar to Alexander the Great. For example, toward the end of the Italian wars, a conflict between France and the "Imperial" forces (Spain and most of Germany and Austria) that was fought mostly in northern Italy between 1464 and 1559, two matched armies met each other at Ceresole, not far from Turin.

They were smaller than most of the armies at the great battles of classical times—only about fifteen thousand on each side—and the year was A.D. 1544, not 332 B.C.. But over the previous century the Europeans had reinvented the principles of a serious body of infantry: uniforms, numbered units, flags to identify them and keep them together, drill, a rigid discipline, marching in step, the lot. And when the two sides lined up one pleasant April morning on two facing ridges with a gentle dip between them, Alexander could have taken command of either side with no more preparation than a crash course in a new language (four languages, actually, as there were Spaniards on one side, French on the other, and Italians and German or Swiss-German mercenaries on both sides).

There were a few tactical variations, caused by the innovation of firearms: the infantry phalanxes were essentially the same, carrying pikes that were no more than glorified spears, but the French had thought it might be useful to place a rank of *arquebusiers* (men armed with heavy matchlock muskets that fired a half-ounce bullet) behind the first rank of pikemen. As Captain Blaise de Montluc explained, "In this way we should kill all their captains in the front rank. But we found they were as ingenious as ourselves, for behind their first line of pikes they had put pistoleers. Neither side fired till we were touching—and then there was wholesale slaughter. Every shot told: the front rank on each side went down. The second and third ranks met over the corpses of their comrades in front, the rear ranks pushing them forward. And as we pushed harder, the enemy tumbled over."[20].

In the end, it came to the same old shoving match that the hoplites knew: the "push of pike," as men of the sixteenth century called it. The French and their Swiss mercenary allies had the advantage of pushing downhill, for the *Landsknechte*, their German mercenary opponents in the center of the Imperial line, had rashly advanced beyond the bottom of the dip and onward, uphill toward the French. When a small force of French heavy cavalry hit the Germans in the flank, their formation folded up, and they were herded into a tightly packed mob where they had no space to use their pikes. Out of seven thousand *Landsknechte*, nearly five thousand were slaughtered. The Italian infantry on the left wing of the Imperial line had already marched off the field to save itself, but when the Spanish and German veterans on the Imperial right tried to retreat through a small wood to their rear, they were quickly cut off by the French cavalry, with the French infantry close behind.

> *And when they descried us only 400 paces away, and with our cavalry ready to charge, they threw down their pikes and surrendered to the horsemen. You might see fifteen or twenty of them round a man at arms, pressing about him and asking for quarter, for fear of us of the infantry who were wanting to cut all their throats. A great many—perhaps half—got killed, the rest were accepted as prisoners.*[21]

Presumably the battle of Ceresole settled something, though nobody remembers exactly what it was. But it was full circle: the Dark Ages and their cavalry interlude were long past, and what happened at Ceresole was indistinguishable, except in minor details, from what had happened at Megiddo three thousand years before, or at Issus halfway between the two.

NOTES

1. Virgil, *The Aeneid*, tr. W. F. Jackson Knight, London: Penguin Books, 1968, pp. 62–65.

2. The eyewitness account of Polybius itself is lost, but this account by Appian is directly based on it. Susan Rowen, *Rome in Africa*, London: Evans Brothers, 1969, pp. 32–33.

3. Ibid.

4. Cornelius Tacitus, *The Histories*, tr. Kenneth Wellesley, London: Penguin Books, 1982, p. 156.

5. Ibid., p. 165.

6. E. R. Chamberlin, *The Sack of Rome*, London: Batsford, 1979, pp. 176–78.

7. Ibid.

8. Ibid.

9. Graham Webster, *The Roman Imperial Army*, London: Adam Charles Black, 1969, p. 221.

10. Thucydides, *History of the Peloponnesian War*, London: Penguin, 1954, p. 392.

11. Herodotus, describing the battle of Marathon in *The Histories*, tr. Aubrey de Selincourt, London: Penguin, 1954, pp. 428–29.

12. F. E. Adcock, *The Greek and Macedonian Arts of War*, Berkeley: University of California Press, 1957, p. 14.

13. Aeschylus, *The Persians*, lines 355 ff. For dramatic purposes, Aeschylus was describing the battle from the Persian side.

14. Thucydides, op. cit., pp. 182–83. Here Phormio addresses the crews of the Athenian fleet before the Battle of Naupactus, 429 B.C. As it turned out, Phormio was lured into the gulf, and lost eleven of his twenty ships there in half an hour.

15. Ibid, pp. 523–24.

16. Keith Hopkins, *Conquerors and Slaves*, Sociological Studies in Roman History, Vol. 1, Cambridge: At the University Press, 1978, p. 33.

17. Ibid, p. 28.

18. Edward N. Luttwak, *The Grand Strategy of the Roman Empire From the First Century A.D. to the Third Century A.D.*, Baltimore: Johns Hopkins Press, 1976, pp. 15, 189.

19. Witold Rodzinski, *A History of China*, Oxford: Pergamon Press, 1979, pp. 164–65.

20. Charles C. Oman, *The Art of War in the Sixteenth Century*, London: Methuen, 1937, pp. 237–38.

21. Ibid., p. 240.

An Assyrian bas-relief from the time of the siege of Troy showing a siege tower, rather like a large horse, assaulting the city of Dabigu. Note the common practice of impaling enemies at upper center, and the realistic throat-cutting and mayhem to the left. *The Campaigns of Tiglath-Pileser III, from the Bronze Gates of Balawat, lower band; Courtesy of The British Museum*

The Greeks peeking out at the Trojans from their wooden
horse, in a version of the event created generations later.
*Pithos from Mykonos of the Greek Wooden Horse; Ar-
chaeological Museum, Mykonos*

Pelting invaders with rocks, Roman soldiers, like the Trojans, defend their besieged fortress against barbarians. *Attack of Dacians on a small fort held by the Romans, Trajan's Column (cast); Alinari/Art Resource*

Early SS methods: the wholesale slaughter of defeated enemies. Rome's Final Solution to the Barbarian Problem. *German prisoners being decapitated, Column of Marcus Aurelius; Alinari/Art Resource*

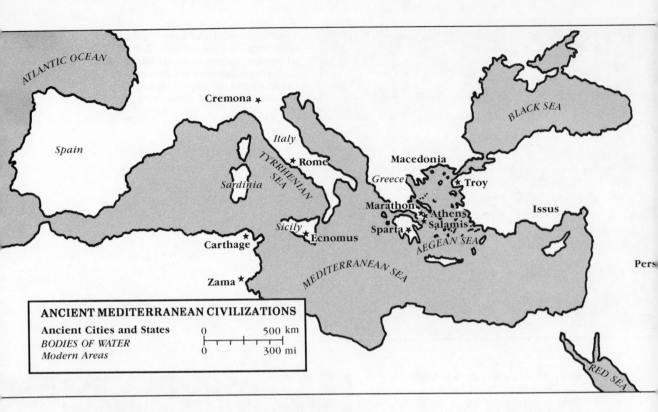

ANCIENT MEDITERRANEAN CIVILIZATIONS

Ancient Cities and States
BODIES OF WATER
Modern Areas

0					500 km
0					300 mi

ATLANTIC OCEAN

Spain

★ Cremona

Italy

TYRRHENIAN SEA

★ Rome

Sardinia

Sicily

★ Ecnomus

Carthage ★

Zama ★

MEDITERRANEAN SEA

Macedonia

Greece

★ Troy

Marathon ★

★ Athens
★ Salamis
Sparta ★

AEGEAN SEA

BLACK SEA

Issus

Pers

RED SEA

The relatively well-documented "middle passage," in
which the great city-states, and a few Eastern empires,
rose and fell according to the fortunes of war. Each state
on this page annihilated one or more of its fellows and
was in turn destroyed.

A healthy and brutal-looking selection of Roman troops, battling their way toward rape and plunder, around the time of the sack of Cremona. *Trajan's Column (cast); Alinari/Art Resource*

Pope Leo I making a fairly miraculous peace with Attila the Hun in the fifth century. Raphael commemorated the event in 1511; only sixteen years later the Spanish sacked Rome. One may imagine the citizens engulfed in the hellish fires on the right. *Raphael, Leo I Meets Attila, Vatican, Stanza, ca. 1511; Scala/Art Resource*

A few hundred men acting in concert, with a common purpose. A Greek hoplite phalanx advancing into battle to the sound of flutes. This is heavy infantry; notice the leg armor, enveloping helmets, and huge shields. *The "Chigi-Kane" vase; Museo Nazionale de Villa Giulia, Rome*

The Greek phalanx drifting to the right, with each man's shield tucked behind his neighbor's. Light infantry is represented by the two archers, Apollo and Artemis, advancing in a skirmish line to the left (their bronze bows have disappeared). *The Battle of the Gods and the Giants, from the north frieze of the Siphnion Treasure-House at Delphi; Delphi Museum*

Greek hoplites advancing. Soldiers, from a Mycenean *crater* dating back thirteen centuries before Christ, dealing with enemies exactly as they had for 2000 years before and would for another 1500 to come. *National Archeological Museum, Athens*

Alexander's army fighting the Persians at a late and exhilarating (for the Greeks) point in the battle, when the phalanx has broken through, the ground is littered with bodies, and the cavalry is mopping up fleeing refugees. *The Alexander Sarcophagus (the Sarcophagus of Abdalonymous); Archaeological Museum, Istanbul*

The remarkable power of discipline and formation, even with primitive weapons. One of the Roman Army's most famous tactics, the "Testudo" or tortoise, in which besieging troops joined their rectangular shields above their heads to create a roof to protect themselves against the shower of weapons, rocks, and boiling oil from above. *Column of Marcus Aurelius; Alinari/Art Resource*

The aquatic version of a land battle between Roman battleships descended from highly efficent Greek triremes. Note the three banks of oars visible on the boats to the right, and the troops, with shields and swords at the ready, who were likely to drown either during the battle or on their way home. *Pompeii, decorative fresco from the Room of the Vettii; Scala/Art Resource*

Hunting down the now-extinct Sarmati, one of Rome's many wars of annihilation. *Trajan's Column (cast); Alinari/Art Resource*

Building one of the many outposts that halted barbarian incursions into the Roman Empire—at least temporarily. *Trajan's Column (cast); Alinari/Art Resource*

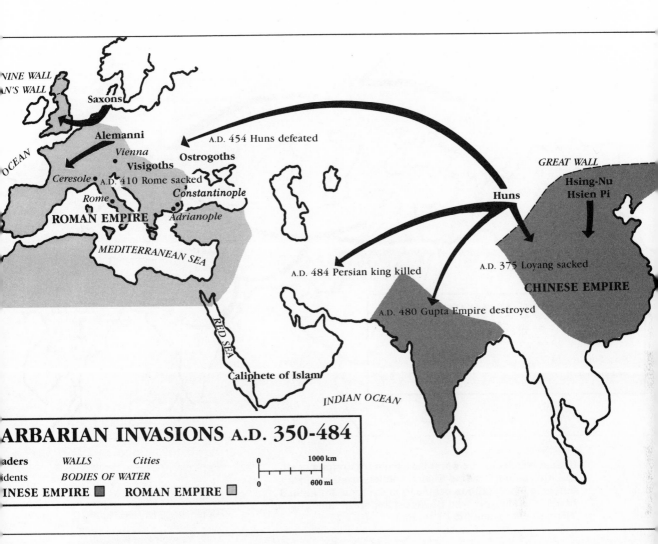

ARBARIAN INVASIONS A.D. 350-484

aders   WALLS   Cities

idents   BODIES OF WATER

INESE EMPIRE   ROMAN EMPIRE

0 — 1000 km

0 — 600 mi

The peril outside. We have forgotten the terror now, but for most of recorded history (and unrecorded history as well) wave after wave of mounted nomads succeeded in destroying settled civilizations in their moments of weakness. These did in the Roman Empire.

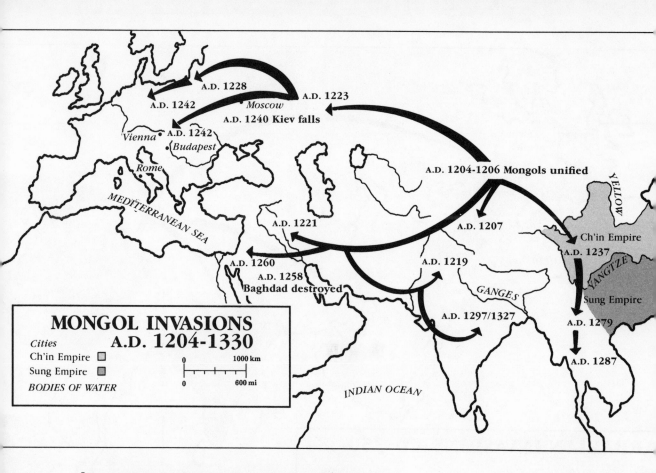

MONGOL INVASIONS
A.D. 1204-1330

Cities
Ch'in Empire ☐
Sung Empire ☐
BODIES OF WATER

0   1000 km

0   600 mi

A.D. 1228
A.D. 1242
Moscow
A.D. 1223
A.D. 1240 Kiev falls
Vienna • A.D. 1242
• *Budapest*
• *Rome*
MEDITERRANEAN SEA
A.D. 1204-1206 Mongols unified
A.D. 1221
A.D. 1207
A.D. 1219
YELLOW
Ch'in Empire
A.D. 1237
A.D. 1260
A.D. 1258
Baghdad destroyed
A.D. 1297/1327
GANGES
YANGTZE
Sung Empire
A.D. 1279
A.D. 1287
INDIAN OCEAN

In some respects, the worst barbarian incursions of all. In China alone, Genghis Khan's soldiers systematically butchered forty million people to make room for animal herds. The Mongols held Budapest and were knocking on Vienna's door when the Khan died.

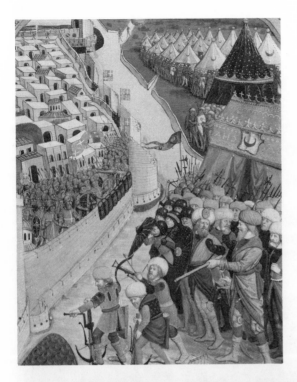

The nomadic invaders neglected mass infantry armies; they clung to their own military style—warfare on horseback—long after they conquered civilized states. *The Siege of Rhodes by the Turks from Caousin's* Relation du Siege de Rhodes; *Bibliothèque Nationale, Paris*

The pathetic spectacle of dismounted knights in their sixty pounds of iron attempting to fight on foot, and how easy they were to dispatch—with sticks or rocks or whatever came to hand—once you knocked them over. *A late fifteenth-century manuscript illumination; The British Museum*

Two solid *tercios* of pikemen twenty or thirty deep in the pike push of a sixteenth-century battle. True to the ideals of his time, Bruegel has emphasized the noble and glorious cavalry in the foreground, but battles were actually decided by infantry (the men being crushed in the center), and cavalry was mostly used for mop-up and skirmishes. *Detail from Peter Bruegel the Elder,* The Suicide of Saul, *1562; Kunsthistorisches Museum, Vienna/Photo Meyer*

3: The Road to Mass Warfare

Blessed be those happy ages that were strangers to the dreadful fury of these devilish instruments of artillery, whose inventor I am satisfied is now in hell, receiving the reward of his cursed invention, which is the cause that very often a cowardly base hand takes away the life of the bravest gentleman.

—Don Quixote

At the time of Ceresole, the most powerful weapons in the world, the great siege cannons, were capable of killing perhaps half a dozen people (if they stood close together) at a range of a few hundred yards. Today, less than four and a half centuries later, the modern counterparts of those weapons, the intercontinental ballistic missiles, can kill several million people at a range of seven or eight thousand miles. The process that has brought us from there to here has not been a simple one (though in retrospect it seems likely that it was inevitable), and only the very last phase of it has been dominated by technology.

"Modern" Europe, whose style of warfare has become the model for most of the world, emerged from its feudal cocoon five or six centuries ago, and only in the last 150 years have its weapons been anything special. But from the start it was evolving a system of war distinguished by its rational and disciplined application of existing technology to battle. Even more importantly, it was becoming a society whose wealth and composition would eventually allow it to make the leap into mass warfare on an unprecedented scale—and mass warfare was the only foundation on which, with the aid of technology, the absurd and lethal phenomenon of total war could ever have been built.

We now tend to identify the invention of gunpowder as the point of departure for the drastic changes that have produced the technologically based total war that threatens our own time. But new technology was only peripheral to the essential early phases of change, in which mercenaries replaced feudal armies, regular armies supplanted the mercenaries, and the regular armies of professional soldiers were finally expanded into mass armies. Firearms played a significant part only in the first step of that process—the reduction of the mounted knight from the leading actor on the battlefield to the position of ornate irrelevance that he occupied by the time *Don Quixote* was written. And even in that stage of the process, firearms may not have been essential to the change.

The explosive results of mixing saltpeter, sulphur, and charcoal were first discovered in China (probably by accident, as the soil near Peking is heavily impregnated with saltpeter). The Sung dynasty was a period of remarkable technological innovation in China, and as early as 1232, Chinese troops defending the city of Loyang against the Mongols used a "thunder bomb," an iron vessel filled with gunpowder and hurled among the besiegers by catapult. The explosion blew those nearby to pieces, and splinters from the casing pierced metal armor.

Within twenty-five years Chinese technicians had developed the "fire lance," a primitive gun consisting of a bamboo tube stuffed with gunpowder which, when ignited, would fire a cluster of pellets about 250 yards. Their Mongol enemies also adopted the new weapon and probably transmitted it to Europe, where Mongol armies were also active. As early as the 1320s, the first real metal guns were being cast in Europe.[1]

From that point onward, the lead in developing firearms passed entirely into European hands. Europe in the fourteenth and fifteenth centuries was an area of rapidly growing wealth and population, straining against the confines of its medieval straitjacket—and also a continent divided into dozens of separate states and torn by constant wars. Any new weapon was welcome, and within two centuries firearms had been elaborated at one extreme into giant cannons able to hurl an iron shot weighing 1,125 pounds at city walls, and at the other into arquebuses (early muskets) that fired half-ounce bullets to an effective range of a hundred yards.

It was even common at one time for historians to give a specific date for the end of the Middle Ages: 1453, when the fourteen miles of walls surrounding the city of Constantinople, which for most of the previous thousand years had been the world's greatest metropolis, were breached by the massed cannon fire of the Turkish army under the young Sultan Mehmet II, and the Byzantine Empire, the last surviving remnant of the Roman Empire, ceased to exist. It seemed a perfectly obvious chain of cause and effect. Cannons could knock over castle walls; therefore the independent power of the feudal nobility was destroyed, and so gunpowder began the march of progress that achieved perfection in the nineteenth century.

The military reality at the time was quite different. The old-style medieval castles and town walls were hopelessly vulnerable to gunfire, but by the seventeenth century new kinds of fortifications were definitely winning the technological race against the cannons of the time. And on the battlefield it was centuries before firearms came into their own. Primitive muskets gradually took over from longbows or crossbows as the principal missile-firing weapon—in 1476 one fifth of the infantry of Milan was already equipped with them, and by a century later archers had disappeared from European armies—but weapons like arquebuses made very little real change in the way battles were fought.[2] They would produce about the same effect as a crossbow and took less training to use, and they made a very satisfactory bang (which was undoubtedly one of the reasons for preferring them), but the arquebusiers remained essentially a secondary element in battle right down to the seventeenth century. The solid core of the army was still the massed ranks of disciplined pikemen who could defend themselves (and the arquebusiers) from cavalry charges and whose clashes with the other side's similarly equipped phalanxes of pikemen generally decided the battle.

What the European states were really doing in the fifteenth and sixteenth centuries was reinventing the infantry armies of classical antiquity—and they were doing it in a specific political and social context. Everywhere it was the monarchs, seeking to increase the power of the central government and undermine the resistance of the old feudal aristocracy, who fostered the new infantry armies. Not only were they more effective militarily, but they saved the king from having to call on the feudal levies of the barons in time of war, which would have given the nobility an opportunity to claw power back from the center in return for its support.

Ideally the monarch would have hired or conscripted his new model army from his own population, and there were numerous attempts to create national militias under the control of the central government. In Spain in 1694, for example, there were 465,000 men registered in the militia. In practice, however, these attempts usually foundered because of the reluctance of the peasantry and the resistance of the aristocracy, which the monarchies were not yet powerful enough to overcome. So it was instead the golden age of mercenaries, who would fight under contract for any government able to pay them: the export of companies of trained mercenary soldiers became practically a national industry in the poorer parts of Europe like Switzerland.[3] And because mercenaries cost so much, armies stayed small—on average only about ten thousand men per side in a sixteenth-century battle.

Feudalism was not destroyed by firearms. The whole basis for the economic and political power of the feudal nobility was being undermined by the shift from agriculture to commerce as the main source of wealth and the growing centralization of political power in the monarchy. Even on the battlefield what destroyed the military predominance of the mounted knight in armor was the reemergence of disciplined infantry armies, with or without firearms. But it was understandable that the old chivalry of Europe, increasingly desperate as its power in the state inexorably declined, should have identified firearms as the root of the trouble. With a few weeks' training a peasant with a musket could kill a knight who had spent his entire life training for battle, a monstrous reversal of the natural order of things. In Europe the feudal aristocracy could not do anything about it because there were too many other factors working against them— but on the other side of the world, where the warrior nobility faced only the threat of firearms and not a wholesale upheaval in the organization of society, they actually managed to buck the trend.

They have not more than five hundred matchlock-men, and if you reckon on them all hitting at the first volley, and also at the second, for after that men shoot wildly, we shall not lose more than a thousand killed and wounded, and that is nothing much.

Gen. Atobe Oinosuke's advice to his lord, Takeda Katsuyori,
before the battle of Nagashino, 1575[4]

Modern European firearms had reached Japan in Portuguese ships in 1542, and within a generation the Japanese were manufacturing cannons and arquebuses that were fully comparable to the contemporary European weapons. By the sixteenth century, when the entire country was caught up in a long civil war, the Japanese were also using their firearms more effectively than the Europeans. In 1567 Lord

Takeda Shingen instructed his officers, "Hereafter, guns will be the most important arms. Therefore decrease the number of spears [per unit], and have your most capable men carry guns." He was killed by a bullet himself six years later.

It was his successor, Takeda Katsuyori, who was reassured by his general in 1575 that he faced only five hundred musketeers at the crucial battle of Nagashino (recently re-created in the superb Japanese film *Kagemusha*). But General Atobe's advice to his master was disastrously wrong, for his enemies, Tokugawa Ieyasu and Oda Nobunaga, had not five hundred but ten thousand arquebusiers. They were drawn up in three ranks and trained to fire in volleys, one rank at a time, so that there was no long pause in the firing during reloading—a practice that did not appear on European battlefields for another half-century. But Takeda took his general's advice and committed all his men in a series of frontal assaults. The defenders stood their ground and fired methodically, mowing down sixteen thousand of Takeda's men. The Takeda clan never recovered from its losses.

> *Nobunaga and I were superior in numbers, and yet though we had a triple stockade in front of us he must come charging down on it. Naturally he got beaten. But if he had taken up a position behind the Takigawa river he could have held us for ten days anyhow and we should have had to retire. . . . It is a pity he was such a fool.* —*Tokugawa Ieyasu*[5]

In 1575, Japanese musketry was already the best in the world, and by the time of the great invasion of Korea in 1590, when three hundred thousand Japanese troops were bogged down by Korean resistance and facing a massive Chinese intervention, no practical Japanese soldier wanted to hear about edged weapons. One Japanese lord wrote home saying, "Please arrange to send us guns and ammunition. There is absolutely no need for spears." Another ordered that his reinforcements should "bring as many guns as possible. . . . Give strict orders that all the men, even samurai, carry guns."

And yet by 1675 there was hardly a gun of any kind to be found in Japan, and they had altogether disappeared from war. It is one of the most extraordinary about-faces in history: the Japanese looked down the road on which firearms were taking them, decided they did not like the destination, and simply turned back. When Perry's "black ships" finally forced Japan to reestablish contact with the rest of the world in 1854, they found a perfectly preserved medieval society, in which the weapons of war were swords, spears, and bows and arrows.

It is true that by 1615 the "Age of the Country at War" was over. Tokugawa's long struggle against his rivals ended in complete victory and inaugurated a period of over two centuries during which Japan had a relatively stable feudal system of government: the urgent pressure for efficiency in war was diminished. But that is not enough to explain the deliberate abandonment of firearms by the Japanese, nor is it to be imagined that seventeenth-century Japanese could foresee the ultimately devastating consequences of future developments in weapons technology. What worried them was the social implications of muzzle-loading muskets in the here and now—and rightly so.

It is not doing too much violence to history to compare the warrior class of samurai in Japan with the feudal nobility of Europe. Both were groups who owed their wealth, power, and social position to their proficiency with arms and derived their own self-respect from it. But proficiency with arms is only an important distinguishing mark if it takes long and arduous training to achieve and has a direct relationship to a man's chances of success and survival in battle—as it does with the sword, the spear, or the bow. Firearms take far less time to master and are much more democratic in their effects: samurai and commoners died with equal speed and equal futility in Takeda's desperate charges at Nagashino.

From the very beginning, the introduction of guns to battle roused resistance in Japan, because they practically abolished the single combats in which samurai could win personal glory—and the professional warrior class in Japan was huge: between 7 percent and 10 percent of the population, compared to less than 1 percent for the feudal nobility in Europe. The samurais' distaste for guns was so great that the majority of Oda's matchlock-men at Nagashino were yeoman farmers—which simply increased the offensiveness of the new weapon to the samurai: they were being killed by their social inferiors.

Once the civil wars and the Korean adventure were over, therefore, the pressure of the samurai became irresistible. In 1607 Tokugawa Ieyasu centralized firearms production at only two centers and created a commissioner of guns to license all orders. In practice only government orders were licensed, and those dwindled away to nothing in the course of the seventeenth century; as their craft was slowly strangled, the best Japanese gunsmiths gradually turned to making swords. Technological change is not irreversible; the ruling military caste in Japan gave up the gun because they feared that its socially leveling implications would ultimately undermine the military equation that kept them at the top of the social order.

There was a similar concern over the social effects of firearms among the professional military class in Europe. At the end of the fifteenth century, Gian Paolo Vitelli, one of the leading Italian *condottieri*, took to plucking out the eyes and cutting off the hands of all the arquebusiers he could capture, considering it disgraceful that noble men-at-arms should be killed from a distance by low-born infantrymen.[6] But Europe was not Japan. It was undergoing not just a military revolution, but far-reaching transformations in the whole structure of political authority and economic productivity that could not be turned back. By the mid-1500s Brescia and the surrounding Val Trompia, the main arms-producing area in Italy, were making twenty-five thousand muskets a year even in peacetime—and managed to quadruple that output during the war against the Turks in 1570–73.

Nevertheless, armies in Europe remained founded on the model perfected by the Spaniards, the most successful military power of the age: solid *tercios* (phalanxes) of pikemen sixteen, twenty, or even thirty ranks deep, with musketeers posted in the corners of the formation and the extremely heavy, just barely mobile field artillery of the time stationed across the front of the line. Cavalry was still present, posted in the wings, but as it too acquired firearms, its importance shrank further; frequently it did no more than trot up to an infantry formation, fire its pistols, retreat, reload, and repeat. But this unwieldy, slowed-down version of classical warfare (and much else) was to change in the cataclysm known as the Thirty Years' War.

From the mid-sixteenth century, Europe was increasingly torn by wars of religion arising out of the Protestant Reformation—notably the Huguenot wars in France in 1562–93 and the eighty-year Dutch revolt against Spanish rule that began in 1567. In the years after 1618 all the particular quarrels coalesced into the first war in which all the European powers became involved. By the time the Thirty Years' War ended in 1648, the international system based on the total sovereignty of the state, which now covers the whole world, was firmly in place, battles had taken on the form they were to retain until little more than a century ago—and eight million people were dead.

There was a genuine element of religious fervor in the war, which tended to make victors even more brutal and intolerant toward losers, but it was governments, not churches, who fought the war. There were also the beginnings of modern nationalism stirring in some of the peoples involved— especially the French, English, Dutch, and Swedish—and governments were quick to enlist those sentiments, like religious sentiments, in support of their policies. But the monarchs and their advisers mainly calculated in terms of power and security—the permanent currency of international politics. Religion had rather the same role in their thinking that ideology has in that of governments today.

Most Catholic and Protestant rulers really believed in their particular version of the truth, used it to justify their actions, and saw other like-minded rulers as their natural allies in the endless, merciless struggle for position, and even sheer survival, among the states of Europe. Most of them could no more have dissected the ideological component in their decisions from their reflexive concern for the state's power than the men of power in Moscow and Washington could do today. But what was actually emerging was a unified system of European states that all saw themselves as being in the game of power: a zero-sum game in which every increase in power for one state was automatically a loss of security for all the others, even if they were as far apart as Sweden and Spain, with little by way of concrete reasons for fighting each other. As the fear of Soviet power has driven Communist China into association with capitalist states today, so the fear of triumphant Catholic "Imperial" (Hapsburg) power drove Catholic France to ally itself with the weakening Protestant powers and prolong the war until the "balance of power" was restored (i.e., the war ended in a draw).

It was the Germans, on whose territory most of the battles of the Thirty Years' War were fought, who paid the price for this policy.

> *Drunk with victory, the troops defied all efforts to control them. . . . Towards midday flames suddenly shot up at almost the same moment at twenty different places. There was no time for Tilly and Pappenheim to ask whence came the fire; staring in consternation, they rallied the drunken, disorderly, exhausted men to fight it. The wind was too strong, and in a few minutes the city was a furnace, the wooden houses crashing to their foundations in columns of smoke and flame. The cry was now to save the army and the imperialist officers struggled in vain to drive their men into the open. Rapidly whole quarters were cut off by walls of smoke so that those who lingered for booty or lost their way, or lay in a drunken stupor in the cellars, alike perished.*[7]

The sack and destruction by fire of Magdeburg, with the death of some forty thousand inhabitants, came in 1631, when the worst phase of the war was just beginning. As ruthless armies of mercenaries marched across Germany season after season, taking whatever they wanted and spreading disease in their wake, the increasingly desperate and starving peasants were repeatedly driven to revolt, only to be ferociously repressed by all sides. The supply arrangements of the armies steadily deteriorated over the long years of the war, and the hungry soldiers' depredations on an already impoverished and denuded countryside grew even greater. Social order among the civilians and military discipline among the soldiers completely broke down over wider and wider areas of the country, and the landscape was filled with desperate bands of refugees and marauding groups of deserters whose behavior was virtually indistinguishable. Murder for a loaf of bread was commonplace, and there were numerous cases of cannibalism. By the time the Treaty of Westphalia brought a peace of exhaustion to Europe in 1648, the population of Germany had fallen from twenty-one million to only thirteen million; the thirty-five thousand villages of Bohemia had been reduced to only six thousand.

It was a century and a half before there was another war in Europe that caused deaths on anything like the same scale, and fully three centuries—almost down to the present—before civilian losses again outnumbered the military casualties. But the caution that restrained the rulers of Europe from engaging in another such bloodbath for so long had little to do with the horrors inflicted on the victims (of whom the overwhelming majority had been German peasants—only 350,000 soldiers were killed). It had a great deal to do with the rulers' vivid recollection that if wars get too badly out of hand, whole states and dynasties can disappear (as so many petty kingdoms did in Germany during the Thirty Years' War).

The primary goal of any state, any dynasty, is survival, and the vivid demonstration of what happens when wars go too far probably explains why the monarchs, even as they consolidated their newly won positions as the absolute rulers of sovereign states, simultaneously behaved as though they were all members of the same club. They would fight wars against each other, seize each other's border provinces or overseas territories, try to undermine each other's power in a hundred ruthless ways, but behind all that was the tacit agreement that no member of the rulers' club—or at least no important member—would ever lose so badly as to disappear from the game entirely. (The one significant exception, Poland, was a weak state partitioned by the unanimous agreement of all its powerful neighbors.) The aims of wars remained remarkably limited in the next 150 years, and the main source of the limitation was the overriding interest of each dynasty in survival.

That is not to say that battles became less violent, for this was the period in which firearms finally became the dominant weapon on the battlefield. The man most responsible for the change, King Gustavus Adolphus of Sweden, ruled a kingdom whose population of less than a million and a half left it in permanent difficulties against the stronger countries that surrounded it—Russia, Poland, and Denmark. Lacking the numbers he needed to fight his neighbors on an equal basis in the standard "push of pike," he set out in 1611 to remedy Sweden's military problems by tactical innovation—and created the first army that Alexander the Great would not have known how to command.

Gustavus Adolphus realized that the solid formations of pikemen modeled on the Spanish *tercios*, which then dominated European battlefields, were ideal targets for gunfire, if only he could get enough of it. So he had the standard Swedish musket redesigned until it was light enough to be used without a wooden rest propping up the front and fitted a wheel lock (rather like the ignition device on a modern cigarette lighter) to it to make it fire more reliably. He then converted two thirds of his infantry into musketeers, operating in ranks only six deep, and took almost all their armor away to make them more mobile.

He wrought the same transformation in artillery, abandoning the usual heavy field pieces drawn by twenty-four horses for light, quick-firing guns using a prepared cartridge that could be pulled by only one or two horses— and so could be moved around on the battlefield, even under fire.

The result of both changes was to make firepower highly effective on the battlefield for the first time. The musket volleys and cannon fire of Gustavus Adolphus's army could shatter a formation of pikemen from a hundred yards away, without ever coming into physical contact with it. And once the enemy formations were disordered by gunfire, his cavalry was trained to charge home with the sword and turn disorder into rout.

In addition to all this, his army was made up not of mercenaries but mostly of Swedes animated by genuine religious and national fervor, thanks to the military reforms of his father, who had required each district of Sweden to furnish a fixed number of men to a standing army. When this army arrived in Germany to rescue the failing Protestant cause in 1630, it demolished the old-style mercenary armies of its imperial (Spanish and Austrian) opponents with convincing efficiency. Gustavus Adolphus himself was killed in battle in 1632, and the Swedish intervention was in the end only one more episode in a seemingly endless war, but every other army in Europe rapidly adopted the revolutionary tactics originated by the Swedish king.

Firearms and not cold steel now decide battles.   —*J. F. Puysegur, 1748*[8]

The proportion of cavalry in European armies fell from almost a half to only a quarter in the century after the Thirty Years' War; infantry had really become the "Queen of Battles." The proportion of pikemen to musketeers also dwindled rapidly, the latter being issued with "plug bayonets" that they could insert into their musket barrels to serve as makeshift pikes if they were faced with a cavalry charge. This did, however, leave them with a particularly unhappy choice as the cavalry neared: whether to try for one last volley and face the risk of not having time to fix bayonets if it did not break the charge, or to plug the bayonets into their muskets early and abandon their firepower. But the invention of the socket bayonet, which left the musket free to fire, eliminated the pike's role entirely, and by 1700 all infantrymen carried muskets.

Moreover, the muskets they carried were now flintlocks, much improved weapons that misfired only twice in every ten shots and, in the hands of a well-trained soldier, could be loaded and fired twice a minute. They were highly inaccurate except at very close range, but that scarcely mattered, since they were not used against individual targets. The infantry battalion's job was to deliver volleys of fire; it could almost be described as a human machine gun with several hundred moving parts (the soldiers), capable of delivering a single burst of fire every thirty seconds.

Toward the end of the eighteenth century the Prussian army even conducted field experiments with their muskets, setting up a canvas target one hundred feet long and six feet high to simulate an enemy unit and having a battalion of Prussian infantry fire volleys at it from various ranges. At 225 yards only 25 percent of the bullets struck this huge target, but at 150 yards 40 percent hit, and at 75 yards, 60 percent of the shots told—which simply confirmed what every practical soldier already knew: fighting had to be done at as close a range as possible.[9]

During the battle of Fontenoy in 1745, for example, the British Guards Brigade, emerging from a sunken road, caught sight of the French infantry. The French officers called out to the British commander, Lord Charles Hay, inviting him to open fire, to which he replied with impeccable courtesy: "No, sir, we never fire first. After you." The British continued to advance (a guardsman in the ranks called out, "For what we are about to receive, may the Lord make us truly thankful") until the French finally let off their volley. And then while they were reloading, the surviving British troops marched on into the distance of only thirty paces and fired an answering volley that killed or wounded nineteen officers and six hundred men of the French in a single second—whereupon the rest understandably broke and fled. The famous command given to the American revolutionary troops at Bunker Hill—"Hold your fire until you see the whites of their eyes"—was not bravado, but the standard tactical doctrine of the time.

The discipline required for soldiers to stand up to this sort of battle was of a new order: the soldier had to go through the several dozen complicated movements necessary to load and aim his musket while facing what amounted to a firing squad only a hundred yards away, without even the emotional release of violent exertion and physical contact with the enemy. Standing in the ranks for hours under steady fire from artillery only five or six hundred yards away, which was often the lot of battalions not directly engaged in the fighting—they could even watch the gunners loading—must have been even worse. To keep men in the lines under such conditions took the most severe discipline: Prussian army regulations stated that "if a soldier during an action looks as if about to flee, or so much as sets foot outside the line, the noncommissioned officer standing behind him will run him through with his bayonet and kill him on the spot."[10]

The casualties in the eighteenth-century battle rivaled anything in ancient warfare, and now they were more evenly shared by the two sides than in the battles of earlier times, because most killing was done at a distance, and there was less chance of a massacre when the losers turned to retreat. Over two fifths of the casualties in a typical battle now came from musket fire, and another two fifths, from field artillery, with under a fifth being caused by swords and bayonets used at close range. But the overall scale of the carnage was undiminished: at Blenheim in 1704, for example, the victors lost 12,500 men (24 percent of their force), and the losers suffered 20,000 killed and wounded (40 percent of their force) in five hours of fighting on a single day. During the Seven Years' War (1756–63) the Prussian army lost 180,000 dead, three times the number it started out with.[11] Its commander, King Frederick the Great, complained that "recruits can replace the numbers lost but not their quality. . . . One commands in the end nothing more than a band of badly drilled and badly disciplined rustics."[12]

And yet the century and a half between the Thirty Years' War and the French Revolution (1648–1789) truly was an era of limited war. The battles were terrible, but they didn't happen very often. The armies grew larger—the average number of soldiers present on each side on the battlefield had risen from ten thousand to thirty thousand during the Thirty Years' War, and it jumped again to hover around the hundred thousand mark in the biggest battles of the eighteenth century—but they also grew steadily more isolated from civilian society both in their social composition and in their operations: mostly they fought each other and left the civilians alone.

Wars were almost constant, but their political consequences were curiously small, at least in Europe: a province or a few fortresses would change hands here, some overseas colonies there, and a different candidate might gain a throne somewhere, but there was little disturbance to the steady growth of population, prosperity, and industry across most of the continent. At the height of the Seven Years' War, Laurence Sterne left London for Paris without getting the necessary passport to travel in an enemy country ("it never entered my mind that we were at war with

France"), but nobody stopped him at the French coast, and the French foreign minister courteously sent him one after he had arrived at Versailles.[13]

It could almost be said that the monarchies of eighteenth-century Europe were deliberately excluding the great mass of their subjects from anything to do with war, just as they denied them any role in domestic affairs of state. It was an age of absolutism, and an absolute ruler wants his servants to be obedient instruments of his will, not independent citizens with interests and opinions of their own. The France of Louis XIV was already far wealthier and more populous than the Roman Empire during the Punic wars and could easily have created larger, cheaper armies based on the same principle of a universal obligation for military service—but that Roman army had served a republic, which was not at all what Louis XIV had in mind. The kind of army he and his fellow monarchs chose to create instead imposed very severe limitations on the style of warfare, but they were limitations that they were willing to accept.

By the end of the seventeenth century, all the kingdoms of Europe had created standing armies controlled and paid directly by their own governments. Regular troops had to be paid even in peacetime, but they were more reliable than mercenaries, and they freed the newly absolute monarchs from the necessity of relying on any particular section of the civil population for military help in a crisis, with the concomitant obligations and restraints on the monarch's power that that would imply. Moreover, it was an age intensely conscious of the need to build and safeguard the wealth of the national economy, and the last thing the monarchs wanted was to undermine it by putting several hundred thousand productive citizens into military service.

So the armies of Europe ended up almost everywhere being composed of "nobles and vagabonds." The numerous and still martially inclined nobility of Europe, many of whom were now verging on genteel poverty, were both subsidized and politically neutralized by being granted a near-monopoly on officers' jobs in the new regular armies. They no longer posed a threat to the central government's power in this capacity, as they were merely salaried servants of the state, not the independent commanders of troops they had raised themselves. The officer corps of the European armies became a vast system of outdoor relief for the titled classes (who proceeded to haggle and lobby to preserve and extend their near-monopoly over the officer ranks with a narrow determination worthy of a craft trade union threatened by changing circumstances).

The soldiers commanded by these officers came from the other extreme of the social spectrum: the best were landless peasants, penniless adventurers, and political refugees, but at least as many were drunks, chronic ne'er-do-wells, and outright criminals, for whom the army was the last refuge from starvation or from justice. Up to a third of the troops in the typical European armies were foreigners. Discipline in armies composed of such men could only be maintained by liberal use of the lash, the hangman's noose, and the firing squad: "In general, the common soldier must fear his officers more than the enemy," said Frederick the Great,[14] and Wellington remarked of his troops: "I don't know if they frighten the enemy, but by God they frighten me!"

What had happened, in essence, was that the groups in late seventeenth- and eighteenth-century society whose power and wealth were on the rise—the central government and the urban bourgeoisie—had hired the declining nobility and the down-and-outs of society to fight their wars for them. But the armies were still not cheap, at least in proportion to the resources available to the governments of the day. They had to be kept up to full war strength even in peacetime because it took several years of training to turn a recruit into a useful soldier.

Conditioning, almost in the Pavlovian sense, is probably a better word than *training*, for what was required of the ordinary soldier was not thought, but the ability to perform extremely complicated maneuvers in large formations and to load and fire their muskets completely automatically even under the stress of combat. This was accomplished by literally thousands of hours of repetitive drilling, accompanied by the ever-present incentive of physical violence as the penalty for failure to perform correctly. The trained soldier, however despised as an individual, was therefore an expensive commodity, irreplaceable in the short term, whose life the state was reluctant to squander in battle, a sentiment expressed by Marshal Saxe in 1732: "I do not favor pitched battles, especially at the beginning of a war, and I am convinced that a skillful general could make war all his life without being forced into one."[15]

The loss of a soldier by desertion was as serious as if he were killed in battle, but on the whole, desertion was a bigger problem. The miserable living conditions, the brutal discipline, and the stupefyingly boring training were unappealing enough in peacetime, but when soldiers devoid of patriotic feelings were also faced with the imminent prospect of a battle, their natural instinct was to desert. Despite the most stringent precautions against it, eighty thousand men managed to desert from the Russian army during the Seven Years' War, and seventy thousand from the French.[16] And the necessary precautions imposed very severe limitations on how the armies could operate.

It was practically impossible for an army to live off the land because if the soldiers were allowed to forage for themselves, the army would simply melt away. Therefore, eighteenth-century armies hardly ever cut loose from their supply lines for more than a short time, and the supply arrangements were extremely cumbersome. There had to be some central magazine near the area of operations, prepared long beforehand, which stored huge amounts of food for the troops. (During the Seven Years' War, bread was baked from flour forty years old.) The field ovens could advance up to sixty miles from the magazine in order to bake, and the bread wagons could deliver it another forty miles to the army, but that was the limit. In theory, at least, no army could advance more than a hundred miles into enemy territory without setting up an intermediate magazine. And since even this elaborate supply organization could not possibly bring up the fodder for the forty thousand animals that typically accompanied an army of a hundred thousand men, the armies spent much of their time just moving to new grazing grounds (forty thousand animals went through eight hundred acres a day).[17] This also obliged armies to restrict their campaigning to the months of May through October, when there was grass in the fields, except on the rarest occasions.

So wars tended to be fought in certain well-defined border areas that were full of fortresses, and warfare was a slow and cumbersome business consisting mainly of sieges: in 1708 Marlborough's siege train of eighteen heavy guns and twenty siege mortars required three thousand wagons and sixteen thousand horses to move it and took thirty miles of road. Armies maneuvered to threaten each other's supply lines and force a withdrawal, but actual battles were relatively rare because soldiers were too expensive to waste if an opponent could be forced to withdraw by maneuver, and the armies moved so slowly (except in the most skilled hands) that if either side was reluctant to fight, then the other would have great difficulty in forcing a battle.

All these limitations were reinforced by the limited goals of the wars; they were hardly ever fought for sheer survival. The unwritten understanding was that wars must not be pursued to the point where one power achieved total domination over the others or extinguished its rival utterly. This understanding was enforced by the device rather misleadingly known as the "balance of power": misleading, because it did not then (and does not now) mean that peace is to be ensured through establishing a permanent equality of power between states or alliances. Rather it meant that any country or alliance whose military power grew so great that it threatened the security of the other European states would automatically be confronted with an alliance of all the others—and the mechanism that made the system work was war.

In this, at least, Europe has been unified for over 350 years, since the Thirty Years' War. Almost all its major wars, whatever their specific origin, have rapidly spread to involve all the great powers of the time. By the eighteenth century, moreover, they were already world wars, in the sense that the fighting occurred all over the globe. During the Seven Years' War, for example, there was fighting in every continent except Australia. (In the peace settlement Britain, the biggest winner, kept Canada, Senegal, and some West Indian islands, and retained most of the fruits of Clive's military victories in India, but had to return Cuba, the Philippines, and Argentina to Spain.)

It had been the development of ocean-going sailing ships, the biggest and most complex machines men had ever built, that enabled the Europeans to establish their control over almost half the world during the first period of colonial expansion, in the sixteenth century. They did, of course, need to use military force to complete their conquest of the Western Hemisphere and much of Africa, but it did not require technology and organization of a very high order. Any other civilized domain—the Ottoman Empire in the Middle East, the Mogul Empire in India, or the Chinese

Empire—would have had as little difficulty in subjugating the Stone Age cultures who inhabited those areas of the world if they had possessed the ships and the commercial drive to take them there. As late as 1688, indeed, the military technology and organization of the Muslim world was still roughly comparable with that of Christian Europe, and an Ottoman army was able to besiege Vienna, more than halfway from Istanbul to Paris.

Nor did the technology of weapons change appreciably in the following century and a quarter. The flintlock muskets used at the battle of Blenheim in 1704 differed hardly at all from those employed by European armies of the 1830s, and the same applied to field artillery, warships, and almost every other category of weapon. But the rigid discipline and ruthlessly efficient organization that the Europeans brought to the use of these weapons, backed by their rapidly growing wealth, could not be matched by their opponents elsewhere, and by the eighteenth century other parts of the civilized world were beginning to fall under European rule: the British conquered most of India, and the Ottoman borders began to contract under Austrian and Russian pressure.

To a European of the last generation before the French Revolution, therefore, war would have seemed at worst a bearable evil—and perhaps even a beneficial phenomenon, on balance, since Europe's proficiency in the modern art of war was rapidly giving it the mastery of the whole world at a relatively low cost in money and lives. The incessant wars within Europe itself could not be seen in the same cheerful light, but at least they were well contained. A few areas that had the misfortune to constitute some sort of military crossroads took a severe beating from time to time (the province of Pomerania suffered seventy thousand civilian deaths, one fifth of its population, during the Seven Years' War),[18] but usually the suffering caused by war fell mainly on the soldiers, who lived a life apart from civil society. Cities were not sacked, civilians did not face intolerable demands for their taxes and their sons in order to fight wars, and whole countries did not disappear or dissolve into chaos as a result of war. The institution of war had been brought under control, limited, and rationalized (as that extremely rational age might have put it).

What the eighteenth century did not realize was how fragile all the limitations on war were.

The balance of power will continue to fluctuate, and the prosperity of our own or the neighbouring kingdoms may be alternately exalted and depressed; but these partial events cannot essentially injure our general state of happiness, the system of arts, and laws, and manners, which so advantageously distinguish, above the rest of mankind, the Europeans and their-

colonies. . . . In peace, the progress of knowledge and industry is accelerated by the emulation of so many active rivals: in war, the European forces are exercised by temperate and undecisive contests. —Edward Gibbon, 1782[19]

From this moment until that in which our enemies shall have been driven from the territory of the Republic, all Frenchmen are permanently requisitioned for service in the armies. The young men shall fight; the married men shall forge weapons and transport supplies; the women will make tents and clothes and serve in hospitals. . . . The public buildings shall be turned into barracks, the public squares into munition factories. . . . All firearms of suitable calibre shall be turned over to the troops: the interior will be policed with shotguns and cold steel. All saddle horses shall be seized for the cavalry; all draft horses not employed in cultivation will draw the artillery and supply wagons. —Decree of the National Convention, Paris, 1793[20]

The idyllic world so complacently described by Gibbon had less than a decade to run when he wrote, for it rested on highly unstable foundations. In particular, its restraint in the conduct of war was a highly artificial behavior that depended on the conviction of Europe's absolute monarchs that their common interest in the survival of their dynasties outweighed any disputes that divided them, and that to exploit the military resources of their kingdoms to the full in war would unleash social and political forces that would threaten their thrones. But ideas about equality and democracy, which were fundamentally hostile to the existing order, were the common currency of late eighteenth century thought, and even as Gibbon wrote, the first revolution based on those ideas was triumphing in the United States.

In 1789 the revolution arrived in France. The impact of that upheaval can only be compared to what would be the effect today if Maoists seized power in the United States, for France was then the intellectual and cultural center of Western civilization and by far the biggest country in Europe: even Russia did not overtake France in population until the mid–nineteenth century. Almost all the monarchies of Europe launched their armies against France to stamp out the sacrilegious revolutionaries, and when what was left of the old royal army, aided by volunteers, proved unable to stem the attacks, the National Convention decided on conscription: the *levée en masse*.

The first levy, in February 1793, demanded a quota of men from each district—each local battalion to be united under a banner bearing the inscription "The French people risen against tyranny"—but as the military situation continued to worsen, the convention issued the call for a *levée en masse* in August. By New Year's Day, 1794, the French armies numbered about 770,000 men,[21] and the wars of mass armies that ensued ravaged Europe for the next two decades.

Conscription was not an entirely new idea—as early as 1506 the *Ordinanza* in Florence had decreed obligatory military service for all fit males between eighteen and thirty—but it had never really amounted to more than compulsory selection of an unfortunate minority, nor had it lasted long or been extended to an entire country.

But the French Revolution, with its principles of liberty and equality, first stimulated and then exploited a fervent nationalism which made conscription acceptable. It also made French troops behave differently.

The "nation in arms" produced poorly trained soldiers (by eighteenth-century standards) who had no time to master the intricate drill of close-order formations, but their enthusiasm and numbers made up for it: attacking in clouds of skirmishers and disorderly columns, they often simply overwhelmed their better—trained adversaries. The new French armies moved far faster than before, having abandoned most of the baggage that encumbered the armies of the old regime. Soldiers no longer had tents, but only greatcoats, and if there was no bread they could dig in the fields for potatoes (whose cultivation had spread across Europe in the preceding decades). Battles rarely ended in draws any more—Carnot of the Committee of Public Safety instructed the French armies in 1794 "to act in mass formations and take the offensive. . . . Give battle on a large scale and pursue the enemy till he is utterly destroyed."[22]

The basic principle underlying all this was that whereas the prerevolutionary regular soldiers had been scarce and expensive, the lives of conscripts were plentiful and cheap. The disdain for casualties grew even greater once Napoleon had seized control of France in 1799. "You cannot stop me," he boasted to Count Metternich, the Austrian diplomat; "I spend thirty thousand men a month." It was not an idle boast: the losses of France in 1793–1814 amounted to 1.7 million dead—almost all soldiers—out of a population of 29 million.

Not much was said about the democratic ideals of the revolution after Napoleon made himself emperor in 1804: the war's aim was simply to establish French domination over all of Europe (and thus, in effect, to create a world empire). And yet, by adroit and cynical exploitation of the French appetite for national "glory"—together with all the means of compulsion available to a dictatorial government—Napoleon managed to keep going for another ten years of constant war. Between 1804 and 1813 he drafted 2.4 million men, few of whom were ever released again so long as they were still physically fit (and fewer than half of whom returned home at the end of the empire). "Troops are made to get killed," he once said, though as time went on the conscripts became less willing—by 1810, 80 percent of the annual quota of conscripts failed to appear voluntarily.[23]

If troops had become much cheaper in France, the weapons they used had not, but the revolutionary regime quickly discovered how easy it was for a truly centralized government with dictatorial powers to get more out of the economy than the old monarchy had ever dared to demand. State—owned arms factories multiplied, in which prices and wages were strictly controlled; equipment, food, and horses could simply be requisitioned, with payment made later at government—set prices, or never. And after the conquests began to accumulate, there was so much money coming in from abroad that for a time the wars actually paid for themselves.

It was far more difficult for the opponents of the French, who had to match the size of the revolutionary armies but did not dare to introduce universal conscription for fear that it would destroy the precarious structure that underpinned the monarchies in their countries too. That meant the troops had to be paid for, which imposed an awesome burden on their treasuries. Britain, the richest of the allies, which had to subsidise most of the others, introduced the world's first income tax in 1799 to meet its commitments.

Yet the other countries of Europe had to do whatever was necessary to stop the French, for the rules of war had been changed drastically; the revolutionary armies spread republicanism wherever they went, and Napoleon simply annexed entire kingdoms or turned them into satellites and placed his own relatives or marshals on the thrones. For the governments who fought the French, it was a war for sheer survival, and they would take almost any risk in order to survive—even to the extent of arming the people.

Arming the people became much safer after Napoleon declared himself Emperor of the French and the remaining revolutionary credibility drained away from the French cause. Now the French armies were simply foreigners attacking the motherland, and the monarchs could exploit the national feeling of their own people to mobilize resistance against them. Even Austria, a multinational empire, experimented with a popular militia in 1807 as being the only way "to remedy . . . the paucity of our resources" (though it was considered very dangerous politically by Austrian conservatives, and eventually withered away).[24] In Spain, which was under French occupation for half a decade, nationalist *guerrillas* fighting in the name of the exiled king, backed by a regular British army based in Portugal, inflicted as many casualties on the French over the years as the disastrous Russian campaign did. (The word *guerrilla* was coined in that struggle.)

And when Napoleon, having temporarily managed to subdue every other country on the continent, finally invaded Russia in 1812 with 440,000 men, the Russian response was similar. The campaign is known in Russian history as the "Great Patriotic War," a term revived by the Soviets to describe the struggle against Hitler, and the fighting was made more pitiless by a national antagonism that had simply not existed back in the time of limited wars and professional armies. At the battle of Borodino, the Russians' last stand before Moscow, described in the two eyewitness accounts below, they lost thirty-five thousand men, and the French, thirty thousand.

> *When we reached the crest of the ravine, we were riddled with grapeshot from the battery and several others flanking it, but nothing stopped us. Despite my wounded leg I did as well as my [men] in jumping out of the way of roundshot which ricocheted into our ranks. Whole files, half platoons even, went down under the enemy's fire, and left huge gaps. . . . A Russian line tried to stop us, but at thirty yards range we fired a volley and passed through. Then we dashed towards the redoubt and clambered through the embrasures. I went in just after a piece had been discharged. The Russian gunners received us with handspikes and rammers, and we fought them hand to hand. They were redoubtable opponents. A great many Frenchmen fell into rifle pits, jumbled up with the Russians already occupying them.*
>
> Capt. Charles François, 30th Regiment[25]

It was horrible to see that enormous mass of riddled soldiers. French and Russians were cast together, and there were many wounded men who were incapable of moving and lay in that wild chaos intermingled with the bodies of horses and the wreckage of shattered cannon. —Barclay de Tolly[26]

Napoleon won all the battles, including the crucial battle of Borodino, and even occupied Moscow, but the Russians refused to acknowledge that they were beaten, and he was eventually forced to retreat in the dead of winter through lack of supplies. The Russians had destroyed their own crops and food stocks rather than leave them to the French. Only a few thousand of the French made it out of Russia alive.

By calling up the class of 1814 a year early and drafting all those who had previously had exemptions, Napoleon managed to assemble another large army by the spring of 1813, when he rightly expected all the powers of Europe to attack him in an attempt to exploit his Russian disaster. But he was scraping the bottom of the barrel for manpower by then, and some of the new recruits got as little as a week's training before being thrown into battle. Even more seriously, the Prussians had finally decided to bring in conscription too. There was no kingdom in Europe more autocratic, more riddled with class privileges and inequalities, than Prussia, but by the law of 1813, all male Prussians were made liable for three years' service in the regular army upon reaching twenty, followed by two years in the active reserve and fourteen years in the *Landwehr* (territorial army).[27]

The Prussian army reformers gambled that a combination of patriotism and compulsion would make conscription work even without the revolutionary ideal of the equality of all citizens, that men would be seduced by the promise of an equality in battle that they were denied in their ordinary lives. In token of that, they founded the Order of the Iron Cross at the opening of the new war against Napoleon—a decoration for bravery that broke all the rules of Prussian society by being open equally to peasants, bourgeoisie, and nobles. Its decree stated, "In the present great catastrophe in which everything is at stake for the Nation, the vigorous spirit which elevates the Nation so high deserves to be honoured and perpetuated by some quite peculiar monuments. That the perseverance by which the Nation endured the irresistible evils of an iron age did not shrink to timidity is proved by the high courage which now animates every breast and which could survive only because it was based on religion and true loyalty to King and Country."[28]

"Get me a national army," Marshal Blücher had begged the Prussian reformers, and in 1813 he had one: the *Landwehr* battalions of conscripts tripled the size of his army and played a major part in the two decisive defeats of Napoleon at Leipzig in 1813 and at Waterloo in 1814. "The *Landwehr* battalions were so–so at first," Blücher said, "but after they had tasted plenty of powder, they did as well as the battalions of the Line."[29]

The battles of the Revolutionary and Napoleonic wars were fiercer than those of the eighteenth century and somewhat larger on average—on one or two occasions Napoleon may have had close to two hundred thousand troops on or near the battlefield, though he had great difficulty controlling so many—but they were fundamentally the same sort of battle. The weapons were virtually identical, and the tactics not very much changed. Indeed, a typical Napoleonic battle was still not all that different from one of Alexander the Great's battles, except that firearms had replaced edged weapons for most purposes: about the same number of men arrayed themselves in roughly comparable formations in approximately the same compact space, fought for a similar length of time (perhaps a few hours more, by the nineteenth century), and left about the same proportion dead on the field.

The great change was in the *number* of battles. In classical times or in the Thirty Years' War, there might be three or four battles in a year, and one or two in the whole war wherein the opposing armies exceeded a hundred thousand men in total. During the period 1792–1814 there were forty–nine such battles, and smaller but still major battles occurred on average more than once a week on one or another of the several fronts where campaigns were in progress.[30] The mobilization of whole populations for war had given the generals resources on a previously unheard of scale, and they used them: at least four million people died.

True, that is only half the death toll of the Thirty Years' War, but it is a different phenomenon. The overwhelming majority of those who died in the Thirty Years' War were civilians who fell victim to famine, plague, or murder when a long period of bitter fighting in Central Europe caused social and economic breakdown in a basically poor country. The overwhelming majority of the four million who died in the Revolutionary and Napoleonic wars were soldiers—a figure quite unprecedented in history.

Almost as important is the fact that European society did not break down under the strain. There was hardship, but no starvation, and the warring powers were able to keep at it—and keep their people at it—year after year with no end in sight. The European states had developed the wealth, the organizational techniques, and the methods of motivation needed to fight mass wars with a degree of popular participation that no other civilized society had ever even approached. All that was lacking to transform mass warfare into total war was the technology. But the industrial revolution was already almost a generation old in 1814, and soon it would begin to fill that last remaining gap.

NOTES

1. J. J. Saunders, *The History of the Mongol Conquests*, London: Routledge and Kegan Paul, 1971, pp. 197–98.

2. Malcolm Mallett, *Mercenaries and Their Masters: Warfare in Renaissance Italy*, London: Bodley Head, 1974, p. 157; Malcolm Vale, *War and Chivalry*, London: Duckworth, 1981, pp. 137–38.

3. Andre Corvisier, *Armies and Societies in Europe 1494–1789*, Bloomington, Indiana: Indiana University Press, 1979, p. 28.

4. A. L. Sadler, *The Maker of Modern Japan: The Life of Tokugawa Ieyasu*, London: George Allen and Unwin, 1937, p. 103.

5. Ibid., p. 105.

6. Frederick Lewis Taylor, *The Art of War in Italy, 1494–1529*, Cambridge: Cambridge University Press, 1929, p. 56.

7. C. V. Wedgewood, *The Thirty Years' War*, London: J. Cape, 1938.

8. J. F. Puysegur, *L'art de la guerre par principes et par regles*, Paris, 1748, I.

9. David Chandler, *The Campaigns of Napoleon*, London: Weidenfeld and Nicholson, 1966, p. 342.

10. Edward Mead Earle, ed., *Makers of Modern Strategy*, New York: Atheneum, 1966, p. 56.

11. Hew Strachan, *European Armies and the Conduct of War*, London: George Allen and Unwin, 1983, p. 8.

12. Willerd R. Fann, "On the Infantryman's Age in Eighteenth–Century Prussia," *Military Affairs*, XLI, no. 4 (December 1977), p. 167.

13. Laurence Sterne, *A Sentimental Journey through France and Italy*, New York: Liveright, 1924.

14. Christopher Duffy, *The Army of Frederick the Great*, London: David and Charles, 1974, p. 62.

15. Maurice Saxe, *Reveries, or Memoirs upon the Art of War*, Paris: 1757. Tr. and reissued in Westport, Connecticut: Greenwood Press, 1971.

16. Strachan, op. cit., p. 9.

17. Martin van Crefeld, *Supplying War: Logistics from Wallenstein to Patton*, Cambridge: Cambridge University Press, 1977, p. 38.

18. John Childs, *Armies and Warfare in Europe, 1648–1789*, Manchester, England: Manchester University Press, 1982, p. 158.

19. Edward Gibbon, *The Decline and Fall of the Roman Empire*, New York: The Modern Library, 1932.

20. Maj. Gen. J. F. C. Fuller, *The Conduct of War, 1789–1961*, London: Eyre and Spottiswoode, 1961, p. 32.

21. R. D. Challener, *The French Theory of the Nation in Arms, 1866–1939*, New York: Russell and Russell, 1965, p. 3; Alfred Vagts, *A History of Militarism*, rev. ed., New York: Meridian, 1959, pp. 108–11.

22. Vagts, op. cit., p. 114.

23. Vagts, op. cit., pp. 126–137; John Gooch, *Armies in Europe*, London: Routledge and Kegan Paul, 1980, p. 39.

24. Gunther Rothenburg, *The Art of Warfare in the Age of Napoleon*, London: B. Batsford, 1977, pp. 172–73.

25. Anthony Brett-James, *1812: Eyewitness Accounts of Napoleon's Defeat in Russia*, London: Macmillan, 1967, p. 127.

26. Christopher Duffy, *Borodino and the War of 1812*, London: Seeley Service, 1972, p. 135.

27. David Chandler, *The Campaigns of Napoleon*, New York: Macmillan, 1966, p. 668; Gooch, op. cit., pp. 39–41.

28. Vagts, op. cit., pp. 143–44.

29. Ibid., p. 140.

30. Earle, op. cit., p. 57.

Borodino—the Russians' last stand before Moscow. The soldier-artist Lejeune did not choose to convey the staggering casualties of this battle—"the equivalent of a jumbo jet crashing . . . every three minutes from breakfast to sundown"—but rather France's moment of triumph, when the Russian commander surrendered his sword. *Louis-François Lejeune,* The Battle of Borodino; *Musée de Versailles*

One of the lessons of modern war is that you can win and still lose. Napoleon was forced to retreat from Moscow, not by military defeat, but due to lack of supplies. Four hundred twenty-two thousand troops marched into Russia; only ten thousand escaped. Here a conscripted child and an old veteran await death from wounds, cold, and hunger. *Henri-Félix Emmanuel Philippoteaux,* An Episode from the Russian Retreat; *Musée de Versailles*

A short time after the fall of Constantinople, this artist depicted an Eastern city under siege by cannon. The results were devastating at first, but defenses soon caught up with artillery. *Bombardment of a City, Bibliothèque Nationale (MS5090), Paris*

The Japanese had guns as early as 1542; the *Inatomi Gun Manual* of 1607 gives detailed, illustrated instructions on handling and marksmanship. But guns took all the fun out of being a samurai, and less than a generation later, guns had been entirely rooted out of Japanese society. *Courtesy Noel Perrin, author of* Giving Up the Gun; *Spenser Collection, New York Public Library (Japanese MS 53)*

"The landscape was filled with desperate bands of refugees and marauding groups of deserters . . ." The Thirty Years' War was the first intimation of how badly war could get out of hand if people were emotionally committed and politically unrestrained; it would be 150 years before war would again be fought on this scale. *Detail of* An Episode from the Thirty Years' War; *Vranx and Bruegel, Kunsthistorisches Museum, Vienna/ Photo Meyer KG*

Swedish troops at Dvina in 1701; Alexander the Great wouldn't have known how to command this army. King Gustavus Adolphus' redesigned light musket and mobile field artillery destroyed the ancient tactics of sword and pike push that had ruled the battlefield for thousands of years, and by the eighteenth century, all European armies had been remodeled in the pattern he pioneered. *Daniel Andersson Stawert*, The Battle of Dvina, 1701. *Statens Konstmeer, National Swedish Art Museum, Stockholm*

The curious traveling-carnival nature of the limited wars of the late seventeenth and most of the eighteenth centuries. *Engraving by George Balthasar Probst,* The Encampment of the Austrian Army, *ca. 1760; Courtesy of the Anne S.K. Brown Military Collection, Brown University Library, Providence, Rhode Island*

THE LASH, THE NOOSE, AND THE FIRING SQUAD

The means used to control seventeenth- and eighteenth-century soldiers were brutal. Here, "cowards, traitors to their duty, blasphemers, troublemakers and liars" are punished on the strappado—a device on which people were trussed and hung like game, sometimes with weights. This would dislocate most of their joints, at least, and eventually would break most of their bones. *Jacques Callot,* The Strappado, *from* Miseries of War *series (detail); National Gallery, Washington, D.C.; Rosenwald Collection*

Here "traitors"—that is, deserters—die for their sins. Seventy thousand fled from the French alone during the Seven Years' War. Death by firing squad was not very different from death in battle, where soldiers had to remain in ranks reloading their muskets, in plain sight of the enemy file aiming their next volley. *Jacques Callot,* The Firing Squad, *from* Miseries of War *series (detail); National Gallery, Washington, D.C.; Rosenwald Collection*

"The common soldier must fear his officers more than the enemy." Desertion was a major problem even in peacetime; in war it became so epidemic that public mass executions like this were used to terrorize the soldier into accepting the brutality, boredom, and misery of life in the army. *Jacques Callot,* The Hanging, *from* Miseries of War *series (detail); National Gallery, Washington, D.C.; Rosenwald Collection*

Pavlovian conditioning through thousands of hours of drilling. A truncated version of the eighty-three steps necessary for a seventeenth-century musketeer to load, fire, and reload his musket. *Johann Jacobi von Wallhausen,* Musket Drill *from* L'Art Militaire pour l'Infanterie, *Courtesy Royal Military College of Canada Library, Kingston, Ontario*

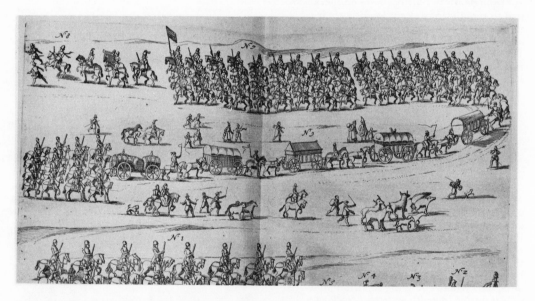

The elaborate supply organization of seventeenth-century war. Tens of thousands of animals—including cows, sheep, and pigs—habitually accompanied large armies, which therefore had to confine their operations to the summer months, when grazing was available. *Johann Jacobi von Wallhausen,* L'Art Militaire à Cheval; *Courtesy Royal Military College of Canada Library, Kingston, Ontario*

"A bearable evil . . ." The expensive and therefore small regular armies of Europe being "exercised by temperate and undecisive contests," as Gibbon put it, in one of the many relatively restrained European wars— less than a generation before Napoleon changed all the rules. *From* Victory of the Prussian Army over Combined Austrian and Saxon Forces near Wilsdery, December 15, 1745; *Courtesy Anne S.K. Brown Military Collection, Brown University Library, Providence, Rhode Island*

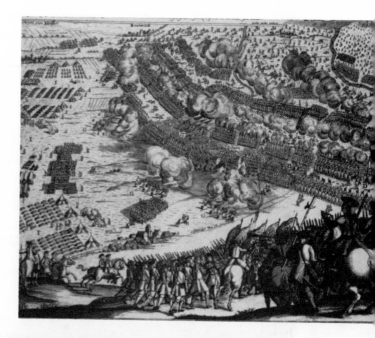

The French Revolution made the rational, restricted wars of the eighteenth century obsolete. The attack on the Tuileries in August of 1792 was the signal for all of Europe to rally to the monarchist cause. Six months later the Revolutionaries were forced to introduce true conscription— and the mass army was born. *Jacques Bertraux,* The Attack on the Tuileries; *Musée de Versailles*

Napoleon squandering cavalry against the solid musket and bayonet wall of the British Square, a formation not very different from the pike *tercios* of centuries before and the spear phalanxes of centuries before that; the great change in battle had not yet come. *Henri-Félix Emmanuel Philippoteaux, Charging the British Square, the Battle of Waterloo; Courtesy of the Victoria and Albert Museum*

Napoleon's rise to power, first as "First Consul" and then as "Emperor of the French," gradually destroyed the ideological attraction of French Republicanism and it became safer for the absolutist governments he was fighting to arm their people against him. *David,* The First Consul Crossing the Alps, May 20, 1800; *Musée de Versailles*

4: Reductio Ad Absurdum: Total War

Restricted warfare was one of the loftiest achievements of the eighteenth century. It belongs to a class of hot-house plants which can only thrive in an aristocratic and qualitative civilisation. We are no longer capable of it. It is one of the fine things we have lost as a result of the French Revolution.
—Guglielmo Ferrero, 1933[1]

He who uses force unsparingly, without reference against the bloodshed involved, must obtain a superiority if his adversary uses less vigour in its application. . . . To introduce into a philosophy of war a principle of moderation would be an absurdity. War is an act of violence pushed to its utmost bounds.
—Karl von Clausewitz, 1819[2]

Ferrero's refined nostalgia for the limited warfare of the eighteenth century contains an elementary truth. Such limitations were part and parcel of an autocratic and hierarchical social order, and could not survive in the new mass societies infected with nationalism. The true military spokesman of the nineteenth century was Karl von Clausewitz, a Prussian veteran of the Napoleonic wars, whose writings on the theory of war became gospel for succeeding generations of soldiers. But one form of restriction from the old way of warfare did survive in an attenuated form for over a century thereafter: by and large, civilians were spared the worst horrors of war.

Once conscripted and put into uniform, of course, citizen-soldiers were fair targets for any weapon the imagination of man could devise, but those who remained at home—and even those who lived in the battle zone— were largely left in peace. There were three reasons for this: the still relatively minor importance of industrial production of weapons and equipment compared to the all-important role of the masses of soldiers themselves; the absence of weapons able to strike at the enemy's centers of production in any case; and a genuine reluctance on the part of soldiers to turn their weapons against civilians. Unfortunately, the last of these proved to be no obstacle when the other two conditions altered.

For forty years after the defeat of Napoleon in 1814—a period as long as has passed since the end of World War II—there was peace between the major European states. It may have been a peace of exhaustion; it was certainly everywhere a peace of conservative reaction to the excesses of the French Revolution. Among the dangerous innovations that were generally discarded was the mass army based on conscription; most of Europe went back to small, professional armies. But in Prussia, the smallest of the great powers in population, conscription was not abandoned, and elsewhere the knowledge of how to create mass armies was never forgotten. By the time the spate of mid-century wars arrived in 1854–70, every major power in Europe except Britain, protected by its navy, had reintroduced conscription—and by this time new technology was beginning to filter into war.

The greatest of the mid-century wars was not fought in Europe at all, however. It was the American Civil War, in which 622,000 American soldiers died—more than in both world wars, Korea, and Vietnam—out of a population only one seventh as big as it is now. Both sides soon resorted to conscription—the Confederacy in 1862 and the Union a year later—and the resulting armies were huge. The U.S. Army enlisted over one and a half million men during the four years of the war, and the Confederates, over three quarters of a million.

The war, coming at a time of transition, was at first a curious and lethal combination of Napoleonic tactics with very different technology. During the previous decade, new rifled muskets had come into general use that effectively quintupled the range at which the average infantryman could hit his opponent. The results were clearly visible at battles like Second Manassas in August 1862, when Stonewall Jackson's eighteen thousand Virginians lined up behind the shelter of a railway cutting to receive the attack of some fifty thousand Northern infantry: "The Federals sprang forward with a long drawn 'huzzah' ringing from their 10,000 throats [of the first division]. On they went until half the distance to the cut, and then the smoke, flash and roar of 4,000 well-aimed guns burst from the Confederate entrenchments, and a wild, reckless and terrifying Southern yell echoed and re-echoed through the woodlands. . . . This last charge met the same disastrous fate that had befallen those preceding."[3]

Gen. A. P. Hill, author of the above passage, wrote in the high romantic style about war, and many of the ordinary soldiers on both sides still clung to the same antique values. At the height of the attack, some Northern officer rode forward through the black powder smoke, well ahead of his troops, and reached the lip of the railway cutting miraculously untouched. For a few seconds he paused there, sword in hand, as useless as he was brave. Some of the Southern soldiers just below him began to yell out, "Don't kill him! Don't kill him!" But within seconds both he and his horse were shot down by less romantic men.

The cry that had gone up was an echo from the eighteenth century, when it had been thought unsporting to aim at individual enemies, especially officers; everybody took his chance equally in the hail of unaimed volley fire. But it was out of place at Second Manassas, where the Confederate troops were aiming and firing individually, not in volleys.

The Northern regiments were using standard Napoleonic tactics, charging in massed formations, and against the smoothbore muskets of Napoleonic times they would probably have won, because they would have come under effective fire only at about two hundred yards. Running men can cover that distance in less than a minute, even while carrying full infantry kit and maintaining their formations, which would have given the Confederate defenders time to fire two or at the most three shots each.

But with their rifled muskets, Jackson's men began picking off the Union troops at almost half a mile. Every Confederate soldier had time to get off at least ten aimed shots, and the result was massacre. It did not matter that the Union troops had rifles too, because it is impossible to deliver carefully aimed rifle fire while running across broken ground, and besides, the Confederates were behind the shelter of the railway embankment. What was being demonstrated in battles like this was the new fact that troops under cover equipped with rifles could stop much larger numbers of infantry attacking across open ground.

> *I had taken part in two great battles, and heard the bullets whistle both days, and yet I had scarcely seen a Rebel save killed, wounded or prisoners. I remember even line officers, who were at the battle of Chancellorsville, said: "Why, we never saw any Rebels where we were; only smoke and bushes, and lots of our men tumbling about," and now I appreciate this most fully. The great art is to conceal men. . . . Put a man in a hole, and a good battery on a hill behind him, and he will beat off three times his number, even if he is not a very good soldier.* —Col. Theodore Lyman, 1869[4]

Not just the muzzle-loading single-shot rifles that produced such havoc at Second Manassas, but forerunners of practically every modern weapon were used in the American Civil War: breech-loading magazine-fed rifles like the seven-shot Henry repeater (the Confederates called it "that damn Yankee gun that can be loaded on Sunday and fired all week"), early hand-cranked machine guns like the Gatling gun, rifled breech-loading cannons, land mines, armored trains, submarines, ironclad warships, and even a primitive form of aerial reconnaissance by means of hot-air balloons. (A young Prussian lieutenant called Ferdinand von Zeppelin was among the European observers who watched the demonstrations of military balloons from the White House lawn.) The troops were moved quickly over long distances on the extensive American railway network—Civil War battles were the first in history in which the infantry did not get there entirely on foot—and the telegraph gave generals a new ability to coordinate the movement of large forces spread out over a wide area.

In a sense, the Civil War happened just in time. Had it been delayed another ten or fifteen years, most of those new weapons would have been available in large numbers and reliable models, and it would have taken on the character of World War I. As it was, they were mostly either rare or unreliable. The great majority of the artillery used, for example, was little improved on that of fifty years previously, so that it actually had not much greater range than the rifled muskets in use. The gunners had to be positioned well behind the front line to protect them from enemy rifle fire, and long-range bombardment was not possible.

The only really new weapon in mass use was the rifle, and casualty figures proved its effectiveness. Out of 144,000 American soldiers for whom the cause of death is known, 108,000 were killed by rifle bullets, and only 12,500 by shell fragments and 7,000 by swords and bayonets. (Twenty years later, when field artillery could fire accurately for over a mile, and shell bursts could produce a thousand fragments lethal at a radius of twenty feet, the figures would have been very different.) Even without modern artillery, Civil War battlefields had taken on an ominously modern aspect by the end. Out of self-preservation the infantry had acquired the habit of digging in whenever they halted, to protect themselves from rifle bullets, and in the lines around Petersburg in 1865 the field entrenchments grew so elaborate—complete with dugouts, wire entanglements, and listening posts—that they foreshadowed the trenches of World War I.

But the multitude of European military observers did not draw the right conclusion from this; it was dismissed as a transient phenomenon due to uniquely North American circumstances. Nor did they appreciate how big a role economic warfare was coming to play. From the beginning of the struggle, the North clamped a tight blockade on the South to cut its overseas trade, and by the end General Sherman (whom the Confederate president, Jefferson Davis, called the "Attila of the American Continent") was deliberately devastating huge areas of the deep South. "We are not only fighting hostile armies but a hostile people," Sherman said, "and must make old and young, rich and poor, feel the hard hand of war."[5]

To those who protested that his methods were immoral, Sherman simply replied: "If the people raise a howl against my barbarity and cruelty, I will answer that war is war. . . . If they want peace they and their relatives must stop the war."[6] He was a twentieth-century man born before his time, but European soldiers preferred to ignore the less appetizing aspects of the American Civil War and go on believing that they could still deliver quick and decisive victories by defeating the enemy's army in the field.

At first there will be increased slaughter—increased slaughter on so terrible a scale as to render it impossible to get troops to push the battle to a decisive issue. They will try to, thinking that they are fighting under the old conditions, and they will learn such a lesson that they will abandon the attempt forever. Then . . . we shall have . . . a long period of continually increasing strain upon the resources of the combatants. . . . Everybody will be entrenched in the next war. —I. S. Bloch, 1897[7]

We listen for an eternity to the iron sledgehammers beating on our trench. Percussion and time fuses, 105's, 150's, 210's—all the calibers. Amid this tempest of ruin we instantly recognize the shell that is coming to bury us. As soon as we pick out its dismal howl we look at each other in agony. All curled and shriveled up we crouch under the very weight of its breath. Our helmets clang together, we stagger about like drunks. The beams tremble, a cloud of choking smoke fills the dugout, the candles go out.

Verdun, 1916[8]

The predictions about the next great war published in Russian in 1897 by Ivan Bloch, a Warsaw banker and ardent pacifist, were logically unassailable. Given the millions of soldiers that each power would call up and rush to the frontiers by rail when war came, and given the firepower now available to each man, stalemate was inevitable. Offensive warfare could not succeed. But no professional soldiers took Bloch's work seriously, and every army went on the offensive simultaneously in 1914, convinced that a quick series of decisive battles in the Napoleonic style (though with far greater numbers of soldiers) would settle the war within six months at the outside.

Within two months, over a million men were dead, and the armies had ground to a halt. Machine weapons—quick-firing artillery and machine guns spewing out six hundred bullets a minute—filled the air with a lethal steel sleet, and anybody trying to move above ground was almost certain to be hit. The act of killing had been mechanized, and men had become the prisoners of machines, trapped below ground level in the proliferating trenches.

And as the trenches spread and linked up with each other, another great revolution in military affairs occurred: the continuous front. Nobody planned it, and nobody expected it. General Foch, sent to the western end of the developing front line in September 1914 after the armies had fought each other to a standstill north and east of Paris, complained, "They have sent me here to maneuver, but things are not going very brightly. This eternal stretching out in a line is getting on my nerves."[9] Within another few weeks, as the Allies and the Germans repeatedly tried to get around the remaining open flank of the trenches, only to collide, halt, and end up in a new stretch of trench, the front reached the sea, and there were no more flanks; it was theoretically possible to walk 475 miles from the English Channel to the border of neutral Switzerland along either of two parallel lines of trench, sometimes as close as ten or twenty yards apart (more usually several hundred), without ever setting a foot on the surface.

The mathematics that created the continuous front were quite straightforward. For almost all of history the weapons in use had forced soldiers to crowd together practically shoulder to shoulder in order to be able to control the space immediately in front of them—only ten feet in front of them in the case of a phalanx of pikemen, but no more than a hundred yards or so even in the case of an eighteenth-century infantry battalion using smoothbore muskets. Battles were therefore extremely congested events occurring in a small space, and relatively compact armies spent most of the rest of their time marching through open country seeking an advantageous position for the critical few hours when they would meet on the battlefield.

But as firepower grew by leaps and bounds in the latter half of the nineteenth century—rifles able to deliver ten shots a minute at a thousand yards, followed by machine guns and modern artillery—dispersion became the key to success. In the American Civil War, attacking troops were already spontaneously abandoning the vulnerable Napoleonic mass formations for a more open order, and the defenders were discovering that it took far fewer men with rifles to hold a given frontage than it had with the old muskets. By the time of the South African War in 1899, the Boers were finding, at battles like Colenso, that they could stop British frontal attacks with only one rifleman every three yards.[10]

All the European armies had professional general staffs long before 1914, and they devoted their time to making elaborate plans for how the next war should be fought. (Indeed, their plans were a major factor in making it likely that war would come.) They all understood the effects of new weapons like the machine gun, which had seen use in small wars and "colonial wars." Even civilians like Hilaire Belloc knew that European troops always beat "natives" because

Whatever happens, we have got

The Maxim gun, and they have not.

But the generals had not done the crucial calculation, which was to multiply the width of the front an individual infantryman could now hold by the millions of men who would be available in a European war. The answer, of course, was that the armies could now spread out to fill all the space available in a continuous front.

And so they did. Not only in France, but across the vast distances of Russia, and later across northern Italy, northern Greece, northeastern Turkey, and even Mesopotamia and Palestine. For the men in the trenches, it was a kind of war such as few soldiers had experienced before. Instead of fighting a battle on one or two days of the year, they were in the field, within shouting distance of the enemy, all the time. Each day they faced the risk of being killed, and each day they endured the misery of living in a ditch.

It's such hell when you're in the front line, especially in the wintertime. It was terrible in the winter. The summertime was not so bad, but you know, it was bad enough; but wintertime was awful. It was no place for a human being to be, really. —Canadian veteran

Constantly having your feet in this gruellike muck caused a complaint which became known as "trench foot." There were dozens of amputation cases in the regiment. —British veteran

Rats bother you; rats eat you if you get wounded, and nobody can look after you. It was a dirty lousy place to live with all the corruption that is known to mankind. —British veteran

The essence of the general's art had always been to maneuver his forces, but now no movement at all was possible until he had broken through the trench lines facing him—and the continuous front meant that *every* attack had to be a frontal attack. Since infantrymen could not hope to survive the hail of fire that would greet them if they tried to advance unaided—that was why they had dug the trenches in the first place—the only way to break through was to eliminate the sources of that fire by shelling the enemy's trenches and gun positions into ruin before the attack. At least that was the theory.

So the trench war became a war of artillery, and over half the casualties were now caused by shellfire. The greatest problem of 1915 for every country was not at the front but at home, where shell production could not keep up with demand. The Russian army's guns fired as many shells in a day as Russian factories could make in a month, and even in Britain, the world's most industrialized country, there was a critical shell shortage in 1915. The demands went on mounting. At the Third Battle of Ypres in 1917, the nineteen-day British bombardment used 4.3 million shells weighing 107,000 tons, a year's production for 55,000 workers.[11]

And still the infantry could not break through, although they died in their millions trying. For though the shells could destroy most of the enemy's machine guns in the first-line trenches, and even the enemy's guns behind the lines, enough defenders always survived to make the advance a slow and costly business, and the bombardments turned the ground into a wilderness of shell holes across which any movement was very difficult. Eventually the attackers might take the enemy's first-line trenches—and by the middle of the war these alone could be a belt up to three thousand yards deep—but by that time the enemy's reserves would have arrived and manned a whole new trench system just to the rear. For over three years, no offensive succeeded in budging the Western Front as much as ten miles.

> . . . the ruddy clouds of brick-dust hang over the shelled villages by day and at night the eastern horizon roars and bubbles with light. And everywhere in these desolate places I see the faces and figures of enslaved men, the marching columns pearl-hued with chalky dust on the sweat of their heavy drab clothes; the files of carrying parties laden and staggering in the flickering moonlight of gunfire; the "waves" of assaulting troops lying silent and pale on the tapelines of the jumping-off places.

> I crouch with them while the steel glacier rushing by just overhead scrapes away every syllable, every fragment of a message bawled in my ear. . . . I go forward with them . . . up and down across ground like a huge ruined honeycomb, and my wave melts away, and the second wave comes up, and also melts away, and then the third wave merges into the ruins of the first and second, and after a while the fourth blunders into the remnants of the others, and we begin to run forward to catch up with the barrage, gasping and sweating, in bunches, anyhow, every bit of the months of drill and rehearsal forgotten.

> We come to wire that is uncut, and beyond we see grey coal-scuttle helmets bobbing about, . . . and the loud crackling of machine-guns changes as to a screeching of steam being blown off by a hundred engines, and soon no

one is left standing. An hour later our guns are "back on the first objective," and the brigade, with all its hopes and beliefs, has found its grave on those northern slopes of the Somme battlefield.[12]

With strategy paralyzed and tactics narrowed to the search for ever bigger bombardments, the war became a simple matter of attrition. New weapons like poison gas only increased the casualties without breaking the deadlock. By 1916, despairing Allied generals were sometimes reduced to the ghastly argument that since they had more men than the Germans, if they traded life for life, they would still have some men left alive when all the Germans were dead. So they would have won.

That was the real meaning of battles like the Somme. The point was not that the British captured only forty-five square miles in a five-month battle at a cost of 415,000 men—over 8,000 men for each useless square mile—but that the Germans were also compelled to sacrifice men and equipment at a similar rate. Battles had become an industrial operation in reverse, in which the rates of destruction at the front matched the rates of production in the industries at home.

It is significant that the phrase "home front" came into use during World War I, when the role of munitions workers, and of civilian production more generally, was becoming as important to victory as the soldiers in the trenches. Without a constant flow of supplies equal to the vast consumption at the front, the soldiers would soon be helpless. And since the mobilization of so huge a number of men left vast gaps in the normal workforce—France put 20 percent of its entire population into uniform, Germany 18 percent, and the other major powers not much less—the remaining adult civilians had to be directed by government into whatever jobs were needed to keep production going. In effect the civilian economy was conscripted too: the governments of Europe quickly took control over labor and raw materials, imposed rationing on all scarce goods, and created true war economies. Women flooded into factories to replace the men at the front, and most production beyond the basic needs of subsistence was diverted into the war effort.

From early in the war, both sides resorted to economic warfare, imposing blockades on each other's seaborne trade. The British did it in the traditional way, by stopping all ships bound for German ports, and their blockade was very nearly leakproof. It took a long time for the full effect to be felt, but in the last two years of the war it is estimated that undernourishment caused an excess of 800,000 civilian deaths in Germany over the peacetime mortality rate.[13] The Germans, denied the use of the sea's surface, resorted to submarines in their counterblockade of Britain. They sank over fifteen million tons of shipping during the war, but only once came close to cutting Britain's vital flow of food and raw materials from overseas.

If the entire civilian population of a nation was now an essential part of its war effort, however, it could be argued that the "home front" was now a legitimate target not merely for the slow-acting weapon of blockade, but for direct armed attack. And by 1915, technology had at last produced a weapon that could strike directly at the enemy's cities and factories: the aircraft.

> *The idea was to equip from twelve to twenty Zeppelins and drill their crews to function as a co-ordinated task force. Each ship would carry about 300 fire bombs. They would attack simultaneously at night. Hence, as many as six thousand bombs would be rained upon [London] at once. . . . When asked for my technical opinion, morality aside, I agreed it was definitely workable.* —Capt. Ernst Lehman, German army zeppelin service[14]

> *We who strike the enemy where his heart beats have been slandered as "baby-killers" and "murderers of women." . . . What we do is repugnant to us too, but necessary. Very necessary. Nowadays there is no such animal as a non-combatant; modern warfare is total warfare. A soldier cannot function at the front without the factory worker, the farmer, and all the other providers behind him. You and I, Mother, have discussed this subject, and I know you understand what I say. My men are brave and honourable. Their cause is holy, so how can they sin while doing their duty? If what we do is frightful, then may frightfulness be Germany's salvation.*
> Letter from Capt. Peter Strasser, head of the German navy's airship division [15]

Bombing civilians in cities—not by accident while trying to hit military targets, but with the deliberate purpose of killing civilians and breaking their morale—was the final step in the brutal logic of total war. If the civilians producing the weapons of war were now the real foundation of a nation's armed strength, then they were actually the most important target of all. It was Germany, whose huge zeppelins were the only aircraft with the range and bomb-carrying capacity to reach an enemy's capital when the war broke out, who initiated the twentieth century's most characteristic form of warfare, but it was just as inevitable as the trenches.

The first major air raid on London came little more than a year after the war's outbreak, on 8 September 1915. Zeppelin L-15 left north Germany late in the afternoon under the command of Capt. Heinrich Mathy, crossing the English coast in Lincolnshire, and followed the main railway line south to London. About 10:40 in the evening he dropped a few bombs on the north London suburb of Golders Green and continued south until he was over Russell Square. Then the rest of the bomb-load—fifteen high-explosive bombs and fifty-odd incendiaries—rained down from eight thousand feet, walking a path of destruction through Bedford Place, Queen's Square, Lamb's Conduit Passage, Red Lion Street, and on to King Edward Street. The worst casualties were at the Dolphin public house on Red Lion Street, where a bomb fell just outside. The front blew in, and the roof came down on the astounded drinkers, leaving seventeen of them dead and injured beneath the rubble.

In all, the raid caused seventy-two casualties and destroyed $2.5 million worth of property.

But both the technology and the spirit of the enterprise retained an amateurish air, on both sides.

> *Well the first job I had after a total of twelve hours in so-called duo and solo was as a night pilot, anti-zeppelin. I was asked by the adjutant if I could fly in the dark. I said I didn't know—I couldn't fly in the daylight, maybe it was easier in the dark. The first night I was there the commanding officer of the station went up on duty and killed himself before he'd got a hundred yards beyond the end flare, so that was my introduction to the game.*
>
> *And then after a flight or two I was sent to start Hornchurch air station as a night-flying anti-zeppelin station. I landed there and the aerodrome consisted of a large field full of sheep, an infuriated farmer, and a still more infuriated dog. So when we'd cleared off the sheep and I'd appeased the farmer and been billeted on him, I formed a flight there which contained amongst others Leefe Robinson—and when I was away on a four-day leave doing something much more dangerous, which was getting married, he went up and he bagged the first zeppelin.*
>
> Sir Arthur Harris, later air marshal and head of RAF Bomber Command, 1942–45

The German raids on Britain in World War I, by zeppelins and later by large two- and three-engined bombers, were tiny by later standards: only four thousand British civilians were killed and wounded throughout the war. But the raids were the precedent and the prototype for Rotterdam, for Dresden, for Hiroshima, for all the cities that have been destroyed from the air in the twentieth century—and for the strategy of nuclear deterrence that now dominates the world. The delay was only due to inadequate technology; after 1915, everybody was a legitimate target.

The transformation of mass warfare in the French revolutionary style into total war in the modern style took little more than a century. Since the Dolphin pub, there have been no barriers of behavior left to breach, only more and more destructive weapons to be used according to principles now universally accepted. And what the governments of Europe who found themselves trapped in the first total war discovered, to their dismay, was that if the means used to fight a war are total, then so must be the ends; it was almost impossible to stop short of total victory for one side and unconditional surrender for the other.

The commercial jealousies, military anxieties, and territorial disputes that caused World War I were not significantly different from those that caused the Seven

Years' War a century and a half before. In the old style of war, the small armies of the two alliances would have fought each other sporadically for a few years (while the vast majority of the citizens of all countries concerned went about their daily affairs undisturbed). Eventually, when one side had proved to be militarily stronger for the moment, a few concessions would have been made by the losers and peace would have returned. A few hundred thousand soldiers would be dead, but no governments would fall, no country would be occupied. The cost may already have been disproportionate to the issues at stake, but at least the governments were able to control it.

The disputes between the rival governments were no more important in 1914, but the techniques of war had completely overpowered the ability of governments to limit their commitment to it. The axiom that force can only be overcome by greater force drove them to make the war total, and the scale of the sacrifices they then had to demand of their citizens required that the purposes of the war must also be great. When sixty million men have been ordered into uniform and sent off to risk their lives; when in France, for example, one in three of the male population (including infants and old men) has been killed or wounded in a period of four years; when the people's willingness to go on making sacrifices has been sustained in every country by hate propaganda that depicts the war as a moral crusade against fathomless evil—then governments cannot just stop the fighting, sort out the petty and obscure Balkan quarrel that triggered it, swap around a few colonies and trade routes, and thank the surviving soldiers and send them home. Total war requires the goal of total victory, and so the propaganda lies become the truth: the future of the nation (or at least the survival of the regime) really does depend on victory, no matter what the war's origins were.

And so those in power, even when they could foresee military collapse or social revolution, even if they could remember what the war had been about when it started (and most of them could not, for they ended up believing their own propaganda), were unwilling and unable to look for a compromise peace. The collapses and revolutions duly came.

The collapse of the Russian army in the field and near-starvation at home brought the (first) Russian revolution in March 1917; in April, fifty-four divisions of the French army (half the total) mutinied after another futile offensive, and nearly twenty-five thousand men were court-martialed after order was restored; in May, four hundred thousand Italian troops simply abandoned the battlefield at Caporetto; and later that month the Chief of the Imperial General Staff in London wrote Gen. Sir Douglas Haig, the commander of the British army in France: "I am afraid there is no getting away from the fact that there is some unrest in the country now as a result partly of the Russian revolution."[16] Meanwhile German occupation troops in Russia were fraternizing with the Bolsheviks, and the Austro-Hungarian empire was teetering on the brink of dissolution into its various national components. But no government stopped fighting voluntarily; they were rightly convinced that by that time their only hope of survival was a *total* military victory.

Some of the governments on the winning side did survive, but none of the losers. Four great empires—German, Russian, Austrian, and Ottoman—were destroyed by the war, and two of them completely dismantled into a welter of new countries and territories. About half the people of Europe, the Middle East, and Africa underwent a radical change of regime or even of citizenship as a result of the war. And several of the new regimes that emerged—in Russia at once, in Italy and Germany later—preserved in peacetime much of the apparatus of total state control over the citizens and the economy that had been invented in order to fight the first total war.

Attrition, in the end, was the main factor that decided who won the war. The Entente powers simply had more men and resources than Germany and its allies (though they had some anxious moments between the time their Russian ally fell out of the war in mid-1917 and the arrival of large numbers of American troops on the Western Front in mid-1918). The scale of losses dwarfed those of any previous war in history. Over eight million soldiers were killed, and about twenty million wounded (many several times). But toward the end of the war there appeared a new weapon that gave some professional soldiers hope that there might be an alternative to the grinding war of attrition in the trenches. It was called the tank.

> Panic spread like an electric current, passing from man to man along the trench. As the churning tracks reared overhead the bravest men clambered above ground to launch suicidal counter-attacks, hurling grenades onto the tanks' roofs or shooting and stabbing at any vision slit within reach. They were shot down or crushed, while others threw up their hands in terrified surrender or bolted down the communication trenches towards the second line.   —German infantryman's first encounter with a tank, 1916[17]

No sooner had the obstacle of the trenches suddenly appeared in late 1914 than the solution occurred to a British staff officer, Col. E. D. Swinton. What was needed, obviously, was a vehicle armored against machine-gun bullets and carrying its own guns, which could roll over shell holes, barbed wire, and trenches on caterpillar tracks. Against much opposition from military conservatives, the idea was adopted by Winston Churchill (even though he was then running the navy), and the earliest production models of the "landships," as they were first called, reached the Western Front in the autumn of 1916.

They were huge, primitive, and horribly uncomfortable vehicles. The eight-man crew, stripped to their waists in the hundred-degree heat, shared the interior with an exposed 105-horsepower Daimler engine. The fumes from the engine and from hot shell cases rolling around on the floor made the atmosphere inside almost unbreathable in combat. There were no springs in the suspension, the noise made voice communications impossible, and it was hard to see hand signals in the semi-darkness, as the only light came through the vision slits. The tanks' top speed was only three and a half miles an hour, and they broke down on average every five or ten miles.

But the first time the tanks went into battle in really large numbers, at Cambrai in November 1917, where 378 were committed, they enabled the British army to advance six miles in six hours, at a cost of four thousand dead and wounded. Earlier the same year, at the Third Battle of Ypres, the British had taken three months to advance a similar distance, and they had lost a quarter-million men doing it. A complete breakthrough was not achieved at Cambrai, or in any of the other tank attacks before the war ended twelve months later, but this was mostly due to the infantry's inability to keep up on foot. However, the plans for 1919, had the war continued, called for a force of several thousand tanks closely supported by aircraft to smash through the enemy's front, with infantry following closely in armored personnel carriers. It seemed that the days of the continuous front were numbered.

During the "twenty-year armistice" between the two wars, numbers of theorists worked on how best to exploit the mobility of tanks, and in 1939–41 it looked as if the Germans, at least, had found a foolproof formula. "Blitzkrieg" (lightning war) involved rapid penetration of an enemy's front by a large force of tanks, closely assisted by ground-attack aircraft and followed by motorized infantry and artillery. Once through the defended zone, the tanks would push on at high speed to the enemy's higher command posts and vital communications centers deep in the rear and spread chaos behind the front, which would then collapse almost of its own accord when the troops holding it found themselves cut off from their own head-quarters and supplies.

Using the blitzkrieg formula, the Germans destroyed the entire Polish army in three weeks in 1939 at a cost of only 8,000 dead, and the following spring in France they were even more successful. Despite the fact that the French and British had more and on the whole better tanks than they did, the Germans' superior tactics allowed them to conquer the Low Countries and France in only six weeks, at a cost of 27,000 dead, 18,000 missing, and 111,000 wounded. The continuous front and its slaughterhouse battles of attrition seemed a thing of the past. But it was all an illusion: what tanks had really done was just to set the continuous front in motion, with disastrous conseqences for civilians.

No innovation in warfare stays a surprise for very long, and by the middle of the war, when German forces were fighting deep inside the Soviet Union, attrition had returned with a vengeance. The solution to the blitzkrieg tactic of rapid penetration was to make the defended zone deeper—many miles deep, with successive belts of trenches, minefields, bunkers, gun positions, and tank traps which would slow down the armored spearheads and eventually wear them away. Sometimes the defense would hold; sometimes there would be a successful breakthrough, but even then, the continuous front would not disappear. It would roll back some dozens or hundreds of miles all along the line and then stabilize again.

The consumption of men and machines in the new style of war was enormous—the Soviets, for example, built approximately 100,000 tanks, 100,000 aircraft, and 175,000 artillery pieces during the war, of which at least two thirds were destroyed in the fighting—but the ability of fully mobilized industrial societies to absorb enormous punishment and still maintain production was seemingly endless. So was the willingness of whole nations in arms, stiffened by patriotism and propaganda and harnessed by totalitarian controls (which were imposed in almost every warring country regardless of its peacetime political system) to accept the most terrible sacrifices without flinching. The Germans ended up with two thirds of all males between the ages of eighteen and forty-five in the armed forces and lost three and a half million military dead,[18] but their army was still fighting in April of 1945 when the two fronts facing the Soviet advance from the east and the Anglo-American advance from the west were practically back to back down the middle of a devastated Germany.

All this would have amounted only to a repetition of World War I with even greater consumption of material and higher military casualties (the notion that World War II was easier on the soldiers is peculiar to the Anglo-Saxon countries and France, whose armies were only fully committed to heavy fighting on a major front for about one year), but for the fact that the continuous front was now in motion. And as it ground across whole countries, it destroyed almost everything in its path.

> Guts splattered across the rubble and sprayed from one dying man onto another; tightly riveted machines ripped like the belly of a cow which has just been sliced open, flaming and groaning; trees broken into tiny fragments; gaping windows pouring out torrents of billowing dust, dispersing into oblivion all that remains of a comfortable parlour . . . the cries of officers and non-coms, trying to shout across the cataclysm to regroup their sections and companies. That is how we took part in the German advance, being called through the noise and dust, following the clouds churned up by our tanks to the northern outskirts of Belgorod. . . .
>
> The burnt-out ruins of Belgorod fell into the hands of [our surviving troops] on the second evening. . . . We had been ordered to reduce the pockets of resistance in the ashes of a suburb called Deptreotka, if I remember correctly. . . . When we reached the end of our sweep, we collapsed at the bottom of a large crater and stared at each other for a long time in dazed silence. None of us could speak. . . . The air still roared and shook and smelled of burning. . . . By the fourth or fifth evening, we had gone through Belgorod without even knowing it.
>
> Guy Sajer, an Alsatian conscript in the German army[19]

Belgorod, a city in southern Russia, had a population of 34,000 people before the front moved east across it for the first time in October 1941—and that time it was lucky. Von Reichenau's Sixth Army took it "on the run," and although there were two days of fighting around the city, most of the buildings and most of the citizens survived. Twenty months later it was liberated by Soviet troops as the front moved west again after the Sixth Army was destroyed at Stalingrad, and again it was relatively lucky: the Germans did not have time to destroy it as they retreated.

But then Belgorod was retaken by the "Gross Deutschland" Division (in which Sajer was serving), at the beginning of the great German offensive around Kursk in July 1943, in which 6,000 tanks, 30,000 guns, and 2 million men fought along a front of hundreds of miles. When the German tanks had finally been halted by the deep Russian defenses, the Soviet counterattack began with 70 tanks and 230 guns to each kilometer, and in mid-August Belgorod was liberated for a second time, after street-fighting (or rather, fighting in the ruins) that killed another 3,000 soldiers within the city limits. And at the end of all that, only 140 of Belgorod's 34,000 people were left; the rest were refugees, conscripts, or dead.

Belgorod had no military importance; it just got in the way. The front moved across it four times, and it was practically extinguished. And what happened there happened to tens of thousands of other towns and villages. World War II killed at least twice as many soldiers as World War I, but it also killed almost twice as many civilians as soldiers. It was the first European war since the Thirty Years' War in which the civilian casualties outnumbered the military. Most of the civilians died more or less by accident, as an incidental by-product of the fighting: the continuous front moved through every city and hamlet in entire countries, sending tens of millions of civilians into flight as refugees or killing them in the rubble of their own homes. So great was the destruction and disorganization that the casualty figures are not reliable even to the nearest million, but on average the countries from Germany eastward, where the fighting was most intense and prolonged, lost about 10 percent of their populations killed.

Civilian casualties of roughly the same order have occurred on the few occasions since 1945 (like Korea) when regular armies in continuous fronts have fought their way through heavily populated territory.

The disintegration of nations in the last war was brought about by the actions of the armies in the field. [In the future] it will be accomplished directly by . . . aerial forces. . . . War will be waged essentially against the unarmed populations of the cities and great industrial centres. . . . A complete breakdown of the social order cannot but take place in a country subjected to this kind of merciless pounding. . . . It will be an inhuman, atrocious performance, but these are the facts. —Gen. Giulio Douhet, 1921[20]

There are a lot of people who say that bombing can never win a war. Well, my answer to that is that it has never been tried yet, and we shall see.
Air Marshal Sir Arthur Harris, head of RAF Bomber Command, 1942–45

At least 97 percent of the forty million people who were killed in World War II were *not* killed by air raids on cities, and it is very hard for even the most devoted admirers of "strategic bombardment" to make a convincing argument that it won the war. But it was only due to the lack of adequate technological capabilities that the bombers took so long to fulfill their promise of instant, decisive destruction from the skies; the will to do it was certainly there.

Bombing is the natural weapon—the *reductio ad absurdum*—of total war, and it was particularly attractive to those theorists between the wars who wished to avoid another bloody struggle in the trenches. The earliest and most influential was an Italian general called Giulio Douhet, who had proposed an independent Italian bombing force of five hundred multi-engine aircraft to attack Austro-Hungarian communications as early as 1915. (Italy had been the first country to use aircraft for bombing, in its war against the Turks in Libya in 1911.) General Douhet became commissioner of aviation after Mussolini's coup in Italy in 1922, but his greatest influence was in Britain and the United States, technologically oriented countries that would rather spend money than lives in war. The principal American bomber of World War II, the B-17, was flight-tested in 1935, and the Royal Air Force's four-engined bombers were designed in the same year.

The first major attacks on cities during World War II, however, were made by the Luftwaffe—on Warsaw, Rotterdam, and then on most of the major British cities—although the German air force had never been primarily intended or designed for that role.

> *There was a mist over the town as men and women began to crawl out of their shelters, look for their friends and survey the ruins of their city. They could hardly recognise it. . . . Hardly a building remained standing. It was impossible to see where the central streets we knew so well had been. Fires were still raging in every direction and from time to time we heard the crash of a fallen roof or wall. . . . It seemed so hopeless with our homes and shops and so much of our lovely old city in ruins. You might say we were dazed.*
>
> BBC interview after the bombing of Coventry, 14–15 November 1940[21]

Forty thousand civilians were killed in the German blitz on British cities between September 1940 and May 1941, but casualties on this scale (one in a thousand of the population) had none of the effects predicted by Douhet. Indeed, the losses were one fourteenth of what the British had expected and had been prepared to accept. (The government had made plans for mass graves.) German bomber technology was simply not up to the job.

Neither were British and American bombers in 1942–43. They lacked the numbers, and the freedom to operate at will in German skies, needed to achieve the purpose for which they were created—the wholesale destruction of German cities and industry. But there was no question, in the minds of the British and American advocates of strategic bombardment at least, that that was the quick and efficient road to victory. In 1942, Lord Cherwell wrote: "Investigation seems to show that having one's house demolished is most damaging to morale. People seem to mind it more than having their friends or even relatives killed. At Hull, signs of strain were evident, though only one-tenth of the houses were demolished. On the above figures we should be able to do ten times as much harm to each of the fifty-eight principal German towns. There seems little doubt that this would break the will of the people."[22]

Up to that time the British air force, in its raids on Germany, had been trying to hit specific industrial targets (for efficiency's sake, not out of moral compunction), although even then the policy was not very strictly observed—especially since the strength of German air defenses forced the bombers to fly at night.

> *We didn't worry too much about not hitting the military targets we were after. Really, I suppose one thought we were at war with Germany and so long as we dropped our bombs we were doing some damage somewhere, although the ruling was that if we couldn't see our target we were to bring our bombs back, but nobody did this. . . . If the target was covered in cloud but you knew you were over a town somewhere you dropped the bombs, and when you got back at the de-briefing you said there was a hole in the cloud and you bombed through the hole—the next raid after Coventry we were briefed not to bring our bombs back. . . . That was the first time we were briefed to do that, after Coventry.*
>
> *Rupert Oakley, RAF Bomber Command pilot (seventy-three missions)*

But in early 1942, Air Marshal Harris took over Bomber Command, and dropped the pretense that the bombing had any more precise objective than the German civilian population. His stated reasons were technical, but the new policy conformed entirely with the ideas first expressed by Douhet:

> *. . . a fellow called Butt was asked to report on the examination of photographs taken by bombers and he came to the conclusion that the average bomb never hit within five miles of its target. . . . With my experience in night flying which was, compared with most people in the service in those days, rather more than most, it was only what I expected, and I realised that the answer to it was simply to mass-bomb large targets, and not try to pick out targets where they make ball-bearings or knitting machines or tie-pins or anything. . . .*

The policy of "mass bombing" that Harris initiated with the thousand-bomber raid on Cologne in April 1942 resulted in the progressive devastation, over the next three years, of almost every major city in Germany: 593,000 German civilians were killed, and over 3.3 million homes destroyed. But the cost to Britain was also high: 46,000 British aircrew were killed, and as much as one third of British military and civilian manpower and industrial resources was devoted to supporting Bomber Command in the latter years of the war.[23]

It seemed as though the whole of Hamburg was on fire from one end to the other and a huge column of smoke was towering well above us—and we were on 20,000 feet!

Set in the darkness was a turbulent dome of bright red fire, lighted and ignited like the glowing heart of a vast brazier. I saw no streets, no outlines of buildings, only brighter fires which flared like yellow torches against a background of bright red ash. Above the city was a misty red haze. I looked down, fascinated but aghast, satisfied yet horrified.

It was as if I was looking into what I imagined to be an active volcano. . . . There were great volumes of smoke and, mentally, I could sense the great heat. Our actual bombing was like putting another shovelful of coal into the furnace. —RAF aircrew over Hamburg, 28 July 1943[24]

The British bombers on this occasion were using the standard mix of bombs: huge numbers of four-pound incendiaries to start fires on roofs and thirty-pound ones to penetrate deeper inside buildings, together with four thousand-pound high-explosive bombs to blow in doors and windows over wide areas and fill the streets with craters and rubble to hinder fire-fighting equipment. But on a hot, dry summer night with good visibility, the unusually tight concentration of the bombs in a densely populated working-class district created a new phenomenon in history: a firestorm.

Eventually it covered an area of about four square miles, with an air temperature at the center of eight hundred degrees Celsius and convection winds blowing inward with hurricane force. One survivor said the sound of the wind was "like the Devil laughing," and another compared the noise of the firestorm to "an old organ in a church when someone is playing all the notes at once." Practically all the apartment blocks in the firestorm area had underground shelters, but nobody who stayed in them survived; those who were not cremated died of carbon monoxide poisoning. But to venture into the streets was to risk being swept by the wind into the very heart of the firestorm.

Mother wrapped me in wet sheets, kissed me, and said, "Run!" I hesitated at the door. In front of me I could see only fire—everything red, like the door to a furnace. An intense heat struck me. A burning beam fell in front of my feet. I shied back but then, when I was ready to jump over it, it was whirled away by a ghostly hand. The sheets around me acted as sails and I had the feeling that I was being carried away by the storm. I reached the front of a five-storey building . . . which . . . had been bombed and burned out in a previous raid and there was not much in it for the fire to get hold of. Someone came out, grabbed me in their arms, and pulled me into the doorway. —Traute Koch, fifteen in 1943

We came to the door which was burning just like a ring in the circus through which a lion has to jump. Someone in front of me hesitated. I pushed her out with my foot; I realised it was no use staying in that place. The rain of large sparks, blowing down the street, were each as large as a five-mark piece. I struggled to run against the wind but could only reach a house on the corner of the Sorbenstrasse. . . .

We . . . couldn't go on across the Eiffestrasse because the asphalt had melted. There were people on the roadway, some already dead, some still lying alive but stuck in the asphalt. They must have rushed onto the roadway without thinking. Their feet had got stuck and then they had put out their hands to try to get out again. They were on their hands and knees screaming.

Kate Hoffmeister, nineteen in 1943[25]

Forty-thousand people died in Hamburg in about two hours. If the Royal Air Force had been able to produce that result every time, its bombers would have ended the war in six months. But only once more, at Dresden in 1945, were all the circumstances right to produce a firestorm. The usual consequences were far less impressive. Over the whole war, the average result of a single British bomber sortie with a seven-man crew was less than three dead Germans, of whom perhaps one might be a production worker—and after an average of fourteen missions, the bomber crew themselves would be dead or, if they were very lucky, prisoners. Moreover, since the damage was done piecemeal over a long period of time, German industrial production for military purposes actually managed to continue rising until late 1944. The theory of strategic bombardment was sound, but the practice was a very expensive aerial equivalent of trench warfare.

The American air force had at least as much effect on German war production by concentrating on daylight precision bombing of "bottleneck" industrial targets. In the war against Japan, where it used huge B-29 bombers and more "British" tactics, the flimsy wooden buildings and crowded conditions of Japanese cities produced a thoroughly satisfactory result. Soon after Dresden, on 9 March 1945, Gen. Curtis E. LeMay ordered the first mass low-level night raid on Tokyo, using only incendiary bombs. "The area attacked was . . . four miles by three . . . with 103,000 inhabitants to the square mile. . . . 267,171 buildings were destroyed—about one-fourth of the total in Tokyo—and 1,008,000 persons were rendered homeless. . . . In some of the smaller canals the water was actually boiling."[26]

By 1945, at least in the particular case of Japan, strategic bombardment was actually working the way the theorists had envisaged: only three hundred thousand Japanese civilians were killed by the bombing, but about twenty-two million—a third of the population—were living in temporary shelters amid the burnt-out cities or had fled into the countryside. "The Twentieth [U.S.] Air Force was destroying Japanese cities at . . . [a] cost to Japan [that] was fifty times the cost to us," reported Gen. "Hap" Arnold, head of the U.S. Army Air Force.[27] But even in these dire circumstances, the almost limitless resilience and determination of the fully mobilized modern nation-state would have prevented a Japanese surrender and necessitated a full-scale invasion of the home islands, costing millions more lives—if an almost magical American weapon had not broken the spell imposed on the Japanese government by total war.

We were not expecting an air raid, but high up in the sky I heard an American bomber, a B-29. I thought it was strange. —Mrs. Ochi, Hiroshima

I saw a perfectly outlined city, clear in every detail, coming in. The city was roughly about four miles in diameter. By that time we were at our bombing altitude of thirty-two thousand feet. The navigator came up— looking over my shoulder, he said: "Yes, that's Hiroshima, there's no doubt about it." We were so well on the target that the bombardier says: "I can't do anything, there's nothing to do." He says: "It's just sitting there."

Col. Paul Tibbetts, pilot, Enola Gay

The U.S. government had begun the Manhattan Project in June 1942 after repeated warnings from refugee scientists that they suspected Germany was working to develop an atomic bomb. That worry was mistaken, in fact, but it was not unjustified, for it was a reasonable assumption by the mid-twentieth century that any scientific or technological development with military implications would be exploited for use in total war. The British certainly were investigating nuclear weapons already (though they and the Canadians accepted subsidiary roles in the Manhattan Project after 1942), and both the Russians and the Japanese had nuclear weapons programs by 1944.[28] And the Germans, though neglecting nuclear weapons, were busy developing the ancestors of the devices that are the principal means of delivering nuclear weapons today: the cruise missile (V-1), of which they launched 10,500 against Britain in 1944, and the long-range ballistic missile (V-2), of which 1,115 fell on or near London. Given the context of total war and the certainty that every potential weapon would be used with utter ruthlessness, it is scarcely surprising that most scientists everywhere placed their services at the disposal of the country of their birth (or their choice).

Even so, some of the nuclear physicists who had worked on the Manhattan Project for three years had second thoughts when, in July of 1945, they moved into an old ranch house in the New Mexico desert to do the final assembly and testing of the first atomic bomb. But it was too late to change their minds. They had delivered into the hands of the government a weapon that would at last fulfill all the promises of the strategists of aerial bombing about cheap and reliable mass destruction from the air. At 5:30 in the morning, the test went off perfectly, and the awestruck scientists contemplated what they had done.

> *We knew the world would not be the same. A few people laughed. A few people cried. Most people were silent. I remembered the line from the Hindu scripture—the* Bhagavad-gita. *Vishnu is trying to persuade the prince that he should do his duty and to impress him, takes on his multi-armed form and says, "Now I am become Death, the destroyer of worlds." I suppose we all felt that, one way or another.*
>
> Robert Oppenheimer, leader of the scientific team at Los Alamos

Scientifically the atomic bomb was an advance into unknown territory, but militarily it was simply a more cost-effective way of attaining a goal that was already a central part of strategy: a means of producing the results achieved at Hamburg and Dresden cheaply and reliably every time the weapon was used. (Even at the time, the $2 billion cost of the Manhattan Project was dwarfed by the cost of trying to destroy cities the hard way, using conventional bombs.) And there was no moral question in most people's minds about the ethics of using weapons of mass destruction against defenseless cities; that question had effectively been foreclosed over the Dolphin pub thirty years before.

> *In those days when one was told, "This is what you're going to do," you just saluted and said, "Yes, sir!" We had worked so long and so hard to perfect the weapon, to adapt the airplanes to carry that weapon, and to train ourselves to do the job—it seemed to be routine.* —Col. Paul Tibbetts

On 6 August 1945, Colonel Tibbetts's crew dropped the weapon on Hiroshima, and total war came fully into its inheritance: seventy thousand people were killed in less than five minutes by a single aircraft carrying a single bomb. Afterward, he said, "I couldn't see any city down there, but what I saw was a tremendous area covered by—the only way I could describe it is—a boiling black mass."

> *It was as if the sun had crashed and exploded. Yellow fireballs were splashing down. [Afterward, on the riverbank], there were so many injured people that there was almost no room to walk. This was only a mile from where the bomb fell. People's clothes had been blown off and their bodies burned by the heat rays. They looked as if they had strips of rags hanging from them. They had water blisters which had already burst, and their skins hung in tatters. I saw people whose intestines were hanging out of their bodies. Some had lost their eyes. Some had their backs torn open so you could see their backbones inside. They were all asking for water.*
>
> Mrs. Ochi

> *If I were given a similar situation in which this country was at war, risking*

*its future, the circumstances being as they were at that time, I don't think
I would hesitate one minute to do it over.*   —Col. Paul Tibbetts

Colonel Tibbetts is only unusual for what he did. His attitudes toward war are those that still dominate the world, although the weapons of mass destruction have grown still more efficient in the four decades since he dropped his relatively puny bomb on Hiroshima. The disproportion between ends and means in warfare has widened into an unbridgeable chasm: the causes and the various national war aims of this century's wars are no more profound or complex than those that sent Tuthmose III's army marching into Palestine three thousand years ago, but the means by which wars can now be fought have placed the whole human race on a permanent thirty minutes' notice of extinction.

As Gen. Douglas MacArthur testified to the U.S. Congress at the end of his career: "You have got to understand the history of war. . . . With the scientific methods which have made mass destruction reach appalling proportions, war has ceased to be a sort of roll of the dice. . . . If you have another world war. . . . only those will be happy that are dead. . . . I understand . . . that you cannot abolish war unless others do it. . . . The only way that you can meet force is by force . . . and you have to provide for that. But sooner or later, if civilisation is to survive, . . . war must go."[29] But there was clearly a long way to go. Only two years before, MacArthur himself had sought permission to use nuclear weapons on the Chinese during the Korean War.

Every era tends to dramatize its own dilemmas, and half the ages of mankind have believed the end of the world was nigh. Certainly if we succeed in solving the problem of war, later eras of human history will have their own dangers and difficulties to cope with, but the rest of human history stands little chance of happening at all if this era fails in its task of finding a way to abolish war.

NOTES

1. Guglielmo Ferrero, *Peace and War*, London: Macmillan, 1933, pp. 63-64.

2. Karl von Clausewitz, *On War*, tr. Col. J.J. Graham, London: Trubner, 1873, I, p.4.

3. Frank E. Vandiver, *Mighty Stonewall*, New York: McGraw-Hill, 1957, p. 366.

4. Col. Theodore Lyman, *Meade's Headquarters, 1863–1865*, Boston, Massachusetts: Massachusetts Historical Society, 1922, pp. 101, 224.

5. Frederick Henry Dyer, *A Compendium of The War of the Rebellion*, New York, New York: T. Yoseloff, 1959.

6. *Personal Memoirs of General W.T. Sherman*, Bloomington, Indiana: Indiana University Press, 1957, II, p. 111.

7. I. S. Bloch, *The War of the Future in Its Technical, Economic and Political Relations.* English translation by W. T. Stead entitled *Is War Impossible?*, 1899.

8. Jacques d'Arnoux, "Paroles d'un Revenant," in Lt. Col. J. Armengaud, ed. *L'atmosphere du Champ de Bataille*, Paris: Lavauzelle, 1940, pp. 118–19.

9. André Tardieu, *Avec Foch: Août-Novembre 1914*, Paris: Ernest Flammarion, 1939, p. 107.

10. J. F. C. Fuller, *The Second World War, 1939–1945: A Strategic and Tactical History*, New York: Duell, Sloan and Pearce, 1949. p. 140.

11. Ibid., p. 170.

12. Henry Williamson, *The Wet Flanders Plain*, London: Beaumont Press, pp. 14–16. Williamson was nineteen years old during the Battle of the Somme.

13. Arthur Bryant, *Unfinished Victory*, London: Macmillan, 1940, p. 8.

14. Aaron Norman, *The Great Air War*, New York: Macmillan, 1968, p. 353.

15. Ibid., p. 382.

16. Sir William Robertson, *Soldiers and Statesmen*, London: Cassell, 1926, I, p. 313.

17. Bryan Perret, *A History of Blitzkrieg*, London: Robert Hale, 1983, p. 21.

18. Theodore Ropp, *War in the Modern World*, rev. ed., New York: Collier, 1962, pp. 321, 344.

19. Guy Sajer, *The Forgotten Soldier*, London: Sphere, 1977, pp. 228–30.

20. Giulio Douhet, *The Command of the Air*, London: Faber & Faber, 1943, pp. 18–19.

21. Norman Longmark, *Air Raid: The Bombing of Coventry 1940*, London: Hutchinson, 1976, p. 146.

22. Max Hastings, *Bomber Command*, London: Pan Books, 1979, p. 149.

23. Ibid., p. 423.

24. Martin Middlebrook, *The Battle of Hamburg*, Allan Lane: London, 1980, p. 244.

25. Ibid., pp. 264–67.

26. Craven and Cate, *US Army Air Forces*, Chicago: University of Chicago Press, 1948, vol. 5, pp. 615–17.

27. H. H. Arnold, *Report . . . to the Secretary of War, 12 November 1945*, Washington: U.S. Government Printing Office, 1945, p. 35.

28. Leonard Bickel, *The Story of Uranium: The Deadly Element*, London: Macmillan, 1979, pp. 78–79, 198–99, 274–76.

29. William Manchester, *American Caesar: Douglas MacArthur 1880–1964*, London: Hutchinson, 1979, pp. 612, 622–23.

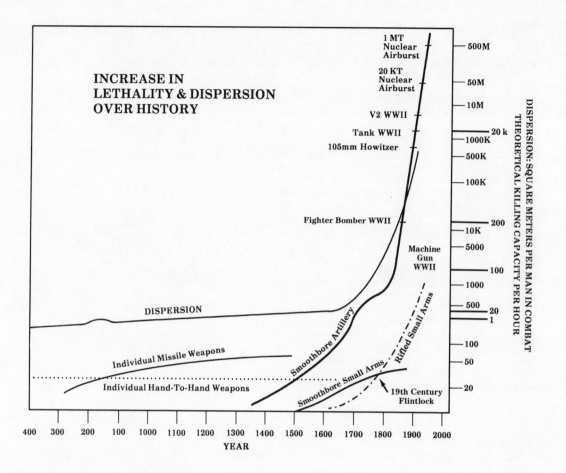

The great change on the battlefield did not come with
gunpowder, but with the development of modern artillery
and the rifled musket. *Courtesy of HERO Books, Fairfax,
Virginia, adapted from* The Evolution of Weapons and
Warfare *by T. N. Dupuy*

The first modern total war was the American Civil War, where more Americans were killed than in the First and Second World Wars, Korea, and Vietnam combined. Collecting remains of the dead on the battlefield, Cold Harbor, Virginia, April 1865. *Courtesy of the Library of Congress (B811 918)*

The North mobilized industrially for the war just as any nation would today. The South relied heavily on things like horsemanship and "the fightin' ability of Southern gentlemen." *From* Asher and Adams' Pictorial Album of American Industry, 1876; *Courtesy of the Hagley Museum and Library, Greenville, Delaware*

THE FORERUNNERS OF ALL MODERN WEAPONS

The American Civil War was the testing ground for war as we know it today. Here soldiers guard breech-loading smooth-bore cannons on armored trains. *Courtesy of the Library of Congress (B8171 1171)*

Aerial reconnaissance: Prof. Thaddeus S. Lowe observing the Battle of Fair Oaks from his balloon, 31 May 1862. Young Ferdinand von Zeppelin was one of the first Europeans to see this new American war technology in action. *Courtesy of the Library of Congress (B8171 2348)*

The telegraph first came into use to coordinate troop activity over a wide area in the 1860s; the same functions is now served by radio. *Courtesy of the Library of Congress (B8184 10497)*

Fort Mahone or "Fort Damnation," Petersburg, Virginia, in 1865; complete with dug-outs, wire entanglements, listening posts and all the necessities of trench warfare. *Courtesy of the Library of Congress (B811 3182)*

Gen. William T. Sherman, "the Attila of the American Continent." "War is war," he was fond of saying when anyone criticized his methods. *Courtesy of the Library of Congress (BH83 1470)*

Two months after the outbreak of World War I, a million men were dead, and all the armies on both sides had ground to a halt. Field Marshal Sir Douglas Haig was only one of the many puzzled officers trying to find a way around the continuous front. *Courtesy of the Imperial War Museum (Q23636)*

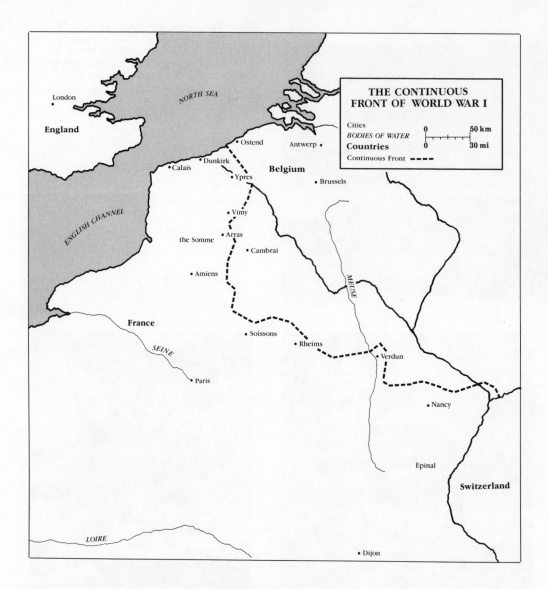

The day of the small, congested, isolated battle was over.
François I's victory at Ceresole in 1544 probably covered
an area of a few hundred yards. Napoleon's at Borodino
extended over perhaps two miles. But the battle of the
Somme took up more than twenty-five square miles; in a
sense, World War I was one enormous battle on each front.

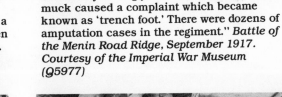

"It's such hell when you're in the front line. . . . It was no place for a human being to be, really." A flooded dugout in a front-line trench, January 1917. The men often managed to smile for the cameras. *Courtesy of the Imperial War Museum (Q4665)*

"Constantly having your feet in this gruel-like muck caused a complaint which became known as 'trench foot.' There were dozens of amputation cases in the regiment." *Battle of the Menin Road Ridge, September 1917. Courtesy of the Imperial War Museum (Q5977)*

"Rats bother you . . . rats eat you if you get wounded." A young Lewis gunner of the York and Lancaster Regiment with the regimental cat, February 1914. The rats gave the cat a practical as well as an emotional value. *Courtesy of the Imperial War Museum (Q8463)*

"It was a dirty, lousy place to live with all the corruption known to mankind." Canadian troops of the 87th Battalion resting near Willerval in April 1918. *Courtesy of the Imperial War Museum (CO2533)*

Soldiers jubilantly unpacking the shipments from home that meant the war could go on, October 1916. *Public Archives of Canada (PA937)*

Spent shellcases along Vimy Ridge, May 1917. Rates of destruction at the front often exceeded rates of production at home; soldiers could use up a month's production in a day's fighting. *Public Archives of Canada (PA 1349)*

The home front was so crucial that civilians were massively recruited into the war effort. This, naturally, made them fair targets. *Women workers in the Assembly Department of the British Munitions Supply Company in Verdun, Quebec, ca. 1916. Public Archives of Canada (PA 24436)*

Cost of the advance: 8000 men per square mile. British troops in a captured German trench, Serre, March 1917. *Courtesy of the Imperial War Museum (Q1787)*

The precedent and the prototype for Rotterdam, Dresden, Hiroshima. The 9 September 1915 Zeppelin raid on White Swan Alley, London. *Courtesy of the Imperial War Museum (LC17)*

One of the four empires destroyed by World War I. Russian revolutionaries storming the Winter Palace in 1917. *(re-enactment for film); TASS from SOVFOTO*

BREAKING THROUGH THE CONTINUOUS FRONT

The first tanks coming off the assembly line. Dark, deafening, hellishly hot inside, and terrifying to their victims, they seemed to promise a solution to the continuous front in 1917. *Public Archives of Canada (PA 5904)*

World War I soldiers greet their first tanks in July 1917. But in the end, all the tanks did was set the continuous front in motion, bringing war to every town and village in its path. *Public Archives of Canada (PA 3022)*

New weapons technology quickly summons up countertechnology: one of the first anti-tank guns bemuses soldiers on the advance east of Arras. *Public Archives of Canada (PA 3055)*

More than twice as many civilians died in the
Second World War as in World War I: most European countries, from Germany eastward,
lost about 10 percent of their population. In a
smashed town like Belgorod, a few survivors
search for their families. *TASS from
SOVFOTO*

5: Anybody's Son Will Do

You think about it and you know you're going to have to kill but you don't understand the implications of that, because in the society in which you've lived murder is the most heinous of crimes . . . and you are in a situation in which it's turned the other way round. . . . When you do actually kill someone the experience, my experience, was one of revulsion and disgust.

I was utterly terrified—petrified—but I knew there had to be a Japanese sniper in a small fishing shack near the shore. He was firing in the other direction at Marines in another battalion, but I knew as soon as he picked off the people there—there was a window on our side—that he would start picking us off. And there was nobody else to go . . . and so I ran towards the shack and broke in and found myself in an empty room.

There was a door which meant there was another room and the sniper was in that—and I just broke that down. I was just absolutely gripped by the fear that this man would expect me and would shoot me. But as it turned out he was in a sniper harness and he couldn't turn around fast enough. He was entangled in the harness so I shot him with a .45 and I felt remorse and shame. I can remember whispering foolishly, "I'm sorry" and then just throwing up. . . . I threw up all over myself. It was a betrayal of what I'd been taught since a child. —William Manchester

Yet he did kill the Japanese soldier, just as he had been trained to—the revulsion only came afterward. And even after Manchester knew what it was like to kill another human being, a young man like himself, he went on trying to kill his "enemies" until the war was over. Like all the other tens of millions of soldiers who had been taught from infancy that killing was wrong, and had then been sent off to kill for their countries, he was almost helpless to disobey, for he had fallen into the hands of an institution so powerful and so subtle that it could quickly reverse the moral training of a lifetime.

The whole vast edifice of the military institution rests on its ability to obtain obedience from its members even unto death—and the killing of others. It has enormous powers of compulsion at its command, of course, but all authority must be based ultimately on consent. The task of extracting that consent from its members has probably grown harder in recent times, for the gulf between the military and the civilian worlds has undoubtedly widened: civilians no longer perceive the threat of violent death as an everyday hazard of existence, and the categories of people whom it is not morally permissible to kill have broadened to include (in peacetime) the entire human race. Yet the armed forces of every country can still take almost any young male civilian and turn him into a soldier with all the right reflexes and attitudes in only a few weeks. Their recruits usually have no more than twenty years' experience of the world, most of it as children, while the armies have had all of history to practice and perfect their techniques.

Just think of how the soldier is treated. While still a child he is shut up in the barracks. During his training he is always being knocked about. If he makes the least mistake he is beaten, a burning blow on his body, another on his eye, perhaps his head is laid open with a wound. He is battered and bruised with flogging. On the march . . . they hang heavy loads round his neck like that of an ass.
— *Egyptian, ca. 1500* B.C.[1]

The moment I talk to the new conscripts about the homeland I strike a land mine. So I kept quiet. Instead I try to make soldiers of them. I give them hell from morning to sunset. They begin to curse me, curse the army, curse the state. Then they begin to curse together, and become a truly cohesive group, a unit, a fighting unit. —Israeli, ca. A.D.1970[2]

All soldiers belong to the same profession, no matter what country they serve, and it makes them different from everybody else. They have to be different, for their job is ultimately about killing and dying, and those things are not a natural vocation for any human being. Yet all soldiers are born civilians. The method for turning young men into soldiers—people who kill other people and expose themselves to death—is basic training. It's essentially the same all over the world, and it always has been, because young men everywhere are pretty much alike.

Human beings are fairly malleable, especially when they are young, and in every young man there are attitudes for any army to work with: the inherited values and postures, more or less dimly recalled, of the tribal warriors who were once the model for every young boy to emulate. Civilization did not involve a sudden clean break in the way people behave, but merely the progressive distortion and redirection of all the ways in which people in the old tribal societies used to behave, and modern definitions of maleness still contain a great deal of the old warrior ethic. The anarchic machismo of the primitive warrior is not what modern armies really need in their soldiers, but it does provide them with promising raw material for the transformation they must work in their recruits.

Just how this transformation is wrought varies from time to time and from country to country. In totally militarized societies—ancient Sparta, the samurai class of medieval Japan, the areas controlled by organizations like the Eritrean People's Liberation Front today—it begins at puberty or before, when the young boy is immersed in a disciplined society in which only the military values are allowed to penetrate. In more sophisticated modern societies, the process is briefer and more concentrated, and the way it works is much more visible. It is, essentially, a conversion process in an almost religious sense—and as in all conversion phenomena, the emotions are far more important than the specific ideas.

The Soviet soldier is powerful and renowned not only because of his weapons. He possesses high moral-combat qualities. The Communist Party has armed him with invincible Marxist-Leninist teachings which contain an inexhaustible source of ideological maturity and Communist conviction for all personnel of the armed forces. —Marshal A. A. Grechko, Soviet army, 1975[3]

When I was going to school, we used to have to recite the Pledge of Allegiance every day. They don't do that now. You know, we've got kids that come in here now, when they first get here, they don't know the Pledge of Allegiance to the flag. And that's something—that's like a cardinal sin. . . . My daughter will know that stuff by the time she's three; she's two now and she's working on it. . . . You know, you've got to have your basics, the groundwork where you can start to build a child's brain from. . . .
USMC drill instructors, Parris Island recruit training depot, 1981

That is what the rhetoric of military patriotism sounds like, in every country and at every level—and it is virtually irrelevant so far as the actual job of soldiering is concerned. Soldiers are not just robots; they are ordinary human beings with national and personal loyalties, and many of them do feel the need for some patriotic or ideological justification for what they do. But which nation, which ideology, does not matter: men will fight as well and die as bravely for the Khmer Rouge as for "God, King, and Country." Soldiers are the instruments of politicians and priests, ideologues and strategists, who may have high national or moral purposes in mind, but the men down in the trenches fight for more basic motives. The closer you get to the front line, the fewer abstract nouns you hear.

Armies know this. It is their business to get men to fight, and they have had a long time to work out the best way of doing it. All of them pay lip service to the symbols and slogans of their political masters, though the amount of time they must devote to this activity varies from country to country. It is less in the United States than in the Soviet Union, and it is still less in a country like Israel, which actually fights frequent wars. Nor should it be thought that the armies are hypocritical—most of their members really do believe in their particular national symbols and slogans. But their secret is that they know these are not the things that sustain men in combat.

What really enables men to fight is the their own self-respect, and a special kind of love that has nothing to do with sex or idealism. Very few men have died in battle, when the moment actually arrived, for the United States of America or for the sacred cause of Communism, or even for their homes and families; if they had any choice in the matter at all, they chose to die for each other and for their own vision of themselves.

Once you get out there and you realize a guy is shooting at you, your first instinct, regardless of all your training, is to live. . . . But you can't turn around and run the other way. Peer pressure, you know? There's people here with you that have probably saved your life or will save your life in the future; you can't back down. —USMC Vietnam veteran

This is going to sound really strange, but there's a love relationship that is nurtured in combat because the man next to you—you're depending on him for the most important thing you have, your life, and if he lets you down you're either maimed or killed. If you make a mistake the same thing happens to him, so the bond of trust has to be extremely close, and I'd say this bond is stronger than almost anything, with the exception of parent and child. It's a hell of a lot stronger than man and wife—your life is in his hands, you trust that person with the most valuable thing you have. And you'll find that people who pursue the aphrodisiac of combat or whatever you want to call it are there because they're friends, the same people show up in the same wars time and again.

Capt. John Early, ex-U.S. Army, Vietnam, ex-mercenary, Rhodesia

John Early is an intelligent and sensitive man who became a combat junkie ("I'm a contradiction in terms, and I can't explain it") and as such he is a rarity. For most men, the trust and intimacy of a small unit in combat never compensate for the fear and revulsion. But the selfless identification of the soldier with the other men in his unit is what makes armies work in combat, and the foundations for it must be laid in peacetime. "Fighting is a social art, based upon collective activity, cooperation and mutual support," an Israeli soldier observed. "This utter reliance on others is an integral part of the effort to meet the enemy irrespective of odds, and it largely determines men's willingness to risk their lives in pressing the attack. . . . In short there is rarely brotherhood in facing death when there is none in peace."[4]

The way armies produce this sense of brotherhood in a peacetime environment is basic training: a feat of psychological manipulation on the grand scale which has been so consistently successful and so universal that we fail to notice it as remarkable. In countries where the army must extract its recruits in their late teens, whether voluntarily or by conscription, from a civilian environment that does not share the military values, basic training involves a brief but intense period of indoctrination whose purpose is not really to teach the recruits basic military skills, but rather to change their values and their loyalties. "I guess you could say we brainwash them a little bit," admitted a U.S. Marine drill instructor, "but you know they're good people."

The duration and intensity of basic training, and even its major emphases, depend on what kind of society the recruits are coming from, and on what sort of military organization they are going to. It is obviously quicker to train men from a martial culture than from one in which the dominant values are civilian and commercial, and easier to deal with volunteers than with reluctant conscripts. Conscripts are not always unwilling, however; there are many instances in which the army is popular for economic reasons.

In early modern Europe, for example, military service was always intensely unpopular with the mass of the population, and most soldiers were drawn from the most deprived and desperate groups on the margins of society. That changed suddenly in the nineteenth century, with conscription—and, strangely, at the same time military service became extremely popular. The fervent nationalism of the nineteenth century had much to do with it, but meat probably had even more.

In the army, the conscripts were fed meat every day and were issued two pairs of boots and a change of underwear—which was more than most of them had back on the farm or in the back streets of the cities. Most armies in the Third World still benefit from this kind of popularity today and have five or ten applicants for every available place (in some countries it is necessary to bribe the recruiter to get in). But even in the industrialized nations of the late twentieth century, in which the average civilian's living standard has long since overtaken that of the private soldier and the white heat of nationalism has subsided somewhat, armies have no difficulty in turning recruits, whether conscripts or not, into soldiers.

A more complex question is what kind of soldier (or sailor, or airman) the recruit must now be turned into. This is usually seen mainly in terms of the increased requirement for technical knowledge brought about by modern weapons, but that is not really a problem of basic training. The crux of the issue is the kind of social environment the recruit will eventually have to fight in.

For all of military history down to less than a century ago, the answer was invariably the same: an extremely crowded one, with his comrades all around him. In a Roman legion, on the gun deck of a seventeenth-century warship, or in a Napoleonic infantry battalion, the men fought close together, and the presence of so many others going through the same ordeal gave each individual enormous moral support—and exerted enormous moral pressure on him to play his full part. So long as you drilled the recruit to the point of boredom and beyond in the use of his sword, cannon, or musket; instilled in him a loyalty to his legion, ship, or regiment; and put him in mortal fear of his officers, he would probably perform all right on the day of the battle.

To a very large extent the crews of modern ships and aircraft (and even tanks)—all the men who fight together from inside machines—are still living in the same social environment, though the crowds have thinned out noticeably. And when men go into battle in the presence of their peers, the same principles of training will still produce the same results. But for the infantry, who fought shoulder to shoulder all through history, the world has been turned upside down.

Even after the continuous front emerged in World War I, infantrymen could still usually see their whole company in an attack, but the dispersion forced on them by modern firepower has reduced the group who will actually be within sight or hearing of each other in a typical position to ten men or less—and even they will probably be spread out over a considerable area. For the foot soldier, the battlefield has become a desperately lonely place, deceptively empty in appearance but bristling with menace, where he can expect neither direct supervision by his officer or NCO in combat, nor the comforting presence of a group of other men beside him.

The more sophisticated forms of infantry basic training have now recognized that fact, and in the latter phases of the training, they place far greater stress on "small-group dynamics": building the solidarity of the "primary group" of five to ten men who will be the individual's only source of succor and the only audience of his actions in combat. Far greater dependence must now be placed on the individual soldier's initiative and motivation than ever before, and so armies have to try harder. But for all that, the fundamentals of basic training have not changed.

Even in countries where the regime demands that all policies, including military ones, be chosen and justified solely in terms of the official state ideology, professional soldiers always manage to get around it and deal with military problems in terms of human realities. In the Soviet Union, for example, the official position is that the soldier is only as good as his ideology. "Courage, bravery and heroism can be displayed by soldiers on a mass scale . . . only if they are linked with the noble ideals [of Marxism-Leninism], with the conviction that the purpose of the army and its war aims correspond to the interest of the people. . . ."[5] The Soviet Army does not—publicly—demur.

It has the advantage, of course, of drawing its conscripts from a highly regimented totalitarian society in which the citizens are habituated to public displays of orthodoxy and obedience to authority, and where "each teacher must explain to the student the policies of the Communist Party and the Soviet government concerning the country's defense, the requirement for and importance of military service, and the need to develop the moral-political qualities required by future soldiers."[6] Moreover, all teenagers between sixteen and eighteen are expected to participate in premilitary training clubs, which teach them basic military skills. On the other hand, the army only gets to give its conscripts a few weeks of concentrated basic training before they take the military oath.

It is all, however, just another example of the *pokazhuka* (shadow-play) that pervades Soviet society. In fact, "at all rank levels in the Soviet army, the proposition that ideology is an important factor in motivating soldiers to fight is simply not strongly held. . . . The forces that motivate the soldier in combat are those generated internally within the group and have no relationship to ideology."[7]

The same realism prevails among professional soldiers in other armies that are forced by the totalitarian regimes they serve to pretend in public that the official ideology supersedes all practical military wisdom. Postwar studies showed, for example, that the Nazi trappings of the German army had nothing to do with the fact that its units held together extraordinarily well under extreme combat stress; the German army was just very good at encouraging and sustaining the essential loyalty in the "primary groups" within its units.[8] (No doubt competent Iranian regular officers today are surreptitiously basing their training on the creation of exactly that kind of small-group bond in their units, while giving appropriate lip service to Islamic fervor.)

Soviet soldiers do get proper basic training, of course; it just happens largely under other names and over a more extended period of time. Indeed, the entire two years a Soviet conscript spends in the army are passed in conditions that would appear to most Western soldiers as a somewhat relaxed version of the basic training regime. And since Russia is in many ways a nineteenth-century society where patriotism is an absolute value and where loyalty to a chosen circle of close friends is sacrosanct, the Soviet army does not have quite as much need for the sharply defined intensive period of basic training that is typical elsewhere.

In Western Europe the gap between military and civilian mores is far wider. West German conscripts are sent to the training company of the battalion in which they will serve for a six-week crash course in becoming a soldier. The volunteers who fill the British army's ranks follow a three-day "orientation" course (during which 25 percent of them drop out) with sixteen weeks of instruction at a regimental training depot, of which about the first half could properly be called basic training. And in the United States, where the contrast between the austerity, hierarchy, and discipline of military life and the prevailing civilian values is most extreme, basic training—the conversion of young civilian males into soldiers—is given a greater emphasis than almost anywhere else.

The degree of emphasis, however, depends heavily on what the American volunteer is going to do in military life. The great majority of military personnel in the armed forces of all industrialized countries these days are not combat soldiers, and a man or woman whose time will be spent in manning one of the navy's radar sets or filing air force documents does not need to learn the very special attitudes and loyalties that are necessary in ground combat. Learning to look military, obey orders, and perform their jobs will suffice. But the U.S. Army, which reckons that all its members could, under some circumstances, find themselves in a combat zone, insists on seven weeks' basic training, followed by advanced individual training in a specific trade—and the U.S. Marine Corps gives eleven weeks of basic training to every man and woman who joins the Corps.

It is a very old-fashioned organization (the last of the U.S. armed forces to get its hands on any desirable piece of new weapons technology), which clings to the belief that every Marine must be a qualified combat rifleman first, even if his subsequent specialty will be cooking or supply. It is also an elite assault force, whose battle doctrine accepts the necessity, on occasion, of trading casualties for time. The entire orientation of the Marine Corps is toward the demands of combat: it informs everything the Corps does.

This makes the Marines atypical of contemporary armed forces in the United States or anywhere else, which generally consist of very large numbers of pseudo-military personnel doing technical, administrative, and even public relations jobs, surrounding a much smaller combat core. The Marines is almost all core. But for this very reason it is a virtually ideal case study in how basic training works: it draws its recruits from the most extravagantly individualistic civilian society in the world and turns them into elite combat soldiers in eleven weeks.

It's easier if you catch them young. You can train older men to be soldiers; it's done in every major war. But you can never get them to believe that they like it, which is the major reason armies try to get their recruits before they are twenty. There are other reasons too, of course, like the physical fitness, lack of dependents, and economic dispensability of teenagers, that make armies prefer them, but the most important qualities teenagers bring to basic training are enthusiasm and naiveté. Many of them actively want the discipline and the closely structured environment that the armed forces will provide, so there is no need for the recruiters to deceive the kids about what will happen to them after they join.

There is discipline. There is drill. . . . When you are relying on your mates and they are relying on you, there's no room for slackness or sloppiness. If you're not prepared to accept the rules, you're better off where you are.

British army recruiting advertisement, 1976

People are not born soldiers, they become soldiers. . . . And it should not begin at the moment when a new recruit is enlisted into the ranks, but

Young civilians who have volunteered and have been accepted by the Marine Corps arrive at Parris Island, the Corps's East Coast facility for basic training, in a state of considerable excitement and apprehension: most are aware that they are about to undergo an extraordinary and very difficult experience. But they do not make their own way to the base; rather they trickle in to Charleston airport on various flights throughout the day on which their training platoon is due to form, and are held there, in a state of suppressed but mounting nervous tension, until late in the evening. When the buses finally come to carry them the seventy-six miles to Parris Island, it is often after midnight—and this is not an administrative oversight. The shock treatment they are about to receive will work most efficiently if they are worn out and somewhat disoriented when they arrive.

The basic training organization is a machine, processing several thousand young men every month, and every facet and gear of it has been designed with the sole purpose of turning civilians into Marines as efficiently as possible. Provided it can have total control over their bodies and their environment for approximately three months, it can practically guarantee converts. Parris Island provides that controlled environment, and the recruits do not set foot outside it again until they graduate as Marine privates eleven weeks later.

> *They're allowed to call home, so long as it doesn't get out of hand—every three weeks or so they can call home and make sure everything's all right, if they haven't gotten a letter or there's a particular set of circumstances. If it's a case of an emergency call coming in, then they're allowed to accept that call; if not, one of my staff will take the message. . . .*
>
> *In some cases I'll get calls from parents who haven't quite gotten adjusted to the idea that their son had cut the strings—and in a lot of cases that's what they're doing. The military provides them with an opportunity to leave home but they're still in a rather secure environment.*
>
> *Captain Brassington, USMC*

For the young recruits, basic training is the closest thing their society can offer to a formal rite of passage, and the institution probably stands in an unbroken line of descent from the lengthy ordeals by which young males in precivilized groups were initiated into the adult community of warriors. But in civilized societies it is a highly functional institution whose product is not anarchic warriors, but trained soldiers.

Basic training is not really about teaching people skills; it's about changing them, so that they can do things they wouldn't have dreamt of otherwise. It works by applying enormous physical and mental pressure to men who have been isolated from their normal civilian environment and placed in one where the only right way to think and behave is the way the Marine Corps wants them to. The key word the men who run the machine use to describe this process is *motivation*.

> *I can motivate a recruit and in third phase, if I tell him to jump off the third deck, he'll jump off the third deck. Like I said before, it's a captive audience and I can train that guy; I can get him to do anything I want him to do. . . . They're good kids and they're out to do the right thing. We get some bad kids, but you know, we weed those out. But as far as motivation— here, we can motivate them to do anything you want, in recruit training.*

USMC drill instructor, Parris Island

The first three days the raw recruits spend at Parris Island are actually relatively easy, though they are hustled and shouted at continuously. It is during this time that they are documented and inoculated, receive uniforms, and learn the basic orders of drill that will enable young Americans (who are not very accustomed to this aspect of life) to do everything simultaneously in large groups. But the most important thing that happens in "forming" is the surrender of the recruits' own clothes, their hair—all the physical evidence of their individual civilian identities.

During a period of only seventy-two hours, in which they are allowed little sleep, the recruits lay aside their former lives in a series of hasty rituals (like being shaven to the scalp) whose symbolic significance is quite clear to them even though they are quite deliberately given absolutely no time for reflection, or any hint that they might have the option of turning back from their commitment. The men in charge of them know how delicate a tightrope they are walking, though, because at this stage the recruits are still newly caught civilians who have not yet made their ultimate inward submission to the discipline of the Corps.

> *Forming Day One makes me nervous. You've got a whole new mob of recruits, you know, sixty or seventy depending, and they don't know anything. You don't know what kind of a reaction you're going to get from the stress you're going to lay on them, and it just worries me the first day.*

> *Things could happen, I'm not going to lie to you. Something might happen. A recruit might decide he doesn't want any part of this stuff and maybe take a poke at you or something like that. In a situation like that it's going to be a spur-of-the-moment thing and that worries me.* —USMC drill instructor

But it rarely happens. The frantic bustle of forming is designed to give the recruit no time to think about resisting what is happening to him. And so the recruits emerge from their initiation into the system, stripped of their civilian clothes, shorn of their hair, and deprived of whatever confidence in their own identity they may previously have had as eighteen-year-olds, like so many blanks ready to have the Marine identity impressed upon them.

The first stage in any conversion process is the destruction of an individual's former beliefs and confidence, and his reduction to a position of helplessness and need. It isn't really as drastic as all that, of course, for three days cannot cancel out eighteen years; the inner thoughts and the basic character are not erased. But the recruits have already learned that the only acceptable behavior is to repress any unorthodox thoughts and to mimic the character the Marine Corps wants. Nor are they, on the whole, reluctant to do so, for they *want* to be Marines. From the moment they arrive at Parris Island, the vague notion that has been passed down for a thousand generations that masculinity means being a warrior becomes an explicit article of faith, relentlessly preached: to be a man means to be a Marine.

There are very few eighteen-year-old boys who do not have highly romanticized ideas of what it means to be a man, so the Marine Corps has plenty of buttons to push. And it starts pushing them on the first day of real training: the officer in charge of the formation appears before them for the first time, in full dress uniform with medals, and tells them how to become men.

> *The United States Marine Corps has 205 years of illustrious history to speak for itself. You have made the most important decision in your life . . . by signing your name, your life, your pledge to the Government of the United States, and even more importantly, to the United States Marine Corps—a brotherhood, an elite unit. In 10.3 weeks you are going to become a member of that history, those traditions, this organization—if you have what it takes.*
>
> *All of you want to do that by virtue of your signing your name as a man. The Marine Corps says that we build men. Well, I'll go a little bit further. We develop the tools that you have—and everybody has those tools to a certain extent right now. We're going to give you the blueprints, and we are going to show you how to build a Marine. You've got to build a Marine—you understand?*
> —Captain Pingree, USMC

The recruits, gazing at him with awe and adoration, shout in unison, "Yes, sir!" just as they have been taught. They do it willingly, because they are volunteers— but even conscript tend to have the romantic fervor of volunteers if they are only eighteen years old. Basic training, whatever its hardships, is a quick way to become a man among men, with an undeniable status, and beyond the initial consent to undergo it, it doesn't even require any decisions.

> *I had just dropped out of high school and I wasn't doing much on the street except hanging out, as most teenagers would be doing. So they gave me an opportunity—a recruiter picked me up, gave me a good line, and said that I could make it in the Marines, that I have a future ahead of me. And since*

I was living with my parents, I figured that I could start my own life here and grow up a little.   —*USMC recruit, 1982*

I like the hand-to-hand combat and . . . things like that. It's a little rough going on me, and since I have a small frame I would like to become deadly, as I would put it. I like to have them words, especially the way they've been teaching me here.   —*USMC recruit (from Brooklyn), Parris Island, 1982*

The training, when it starts, seems impossibly demanding physically for most of the recruits—and then it gets harder week by week. There is a constant barrage of abuse and insults aimed at the recruits, with the deliberate purpose of breaking down their pride and so destroying their ability to resist the transformation of values and attitudes that the Corps intends them to undergo. At the same time the demands for constant alertness and for instant obedience are continuously stepped up, and the standards by which the dress and behavior of the recruits are judged become steadily more unforgiving. But it is all carefully calculated by the men who run the machine, who think and talk in terms of the stress they are placing on the recruits: "We take so many c.c.'s of stress and we administer it to each man—they should be a little bit scared and they should be unsure, but they're adjusting." The aim is to keep the training arduous but just within most of the recruits' capability to with-stand. One of the most striking achievements of the drill instructors is to create and maintain the illusion that basic training is an extraordinary challenge, one that will set those who graduate apart from others, when in fact almost everyone can succeed.

There has been some preliminary weeding out of potential recruits even before they begin training, to eliminate the obviously unsuitable minority, and some people do "fail" basic training and get sent home, at least in peacetime. The standards of acceptable performance in the U.S. armed forces, for example, tend to rise and fall in inverse proportion to the number and quality of recruits available to fill the forces to the authorized manpower levels. (In 1980, about 15 percent of Marine recruits did not graduate from basic training.) But there are very few young men who cannot be turned into passable soldiers if the forces are willing to invest enough effort in it.

Not even physical violence is necessary to effect the transformation, though it has been used by most armies at most times.

It's not what it was fifteen years ago down here. The Marine Corps still occupies the position of a tool which the society uses when it feels like that is a resort that they have to fall to. Our society changes as all societies do, and our society felt that through enlightened training methods we could still produce the same product—and when you examine it, they're right. . . . Our 100 c.c.'s of stress is really all we need, not two gallons of it, which is what used to be. . . . In some cases with some of the younger drill instructors it was more an initiation than it was an acute test, and so we introduced extra officers and we select our drill instructors to "fine-tune" it.

Captain Brassington, USMC

There is, indeed, a good deal of fine-tuning in the roles that the men in charge of training any specific group of recruits assume. At the simplest level, there is a sort of "good cop—bad cop" manipulation of the recruits' attitudes toward those applying the stress. The three younger drill instructors with a particular serial are quite close to them in age and unremittingly harsh in their demands for ever higher performance, but the senior drill instructor, a man almost old enough to be their father, plays a more benevolent and understanding part and is available for individual counseling. And generally offstage, but always looming in the background, is the company commander, an impossibly austere and almost godlike personage.

At least these are the images conveyed to the recruits, although of course all these men cooperate closely with an identical goal in view. It works: in the end they become not just role models and authority figures, but the focus of the recruits' developing loyalty to the organization.

I imagine there's some fear, especially in the beginning, because they don't know what to expect. . . . I think they hate you at first, at least for a week or two, but it turns to respect. . . . They're seeking discipline, they're seeking someone to take charge, 'cause at home they never got it. . . . They're looking to be told what to do and then someone is standing there enforcing what they tell them to do, and it's kind of like the father-and-son game, all the way through. They form a fatherly image of the DI whether they want to or not.
—Sergeant Carrington, USMC

Just the sheer physical exercise, administered in massive doses, soon has the recruits feeling stronger and more competent than ever before. Inspections, often several times daily, quickly build up their ability to wear the uniform and carry themselves like real Marines, which is a considerable source of pride. The inspections also help to set up the pattern in the recruits of unquestioning submission to military authority: standing stock-still, staring straight ahead, while somebody else examines you closely for faults is about as extreme a ritual act of submission as you can make with your clothes on.

But they are not submitting themselves merely to the abusive sergeant making unpleasant remarks about the hair in their nostrils. All around them are deliberate reminders—the flags and insignia displayed on parade, the military music, the marching formations and drill instructors' cadenced calls—of the idealized organization, the "brotherhood" to which they will be admitted as full members if they submit and conform. Nowhere in the armed forces are the military courtesies so elaborately observed, the staffs' uniforms so immaculate (some DIs change several times a day), and the ritual aspects of military life so highly visible as on a basic training establishment.

Even the seeming inanity of close-order drill has a practical role in the conversion process. It has been over a century since mass formations of men were of any use on the battlefield, but every army in the world still drills its troops, especially during basic training, because marching in formation, with every man moving his body in the same way at the same moment, is a direct physical way of learning two things a soldier must believe: that orders have to be obeyed automatically and instantly, and that you are no longer an individual, but part of a group.

The recruits' total identification with the other members of their unit is the most important lesson of all, and everything possible is done to foster it. They spend almost every waking moment together—a recruit alone is an anomaly to be looked into at once—and during most of that time they are enduring shared hardships. They also undergo collective punishments, often for the misdeed or omission of a single individual (talking in the ranks, a bed not swept under during barracks inspection), which is a highly effective way of suppressing any tendencies toward individualism. And, of course, the DIs place relentless emphasis on competition with other "serials" in training: there may be something infinitely pathetic to outsiders about a marching group of anonymous recruits chanting, "Lift your heads and hold them high, 3313 is a-passin' by," but it doesn't seem like that to the men in the ranks.

Nothing is quite so effective in building up a group's morale and solidarity, though, as a steady diet of small triumphs. Quite early in basic training, the recruits begin to do things that seem, at first sight, quite dangerous: descend by ropes from fifty-foot towers, cross yawning gaps hand-over-hand on high wires (known as the Slide for Life, of course), and the like. The common denominator is that these activities are daunting but not really dangerous: the ropes will prevent anyone from falling to his death off the rappelling tower, and there is a pond of just the right depth—deep enough to cushion a falling man, but not deep enough that he is likely to drown—under the Slide for Life. The goal is not to kill recruits, but to build up their confidence as individuals and as a group by allowing them to overcome apparently frightening obstacles.

> *You have an enemy here at Parris Island. The enemy that you're going to have at Parris Island is in every one of us. It's in the form of cowardice. The most rewarding experience you're going to have in recruit training is standing on line every evening, and you'll be able to look into each other's eyes, and you'll be able to say to each other with your eyes: "By God, we've made it one more day! We've defeated the coward."* —Captain Pingree, USMC

> *Number on deck, sir, forty-five . . . highly motivated, truly dedicated, rompin', stompin', bloodthirsty, kill-crazy United States Marine Corps recruits, SIR!* —Marine chant, Parris Island, 1982

If somebody does fail a particular test, he tends to be alone, for the hurdles are deliberately set low enough that most recruits can clear them if they try. In any large group of people there is usually a goat: someone whose intelligence or manner or lack of physical stamina marks him for failure and contempt. The competent drill instructor, without deliberately setting up this unfortunate individual for disgrace, will use his failure to strengthen the solidarity and confidence of the rest. When one hapless young man fell off the Slide for Life into the pond, for example, his drill instructor shouted the usual invective—"Well, get out of the water. Don't contaminate it all day"—and then delivered the payoff line: "Go back and change your clothes. You're useless to your unit now."

"Useless to your unit" is the key phrase, and all the recruits know that what it means is "useless *in battle*." The Marine drill instructors at Parris Island know exactly what they are doing to the recruits, and why. They are not rear-echelon people filling comfortable jobs, but the most dedicated and intelligent NCOs the Marine Corps can find; even now, many of them have combat experience. The Corps has a clear-eyed understanding of precisely what it is training its recruits for—combat—and it ensures that those who do the training keep that objective constantly in sight.

The DIs "stress" the recruits, feed them their daily ration of synthetic triumphs over apparent obstacles, and bear in mind all the time that the goal is to instill the foundations for the instinctive, selfless reactions and the fierce group loyalty that is what the recruits will need if they ever see combat. They are arch-manipulators, fully conscious of it, and utterly unashamed. These kids have signed up as Marines, and they could well see combat; this is the way they have to think if they want to live.

I've seen guys come to Vietnam from all over. They were all sorts of people that had been scared—some of them had been scared all their life and still scared. Some of them had been a country boy, city boys—you know, all different kinds of people—but when they got in combat they all reacted the same—99 percent of them reacted the same. . . . A lot of it is training here at Parris Island, but the other part of it is survival. They know if they don't conform—conform I call it, but if they don't react in the same way other people are reacting, they won't survive. That's just it. You know, if you don't react together, then nobody survives. —USMC drill instructor, Parris Island, 1982

When I went to boot camp and did individual combat training they said if you walk into an ambush what you want to do is just do a right face—you just turn right or left, whichever way the fire is coming from, and assault. I said, "Man, that's crazy. I'd never do anything like that. It's stupid."

The first time we came under fire, on Hill 1044 in Operation Beauty Canyon in Laos, we did it automatically. Just like you look at your watch to see what time it is. We done a right face, assaulted the hill—a fortified position with concrete bunkers emplaced, machine guns, automatic weapons—and we took it. And we killed—I'd estimate probably thirty-five North Vietnamese soldiers in the assault, and we only lost three killed. I think it was about two or three, and about eight or ten wounded.

But you know, what they teach you, it doesn't faze you until it comes down to the time to use it, but it's in the back of your head, like, What do you do when you come to a stop sign? It's in the back of your head, and you react automatically.
—USMC sergeant, 1982

Combat is the ultimate reality that Marines—or any other soldiers, under any flag—have to deal with. Physical fitness, weapons training, battle drills, are all indispensable elements of basic training, and it is absolutely essential that the recruits learn the attitudes of group loyalty and interdependency which will be their sole hope of survival and success in combat. The training inculcates or fosters all of those things, and even by the halfway point in the eleven-week course, the recruits are generally responding with enthusiasm to their tasks.

But there is nothing in all this (except the weapons drill) that would not be found in the training camp of a professional football team. What sets soldiers apart is their willingness to kill. But it is not a willingness that comes easily to most men—even young men who have been provided with uniforms, guns, and official approval to kill those whom their government has designated as enemies. They will, it is true, fall very readily into the stereotypes of the tribal warrior group. Indeed, most of them have had at least a glancing acquaintance in their early teens with gangs (more or less violent, depending on, among other things, the neighborhood), the modern relic of that ancient institution.

And in many ways what basic training produces is the uniformed equivalent of a modern street gang: a bunch of tough, confident kids full of bloodthirsty talk. But gangs don't actually kill each other in large numbers. If they behaved the way armies do, you'd need trucks to clean the bodies off the streets every morning. They're held back by the civilian belief—the normal human belief—that killing another person is an awesome act with huge consequences.

There is aggression in all of us—men, women, children, babies. Armies don't have to create it, and they can't even increase it. But most of us learn to put limits on our aggression, especially physical aggression, as we grow up. It is true even of New York gangs wearing their colors and looking as mean as they possibly can, or of British football fans who appear to be restaging the battle of Agincourt on the terraces. They make a very careful distinction between aggressive display and actual violence, and most of what seems to be violence is mime.

You can look at the patterns of aggression and fights that most kids are into, and you find a very orchestrated, highly ritualized pattern by and large. The ritual . . . ensures that not too many people get hurt, and there are of course strong parallels between that pattern of behavior and the pattern of so-called primitive tribesmen and warriors.

There is a lot of talk about violence, far out of proportion to the amounts of violence that actually take place. . . . There is a very tiny, tiny level of violence at British football games. It's very hard to get this idea across to a lot of people who have been led to assume that what goes on on the football terraces is bloody, dangerous, and random. In fact what you have there is a perfect illusion of violence: a very high level of aggression, of competitiveness, of two rival groups coming together, but what goes on there is in terms of symbolic exchanges, in terms of chants, dress, gesture, and what have you. . . .   —Peter Marsh, social psychologist, Oxford

People really do get hurt once in a while, of course, but anyone who has ever run with a gang knows that it is far less dangerous than it looks. There is the occasional psychopath who really wants to slice people open, but most of the kids are more interested in status, display, profit—and damage limitation. That is the warrior tradition that armies are exploiting in basic training, but it isn't enough. The business of armies, in the end, is killing, and so a crucial part of training people to be soldiers is teaching them to ignore the limits they normally place on the actual use of violence, so that in the right circumstances, against the "enemy," they will go all the way and actually kill him. For the vast majority of people, killing has to be taught—though there are exceptions.

Most mercenaries are there because of their friends . . . and they're there because they feel important, and it makes them feel good to win, because they're playing a game. . . . It's a very exuberant feeling, combat.

There's a euphoric effect whenever you make contact with an enemy unit or you're ambushed and you can feel the volume of fire start to build up, and you know that the decisions you make have to be absolutely correct because if they're not somebody's going to be killed or maimed, and that's a tremendous responsibility.

You stay scared, all the time. When you're on patrol you never ever know what's going to happen, and that heightens your senses. You're extremely aware; it's almost like you can feel the texture of the air around you, and it just makes you feel extremely alive, and a lot of people like that. . . .
                                                                    Capt. John Early

There is such a thing as a "natural soldier": the kind of man who derives his greatest satisfaction from male companionship, from excitement, and from the conquering of physical and psychological obstacles. He doesn't necessarily want to kill people as such, but he will have no objections if it occurs within a moral framework that gives him a justification—like war—and if it is the price of gaining admission to the kind of environment he craves. Whether such men are born or made, I do not know, but most of them end up in armies (and many move on again to become mercenaries, because regular army life in peacetime is too routine and boring).

But armies are not full of such men. They are so rare that they form only a modest fraction even of small professional armies, mostly congregating in the commando-type special forces. In large conscript armies they virtually disappear beneath the weight of numbers of more ordinary men. And it is these ordinary men, who do not like combat at all, that the armies must persuade to kill. Until only a generation ago, they did not even realize how bad a job they were doing.

Armies had always assumed that, given the proper rifle training, the average man would kill in combat with no further incentive than the knowledge that it was the only way to defend his own life. After all, there are no historical records of Roman legionnaires refusing to use their swords, or Marlborough's infantrymen refusing to fire their muskets against the enemy. But then dispersion hit the battlefield, removing each rifleman from the direct observation of his companions—and when U.S. Army Colonel S. L. A. Marshall finally took the trouble to inquire into what they were doing in 1943–45, he found that on average only 15 percent of trained combat riflemen fired their weapons at all in battle. The rest did not flee, but they would not kill—even when their own position was under attack and their lives were in immediate danger.

> *The thing is simply this, that out of an average one hundred men along the line of fire during the period of an encounter, only fifteen men on average would take any part with the weapons. This was true whether the action was spread over a day, or two days or three. . . . In the most aggressive infantry companies, under the most intense local pressure, the figure rarely rose above 25% of total strength from the opening to the close of an action.*
>
> Col. S. L. A. Marshall[9]

Marshall conducted both individual interviews and mass interviews with over four hundred infantry companies, both in Europe and in the Central Pacific, immediately after they had been in close combat with German or Japanese troops, and the results were the same each time. They were, moreover, as astonishing to the company officers and the troops themselves as they were to Marshall; each man who hadn't fired his rifle thought he had been alone in his defection from duty.

Even more indicative of what was going on was the fact that almost all the crew-served weapons had been fired. Every man had been trained to kill and knew it was his duty to kill, and so long as he was in the presence of other soldiers who could see his actions, he went ahead and did it. But the great majority of the riflemen, each unobserved by the others in his individual foxhole, had chosen not to kill, even though it increased the likelihood of his own death.

It is therefore reasonable to believe that the average and healthy individual—the man who can endure the mental and physical stresses of combat—still has such an inner and usually unrealized resistance towards killing a fellow man that he will not of his own volition take life if it is possible to turn away from that responsibility. . . . At the vital point he becomes a conscientious objector, unknowing. . . .

I well recall that in World War I the great sense of relief that came to troops when they were passed to a quiet sector such as the old Toul front was due not so much to the realization that things were safer there as to the blessed knowledge that for a time they were not under the compulsion to take life. "Let 'em go; we'll get 'em some other time," was the remark frequently made when the enemy grew careless and offered himself as a target.

Col. S. L. A. Marshall[10]

By World War II, with the increasing dispersion of infantrymen and their escape from direct observation by their comrades, that fundamental disinclination to kill had become the dominating factor even when a unit was directly engaged in heavy combat. And there is no reason to believe that the phenomenon Marshall found in the American army was any different in the German or Soviet or Japanese armies; there were no comparable studies made, but if a higher proportion of Japanese or Germans had been willing to kill, then the volume of fire they actually managed to produce would have been three, four, or five times greater than a similar number of Americans—and it wasn't. Men will kill under compulsion—men will do almost anything if they know it is expected of them and they are under strong social pressure to comply—but the vast majority of men are not born killers.

There has never, of course, been a similar problem with getting artillerymen or bomber crews or naval personnel to kill. Partly it is the same pressure that keeps machine-gun crews firing—they are being observed by their fellows—but even more important is the intervention of distance and machinery between them and the enemy; they can pretend they are not killing human beings.

It may be significant, in this regard, that the U.S. Air Force discovered during World War II that less than 1 percent of its military pilots became "aces"—five kills in aerial combat—and that these men accounted for roughly 30 to 40 percent of all enemy aircraft destroyed in the air, while the majority of fighter pilots never shot anybody down. But these fighter pilots, at least during World War II, were almost always in single-seat aircraft and could often see that inside the enemy aircraft was another human being.[11] On the whole, however, distance is a sufficient buffer: gunners fire at grid references they cannot see; submarine crews fire torpedoes at "ships" (and not, somehow, at the people in the ships); pilots launch their missiles at "targets."

I would draw one distinction between being a combat aviator and being someone who is fighting the enemy face-to-face on the ground. In the air environment, it's very clinical, very clean, and it's not so personalized. You see an aircraft; you see a target on the ground—you're not eyeball to eyeball with the sweat and the emotions of combat, and so it doesn't become so emotional for you and so personalized. And I think it's easier to do in that sense—you're not so affected. —Col. Barry Bridger, U.S. Air Force

But for the infantry, the problem of persuading soldiers to kill is now a major one, because the dispersion that has created the problem will only increase with time. That an infantry company in World War II could wreak such havoc with only about one seventh of the soldiers willing to use their weapons is a testimony to the lethal effects of modern firepower, but once armies realized what was actually going on, they at once set about to raise the average.

Proficiency at bayonet practice and on the rifle range was no longer enough; soldiers had to be taught, very specifically, to kill. "We are reluctant to admit that essentially war is the business of killing," Marshall wrote in 1947, but it is readily enough admitted now. When he was sent back to make the same kind of investigation during the Korean War in the early 1950s, he found that, with the new training, 50 percent of infantrymen were firing their weapons—and in some perimeter defense crises, almost everybody did.[12]

The reshaping of the recruits' attitudes toward actual violence begins quite early in the training, with an exercise known as "pugil-sticks." Recruits are matched up in pairs, helmeted and gloved, given heavily padded sticks, and made to fight each other in a style that would certainly cause numerous deaths if not for all the padding. And the rhetoric of the instructor makes it clear what is required of them.

You have got to be very aggressive! Once you've got your opponent on the run, that means you go on and strike with that first killing blow. Recruit, you don't stop there! Just because you made contact that don't mean you stop. You don't cut him no slack! Don't give him room to breathe, stay on top of him . . . keep pumping that stick. That means there should be nothin' out here today but a lot of groanin', moanin', a lot of eyeballs fallin'—a lot of heads rollin' all over the place.

Later, the recruits spend much of their time practicing with the weapons that will really be the tools of their trade: rifles, bayonets ("cut on the dotted line"), grenades, and the like. With those weapons, of course, there is no dividing recruits into teams and letting them behave as they would in real combat. But if you can't actually blow your enemy up in basic training, you can certainly be encouraged to relish the prospect of his demise, and even the gory manner of it.

Well, first off, what is a mine? A mine is nothing more, privates, than an explosive or chemical substance made to destroy and kill the enemy. You want him. . . . You want to rip his eyeballs out, you want to tear apart his love machine, you want to destroy him, privates, you don't want to have nothing left of him. You want to send him home in a Glad Bag to his mommy!

Hey, show no mercy to the enemy, they are not going to show it on you. Marines are born and trained killers; you've got to prove that every day. Do you understand? —lecture on the use of mines, Parris Island, 1982

And the recruits grunt loudly with enthusiasm, as they have been taught, although most of them would vomit or faint if they were suddenly confronted with someone whose genitals had been blown off by a mine. Most of the language used in Parris Island to describe the joys of killing people is bloodthirsty but meaningless hyperbole, and the recruits realize that even as they enjoy it. Nevertheless, it does help to desensitize them to the suffering of an "enemy," and at the same time they are being indoctrinated in the most explicit fashion (as previous generations of soldiers were not) with the notion that their purpose is not just to be brave or to fight well; it is to kill people.

The Vietnam era was, of course, then at its peak, you know, and everybody was motivated more or less towards, you know, the kill thing. We'd run PT in the morning and every time your left foot hit the deck you'd have to chant "kill, kill, kill, kill." It was drilled into your mind so much that it seemed like when it actually came down to it, it didn't bother you, you know? Of course the first one always does, but it seems to get easier—not easier, because it still bothers you with every one that, you know, that you actually kill and you know you've killed. —USMC Sergeant (Vietnam veteran), 1982

Most of the recruits have never seen anybody dead (except laid out in a coffin, perhaps) before they arrive at Parris Island, and they still haven't when they leave. But by then they also half-inhabit a dream world in which they have not just seen dead people, but killed them themselves, again and again. And it's all right to do it, because they've been told again and again, by everyone they respect, that the enemy, whoever he may be, is not really a full human being like themselves; it is permissible and praiseworthy to kill him.

The idea of me killing a person when I first came down here just . . . you know, it was unheard of, you didn't do that. It was like squirrel hunting without a license—you didn't do things like that. But once you came here and they motivated you and just kept you every day constantly thinking about it, and by the time you left here—it's something you still don't want to do, but you've got it in your mind that you want to do it so bad that you actually go out and do it when you have to. It seemed like it was a lot easier, because of the motivation here. —Parris Island graduate, 1968

Sometimes the drill instructors make you feel like you're going to like it. Like the war—goin' out and killing people. They psych your mind out for you. . . . I haven't done it. I can't say whether I'd like it or not because I never killed anybody, you know? I'd go out there if I had to, though.
Parris Island graduate, 1982

But the question naturally arises: if the great majority of men are not instinctive killers, and if most military killing these days is in any case done by weapons operating from a distance at which the question of killing scarcely troubles the operators—then why is combat an exclusively male occupation? The great majority of women, everyone would agree, are not instinctive killers either, but so what? If the remote circumstances in which the killing is done or the deliberate conditioning supplied by the military enable most men to kill, why should it be any different for women?

My own guess would be that it probably wouldn't be very different; it just hasn't been tried very extensively. But it is an important question, because it has to do with the causes and possible cure of war. If men fight wars because that is an intrinsic part of the male character, then nothing can abolish the institution of warfare short of abolishing the male half of the human race (or at least, as one feminist suggested, disfranchising it for a hundred years).

If, on the other hand, wars are a means of allocating power between civilized human groups, in which the actual soldiers have always been male simply because men were more suited to it by their greater physical strength and their freedom from the burden of childbearing, then what we are discussing is not Original Sin, but simply a mode of social behavior. The fact that almost every living male for thousands of generations has imbibed some of the warrior mystique is no proof of a genetic predisposition to be warlike. The cultural continuity is quite enough to transmit such attitudes, and men were specialized in the hunting and warrior functions for the same physical reasons long before civilized war was invented.

It was undoubtedly men, the "hunting" specialists, who invented civilized war, just as it was probably women, specializing in the "gathering" part of the primitive economy, who invented agriculture. That has no necessary relevance today: we all eat vegetables, and we can all die in war. It is a more serious allegation against males to say that all existing forms of political power have been shaped predominantly by men, so that even if wars are about power and not about the darker side of the masculine psyche, war is still a male problem. That has unquestionably been true through all of history (although it remains to be proven that women exercising power respond very differently to its temptations and obsessions). But there is no need to settle that argument; if war and masculinity are not inseparable, then we have already moved onto negotiable ground. For the forms of political power, unlike psyches, are always negotiable.

Unfortunately there is little direct support for this optimistic hypothesis in the prevailing current of opinion among soldiers generally, where war and maleness are indeed seen as inseparable. To say that the combat branches of the armed forces are sexist is like remarking that gravity generally pulls downward, and nowhere is the contempt for women greater than at a recruit training base like Parris Island. The DIs are quite ruthless in exploiting every prejudice and pushing every button that will persuade the recruits to accept the value system they are selling, and one of those buttons (quite a large one) is the conviction of young males—or at least the desire to be convinced—that they are superior to young females. (After all, even recruits want to feel superior to somebody, and it certainly isn't going to be anybody in their immediate vicinity at Parris Island.)

When it's all boys together, especially among the younger men, Marine Corps slang for any woman who isn't the wife, mother, or daughter of anyone present is "Suzie." It is short for "Suzie Rottencrotch"—and Suzie crops up a lot in basic training. Even when the topic of instruction is hand and arm signals in combat.

> *Privates, if you don't have a little Suzie now, maybe you're going to find one when you get home. You bet. You'll find the first cheap slut you can get back home. What do you mean, "No"? You're a Marine, you're going to do it.*

> *If we get home with little Suzie . . . we're in a nice companionship with little Suzie and here you are getting hot and heavy and then you're getting ready to go down there and make that dive, privates, and Suzie says . . . Suzie says it's the wrong time of the month. Privates, if you don't want to get back home and indulge in this little adventure, you can show your girlfriend the hand and arm signal for "close it up."*

> *And you want her to close up those nasty little thighs of hers, do you not, privates? The hand and arm signal: the arms are laterally shoulder height, the fingers are extended, and the palms are facing toward the front. This is the starting position for "close it up" [tighten up the formation]: just like closing it up, bring the arms together just like that.*

> *Privates, in addition, I want you to dedicate all this training to one very special person. Can anyone tell me who that is, privates?*

> *(Voice) The Senior Drill Instructor, sir?*

> *No, not your Senior Drill Instructor. You're going to dedicate all this training, privates, to your enemy . . . to your enemy. To your enemy: the reason being,*

so he can die for his country. So who are we going to dedicate all this training to, privates? —*lecture on hand and arm signals, Parris Island, 1982*

And they shouted enthusiastically: "The enemy, sir! The enemy, sir!" It would not be instantly clear to the disinterested observer from Mars, however, why these spotty-faced male eighteen-year-olds are uniquely qualified to kill the enemy, while their equally spotty-faced female counterparts get to admire them from afar (or so the supposition goes), and get called Suzie Rottencrotch for their trouble.

Interestingly, it isn't entirely clear either to the senior military and civilian officials whose responsibility it is to keep the organization filled up with warm bodies capable of doing the job. Women are not employed in combat roles in the regular armed forces of any country (though increasing numbers of women have been admitted to the noncombat military jobs in the course of this century). But in the last decade the final barrier has come under serious consideration. It was, unsurprisingly, in the United States, where the problems of getting enough recruits for the all-volunteer armed forces converged with the changes of attitude flowing from the women's liberation movement, that the first serious proposals to send women into combat were entertained, during the latter years of the Carter administration.

There is no question but that women could do a lot of things in the military. So could men in wheelchairs. But you couldn't expect the services to want a whole company of people in wheelchairs.
Gen. Lewis B. Hershey, former director, Selective Service System, 1978[13]

If for no other reason than because women are the bearers of children, they should not be in combat. Imagine your daughter as a ground soldier sleeping in the fields and expected to do all the things that soldiers do. It represents to me an absolute horror. —*Gen. Jacqueline Cochran, U.S. Air Force*[14]

Despite the anguished cries of military conservatives, both male and female, the reaction of younger officers in the combat branches (all male, of course) was cautious but not entirely negative. The more intelligent ones dismissed at once arguments about strength and stamina—the average American woman, one pointed out, is bigger than the average Vietnamese man—and were as little impressed by the alleged special problems arising from the fact that female soldiers may become pregnant. In the noncombat branches, the army loses less time from its women soldiers due to pregnancy than it loses from desertion, drug abuse, and alcoholism in its male soldiers.

More important, few of the male officers involved in the experimental programs giving combat training to women recruits in the late 1970s had any doubt that the women would function effectively in combat. Neither did the women themselves. Despite their lack of the traditional male notions about the warrior stereotype, the training did its job. As one female trainee remarked: "I don't like the idea of killing anything . . . [and] I may not at this moment go into combat. But knowing that I can fire as well as I can fire now, knowing that today, I'd go in. I believe in my country . . . I'd fight to keep it."

The one major reservation the male officers training the "infantrywomen" had was about how the presence of the women in combat would affect the men. The basic combat unit, a small group of men bound together by strong male ties of loyalty and trust, was a time-tested system that worked, and they were reluctant to tamper with it by adding an additional, unknown factor to the equation.

In the end a more conservative administration canceled the idea of introducing women to American combat units, and it may be some years yet before there are female soldiers in the infantry of any regular army. But it is manifestly sheer social conservatism that is retarding this development. Hundreds of thousands, if not millions, of women have fought in combat as irregular infantry in the past half-century, from the Yugoslav and Soviet partisans of World War II to Nicaragua in 1978–79. They performed quite satisfactorily, and so did the mixed units of which they were members. There are numerous differences of detail between guerrilla and regular army units, but none of them is of the sort to suggest that women would not fight just as well in a regular infantry battalion, or that the battalion would function less well if women were present.

The point of all this is not that women should be allowed (or indeed compelled) to take their fair share of the risks in combat. It is rather that war has moved a very long way from its undeniably warrior male origins, and that human behavior, male or female, is extremely malleable. Combat of the sort we know today, even at the infantryman's level—let alone the fighter pilot's—simply could not occur unless military organizations put immense effort into reshaping the behavior of individuals to fit their unusual and exacting requirements. The military institution, for all its imposing presence, is a highly artificial structure that is maintained only by constant endeavor. And if ordinary people's behavior is malleable in the direction the armed forces require, it is equally open to change in other directions.

In basic training establishments, however, the malleability is all one way: in the direction of submission to military authority and the internalization of military values. What a place like Parris Island produces when it is successful, as it usually is, is a soldier who will kill because that is his job.

The motivation it takes to look down the sights of your rifle and pull the trigger and kill the guy—that's the motivation it takes; that's what you get paid to do. Just like being a bag-boy in a supermarket. You know, if that's what you get paid to do is bag groceries, you bag groceries. If you get paid

*to look down your sights and pull the trigger and kill a man, that's what
you do.*   *—career sergeant, USMC, 1982*

The vast majority of soldiers who go through basic training never have to kill
anybody, of course, and on other counts it does work a considerable transformation
in their general behavior, though not in their fundamental character. This change
tends to be in the direction of more self-discipline, more sense of responsibility, and
greater maturity, none of which is to be regretted. A lot of what happens in basic
training is good for the kids who go through it. I have always believed that even the
very tame version of it I underwent at the hands of the Royal Canadian Navy when I
had just turned seventeen was the most important turning point in my life, and
that I would probably have come to an early bad end otherwise.

But, of course, the navy spent relatively little time training me to kill the
enemy with rifles, knives, and bare hands, as there is not much call for that on
warships. For those destined to see ground combat, the key question is whether
basic training actually prepares them for battle—to which the answer is an une-
quivocal yes and no. No, because *nothing* can prepare a man for the reality of combat:
killing is still very hard.

> *I think that if the recruits who leave here now were to go into combat, it
> would take somebody with combat experience, somebody who had . . . been
> in combat and had actually had to kill, to motivate them to the point where
> they would do it. And once the first one went down, then it would be a lot
> easier.*   *—USMC drill instructor, Parris Island, 1982*

But also yes, because the training at Parris Island—or any competent recruit
training center—has given the recruits everything they can possibly expect to
possess before they have seen combat: the skills and reactions that will help them
to survive personally, the attitudes that will quickly transform any combat unit into
a closed circle of mutual loyalty, and an almost laughably high confidence in themselves that will carry them as far as the battlefield.

> *I'd like to be the first on the beach. I'm not scared at all, because when I
> came here I never thought I'd jump off a fifty-foot tower or throw a grenade.
> The drill instructors build your confidence up. Right now I feel I can do
> anything.*   *—graduating recruit, Parris Island, 1982*

He felt that way even though he had been told repeatedly that doing this job
might require that he die. The knowledge may not really have struck home—eighteen-year-olds will not truly believe in the possibility of their own deaths until and
unless they see combat and live long enough to understand what is going on—but
the Marine Corps does not avoid the question. On the contrary, it puts a considerable
effort into telling the recruits why they must, under certain circumstances, throw
their lives away. It happens in the latter part of their training, when the emphasis

is shifting increasingly to how Marines should behave in combat, and though they may not understand the logic that makes the individual's self-sacrifice good for the organization, they are by then more than ready to understand it emotionally.

> *A Marine is lying out in the middle of a paddy and he's wounded. He's not crying for Mom! He's wounded. He might be moaning a little bit; he might be cussin', because he's mad. Another Marine that's in safety because he got behind a dike—he's real safe, but he crawls out into that paddy, and he pulls that wounded Marine to safety, risking his own life, when probably the Marine's going to bite the bullet! He's going to die! And probably the one that goes out and tries to save him is going to die!*
>
> *Why is that done? You ask yourself that question. And you don't check out the Marine's name; you don't check out where he came from. . . . All you care about is—he's a Marine, and he's in your unit. He's one of you.*
>
> Captain Pingree, USMC, 1982

Not always, but very often, people do behave that way in combat. It is certainly the way the Marine Corps wants its men to behave in combat, for the severely practical reason that men will be more willing to risk their lives if they are confident that the others in their unit will take equally great risks to save them if they get in trouble. But the practical necessities and the romantic vision of soldiering are inextricably mixed. In battle the unit will become the only important thing in the infantryman's universe; nothing outside it matters, and no sacrifice for the other men in it is too great.

> *I remember one occasion in which two army officers from another unit came up on the line. They were rather bossy and arrogant, and they wanted to know where the front was, and the sergeant said to them, "You go right down there," and they did and they were instantly cut to pieces [by Japanese machine guns]. Civilians have a great deal of trouble handling that, but the veteran understands it perfectly. You don't love anybody who is not yours.*
>
> *You're dealing with excesses of love and hate, and among men who fight together there is an intense love. You are closer to those men than to anyone except your immediate family when you were young. . . . I was not a brave young man [but after I was wounded] I went back because I learned that my regiment was going to . . . land behind the Japanese lines, and I felt that if I were there I might save men who had saved my life many times, and the thought of not being there was just intolerable. I missed them, I yearned for them—it was, as I say, a variety of love, and I was joyful to be reunited with them. It didn't last long—two days later I was hit much harder, and I was out of the war for good.* —William Manchester

Only the experience of combat itself will produce such devotion and selfless-ness in men, but basic training is the indispensable foundation for it. Despite the ways in which it has been altered to take into account the changes in the battlefields soldiers inhabit and the societies they serve, basic training has been essentially the same in every army in every age, because it works with the same raw material that's always there in teenage boys: a fair amount of aggression, a strong tendency to hang around in groups, and an absolutely desperate desire to fit in. Young men are not natural soldiers any more than they are natural carpenters or accountants, but it's a trade almost anybody can learn. Soldiering takes up a much bigger part of your life than most jobs, but it doesn't take a special kind of person: anybody's son will do. Perhaps anybody's daughter would too.

Moreover, the men like Captain Pingree who teach the recruits how to kill and how to die are not cynical in their manipulation of the minds of impressionable teenagers; they believe every word they say. And if you accept the necessity of armed force in the world as it is—as Captain Pingree does—then he is absolutely right. More than that, he is admirable, for he asks nothing of the recruits that he is not willing to do himself.

The essence of the soldier's trade is self-sacrifice—on behalf of one's fellow soldiers, in practice, but in a more distant sense also on behalf of the community one serves. It will not do to mock Captain Pingree or his counterparts in a hundred other countries—nor even to patronize the callow boys whom they so efficiently turn into soldiers—until we whom they serve have changed our political behavior enough to make their profession redundant. Soldiers are not criminals; they are mostly honorable men doing the difficult and sometimes terrifying job the rest of us have asked them to do.

NOTES

1. Leonard Cottrell, *The Warrior Pharaohs*, London: Evans Brothers, 1968.

2. Samuel Rolbart, *The Israeli Soldier*, New York: A. S. Barnes, 1970, p. 206.

3. A. A. Grechko, *The Armed Forces of the Soviet State*, Washington: U.S. Government Printing Office, 1975, p. 348.

4. Rolbart, op. cit., p. 58.

5. Richard A. Gabriel, *The New Red Legions: An Attitudinal Portrait of the Soviet Soldier*, Westport, Connecticut: Greenwood Press, 1980, p. 188.

6. Harriet Fast Scott and William F. Scott, *The Armed Forces of the USSR*, Boulder, Colorado: Westview Press, 1979, p. 311.

7. Gabriel, op. cit., p. 192.

8. Edward A. Shills and Morris Janowitz, "Cohesion and Disintegration in the German Wehrmacht in World War II," *Public Opinion Quarterly* XXI (1948), pp. 281–315.

9. S. L. A. Marshall, *Men Against Fire*, New York: Wm. Morrow, 1947, pp. 56–57.

10. Ibid., p. 79.

11. G. Gurney, *Five Down and Glory*, New York: Putnam's, 1958.

12. Peter Watson, *War on the Mind: The Military Uses and Abuses of Psychology*, London: Hutchinson, 1978, p. 45.

13. Patricia M. Murphy, "What's a Nice Girl Like You Doing in a Place Like This," *Air University Review*, Sept.–Oct. 1978, p. 75.

14. Maj. Robert L. Nabors, "Women in the Army: Do They Measure Up?" *Military Review*, LXII, no. 10 (Oct. 1982), p. 60.

The military—an institution so strong and so subtle that it can reverse the moral training of a lifetime. In only a few weeks, any young man can be trained to kill, even from hiding. Here, a young soldier shoots at snipers in Vietnam. © *P. J. Griffiths/MAGNUM*

Every little boy's dream of himself as the dashing commando. Sergeant H. A. Marshall, a sniper with the Calgary Highlanders, Belgium, 1944. *Ken Bell/DND/Public Archives of Canada (PA 1404080)*

Recruits usually have less than twenty years' experience in the world, mostly as a child.

Unidentified Confederate soldier. *Courtesy of the Valentine Museum, Richmond, Virginia*

Cpl. Donald Ward, 1st Tank Battalion, near Da Nang, Vietnam. *U.S. Defense Department Photo/Marine Corps*

Pvt. Edwin Francis Jennison, 2nd Louisiana Cavalry, 1 July 1862. *The Library of Congress (B8184 10037)*

The crowded battle environment is a thing of the past. For the soldier alone in his foxhole, the battlefield becomes a desperately lonely place, with no direct supervision and not even the comfort of other men nearby. Dugout near Ismailiya on the west bank of the Suez. © *Micha Bar-Am/MAGNUM*

The most "extravagantly individualistic" society in the world requires fairly strong means to turn recruits into a functioning unit in only a short period of time. The first ritual involves being shorn, literally, of any civilian identity. Given total control for a few weeks, the army can almost guarantee a conversion. © *Hiroji Kubota/MAGNUM*

The benevolent and understanding officer, available for fatherly comfort as well as demanding high performance. Lieutenant-Colonel Sterne being benevolent to Private Rothwell, one of the first Canadians to be released from Communist captivity in Korea, August 1953. *George Marwich/DND/Public Archives of Canada (PA 140412)*

The apparent inanity of practicing close-order drills more than a century after mass formations were any good on the battlefield serves the dual purpose of teaching recruits to obey orders physically and automatically, not as individuals but as elements in a group. Soviet trainees drilling in June of 1980. *TASS from SOVFOTO*

The patterns of aggression in primitive societies and even urban gangs are orchestrated and ritualized to ensure not too many people get hurt. This group of Yanomamo in South America are letting off steam with a display of aggression just prior to a ritual confrontation with another tribe. *From* Yanomamo: The Fierce People, *Second Edition by Napoleon Chagnon. Copyright © 1977 by Holt, Rinehart & Winston. Reprinted by permission of CBS College Publishing*

There probably is such a thing as a "natural soldier," but it isn't so much killing as an environment of danger and excitement that he craves. Armies are not full of such men. They are rare, and congregate mostly in commando special forces or mercenary groups. An American fighting with Salvadoran guerrillas. © *Susan Meiselas/ MAGNUM*

At the end of World War II, the U.S. military discovered, to their great surprise, that only 15 percent of trained riflemen fired their weapons in combat—a statistic that probably held true for all armies. The rest didn't run, but they wouldn't kill. Basic training was drastically changed to emphasize actually killing, not just being brave and doing your duty. Now at least 50 percent of all weapons are fired in battle. Marine recruits practicing. © *Hiroji Kubota/MAGNUM*

The easily fueled conviction of young males that they are superior to young females has somehow become one of the foundations of military training. A mercenary in El Salvador with all the accoutrements of a Real Man. © *Eugene Richards/ MAGNUM*

Marine recruits in San Diego chanting for blood, and learning to relish the prospect of other people's gory deaths. © *Hiroji Kubota/MAGNUM*

Concentration camps were staffed, whenever possible, with thugs and sadists. These S.S. women at Belsen-Belsen were as expert at brutality as their male counterparts. *Courtesy of the Imperial War Museum (BU4065)*

Women have almost always fought side by side with men in guerrilla or revolutionary wars, and there isn't any evidence they are significantly worse at killing people—which may or may not be comforting, depending on whether you see war as a male problem or a human one. Volunteers for the militia in Nicaragua. *© Susan Meiselas/MAGNUM*

He's one of you. The fierce bond, "greater than that of man and wife," that operates in small military groups. American anti-aircraft troops with a captured Japanese gun at Hollandia, New Guinea, May 1944. *UPI/ Bettman Newsphotos*

6: The Profession of Arms

Soldiers are the tradesmen of killing, but officers are the managers of violence.

—Harold Lasswell

The rigid division of all military organizations into officers and enlisted men, two entirely separate hierarchies of people covering roughly the same span of age and often, at the more junior levels, doing much the same kind of job, is so universal that it is rarely considered remarkable. Yet armed forces have the most meticulously stratified system of rank to be found anywhere, and they positively flaunt it.

Among all the intricate distinctions of rank, it is the gulf between the officers and the other ranks that is most distinctive and important. Army lieutenants at the age of nineteen or twenty will normally be placed in charge of a body of enlisted men who are older and more experienced than themselves. The army will expect them to rely heavily on the judgment of their NCOs, but the final decision and the ultimate responsibility are theirs. Indeed, the nineteen-year-old lieutenant is legally of a higher rank than the most experienced and trusted noncommissioned officer in the army (though he would be wise not to exercise his authority without careful consideration). Moreover, in all armies it is deliberately made very difficult to transfer from the enlisted ranks to the officer caste.

The origins of the officer/man distinction are political and social. For most of history, those who ruled the state and employed the army also commanded it. Military leadership was not only part of their main job, that of protecting the state's interests in a dangerous world, it was also necessary for their own safety. If they did not control the army, it could be used by those who did to challenge their power. The profound social divide between officers and men in modern armed forces based on the European model (that is, almost all of them) is a relic of the military organization of feudal Europe, in which the nobility specialized in leadership in war, and it is probably broader than is strictly necessary—but the fundamental principle of hierarchy is quite functional in military terms.

Armies exist ultimately to fight battles—the most complex, fast-moving, and essentially unpredictable collective enterprises (not to mention the most dangerous and confusing) that large numbers of human beings engage in—and that purpose conditions almost everything about them. It guarantees them their high position in the list of priorities of every government (for historically the outcome of those battles has mattered greatly to the armies and to their owners). It also explains why they are so different from other human organizations, and so similar from one country to another.

The government and society of the United States are greatly different from those of the Soviet Union or Egypt, but their armies are so close in structure and in spirit that their officers, when they come into contact, cannot help recognizing their common membership in a single, universal profession whose characteristics everywhere are shaped by the demands of battle. Not only the system of military rank, but all the most striking characteristics of armies—the rote learning and standardization, the seemingly contradictory emphases on strict obedience and individual initiative (both of which may be described as "heroism," depending on the circumstances), even their typical social conservatism—are intimately connected with the fact that armies are in the business of imposing order upon chaos, and of forcing men to do what they very much do not want to do. The key problem in fighting a battle has always been control: he who is less badly informed and less disorganized wins.

War is the province of uncertainty; three-fourths of the things on which action in war is based lie hidden in the fog of greater or less uncertainty.

Karl von Clausewitz

Their Majesties lunch with Doris and me, quite simply, at Government House. The King seemed anxious, but he did not . . . really comprehend the uncertainty of the result of all wars between great nations, no matter how well prepared one may think one is. —*Gen. Douglas Haig, 11 August 1914*[1]

The armed forces are often deprecated for their persistent—and persistently unsuccessful—attempts to reduce all action to routines, rules, and regulations. But all it amounts to, in practice, is a desperate and never more than partially successful attempt to reduce the immense number of variables with which the professional officer must contend. To a limited extent the wild card represented by the unpredictable behavior of his own people under stress can be brought under control by the imposition of uniform training and indoctrination, but there is no comparable way to confine the interplay of will, art, and chance between opponents on the battlefield to a predictable pattern.

Armies try, certainly—there are as many lists of "Principles of War" as there are general staffs, each consisting of ten or a dozen platitudes that are mostly either self-evident or useless to the man who has to take the decision under fire—but combat is an environment that cannot be mastered by set rules. Tactics and strategy must be learned and plans made, but the unpredictable and uncontrollable elements are so large that even the best plans, carried out by the most competent and daring officers, will often fail—and will always change.

Q. Can you tell me how a battle works?

A. Well, in my opinion a battle never works; it never works according to plan. . . . The plan is only a common base for changes. It's very important that everybody should know the plan, so you can change easily. But the modern battle is very fluid, and you have to make your decisions very fast—and mostly not according to plan.

Q. But at least everybody knows where you're coming from?

A. And where you're going to, more or less.

Gen. Dan Laner, Israeli Defense Forces commander, Golan Heights, 1973

Combat at every level is an environment that requires officers to make decisions on inadequate information, in a hurry, and under great stress, and then inflicts the death penalty on many of those who make the wrong decision—and on some of those who have decided correctly as well. In such an environment, officers must rely on rules of thumb that are no more than rough calculations, distilled from much past experience, of the odds that a given action will succeed. On the whole, officers will cling to these rules even if the laws of chance occasionally betray them.

As we were going into the position, there was a large rice field we had to walk across, and I remember that I had to send somebody else across first. And you think, "Well, who do I send? Do I go myself?" But being the leader you can't afford that. You had to send somebody across, and if you sat back and thought about it you would say, "Am I sacrificing this individual? Am I sending him out there to draw fire?"

That may be part of it, but it's better to send an individual than walk out there with your entire force. And I remember pointing to an individual and telling him to go. Now there was one moment of hesitation, when he looked at me: "Do you mean me? Do you really mean it?" And the look I must have given him—he knew that I meant it, and he went across the field.

Everybody was watching that individual. I started sending them across in twos, and it was no problem. Then I took my entire force across. When we were about halfway across, they came up behind us, the VC [Viet Cong], and they were in spiderholes, and they caught most of my unit in the open.

Now tactically I had done everything the way it was supposed to be done, but we lost some soldiers. There was no other way. We could not go around that field; we had to go across it. So did I make a mistake? I don't know. Would I have done it differently [another time]? I don't think I would have, because that's the way I was trained. Did we lose less soldiers by my doing it that way? That's a question that'll never be answered.

Maj. Robert Ooley, U.S. Army

The battle drills in which Major Ooley was trained were worked out by experienced professional soldiers, with the aim of minimizing the chance of an unpleasant surprise and limiting the damage done if the surprise happens anyway. Tactical doctrines like these are constantly updated in the light of new experience, and the same process of analysis is applied to operations all the way up to the level of entire armies. An enormous amount of effort now goes into the attempt to create rules that will give modern officers at least some general guidelines on how to combine all the resources under their command successfully on the battlefield; the tactical manuals of today's armies can run into hundreds of pages.

Yet in the end, the product of all this effort is the same, at every level of command: usually no more than programmed uncertainty and never a reliable guide to success. The official doctrines concentrate on manipulating what can be calculated and rationally planned in war, but the large incalculable elements are at best partly constrained by them—the rest is just hidden by the planning process. But on the battlefield, the uncertainties cannot be hidden, and real combat is just as much a gamble for General Yossi Ben-Chanaan, who has fought in a number of short, victorious wars, as for Major Ooley, who fought a long, losing war.

Ben-Chanaan commanded a tank brigade on the Golan Heights during the 1973 war in the Middle East, and on the sixth day of the war, with only eight tanks left, he succeeded in penetrating the Syrian front line.

. . . and once we arrived to the rear we took position, and all their positions were very exposed. We opened fire, and for about twenty minutes we destroyed whoever we could see, because we were in a great position there.

I decided to charge and try to get that hill, but I had to leave a couple of tanks in cover, so I charged with six tanks. [The Syrians] opened fire from the flank with antitank missiles, and in a matter of seconds, three out of the six tanks were blown up. There was a big explosion in my tank. I blew out, and I was left there. . . . And also the whole attack was a mistake, I think.

General Ben-Chanaan is a very competent officer, but his attack failed and some of his men died. Yet if there had not been Syrian antitank missiles off on his flank (which he could not possibly have known one way or the other), his attack would probably have succeeded, and a vital hill would have been taken by the Israelis at the critical time. Many Israelis who died in the subsequent fighting might now be alive, and the armistice line might be a good deal closer to Damascus. At the time, the gamble seemed worth it to Ben-Chanaan; he took a chance, and he was wrong. There are so many variables in combat that a commander cannot control, and so many things that he simply does not know.

Military officers, to be successful in combat, need a very high tolerance for uncertainty. This may seem one of the attributes least likely to be present in the armed forces, with their identical uniforms and rigid system of ranks, their bureaucratic standardizations (of everything from "Swords, Ceremonial, Officers, for the Use of" to the format in which a commander must compose his operational orders), and their apparently generalized intolerance for deviations from the norm of any sort. Yet in fact these are two sides of the same coin.

It is not necessary for Acme Carpet Sales or the Department of Motor Vehicles to regiment their employees and rigidly routinize every aspect of their work, for they operate in an essentially secure and predictable environment. The mail will be delivered each morning, the sales representatives will not be ambushed and killed on the way to their afternoon appointments, and the secretarial pool will not be driven to mass panic and flight by mortar rounds landing in the parking lot. Armies in peacetime look preposterously overorganized, but peace is not their real working environment.

In battle, however, the apparent lunacies of orders given and acknowledged in standard forms, of rank formalized to an extent almost unknown elsewhere, of training that ensures that every officer will report his observations of enemy movements in *this* format rather than some other, when there seems no particular virtue in doing it one way rather than another, all find their justification by bringing some predictability and order to an essentially chaotic situation. Yet at the same time, officers must never allow themselves to become mere bureaucrats and administrators, or they will be quite useless in combat. It is a difficult balance to maintain, and sometimes—especially in peacetime—whole armies can succumb to the managerial delusion.

The most seductive temptation armies face at present comes from what has been called the "navalization" of land warfare: the post-1945 phenomenon in which the troops of the fully mechanized armies of the great powers are almost all expected to go into battle in machines. The tanks, armored personnel carriers, SAM batteries, and the like can all theoretically be controlled by radio from a battalion or divisional headquarters where calm and rationality prevail, and where the "big picture" is available in real time and in accurate detail from a multitude of electronic intelligence-gathering devices: land battle as a video game. Army officers have at last been presented with the temptation to which their colleagues of the other services have long since surrendered.

For practical purposes, navies are as old as armies, but they have always lived and fought in what was, by contemporary standards, a high-technology environment. They have never faced the same acute problems of control as armies, since their men are all contained within their ships and are less often exposed to physical terror. By and large, naval officers have tended to view human behavior in the same essentially pessimistic way as their army counterparts, but their view of battle has always been simpler. Battle at sea is a complicated and unpredictable problem, but all the relevant factors depend either on technology or on human decisions made in relatively unharassed circumstances by a commanding officer who knows that all his ships will obey his orders so long as they are afloat, and that the fears of individual sailors will probably not sabotage his plans.

Air forces are even further removed from the problems army officers face. They are organizations in which the majority of the actual combatants (and casualties) are themselves officers, and in which combat, for those who experience it, is usually a series of brief incidents in a style of living that otherwise retains much of the character of peacetime routine, and even of civilian life. Problems of discipline and morale are far less acute, and air forces on the whole do not take the tragic view of human nature. Indeed, they are prone to the optimistic assumption that correct managerial techniques and appropriate technology will solve virtually any problem.

With the proliferation of machines and instantaneous communications among ground forces, this kind of attitude is now making inroads even in armies. Its attraction is great, for ground combat would be a great deal more manageable if it could be reduced simply to a complex logistical operation decided ultimately by rates of attrition of material—and the physical environment in which modern army commanders work makes this illusion more plausible.

Even a battalion of eight hundred men will typically be spread out over several square miles in modern war, and the enormous rates of consumption of fuel, ammunition, and other stores mean that organizing supplies becomes a critical factor. Most of the time, the practical side of the battalion commander's job is somewhere between that of a personnel manager and an air traffic controller: he could get killed doing it and so could his officers, but the fact that so large a part of their effort is directed simply at controlling and monitoring the expenditure of vehicles, troops, and ammunition irresistibly fosters a managerial perspective.

The most significant difficulty for us is the proper way of putting combat power to work on the battlefield. Who controls the fires? Do we let the individual gunner fire each missile? We expended a heck of a lot of missiles in this last battle, shooting at targets that might have been destroyed with *artillery or another means, and you know, each one of those missiles is $2,500 to $3,000 apiece.*

Lt. Col. James Bigelow, 1st Battalion, 5th Cavalry, U.S. Army

Colonel Bigelow spoke in this vein in the middle of a heavily computerized battalion staff exercise carried out in a simulated command post in a building at the Army Staff College at Fort Leavenworth, Kansas, and no doubt the setting influenced his remarks. He is a Vietnam combat veteran who knows that real battle is not an exercise in accountancy, and his more usual attitude is of an older tradition. Battle, he believes, is "a question of 'Follow me; do as I do.' It's a question of confidence, and I tell all my people that the only thing I'm interested in is killing more Russians, lots of Russians."

It is not only realism that drives military officers to cling to these attitudes; there is also the question of self-esteem. Officers have traditionally seen themselves as warriors, not administrators, even though they have always been a mixture of both. A warrior is a man of honor whose actions, however much death and destruction they cause, are justified by the warrior's special moral code. They organize people to kill, but they are not murderers; they die, but they are not accident victims. To accept that technology is more important than human will is to reduce their own efforts, and perhaps their own deaths, to insignificance, so combat officers in every army tend to reject the notion strongly.

The most important thing is the man who is using the weapons. It doesn't matter what the weapons are. Assuming he knows how to use the weapons and is well trained, the soldier or officer who will win is the one who thoroughly understands the goals of the war, who is striving to achieve those goals, and who is ready to sacrifice his life in the name of those goals. —Gen. Rair Simonyan, Soviet army

The history of the modern military establishment can be described as a struggle between heroic leaders, who embody traditionalism and glory, and military "managers." . . . Military managers . . . are aware that they direct combat organizations . . . but they are mainly concerned with the most rational and economic ways of winning wars or avoiding them. . . . Heroic leaders . . . would deny that they are anti-technological, but for them the heroic traditions of fighting men, which can only be preserved by military honor, military tradition, and the military way of life, are crucial. —Morris Janowitz, The Professional Soldier[2]

Despite the faint traces of Soviet political rhetoric and American sociological jargon, both men are expressing the same traditional soldier's conviction that battle is not a statistical operation and that it cannot be won with a managerial approach. It is true; the traditional soldiers are still right. But armies also contain many officers whose bent is managerial rather than "heroic" these days, and the temptation to believe that all the human imponderables of combat can be reduced to simple equations is very seductive. If it were true, ground combat would become a predictable science, not an arcane art in which the good commander's chance of success is only about the same as the good poker player's chance of winning on a given evening (for the same sort of reasons).

Moreover, the technological and logistical elements of warfare, being much more amenable to the planning process, have tended to get an undue share of attention in peacetime armies (on much the same principle that impels the drunk to look for his lost car keys not where he dropped them, but over by the street lamp where the light is better). This has led a number of armies—most notably that of the United States, the ultimate technological society—to exalt the role of the manager and the planner over that of the traditional fighting commander, whose worth cannot be evaluated until the shooting starts, and so to grant competent administrators and technocrats greater resources and more rapid promotion. There is such a thing as national style in armies (whose members, after all, share most of the basic values and assumptions of the civilian society from which they are drawn). In the particular case of the U.S. Army, the "managers" had almost entirely taken over by the late 1960s.

The two largest influences in shifting the U.S. Army in this direction were the traditional American belief that industrial productivity and firepower can be an adequate substitute for the expenditure of American lives in combat and the staff officer's instinctive search for quantifiable data and predictability in war. The result was an extraordinarily mechanistic approach to the highly volatile and intensely human subject of warfare.

U.S. tactics for a possible war in Europe have been defined for decades in pseudoindustrial terms—target acquisition, rates of delivery of firepower, and the like—but the managerial delusion undoubtedly reached its apotheosis in Vietnam. Computers told the Americans they were winning the war ("garbage in, garbage out"), while the North Vietnamese, combining a traditional fighter ethic among the troops and commanders with a subtle political strategy, steadily eroded the military and political capacity of their superpower opponent to continue the struggle.

> *You really had a mentality in the U.S. Army in Vietnam which had very little to do with war and fighting in the conventional historical sense. The officers and the men quite frequently were more involved in typing and driving trucks around than they were in fighting, and in many cases it meant that the morale of a unit was not that of a fighting unit; it was an administrative unit that happened to get people killed up in the front of it. There eventually developed a considerable difference in the attitudes of the front-line soldiers versus the people in the rear, who were usually given various nicknames by the people in front, like remfs—rear-echelon motherfuckers.* —Tom Tulenko, U.S. Army advisor, Vietnam, 1970–71

In the bitter aftermath of that experience, U.S. Army officers have recovered some of their profession's ingrained pessimism about the degree to which battle can be programmed and controlled. The temptation to believe otherwise still lurks in the background, but despite all the attempts armies make to reduce the areas of uncertainty in war and all the devices they employ to contend with it, warfare continues to present a formidable resistance to predictability. Ground combat always means a serious threat to officers' control over their troops. Indeed, while attrition dominates in air and naval warfare, which is essentially a war of machines, the goal of combat in ground warfare is always the disintegration of the other side's organization and control. Physical destruction is only the means to that end; land battle is still, in the end, as much a struggle of morale as of machines.

Politicians may . . . pretend that the soldier is ethically in no different position than any other professional. He is. He serves under an unlimited liability, and it is the unlimited liability which lends dignity to the military profession. . . . There's also the fact that military action is group action, particularly in armies. . . . The success of armies depends to a very high degree on the coherence of the group, and the coherence of the group depends on the degree of trust and confidence of its members in each other.

Now what Arnold Toynbee used to call the military virtues—fortitude, endurance, loyalty, courage, and so on—these are good qualities in any collection of men and enrich the society in which they are prominent. But in the military society, they are functional necessities, which is something quite, quite different. I mean a man can be false, fleeting, perjured, in every way corrupt, and be a brilliant mathematician, or one of the world's greatest painters. But there's one thing he can't be, and that is a good soldier, sailor, or airman. Now it's this group coherence and the unlimited liability which, between them, set the military professional apart, and I think will continue to do so.
                                                           —*Gen. Sir John Hackett*

There are bad officers, of course, of whom none of this is true, but General Hackett is right: the lack of those virtues is what makes them bad officers. In a way, he is simply offering a general and somewhat romanticized formulation of the state of grace amid evil that does prevail, by necessity, among front-line soldiers: the same phenomenon that a private soldier described in talking of "the friendly helpfulness and almost gaiety that increases until it is an almost unbelievably tangible and incongruous thing as you get nearer to the front. A cousin writing to me recently . . . said, 'Men are never so loving or so lovable as they are in action.' That is not only true, it is the beginning and end of the matter."[3] But it is not the end of the matter for officers, although they run the same risks and share the same bonds of mutual loyalty. They must use up their men's lives in order to win (or rather in the hope of winning) battles, and it results in a very particular mentality.

You've got to keep distant from [your soldiers]. The officer-enlisted man distance helps. This is one of the most painful things, having to withhold sometimes your affection for them, because you know you're going to have to destroy them on occasion. And you do. You use them up: they're material. And part of being a good officer is knowing how much of them you can use up and still get the job done. —Paul Fussell, infantry officer, World War II

Officers play a very large role in battles, and their casualties are usually higher proportionally than those of the enlisted men. The brief life expectancy of infantry lieutenants on the Western Front in World War I is legendary, but the figures were actually worse in World War II.

It occurred to me to count the number of officers who had served in the Battalion since D-Day. Up to March 27th, the end of the Rhine crossing [less than ten months] . . . I found that we had had 55 officers commanding the twelve rifle platoons, and that their average service with the Battalion was 38 days. . . . Of these 53% were wounded, 24% killed or died of wounds, 15% invalided, and 5% survived. —Col. M. Lindsay, 1st Gordon Highlanders[4]

In general, officer casualties in the British and American armies in World War II, in the rifle battalions that did most of the fighting, were around twice as high proportionally as the casualties among enlisted men.[5]

Nevertheless, there is a fundamental difference in the officer's experience of battle. He feels as much fear and is exposed to as much danger as his men, but except in the most extreme circumstances, he will not be using a weapon himself. His role is to direct those who do and make them go on doing it. The task officers must perform and the circumstances in which they must do it have instilled in them a very special view of the world and how it works.

I went where I was told to go and did what I was told to do, but no more. I was scared shitless just about all the time.

James Jones, infantry private, World War II

If blood was brown, we'd all have medals.

Canadian sergeant, northwest Europe, 1944–45

Fear is not just a state of mind; it is a physical thing. With its useful mania for questionnaires, the U.S. Army set out during World War II to find out just how much fear affected the ability of soldiers to perform on the battlefield. In one infantry division in France in August 1944, 65 percent of the soldiers admitted that they had been unable to do their jobs properly because of extreme fear on at least one occasion, and over two fifths said it had happened repeatedly.

In another U.S. infantry division in the South Pacific, over two thousand soldiers were asked about the physical symptoms of fear: 84 percent said they had a violent pounding of the heart, and over three fifths said they shook or trembled all over. Around half admitted to feeling faint, breaking out in a cold sweat, and feeling sick to their stomachs. Over a quarter said they had vomited, and 21 percent said they had lost control of their bowels.[6] These figures are based only on voluntary admissions, of course, and the true ones are probably higher in all categories, especially the more embarrassing ones. James Jones's remark about being "scared shitless" was not just a colorful expression.

This is the raw material with which officers must conduct their battles: men whose training and self-respect and loyalty to their close friends around them are very nearly outweighed by extreme physical terror and a desperate desire not to die. Soldiers in battle, however steady they may appear, are always a potential mob capable of panic and flight, and armies must expend an enormous amount of effort, beginning in basic training and continuing on the battlefield, to keep them in action.

The officer's task has grown even more difficult over time, for he no longer has all his men lined up in ranks under the eagle eyes of his NCOs, in a situation in which as long as they continue to go through the mechanical motions of loading and firing, they are being militarily effective. Modern ground forces fight in circumstances of extreme dispersion in which it is impossible for the officer to exercise direct supervision and control over his men's actions. Though the structure of command, compulsion, and punishment for poor performance remains in place, the officer must now rely much more on persuasion and manipulation of his men.

> *You lead by example. I don't think it was unknown that I was afraid to be shot at. I didn't like it; I don't think anybody does, but I did what had to be done, given the situation at any given time, and I think that's a contagious-type thing. When the shooting starts and things start happening, you do what has to be done, and other people start doing what has to be done, and it's a team effort.* —Lt. Col. Michael Petty, U.S. Army, Vietnam, 1969–71

If too many soldiers in a unit fail to do their jobs, nobody is likely to survive. This approach to leadership, therefore, often produces acceptable results, especially in small wars like Vietnam, in which casualties are relatively low (only about one in fifty of the U.S. soldiers who served in Vietnam was killed), and episodes of intensive combat are generally brief and intermittent. It was the collapse of morale, not the attrition of combat, that destroyed the U.S. Army's fighting capability in Vietnam.

But in large-scale warfare between regular armies, things are different, and have been for at least the past two generations. In any big battle down to the latter part of the nineteenth century, the dead and wounded on a single day of fighting could amount to up to 40 or 50 percent of the men engaged, and the average figure was rarely less than 20 percent. Given a couple of battles a year, the infantryman stood an even chance of being killed or wounded for each year the war continued—a very discouraging prospect. But for 363 days of the year, it was merely a hypothetical prospect, for he was not in battle or even in close contact with the enemy on those days. He might be cold, wet, tired, and hungry much of the time—if it was the campaigning season and the army was maneuvering around the countryside—but for a good part of the year he was probably billeted somewhere indoors at night. In such circumstances the high probability that he would be dead or wounded within the year could be dealt with in the same sort of way that everybody deals with the eventual certainty of death.

The navies and air forces of today fight a kind of war that is still recognizably the same in its psychological effects. On a warship there is the constant psychological strain of being below deck knowing that a torpedo could hit at any time, but actual close contact with an enemy rarely averages more than a few hours a month. Even the bomber crews of World War II, whose life expectancy was measured in months, were still fighting that kind of war, although in an extreme form: in between the brief moments of stark terror when the flak or the fighters came too close, they slept between clean sheets and might even get to the pub some evenings. But for armies, things have changed irreversibly.

> *There is no such thing as "getting used to combat." . . . Each moment of combat imposes a strain so great that men will break down in direct relation to the intensity and duration of their exposure.*
>
> U.S. Army psychological investigation into the effects of combat[7]

The most striking visible sign of the change that has made ground warfare so much harder on the soldiers, paradoxically, is a steep drop in the casualty toll in a day of battle. Unlucky small units can still be virtually exterminated in an hour when something goes badly wrong, but the average daily loss for a division-sized force in intensive combat in World War II was about 2 percent of its personnel. For entire armies, the casualties even on the first day of a great offensive rarely amount to 1 percent. The lethality of weapons has increased several thousandfold since the time of Napoleon, but the extent to which the potential targets of those weapons have spread out is even greater, and it is certainly far safer to be a soldier on any given day of battle in the twentieth century than it was a hundred or a thousand years ago. The problem for the soldiers is that battles can now continue for weeks, with individual units being sent back in at frequent intervals, and the battles follow each other in quick succession.

In terms of overall casualties per year, the loss rate is cumulatively about the same as it was in earlier times, with combat infantrymen facing at best an even chance of death or a serious wound within a year. But the psychological effect is very different. Being in contact with the enemy and exposed to the elements most of the time, being shelled every day, and living amid constant death gradually erodes men's desperate faith in their own hope of survival and eventually destroys everybody's courage and will. Anyone can be brave once, but nobody can go on forever: "Your courage flows at its outset with the fullest force and thereafter diminishes; perhaps if you are very brave it diminishes imperceptibly, but it does diminish . . . and it can never behave otherwise," wrote a British soldier who had been through too much.[8]

The U.S. Army concluded during World War II that almost every soldier, if he escaped death or wounds, would break down after 200 to 240 "combat days"; the British, who rotated their troops out of the front line more often, reckoned 400 days, but they agreed that breakdown was inevitable. The reason that only about one sixth of the casualties were psychiatric was that most combat troops did not survive long enough to go to pieces.

The pattern was universal, in all units of every nationality on all fronts. After the first few days of combat, in which the members of a fresh unit would show signs of constant fear and apprehension, they would learn to distinguish the truly dangerous phenomena of combat from the merely frightening, and their confidence and performance steadily improved. After three weeks they were at their peak—and then the long deterioration began. By the sixth week of continuous combat, two Army psychiatrists who accompanied a U.S. infantry battalion in 1944 reported, most soldiers had become convinced of the inevitability of their own death and had stopped believing that their own skill or courage could make any difference: "As far as they were concerned the situation was one of absolute hopelessness. . . . The soldier was slow-witted. . . . Mental defects became so extreme that he could not be counted on to relay a verbal order. . . . He remained almost constantly in or near his slit trench, and during acute actions took little or no part, trembling constantly." At this point the "two thousand-year stare" appeared (in Vietnam it was known as the "thousand-yard stare"), and the next stage was catatonia or total disorientation and breakdown.[9]

The amount of time it took soldiers to reach this point varied from individual to individual and could be greatly extended if they had some periods of relief from combat, but almost everybody was bound to get there eventually. The principal reason that relatively few entire units collapsed was that the same combat environment that produced these symptoms also caused so many casualties that there was a constant flow of replacements. (The Soviet army's casualties in 1943, for example, were 80 percent of the forces engaged, and the same in 1944.) Most units in prolonged combat in modern war, therefore, consist of an uneasy mixture of some utterly green and unsure replacements, some surviving veterans of many months of combat, most of whom are nearing collapse, and a proportion of soldiers—the larger the better, from the unit's point of view—who are still in transition from the former stage to the latter.

Given the prevailing uncertainty about the most vital and basic questions in battle (Where is the enemy? Will we be alive an hour from now?) that both commanders and troops must tolerate, every element of stability and familiarity that can be provided is most valuable. This is why many armies place such emphasis on a stable regimental system in which men have served together for a long time, and on the preservation of traditions that will give men under great stress a collective memory and example of how other men have behaved in similar circumstances (even if this often involves a considerable distortion of history).

This is the reality that an officer must deal with (if he is not yet too far gone himself to cope with it), and except in the very first experiences of a unit in combat he must reckon at best with the state of mind described by Brig. Gen. S. L. A. Marshall:

> *Wherever one surveys the forces of the battlefield, it is to see that fear is general among men, but to observe further that men commonly are loath that their fear will be expressed in specific acts which their comrades will recognize as cowardice. The majority are unwilling to take extraordinary risks and do not aspire to a hero's role, but they are equally unwilling that they should be considered the least worthy among those present. . . .*

> *The seeds of panic are always present in troops so long as they are in the midst of physical danger. The retention of self-discipline . . . depends upon the maintaining of an appearance of discipline within the unit. . . . When other men flee, the social pressure is lifted and the average soldier will respond as if he had been given a release from duty, for he knows that his personal failure is made inconspicuous by the general dissolution!*[10]

The experienced professional officer takes an unromantic view of men's behavior under stress and believes that all his efforts in war amount to no more than trying to build shaky bridges across chaos with highly volatile human material. A young American infantry officer was strikingly frank about these realities to the survivors of his company in a postcombat debriefing that Marshall attended after the company had assaulted a small German fort outside Brest in 1944. The men had made a remarkable seven hundred-yard charge across an open field, which caused most of the German garrison to flee, and reached the cover of a hedgerow only fifteen yards from the fort. But they could not then be persuaded to get up and cross the scant remaining distance for seven hours, although only a handful of German defenders remained.

> *You have a plan. You have an objective. Your men get started with the objective in mind. But in the course of getting to the objective and taking up fire positions, disorganization sets in. The men look for cover and that scatters them. Fire comes against them and that scatters their thoughts. They no longer think as a group but as individuals. Each man wants to*

stay where he is. To get them going again as a group, an officer must expose himself to the point of suicide. The men are in a mental slump; they always get that way when they have taken a great risk. . . . It is harder to get men to mop up after a charge than to get them to charge.

Lt. Robert W. Rideout, Brest, 1944[11]

Marshall offers dozens of instances of the "lightning emotional changes" of men in combat, which will cause "the same group of soldiers [to] act like lions and then like scared hares within the passage of a few minutes." He is also acutely aware of how easily the apparent authority of officers can be undermined by the reluctance of the soldiers. They may, for example, seize upon the failure of some promised element of support for an attack (tanks, an artillery barrage, etc.) to arrive at the right time in the promised quantities: "The men squat in their foxholes and count. If they see a default anywhere they feel this gives them a moral excuse to default in their portion. They procrastinate and argue. . . . " In the end the attack goes off halfheartedly, without hope of success. "The rule for the soldier," Marshall concludes, "should be that given the Australian mounted infantryman when he asked the Sphinx for the wisdom of the ages: 'Don't expect too much!' "[12]

Everything army officers know about the behavior of men in combat leads them toward the same conclusion: that man is a frail and fallible creature who requires strong leadership and firm discipline in order to behave properly and function effectively. This fundamental pessimism about the limits of heroism and idealism is the central phenomenon in the professional soldiers' world. Such pessimism plays a very large part in defining the "military mind" despite all of the counterrhetoric about heroism and idealism in which some soldiers indulge on public occasions.

On the outermost margins of human experience, where they must operate in combat, military officers' assumptions about human nature are absolutely right, and they would be less than professional if they did not recognize them. And this essentially tragic view of human nature is reinforced and broadened by what they know about the nature of battle itself: that it is an environment where nothing works reliably, and no plan or stratagem succeeds for very long. A profession that knows that its basic function—waging and winning wars—can never be reduced to a rational, predictable, controllable activity, despite all the effort and intelligence that men devote to it, is bound to take a rather jaundiced view of the perfectibility of human institutions.

The military ethic emphasizes the permanence of irrationality, weakness and evil in human affairs. It stresses the supremacy of society over the individual and the importance of order, hierarchy and division of function.

It accepts the nation state as the highest form of political organization and recognizes the continuing likelihood of war among nation states. . . . It exalts obedience as the highest virtue of military men. . . . It is, in brief, realistic and conservative.
— *Samuel Huntington*[13]

Much of Huntington's classic definition of the "military mind" would have applied to long-serving military officers of the distant past, but there is an added dimension to it now, for it represents the outlook of a separate and specialized profession. Although there have always been full-time specialists in the military art at the lower levels of armies' command structures, it is only in the past few centuries that there has come into existence in every country an autonomous body of people— the professional military officers—whose sole task is to maintain the armed forces in peacetime and lead them in war.

Profession is the correct word for the calling of the career officer today, in much the same sense that the word is applied to older professions like medicine or the law. The officer corps is a self-regulating body of men and women with expert knowledge of a complex intellectual discipline. It has a monopoly of the exercise of its function, and the exclusive right to select and train those new members who will be admitted to the discipline. Its client is society as a whole (through the mediation of the government, its sole employer), and it enjoys special privileges in compensation for its grave responsibilities. And, like any other profession, it also has a wide range of corporate interests and views to defend and advance. There were wars long before there was a professional officer corps, but the existence of an entire profession dedicated to the study of military affairs and the enhancement of military techniques has certainly influenced the character of wars and perhaps their frequency as well.

If you believe the doctors, nothing is wholesome; if you believe the theologians, nothing is innocent; if you believe the soldiers, nothing is safe.

Lord Salisbury

The professional military officer's view of the world is not merely the fruit of his personal experience of the realities of combat; indeed, in many instances he has not personally seen combat. Most armies, most of the time, are remarkably nonviolent organizations. The major European armies have been at war with each other for less than 10 percent of the past 150 years. But every nation's armed forces now consciously educates its officers in the perspectives and values appropriate to their profession, as much as in the technical aspects of their job, and at the summit of the organization is an institution that concentrates all this in a particularly potent form: the general staff.

The birth date of the military profession as an autonomous body with its own corporate views and interests, derived from its professional responsibilities and not from mere personal ambitions, was 25 November 1803, when the first true general staff was created in Prussia. Its intended function was to apply to war the same principles of rational organization and planning that were already transforming civil society in Europe. The Prussian general staff's long-range task was to develop fundamental principles for military operations that would provide guidance for commanders in all circumstances; its shorter-term duties were to prepare detailed war plans and solve current military problems.

> *The only title to an officer's commission shall be in time of peace, education and professional knowledge; in time of war, distinguished valor and perception. From the entire nation, therefore, all individuals who possess these qualities are eligible for the highest military posts. All previously existing class preference in the military establishment is abolished, and every man, without regard to his origins, has equal duties and equal rights.*
>
> decree on selection of officers, Prussian army, 1808[14]

Within only a few years of the creation of the general staff, the shock of defeat by Napoleon drove the Prussian army to cast aside all the traditions that had made eighteenth-century warfare an ad hoc business run by amateur officers whose main qualification was aristocratic birth. Entry into the officer corps now depended on high educational qualifications and examinations on military subjects, and promotion was largely governed by performance reports and further exams. In 1810, the army founded a staff college (the *Kriegsakademie*) where a small number of gifted middle-rank officers attended an extremely demanding one-year course in subjects ranging from military history, tactics, and military administration to foreign languages, mathematics, and "special geography and geology"—and in due course it became the rule that only *Kriegsakademie* graduates could be promoted to high rank or appointed to the general staff. In less than a decade, Prussia had laid all the necessary foundations for a fully professional officer corps.[15]

The controlling assumption behind all these changes was the Prussian army's realization, born of defeat at the hands of Napoleon, that the aristocracy's pretensions to an inborn talent for war were hollow, and that no country could afford to gamble on a self-taught military genius like Frederick the Great or Napoleon turning up to save it at the crucial moment. Instead, the Prussian military reformers had concluded that the "art of war," like law or medicine or any other profession, was actually a body of technical knowledge and inherited practical experience that could be formulated and taught in such a way that men of ordinary intelligence and personality could become extremely competent in it.

It was typical of the great intellectual vigor of Prussian military thought at the time that one of the *Kriegsakademie*'s first directors was Karl von Clausewitz, who wrote the first (and still the most perceptive) general study of the theory and practice of war, called simply *On War*, during his term there. In the end, every other major power imitated the Prussian innovations and professionalized its own armed forces, but in some cases it took almost a century. The enormous practical advantage that the Prussian army (and its successor, the German army) gained from this early adoption of a rigorously professional approach to war was still very evident only forty years ago.

> *One of the things that emerged from our study of operations on the Western Front and in Italy in World War II was that there was a consistent superiority of German ground troops to American and British ground troops. As a retired American army officer this didn't particularly please me, but I can't deny what my numbers tell me. . . . I had assumed that by 1944 we would have learned enough that we would be approximately equal, [but] in combat units 100 Germans in mid-1944 were the equivalent of somewhere around 125 American or British soldiers. . . . At about the same time 100 Germans were the equivalent of about 250 Russians. . . . Now this doesn't mean that the average German was any more intelligent, any braver, any stronger, any more motivated than the average Russian, but it means that when they were put together in combat units . . . the Germans used their weapons and equipment 2.5 times better than did the Russians.*
>
> *What [the Germans] did, in effect, was to institutionalize military excellence . . . and more than any other single factor it was the German general staff that made the difference. . . . There were generals in World War II, Russian generals, American generals, British generals, who were as good as the best of the Germans, but the Germans had about ten times as many very good generals.*
> —Col. T. N. Dupuy, U.S. Army ret'd.

In the end the Germans lost World War II, as they had World War I; good generalship is only one factor, and a relatively minor one, in total war. The early professionalization of the German officer corps ensured a high level of technical competence throughout the armed forces, but what Germany really needed to avoid the catastrophic defeats of 1918 and 1945 was the kind of strategic foresight that would have kept the nation from getting into wars in which it faced overwhelming enemy superiority in numbers and resources in the first place. This is what general staffs are supposed to provide—but even allowing for the fact that they usually do not control all the diplomatic, political, economic, and emotional factors that go into their country's choice of enemies, they have not historically done very well at this task.

It was Clausewitz who first drew a clear distinction between war as an independent field of activity with its own rules and logic, and the subordinate relationship of war to the general political objectives of the state. Armies do not exist for their own purposes; they are hirelings of the state, and all their plans and actions, however logical in terms of simply "winning" a battle or a war, must submit to the test of whether they actually further the political purposes of the state. This is the standard relationship of any profession to its clients. In the military case, however, the tail has often ended up wagging the dog.

The classic example was the Schlieffen Plan, drawn up by the Chief of the German General Staff in the first decade of this century, on the assumption that in any European war Germany would have to fight on two fronts—against Russia and France. Bearing in mind the smaller physical size of France and Russia's army probably being only partially mobilized, Schlieffen concluded that the solution to Germany's military problem would be to attack France with almost the entire German army at the very outbreak of war (leaving only about one ninth of it to cover the Russian frontier) and to win a decisive victory against France within six weeks.

Even as a purely technical military solution, it had grave defects; politically it was a horror. To find the space necessary to move his huge army into France quickly and to take the French in the rear, Schlieffen planned an attack through neutral Belgium (although that would almost certainly bring Britain into the war against Germany too). Far worse, his plan committed Germany to attack France at the start of *any* war, even if the actual cause of the war should lie (as it eventually did) at the other end of Europe. His planning gave Germany's civil authorities no political options—and the elaborate technical considerations that governed the process of mobilization for war left the civilians in a very weak position to demand changes when the crisis was upon them.

Mobilization plans were an obsession with the general staffs of all the European powers before 1914. They all believed that the first battles of a war would be decisive. It was therefore crucial to get the millions of army reservists to the frontiers, ready to fight, as quickly as possible. To that end they all prepared mobilization schedules filling entire volumes, which consisted mainly of elaborately interlocking timetables for the movement of those troops to the frontiers by train.

In theory, mobilization is a military precaution and a diplomatic warning, not an irrevocable declaration of war. In practice, once the first European power mobilized, every country found itself on a nonstop train to war. The general staffs elsewhere demanded that their own governments mobilize immediately in response— otherwise they could not guarantee the safety of the frontiers when the enemy's mobilization was completed. And then, whenever the increasingly frightened governments tried to draw back from the headlong rush to war, the general staff planners pointed out that the mobilization schedules would be hopelessly disrupted if they were stopped midway. There would be troops and trains stranded all over the place, often without the fuel and food they required, and it might take weeks to start the process moving again once it stopped.

The operation was successful, but the patient died (as a different profession would put it). The governments of Europe believed what they were told by their military professionals, and the trains delivered them punctually into World War I. (Any similarities with the present mobilization and war plans of NATO and the Warsaw Pact are, of course, purely coincidental.)

Armed forces are given vast resources over long years by governments, on the tacit assumption (by the latter) that this will buy them military security. Moreover, professional soldiers will generally pander to this illusion in peacetime to the extent necessary to extract the money they want for new weapons or other military measures, promising that they will solve some security problem or other. The more serious officers themselves realize that there can be no certainty of success in war, but naturally they find it very embarrassing to have to admit this to their civilian clients and will generally avoid doing so for as long as possible. One of the likeliest places for peace to founder is in the gap between civilian and military assumptions about the predictability of the outcome of war.

The professionalization of the world's armed forces has not been an unalloyed benefit, even in circumstances short of overt crisis. The rivalries between the three or more separate services maintained by most countries frequently lead to an exaggeration of the alleged threats facing a country in order to justify the acquisition of some specific new weapon by a particular service or generally to advance its cause in the perennial interservice competition for resources. This phenomenon has much to do with technological change and the matrix of interlocking interests known in the United States as the "military-industrial complex," but the fact that all senior officers are now career professionals—whose promotion prospects and reputation depend mainly on the opinion of their peers within the same service—tends to stifle any broader critical analysis of arms policies from within the services themselves.

Moreover, since it is the professional duty of military officers to identify threats to the security of the state, they are constantly searching for potential dangers abroad—and virtually every other state within military reach constitutes such a threat simply by virtue of having armed forces of its own. The planning reflex of general staffs provides governments with detailed and regularly updated scenarios for conflicts in unlikely places with improbable enemies (as late as the 1920s military planners in the United States and Canada were maintaining carefully worked out plans to invade each other), which on occasion can lend undue military importance to minor incidents and alarms. After World War II, for example, the United States divided the entire world into a series of military zones that were the responsibility of various military commands, with the inevitable result that any event anywhere by definition became potentially a matter of military concern for the United States.

General staffs did not create the international environment in which wars are inevitable, but they have certainly contributed to some wars and to many arms races by spreading their professional perceptions of insecurity in their own countries and creating corresponding feelings of insecurity in other countries by their weapons acquisitions. And in many states where the civil institutions are weak, the emergence of a professional military institution has even led to repeated military coups as the officer corps enforces its view of the world on the rest of the community or reacts against civilians who are unwise enough to challenge its corporate privileges.

Officers in countries where civil-military relations have never fallen to this level of discord see such behavior as unprofessional, but the fact remains that the era of military coups in various parts of the world roughly coincides with the emergence of an autonomous military profession in the region. Professional officer corps are organizations with strong corporate views and interests and sufficient resources to overcome or suppress most rival institutions in the state if they choose to do so.

Notwithstanding all the foregoing disadvantages and derelictions of duty of professional armed forces, however, one thing can be said with confidence: the military profession, especially in the great powers, hardly ever wants war. As a czarist officer once remarked, war "spoils the armies."

Under the stress of total war, many armies have gone to the verge of collapse or beyond. The Russian army dissolved in 1917, and the French and Italian armies came close to following suit. The Austrian and German armies collapsed in 1918, and the British army hovered on the brink for a time. The French army did collapse in 1940, and the Italians in 1943.

There is, moreover, no reliable means of predicting when collapse may occur. A combination of huge casualties and demoralization at home destroyed the Russian army's will to fight in 1917, while similar circumstances did not cause the Soviet army to collapse in 1942. The French mutinies of 1917, which were a spontaneous outburst of resentment by the men in the trenches, who felt their lives were being wasted in futile and foredoomed offensives, were contained (barely) by the decisive actions of the high command, whereas the disintegration of the French army in 1940 was mainly due to demoralization and despair in the high command: Most French troops fought very hard in 1940, and with more intelligent control from the center, they might even have succeeded in creating a new Western Front rather than being destroyed piecemeal by the German attack. But though the causes of collapse are unpredictable, it is clear to professional soldiers that mass armies, for all their enormous power, are also very fragile. And if they break, everything can be lost.

Professional military men always want to prepare for war, for "nothing is safe," but they are almost invariably reluctant to actually enter into war—this was as true of the military profession in the fascist states as in any others—because they are too aware of the sheer unpredictability of the outcome. Most of the exceptions to this generalization are in fact military-ruled states where the leaders of the armed forces have assumed the powers and some of the attitudes of politicians and have lost their professional military perspective.

Soldiers are not, on the whole, warmongers, but the "military mind"—the professional military perspective on human affairs—nevertheless exercises an enormous influence on how the business of mankind is conducted. The perspective is by no means arbitrary or narrowly self-serving; it is grounded in the military officers' recognition of the unpleasant realities of their profession.

They know that human beings under stress are usually not heroic, that the world is a far less rational and predictable place than most civilians like to pretend, and that deadly conflict between nations is an intrinsic part of the existing international system. They know all these things because the focus of their profession is battle, which makes these truths impossible to ignore. Professional military officers understand in their bones the role of power, compulsion, and brute force in human affairs.

NOTES

1. Robert Blake, ed., *The Private Papers of Douglas Haig, 1914–1919*, London: Eyre and Spottiswoode, 1952, p. 70.

2. Morris Janowitz, *The Professional Soldier*, New York: Free Press, 1964, pp. 21, 35.

3. S. Bagnall, *The Attack*, London: Hamish Hamilton, 1947, p. 21.

4. M. Lindsay, *So Few Got Through*, London: Arrow, 1955, p. 249.

5. John Ellis, *The Sharp End of War*, North Pomfret, Vermont: David and Charles, 1980, pp. 162–64.

6. S. A. Stouffer et al., *The American Soldier*, vol. II, Princeton, New Jersey: Princeton University Press, 1949, p. 202.

7. Lt. Col. J. W. Appel and Capt. G. W. Beebe, "Preventive Psychiatry: An Epidemiological Approach," *Journal of the American Medical Association*, 131 (1946), p. 1470.

8. Bagnall, op cit., p. 160.

9. Appel and Beebe, op. cit.

10. Col. S. L. A. Marshall, *Men Against Fire*, New York: William Morrow and Co., 1947, pp. 149–50.

11. Ibid., p. 191.

12. Ibid., pp. 191, 182, 153.

13. Samuel P. Huntington, *The Soldier and the State*, New York: Vintage, 1964, p. 79.

14. Ibid.

15. Walter Goerlitz, *History of the German General Staff*, New York: Frederick A. Praeger, 1953.

Army officers, "the managers of violence," are carefully selected to include only people who are bound to the state and its rulers by their own interests and ideas. Field Marshal Montgomery visiting General H. S. G. Crerar at Canadian Army Headquarters in The Netherlands, February 1945. *Ken Bell/DND/ Public Archives of Canada (PA 140409)*

The gaiety increases the nearer you get to the front. This snapshot of exuberant German pals was found on one of their bodies. *SOVFOTO*

The life expectancies of World War II bomber crews were measured in months; but between brief moments of stark terror, they slept on clean sheets and had some cushion against the psychological effects of daily combat. *Courtesy of the Imperial War Museum (CH12418)*

Anyone can be brave once, but nobody can go on forever. It is only a matter of time until the psychological strain of modern battle causes depression and breakdown. "The two thousand-yard stare" is the last stage before catatonia or total loss of control. *Tom Lea*, Marines call it the 2000 Yard Stare, *U.S. Army Audio Visual Agency*

Russian soldiers counting bodies in 1915. Continuous exposure to death makes it difficult, with the passage of time, for a soldier to retain any hope for his own survival. In World War II, Soviet casualties for engaged forces were up to 80 percent per year. The soldiers' fears were well-placed. *TASS from SOVFOTO*

The universal pattern: the average soldier would break down after about 250 "combat days," so constant troop rotation became the universal method. The only reason psychological casualty statistics were not higher is that most men didn't survive long enough to go to pieces. Here, exhausted Canadian veterans returning from the trenches pass their replacements, November 1916. *Public Archives of Canada (PA 913)*

The battle environment that produced mental collapse and unpredictable outcomes also caused so many casualties that there was a constant flow of replacements. Canadian wounded being taken to an aid station, September 1916. *Public Archives of Canada (PA 678)*

The officer's fundamental pessimism about his men's heroism or ability to function effectively under stress means that he must call on all his resources of persuasion, example, and plain coercion in battle. Colonel R. F. L. Keller urging members of the 3d Canadian Infantry Division on to glory in Normandy, June 1944. *DND/Public Archives of Canada (PA 115544)*

Land battle as video game—the separation of soldiers from what they're actually doing. A war planning room at the Pentagon. © *Roger Malloch/ MAGNUM*

Military professionals seek to preserve a collective memory of how men have behaved in battle (even if history suffers some distortion in the process). A French-Canadian recruiting poster for World War II presents the soldier as a White Knight on a motorcycle. *Courtesy of the Department of Rare Books and Special Collections of the McGill University Library, Montreal/Photo by Marilyn Aiken*

The temptation to believe that all the human imponderables of combat can be reduced to neat equations was especially strong in the United States and exalted the role of the manager and planner over that of the traditional fighting commander. Here, MACV personnel in Saigon get still more good news about the pacification program. © *P. J. Griffiths/MAGNUM*

The optimistic air force has a natural tendency, from way up there, to believe that correct managerial techniques and appropriate technology will solve any problem. An ebullient squadron commander signals the "A-OK" on returning to his carrier from a strike against North Vietnam, despite the loss of a plane, March 1965. *UPI/Bettman Newsphotos*

The "managerial delusion" reached its apotheosis in Vietnam; the jutting military confidence (and chins) of McGeorge Bundy, Gen. William Westmoreland, and, in the background, Ambassador Taylor, "surveying the political situation" in 1965. *UPI/Bettman Newsphotos*

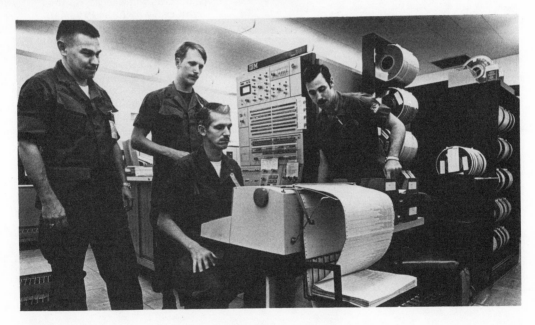

More good news from the computers about the Vietnam War. Despite all attempts to reduce it to science and certainty, warfare continues to be volatile, human, and mostly unpredictable. Here data from the "Hamlet Evaluation System" assures U.S. analysts that they are loved. © *P. J. Griffiths/MAGNUM*

Russian and German troops fraternizing. These soldiers simply stopped fighting each other in June 1917, something no general likes to see. The Russian army had collapsed under a combination of huge casualties and demoralization at home, and the German and Austrian armies would collapse a year later. *TASS from SOVFOTO*

Gen. Hans von Seeckt, on the right, every inch the Prussian professional and a fine example of "the institutionalization of military excellence." Throughout the twenties and thirties he continued to build up the German army, in violation of the Treaty of Versailles. Here he receives birthday congratulations in 1936. *UPI/Bettman Newsphotos*

7: The Army, the State and the People: Power Confounded

The weak in this world can never have peace.

—President Hafiz Assad of Syria 1985

The Siamese twins, army and state, have never been separated since they were born some eight or nine thousand years ago—and most of the time, the state is the stronger of the twins. Armies exist to serve the interests of the states that own them, and their legitimacy comes solely from the fact that they belong to states; similar groups of armed men, if self-employed, are generally known as rebels or bandits. This is the context in which warfare, as opposed to casual and illegitimate violence, must be seen: it is something that states do, and have always done, because they believe it serves their interests. If, for some states at least, warfare is now ceasing to be a rational activity, their difficulty in adjusting to this new situation is hardly surprising. Besides, for most states warfare remains a rational and potentially profitable activity.

There are accidental wars, futile wars, even plainly silly wars (like the Falklands war, for example), but the great majority of wars are fought because the government on at least one side has concluded, after rational calculation, that accepting the consequences of not fighting the war would be worse. The nation would suffer greatly, or disappear, or fail to be born, and so the war is worth it. Even when the decision to fight is not rational from the standpoint of national interest, it generally makes sense in terms of the personal priorities of the decision makers: we will lose face, or the government will fall, or our investments/fellow believers/ ideological allies in Slobbovia will suffer, unless we fight.

It is certainly wrong to blame the military profession in general for the existence of war, and usually it is also wrong to blame particular wars on the soldiers. It is states, and the people who live in them and accept their assumptions about such things as sovereignty, that are responsible for war. Armies in civilized states are, with rare exceptions, instruments of power, not prime movers. Nor is it surprising that this particular kind of instrument should be almost universally available and frequently used.

Force is the ultimate argument in human affairs, and naked military power is the most effective form of force. To the extent that concepts like international law have any substance, they are attempts to contain the most disruptive effects of this fact, but the historical pattern has been that power expands to its potential limits. In the past, those limits were often set by internal constraints like lack of resources or poor communications, but for the major industrialized states of recent times the more important limit has been the external opposition of similarly powerful states.

War is nothing more than the continuation of policy by other means.

Karl von Clausewitz[1]

Great states have no permanent friends, only permanent interests.

Lord Palmerston[2]

There has accumulated over the millennia a vast body of beliefs, habits, and perspectives about the environment in which states operate and about how best to survive within that merciless environment. Almost all individuals who rise to positions of political power in any country come to share the assumptions of this traditional wisdom to a large extent, however different their political beliefs or their specific national situations—and it is a tradition almost totally dominated by the belief that war is theoretically possible at any time between any of the independent states of the world. (That is why the language of diplomacy resembles the obsessively polite intercourse of societies in which dueling is permitted: if you cause somebody to lose face, he may start shooting.)

Yet it is glaringly obvious that the kinds of quarrels that occur between individuals and groups in the civil community over land, money, and rights—and the kinds of suspicion and rivalry that cause people to fear or hate their neighbors—are different only in their petty scale from the kinds of disputes that arise between states. There are only a strictly limited number of areas in which human beings are likely to come into serious conflict, and the list stays about the same at every level from individuals to governments (except that states rarely quarrel about sex). In the civil community, however, these conflicts do not normally lead to fatal violence between individuals or civil war between groups—whereas in the international community they very often lead to war.

States fight wars because, in the end, that is what they are organized to do. The quarrels that are settled by law if they occur within a state are frequently settled by war between states, because there is little international law and no international law enforcement. The need to prepare for and wage war has therefore been the decisive influence on the evolution of the state. It was practically the sole business of the ancient or medieval monarchy, and it accounts for most of the developments in governmental structure and bureaucratic technique that have shaped the modern state. This may seem a circular argument—wars happen between states largely because states are organized to fight wars—but it is nonetheless an accurate description of the present or of any previous historical period. States are principally organizations for the accumulation of power in the pursuit of security, and their most significant distinguishing characteristic is the possession of military forces.

What makes the government of a sovereign state like Greece different in kind from the government of a large city like New York or an extensive province like Bavaria is Greece's ability and even its right (in war) to kill foreigners. The Greek government collects no more taxes than either New York City or Bavaria, and it probably provides fewer services to those it governs—who are not significantly more numerous. It is not even different in having its own laws or in its ability to enforce those laws on its citizens using whatever force may be necessary. But it is totally different in having an army, a navy, and an air force whose purpose is to safeguard its interests by using deadly force against the citizens of other governments. If New York City had similar forces and a similar outlook, then it too would be a sovereign state. Armed forces are the key to the equation—for any state to contemplate giving up the right to have and use them, in the world as it is, is almost unthinkable.

There were two armies, one defeated, the other victorious. To disband the defeated army was no problem. First we licked them, then we disbanded them. As for the victorious army, they were all volunteers who wanted nothing else but to go home. —*José Figueres Ferrer, former president of Costa Rica*

It is possible to have an independent state without an army; Costa Rica has been such a country since 1948. The regular army made the mistake of siding with an unpopular dictator in the two-month civil war of that year, and the rebel army that overthrew him was led by an extraordinary man whose democratic convictions preserved him from the temptations of military-backed absolute power. "Don Pepe" Figueres was also tough and wily enough to stop any of his companions from succumbing to temptation, and he was well aware of the blight that military interventions have cast over Latin American history, "so when I had the chance to abolish the military, I took it."

For over a generation Costa Rica has survived as a democratic state without an army—it has armed police forces, but their training, equipment, and spirit are not even paramilitary—despite the fact that for most of that time its neighbors have been army-ruled dictatorships. It can be done. But Costa Rica is the only independent country in the world that has chosen to live without an army (except for some island mini-states with populations well under a million). And as superpower politics has come to dominate Central America in the aftermath of the Nicaraguan revolution in 1979, Costa Rica has come under increasingly heavy pressure from the United States to recreate an army for possible use against its Marxist neighbors in Nicaragua.

Countries in parts of the world that have historically seen heavy military traffic have never dared to contemplate the Costa Rican solution, even if, like Switzerland, they have adopted a policy of strict and permanent neutrality. Switzerland has not faced a foreign invader since Napoleon, and apart from a brief civil war in 1847 no Swiss military unit has fired a shot in anger for 170 years, but it does not feel safe without an army. One of the traditional requirements of neutrality is that a country be able to prevent any neighboring state from moving across its territory to attack another neighbor, and that requires armed forces.

Despite its mountains and the fact that it isn't on a main invasion route to anywhere, Switzerland feels compelled to maintain a large military potential to make sure its neutrality is respected. The country spends over 2 percent of its gross domestic product on defense, and every male Swiss citizen must do seventeen weeks of recruit training, followed by thirty-two further weeks of reserve refresher training spread over the next thirty years. Every reservist keeps his weapons at home, and the Swiss government counts on having 625,000 trained troops available (10 percent of the entire population) within forty-eight hours of mobilization. And every couple of years there is renewed discussion in the Swiss press about whether the country should invest in nuclear weapons.

Small countries without Switzerland's neutral traditions and out-of-the-way location usually join (or are press-ganged into) military alliances that allegedly guarantee their security. As for the minority of states that have active territorial disputes underway with their neighbors—Israel is able to mobilize almost as many troops as Switzerland out of a population only about half as big, and it spends around a third of its gross national product on defense. It has far more tanks than the French army, more combat aircraft than the West German air force, and it does have nuclear weapons, though it maintains a tactful silence about them. To be a state is to go armed.

To be a state is also, in practice, to fight wars, and the bigger and more powerful the state, the more frequent its wars. The belief that lies at the root of all deterrence theory, either nuclear or conventional—that great military strength is the surest guarantee that a country will be left in peace—is demonstrably false and is indeed the exact reverse of the truth.

During the entire period of modern European history from 1480 to 1940, it has been calculated that there were about twenty-six hundred important battles. The only country that was a leading military power during the whole of that period, France, participated in 47 percent of those battles, and Germany (Prussia), Russia, and Britain all fought in between 22 percent and 25 percent of them. By contrast Spain, which ceased to be a major military power at the beginning of the nineteenth century, soon afterward dropped out of Europe's wars almost entirely and can only offer an attendance record of 12 percent over the whole period, and the Netherlands and Sweden (great powers only for brief periods) were present at only 8 percent and 4 percent of Europe's battles respectively.[3]

By any other yardstick—the amount of time a given European country has spent at war, the number of wars it has participated in, the proportion of its population that has been killed in war over the years—the result is the same. There is a steep and consistent gradient of suffering, in which the most powerful nations fight most often and lose most heavily in lives and wealth. Nor are these facts unique to Europe. For example, the United States, which has been a great power on the make since soon after its independence, has seen only 25 years of its entire history (now over two centuries) in which its army or navy has not been involved in active operations somewhere during some part of the year, while Sweden, which long ago abandoned its great-power ambitions, has not used its armed forces in a war for 170 years.

The practical solace that inoffensive small nations can take from this is severely limited by the fact that the great-power wars of the twentieth century—the two world wars—have shown an irresistible tendency to sweep almost all the smaller countries into the conflagration too. World War I spread to all the European great powers and Japan within a year, pulled the United States in after two and a half years, and had thirty-three belligerents—half the independent states then in existence—by its end; World War II spread to every great power within just over two years, and by 1945 all but six of the world's independent countries were at war. The increasingly rapid and uncontrollable spread of great-power wars is partly due to the sheer technological reach of modern war machines, but it is also undoubtedly related to the growing interdependency of states in trade and to the development of a single worldwide political market in ideas. These latter phenomena are essentially hopeful trends, part of the process that is slowly laying the foundations on which an international system that does not depend on war might eventually be built, but their short-term consequence has unquestionably been to produce not world peace, but true world wars.

Since 1945 there has, however, been an apparent change in the pattern of wars between states. None of the great powers has fought any other great power directly for the past four decades, though almost all of them have fought several wars in smaller countries, which were often seen as "proxies" for their great-power rivals. (This self-restraint is commonly seen as a new and important factor in international affairs, brought on by the fact that all the great powers now possess nuclear weapons or are closely allied to those who do.) "Bilateral" wars between neighboring countries—Israel and the Arab countries, Pakistan and India, Iran and Iraq—have continued to occur at a rate that does not diverge greatly from the historical norm (allowing for the threefold expansion in the number of sovereign states since 1945). But the vast majority of the estimated 21 million people killed in war since 1945 have died in a quite different and seemingly new kind of struggle: guerrilla warfare, "revolutionary war," counterinsurgency campaigns, and the like. Mostly they have been killed by their own fellow citizens, yet few of these conflicts fit the classic model of civil war either.

There have been theorists who have arranged the three potential kinds of armed conflict in the world—"unconventional war," bilateral and "proxy" wars fought with conventional weapons, and great-power nuclear war —into a connected hierarchy: stages of escalation in the same basic conflict, so to speak. These theorists have generally resided in the superpowers, where everything that happens in the world is seen as part of the American-Soviet struggle for dominance, and they should not be taken too seriously. The world is full of people who spend their time concocting or detecting nefarious plots (strategists, in the vernacular), but it is not run with as much competence and foresight as the paranoids think. The Soviet Union occupied Afghanistan in 1979 to rescue a failing Marxist regime in which it had invested too much political capital to write off, not as part of a drive toward "warm-water ports" and the Gulf oil fields; the United States first allowed its former protegee, the Nicaraguan dictator Anastasio Somoza, to be overthrown by domestic rebels in 1979, and then began sponsoring (guerrilla) forces commanded by ex-Somoza officers in an attempt to overthrow the left-wing government created by the Nicaraguan revolutionaries because it is perennially torn between its democratic ideology and its instincts as a great power; and Britain fought Argentina in 1982, not to create a NATO base in the South Atlantic, but simply to avenge an insult to "national honor" and to save a prime minister from electoral defeat.

Nevertheless, there is a new common factor discernible in all the armed conflicts that ravage the contemporary world, and especially in the majority of those conflicts that are irregular in nature. Military power is becoming less effective in achieving decisive, politically satisfactory results at every level of conflict. This is as true for enemies fighting with conventional weapons as for the nuclear-armed great powers, and it is equally true for governments and for insurgents in the lower intensity irregular wars that now account for most of the world's actual killing.

The principal technique which the insurgent groups have used to attack the state in the past half century has been guerrilla warfare; for a time, in the 1950s and early 1960s, it seemed a virtually infallible technique for overthrowing governments. But like the first of the modern methods for seizing state power, the urban uprisings of nineteenth and early twentieth century Europe which drew their inspiration from the French revolution in 1789, guerrilla warfare proved to be a technique that only flourished in a specific environment.

> *Wherever we arrived, they disappeared; whenever we left, they arrived. They were everywhere and nowhere, they had no tangible center which could be attacked.* —French officer fighting Spanish guerrillas, 1812[4]

Guerrilla warfare as a form of resistance to foreign occupation or an unpopular domestic government had been around for the better part of forever, but it gained particular prominence in the Napoleonic wars, when the Spanish (who gave the technique its name) and the Germans waged very large guerrilla campaigns against French occupying forces. But it was not generally regarded as a potentially decisive military technique even as late as World War II, when it was again widely employed against German and Japanese occupation forces, primarily because it lacked an adequate strategy for final victory.

So long as the guerrillas remained dispersed in the hills, forests, or swamps and indulged in only hit-and-run raiding against the government or the foreign occupiers, they could make a quite infernal nuisance of themselves—but they could never clear their opponents out of the urban centers of power. If they came down out of the hills and attempted to do so in open combat, they gave their opponents the target they had been hoping for, and the enemy's regular forces would smash them. Even the Yugoslavs, the most successful guerrilla fighters of World War II, could not have liberated their country unaided; the Germans finally pulled out mainly because the Red Army was sweeping through the Balkans toward them.

What changed after World War II was that the rural guerrilla technique spread into the European colonial empires, at a time when the imperial powers had lost their nerve and were in a gravely weakened economic condition. As in the occupied countries of Europe during the war, the guerrillas in the European colonies after the war had no difficulty in mobilizing many of their newly nationalistic fellow countrymen against the foreign occupiers—and as in the occupied countries of Europe, they had virtually no prospect of winning a military victory against the well-equipped regular forces of the imperial power, though they could turn themselves into an expensive and ineradicable nuisance. What was different, however, was that whereas the Germans in Yugoslavia were fighting a great war in which the very survival of their own regime was at stake, and so were willing to bear the cost of fighting the Yugoslav guerrillas virtually indefinitely, the European powers had no such stake in retaining control of their colonies.

It came down in the end to the fact that if the guerrillas could make it very expensive for the colonial power to stay, and could go on doing so indefinitely, they didn't have to worry about gaining a military victory. The colonial power would eventually decide to cut its losses and go home. This was a reality that had already been demonstrated by the Irish war of independence in 1919–20 and the Turkish war of national resistance against attempted partition by the victorious Entente powers in 1919–22 (the struggle for which the Soviets coined the phrase "national liberation war"). The demonstration was repeated many times in the two decades after 1945, in Indonesia, Kenya, Algeria, Malaya, Vietnam, South Yemen, and many other places. In a few cases, like Malaya, the imperial power managed to hand over control to some local group other than the guerrillas themselves (but this depended mainly on the unusual racial split in Malaya). In the majority of cases, the decolonization process was achieved without a guerrilla war, once the message of their own vulnerability to this technique had been absorbed by the imperial powers.

At the time, the apparently irresistible spread of rural guerrilla wars caused great alarm and despondency in the major Western powers—partly, of course, because it was their own oxen that were being gored. There was also an ideological element, however, in that almost all of these postwar guerrilla movements espoused some variant of the same Marxist ideology propounded by the West's main international rival, the Soviet Union. (And naturally, being Marxists, the guerrillas tended to attribute their successes to ideology rather than to the particular environment they were operating in, and announced this conviction loudly.) This led to a belief in the West that it was Soviet and/or Chinese expansionism, and not simply local resentment of foreign rule, that lay behind these guerrilla wars, and so to the creation of special counterinsurgency forces, especially in the United States, and ultimately to the commitment of U.S. troops to Vietnam under a total misapprehension as to what the war there was about.

In fact, the guerrillas had mostly adopted a Marxist ideology because they could scarcely be expected to adopt the dominant ideology of the imperial powers they were seeking to expel. They thus opted for the expedient of espousing the leading opposition ideology prevailing at the imperial center, Marxism, much as an earlier generation of anti-imperialist revolutionaries in China, Iran, Turkey and Mexico had taken up the then predominant opposition ideology of liberalism a half-century before. The Third World Marxist revolutionaries of the fifties and sixties learned their Marxism in London and Paris, not in Moscow.

The full-scale U.S. military commitment to Vietnam in 1965 was not only made for the wrong reason—to thwart perceived Soviet expansionism acting through the Chinese—but at the wrong time. For by 1965 the wave of guerrilla wars in what we now call the Third World was coming to its natural end, as most of the countries there had already received their independence. Apart from Indochina, only Southern Africa and South Yemen were still the scenes of active guerrilla campaigns against imperial rule. And although it had scarcely been noticed yet, the rural guerrilla technique hardly ever worked against a locally based government supported by a major local ethnic group.

It is far harder to win a guerrilla campaign against one's own government, not only because there is not the natural antipathy against foreign rule to attract recruits to one's cause, but also because a locally based government cannot simply cut its losses and go home if the cost of fighting a counterinsurgency campaign gets too high. It is already home and has nowhere else to go. As a consequence, when fighting against their own government, rural guerrillas *do* have to face the question of how to win final military victory in open battle against the government's regular armed forces—and only three have achieved it: China in 1949, Cuba in 1959, and Nicaragua in 1979.

The technique of rural guerrilla warfare only flourished as long as there were demoralized imperialist governments around to oppose. The world remains littered with rural guerrilla movements today, hanging on in the more rugged parts of dozens of Third World countries, but as the exponents of a minority ideology or the representatives of a minority ethnic group, they have very little prospect of success against local governments that can credibly invoke nationalism on their own side. The era of successful rural guerrilla wars was already in decline when the United States committed its army to Vietnam in 1965.

This fact has been considerably obscured by the American war in Vietnam in 1965–73, which is still widely viewed as a counterguerrilla war. In fact it was nothing of the sort, though a minority of American troops and a majority of South Vietnamese forces were indeed involved in the classic and extremely tedious task of counterinsurgency and internal security operations. Most of the U.S. combat units, however, were fighting a semiconventional "limited war" almost from the day they arrived in the country. This was due primarily to the fact that the North Vietnamese chose to make it that way.

Americans had an image of war . . . which equated guerrilla warfare with a certain very small set of images: basically any kind of jungle warfare must be guerrilla warfare. The guerrilla warfare image and television led everyone to think that everything that was going on in Vietnam was a guerrilla war. They saw newsreel footage of only a few stock images week after week, year after year: people slogging through rice paddies, people going through jungle so thick that you couldn't believe that there could actually be another unit in there fighting you, film footage of villages being bombed.

In all cases you couldn't see the enemy, which seemed to confirm the image of the guerrilla as being very elusive. There you are. You have a lot of heavy forces moving around trying to find him; he fires; he gets you; you don't get him; he runs away; and you've mashed a village or something but you don't get any results.

In fact, quite frequently you had very large and very conventional North Vietnamese forces operating against the Americans just when this newsreel footage was being taken. But the point about newsreel footage is that you virtually never see the enemy, in any war. So the whole Vietnam war seemed to be an anti-guerrilla war, while of course it was nothing of the kind. The American units went into the jungles, up into the highlands in the western part of the country where the enemy lived, going straight for battle against the main enemy in classical old military style, and once they got there it was a conventional American force fighting against a lightly equipped but conventional Asiatic enemy.

Tom Tulenko, military advisor and analyst, Historical Evaluation and Research Organization, Washington, D.C.

For both North Vietnam and the United States, the second Vietnamese war, after the commitment of U.S. combat units in 1965, was much more a limited conventional war than a guerrilla campaign. American strategy was dedicated to stopping the rot in South Vietnam by committing enough combat troops on the ground to take the pressure off the South Vietnamese army (which was very near collapse in 1965), while the offensive element consisted of "limited" but large-scale aerial bombardment of North Vietnam against an expanding list of targets (the theory of escalation) until Hanoi's "threshold of pain" had been reached and it desisted from supporting the guerrilla campaign in the South. The problem was that the threshold of pain of an intensely nationalistic and ruthlessly totalitarian regime like North Vietnam's was not even reached when the Americans had escalated all the way to bombing Hanoi and Haiphong.

The American strategy was founded on the argument (based on ideological preconceptions rather than fact) that the threat to the South Vietnamese regime in 1965 came not from indigenous guerrilla forces enjoying a certain amount of logistical support from the North—which was in fact the case—but rather from the large-scale infiltration of regular North Vietnamese army units down the Ho Chi Minh trail. On this assumption, it was argued that if Hanoi could be forced to stop the infiltration, the problem in South Vietnam would go away.

In fact, however, the dispatch of large numbers of American combat troops to South Vietnam served to turn Washington's mistaken assessment of the situation into an accurate one, for Hanoi responded by sending large forces of its own into South Vietnam. By 1968 the North Vietnamese army was in effective charge of all operations in the south, most of the Vietcong guerrilla cadres had been replaced by regular North Vietnamese military officers, and whole divisions of the North Vietnamese army were operating in the Central Highlands.

In thus providing the Americans with precisely the hard targets they wanted, and standing up to U.S. forces in open battles that cost them enormous casualty tolls, the North Vietnamese were contravening all the traditional rules of rural guerrilla warfare—but they were no longer fighting that kind of war. They were instead working from the analogy of their 1954 battle with the French at Dien Bien Phu, and it hardly mattered whether they won their battles, as they had done in that case, or lost, as they did in the comparable siege of Khe Sanh in 1967–68. The point was that by engaging the Americans in fierce combat—even accepting loss ratios of as much as ten-to-one, which was an inevitable consequence of the vastly superior American firepower—the North Vietnamese could exact that steady and large toll of American casualties that would destroy the American public's will to continue.

It worked precisely as Hanoi had calculated. The Americans hardly ever lost a battle in Vietnam, but it took only three years of combat, culminating in Hanoi's purportedly "suicidal" Tet offensive of 1968, for the North Vietnamese to win the battle on the American home front. Only fifteen-thousand American fatalities in Vietnam were incurred before Tet[5]—to put it at its crudest, a mere one in fifteen thousand of the American population—but even that scale of loss, when combined with the relentless television publicity given to the war, proved more than the American public was willing to bear in such a doubtful cause. After Tet, the Americans stopped looking for fights and started looking for a way out—though it took five years to find the famous "decent interval" that let the Americans leave in 1973 without overt military humiliation, and pretend that it was not a defeat for the U.S. Army when Hanoi collected its victory two years later.

What Vietnam demonstrated was merely that it is as hard for a democratic country to maintain domestic support for an expensive limited war overseas as it is for a comparable counterinsurgency campaign, if the country's own vital interests are not clearly involved in the outcome. This had already been demonstrated in that other American limited war, Korea, which President Eisenhower only managed to conclude more or less satisfactorily, before the home front's patience ran out in 1953 by threatening to escalate to the use of nuclear weapons. The one advantage of total war is that the government doesn't have to worry much about the home front, since national survival is involved; with anything less, in a democracy, the government has problems pretty soon, as it gets caught between those who want to quit and those who want to "solve" the problem by escalating the war.

The Vietnamese nightmare obscured an important development elsewhere, however, for this was precisely the period in which rural guerrilla warfare showed how ineffective it was outside the specific late colonial environment in which it had flourished. There was never any serious attempt to practice it in any industrialized country, but in the middle and late 1960s the Cubans made a concerted effort to extend the technique to the independent states of Latin America. Rural guerrilla movements sprang up in almost all the states of South America, Marxist in orientation and enjoying tacit or even open Cuban support. Without exception, they failed disastrously. The epitome of this failure was "Ché" Guevara's own tragicomic attempt to start such a movement in Bolivia, which ended in his own death.

> *Our isolation continues to be total; various illnesses have undermined the health of some comrades . . . our peasant base is still underdeveloped, although apparantly a program of planned terror will succeed in neutralizing most of them, and their support will come later. We have not had a single recruit (from the peasantry). . . . To sum up, a month in which all has evolved normally considering the standard development of a guerrilla war.*
> —Ché Guevara, Bolivia, April 1967[6]

Six months later Guevara was dead and his little guerrilla band had been broken up—and the same fate eventually attended almost all the other attempts to emulate the Cuban experience that had sprung up in Latin America.

This is not to say, of course, that the technique can never work in independent underdeveloped countries, but it certainly does require that the target government be extraordinarily iniquitous, incompetent, and politically isolated (as in Nicaragua). In most Latin American countries, the guerrillas had been eliminated or reduced to a merely marginal nuisance by 1970. The inescapable conclusion— which was accepted by most Latin American revolutionaries—was that rural guerrilla warfare was another revolutionary technique that had failed.

This realization drove numbers of these disappointed revolutionaries into random terrorism (or rather, "urban guerrilla warfare," as it is now known). In effect, the strategy of the Latin American originators of this doctrine, most notably the

Montoneros of Argentina, the Tupamaros of Uruguay, and Brazilian revolutionaries like Carlos Marighella, was aimed at driving the target regimes into extreme repression.

By assassinations, bank robberies, kidnappings, hijackings, and so on, all calculated to attract maximum publicity in the media and to embarrass the government to the greatest possible extent, the guerrillas sought to provoke the displacement of democratic governments by tough military regimes, or to drive existing military regimes into even stricter and more unpopular security measures. If the regime resorted to counterterror, torture, "disappearances," and death squads, all the better, for the purpose was to discredit the government and alienate it from the population.[7]

> It is necessary to turn political crisis into armed conflict by performing violent actions that will force those in power to transform the political situation of the country into a military situtation. That will alienate the masses, who, from then on, will revolt against the army and the police and blame them for this state of things. —Carlos Marighella[8]

As in the case of rural guerrilla warfare attempted outside the colonial environment, however, the fatal flaw in the urban guerrilla strategy is that it lacks an effective end game. The theory says that when the guerrillas have succeeded in driving the government into a sufficiently repressive posture, the populace will rise up in righteous wrath and destroy its oppressors. But even if the population should decide that it is the government and not the guerrillas that is reponsible for its growing misery, how is it to accomplish this feat? By the urban uprisings that have rarely succeeded since the nineteenth century? Or by the rural guerrilla warfare that has just demonstrated its ineffectiveness?

In a number of Latin American countries, the urban guerrillas did accomplish the first phase of their strategy: the creation of thoroughly nasty and brutally repressive military governments dedicated to destroying them. But what then happened was that these governments proceeded to do precisely that. In every Latin American country where they attempted to use this strategy, the vast majority of the urban guerrillas are now dead or in exile.

> Whether we like it or not, a type of constant revolution has existed since 1789. Each successful revolution has left the state enlarged, better organized, more potent, and with wider areas of influence; that has been the pattern even when revolution has assaulted and attempted to diminish the state. It is a matter of record which no theory can disprove. —Jacques Ellul[9]

All the nongovernmental forms of organized violence which have emerged over the past couple of centuries do not change the basic reality: a world of sovereign and independent states organized for war against each other. Insurgents of any political color, no matter which specific techniques they are using, are an inherently transient phenomenon. Their goal is to seize control of the state, not to destroy it, and they will end up either in government or in shallow graves. Moreover, the struggle will have the effect of expanding the powers of the state, because the need of both sides to mobilize and regiment popular support in an internal war is just as strong as in the great international wars of this century. Whether the insurgents win or lose in the end, the institution of the state will survive and flourish. And states fight wars.

Whenever someone goes to sleep, whenever someone rests for a while and puts off his arms, he is exposed to someone who jumps on his neck. And I certainly believe that the generation that is growing now, my son—I have a five-year-old son, and he will have to fight, and maybe my grandchild will have to fight. And maybe that's the way it should be.

Gen. Yossi Ben-Chanaan, Israeli Defense Forces

Leaving the great powers aside for the moment, the majority of the world's international wars grow out of real and grave disputes between governments in which the interests of their citizens are more or less closely involved. The paradigm for wars in the post-1945 world is Israel, which illustrates in its brief and hectic history virtually all the motives that can drive a state to war.

Israel's first war, occurring in the years immediately before its independence in 1948, was a combination of a classic terrorist campaign against the imperial occupying power, Britain, with a counterinsurgency struggle against what was destined to become the Palestinian minority within the state of Israel (once a sufficient number of Palestinians had fled to turn the rest into a minority). Its second war, in 1948–49, was a desperate defensive battle against the regular armies of Israel's Arab neighbors, in which 1 percent of the new state's population was killed and its very survival was in the balance. At the time, Israel enjoyed the moral support of both superpowers, each of which saw it as a potential friend and ally in a region still otherwise dominated by the European colonial powers—Washington counting on Israel's close financial and sentimental links with the American Jewish community, Moscow on its Eastern European socialist traditions and its anti-imperialist attitudes—while Britain and France, with their extensive interests in the Arab world, officially treated Israel with a coolness verging on hostility.

By 1956, however, British and French colonial interests in the Arab world were under heavy attack (by Nasser's Free Officers in Egypt and the National Liberation Front in Algeria), and Israel found itself conspiring with the old imperial powers to launch an attack on Egypt. Israel's interest in the proceedings was to end attacks from across the Egyptian border and gain the use of the Suez Canal—but it and its European allies were thwarted in their aims and forced to evacuate the

Suez Canal and the Sinai Peninsula by Washington and Moscow, which were both now more interested in gaining the support of the growing number of independent Arab countries.

Israel's close alliance with France (though not with Britain) lasted for another decade and enabled it to lay the foundations for its nuclear weapons program, but the next war, in 1967, saw another change in the alliance. Israel launched the war with a "preemptive" strike against the air forces of its Arab enemies (who were talking loudly about a concerted attack on Israel, though their actual military preparations for it were unconvincing), and France at once broke its defense ties with Tel Aviv. In the meantime, however, the Soviet Union had established substantial diplomatic and military bonds with Israel's most powerful Arab enemies, Egypt and Syria, and so the United States rapidly assumed France's place as Israel's major foreign ally: "The enemy of my enemy [or my enemy's Arab allies] is my friend."

The 1967 campaign developed into a war of conquest which quadrupled the territory under Israeli control and made it impossible even for the most war-weary Arab regimes to talk about a compromise peace settlement with Israel until the military balance had been somewhat restored. That task was accomplished by the Egyptian-Syrian surprise attack of 1973, which was conceived and fought (at least by the Egyptians) as a limited war whose purpose was to dent Israeli military hubris and capture enough territory to force Israel to the negotiating table. The initial Arab onslaught was so effective that Israel reportedly was considering using its nuclear weapons if the military situation continued to deteriorate, but in the end the superior military competence of the Israeli armed forces reversed the situation and left Israel triumphant. Once again, as in 1956, the Soviet Union and the United States had to intervene to forestall the complete destruction of an Egyptian army—and their own forces had been put on a high degree of alert before they managed to formulate a joint approach to the crisis.

Nevertheless, the Egyptian political strategy behind the 1973 war was largely successful: Israel was persuaded to trade territory for peace, and within five years Egypt had signed a peace treaty with Israel in return for the restitution of all its occupied lands. On other fronts the Arab-Israeli wars continue—Israel invaded southern Lebanon in 1978 and drove all the way north to Beirut in 1982, in attempts to suppress Palestinian guerrilla attacks on northern Israel—and the need to keep the Arabs permanently inferior militarily has become a critical issue in Israeli politics. In 1980 a government in the midst of an election campaign turned the odds in its favor by launching a surprise attack on the building site for an Iraqi nuclear reactor which it alleged to be part of an Iraqi nuclear weapons program. In reality, however, since the departure of Egypt from the joint Arab military front, the possiblity of an irreparable Israeli military defeat has dwindled to the vanishing point.

Israel has done very well by war. At a considerable cost in the time and money of its citizens, but no great cost in lives (more Israelis have died in car accidents than in war), Israel has succeeded in carving out the territory of a Jewish nation in the Levant, against the unanimous opposition of all the previous local inhabitants, and gaining a military superiority that makes it very unlikely that its existence can be effectively threatened by those opponents for the foreseeable future. To do so it has had to militarize its own society to an extent that many Israelis consider deeply regrettable, but few would argue with the results. The European Jews who founded Israel, more than any other people in the world, had learned the bitter cost of being without a state and an armed force of their own to protect themselves.

I would say the cultural mood of the average Israeli is that the most important symbol of independence is military power. And there is a danger that out of an objective situation, our existing culture is being too much affiliated with and influenced by the very existence of brutal military force.

Meir Pail, ex-senior IDF officer, member of the Knesset

Look, I don't like to kill people, but I've killed Arabs. Maybe I'll tell you a story. A car came towards us, in the middle of the [Lebanese] war, without a white flag. Five minutes before another car had come, and there were four Palestinians with RPGs in it—killed three of my friends. So this new Peugeot comes towards us, and we shoot. And there was a family there—three children. And I cried, but I couldn't take the chance. It's a real problem. . . . Children, father, mother. All the family was killed, but we couldn't take the chance.

Gaby Bashan, Israeli reservist (severely wounded in Lebanon, 1982)

The brutality is bad at the front, but even worse is the brutalization of attitudes at home: at least the soldiers still see their enemies as human beings and are directly confronted with the horrors that war inflicts on innocent civilian bystanders. In cabinet rooms and living rooms far from the fighting, it is easy to reduce the "enemy" to a faceless, malevolent, unreasoning caricature of a person who therefore can be killed without compunction, and this tendency gets worse the longer a confrontation continues. It need not involve a long series of actual wars like the Arabs and Israelis have experienced. Americans and Russians, used to hostility by decades of cold and tepid war, can contemplate the immolation of millions of "enemies" (some of them not yet old enough to walk) in the other side's cities without losing any sleep; it is the retaliation on their own cities that causes them concern. Killing still bothers soldiers; ordering soldiers to do it bothers civilians less often, so long as the war can be won and the peace settlement is satisfactory.

Unfortunately, though wars can still be won, the peace settlements are rarely satisfactory, at least if the implication is that they will bring lasting peace. The Israelis have "won" all of their wars militarily, but after half a dozen of them they still live in an atmosphere of permanently impending war. Elsewhere it is the same: India and Pakistan have fought three wars but make constant military provisions for a fourth, Korea remains an armed camp over three decades after the shooting ended, Argentina refuses to declare hostilities at an end after the Falklands war, and Britain finds itself building a large permanent garrison in the islands. Wars are not nearly as effective in settling things as they once were.

Some of the reasons have to do with the nature of modern states. Since nationalism has become the basic source of legitimacy for states, the emotional involvement of the populace in the international fortunes of the state has made it far more difficult for governments to accept a defeat, write it off, and go on to other matters. The popular perception is that the insult to national honor must be avenged, and so the sacred cause—Kashmir, the Falkland Islands, or whatever—is cherished by millions of people who have no personal interest in the outcome.

Modern states, moreover, are enormously rich and competent organizations by any previous historical standards. Late twentieth-century Pakistan, for example, has a more efficient centralized government, greater disposable total wealth, and far more educated people than any of the seventeenth-century European great powers, and it also has access to all the technological and scientific capabilities of the era it lives in. The consequence is that a modern state defeated in war has enormous reserves of human and material resources to draw upon, in order to ensure that the next round will not come out the same way; it can escalate the scale of the conflict. In the end, it will probably lose the next round too, for resources are only meaningful in relative terms and its opponent will also be escalating, but few states that have been involved in a major international war since 1945 have been able to get off the escalator afterward. In a number of cases, the escalation is now approaching the level of nuclear weapons, and in at least two instances—the Arab-Israeli and the Indo-Pakistan conflicts—the nuclear threshold has already been crossed (in terms of weapons, though not yet in terms of actual war).

The number and kind of nuclear weapons that are likely to be in the possession of a nongreat power are not "unusable" in quite the same sense as the tens of thousands of warheads to be found in the superpowers' arsenals. The destruction would be enormous if a country like Syria or Pakistan were struck by nuclear weapons, but it would not be a global disaster as long as the fighting did not spread, and it could certainly decide a local war.

The real constraint that makes both the conventional and the hypothetical nuclear forces of nongreat powers incapable of achieving decisive victories anymore is the fact that all the world is now incorporated into the system of great-power competition even in peacetime. Israel cannot go too far against Syria because the Soviet Union would intervene to rescue its client; India could never wage a war against Pakistan to total victory because China would intervene to protect it; China has been unable to reunite the country by seizing Taiwan because the United States will not permit it. The entire world has become a single political arena, and there is almost no dispute in which the great powers do not take opposite sides.

There is one, however, and it is the exception that proves the rule. The war between Iran and Iraq that began in 1980 involved two regimes so unappetizing that, as a member of the State Department in Washington put it, his only regret was that both sides couldn't lose. The Soviet attitude was not greatly different in practice, and both superpowers ended up offering limited support to the Iraq regime, which they regarded as slightly the lesser evil. The result is that the Iraq-Iran war has lasted longer than World War I.

The post-1945 norm, in starkest contrast, is that open international wars between regular armies (almost invariably in Third World countries) rarely last more than a few weeks, because by then the superpower involvement on both sides has become so deep that direct clashes between them become conceivable if the local fighting is not stopped. At that point the superpowers themselves take fright and impose a freeze on the war by using all the levers of diplomatic and financial support and arms supplies that they have at their disposal. Only one of Israel's wars since 1948 has lasted longer than three weeks, and the norm in less sensitive regions of the world still does not exceed a month or two.

The interests of the superpowers generally do not permit decisive victories to occur in wars between their clients (since this would mean that one superpower's influence would grow at the expense of the other's), nor dare they let such wars go on for very long. Even the best-armed of the nongreat powers are therefore not able to translate their military superiority into a satisfactory and lasting victory in their local disputes. Virtually the whole world has been absorbed into the great-power system willy-nilly—and that system, with its nuclear-centered strategy, is an even more extreme example of the way that military power is declining in usability even as it grows in destructiveness.

NOTES

1. Karl von Clausewitz, *On War*, New York: The Modern Library, 1943.

2. W. Baring Pemberton, *Lord Palmerston*, London: Collins, 1954, pp. 220–21.

3. Quincy Wright, *A Study of War*, Chicago: University of Chicago Press, 1964, p. 53.

4. Walter Laqueur, *Guerrilla*, London: Weidenfeld and Nicolson, 1977, p. 40.

5. Stanley Karnow, *Vietnam: A History*, New York: Viking, p. 312.

6. J. Bowyer Bell, *The Myth of the Guerrilla*, New York: Knopf, 1971, p. 231.

7. Robert Moss, *Urban Guerrillas*, London: Temple Smith, 1972, p. 198.

8. Ibid., p. 13.

9. Jacques Ellul, *Autopsy of Revolution*, New York: Knopf, 1971, p. 160.

The remains of the town of Ben Tre after it was saved. © *P. J. Griffiths/MAGNUM*

Costa Rica is the only independent state in the world without an army. This extraordinary man, José Figueres Ferrer, led rebels in deposing an unpopular dictator backed by the military—and abolished both armies when he won. *BLACK STAR*

Rural guerrilla warfare—raids from hills and jungles—on an indigenous government can be an infernal nuisance, but they can rarely drive the government out of the urban centers. If the guerrillas leave the hills they present a clear target; even if the populace rises up to join them, they lack an adequate strategy for final victory. They do, however, provide a strong element of romance. *Insurgents in Cambodia,* © *Al Rockoff*

Guerrillas don't need to worry about
winning wars against an imperial colonial power. All they have to do is keep
up the pressure, and in most cases the
foreigners will eventually decide to cut
their losses and go home. This helicop-
ter is loading last-minute evacuees as
the North Vietnamese take Saigon. *UPI/
Bettman Newsphotos*

The success of many rural guerrilla
movements of the fifties and sixties was
due to local resentment of foreign rule
far more than to ideology or Soviet and/
or Chinese expansionism. As a revolutionary method, it flourished only so
long as there were demoralized imperialist governments to oppose. A local
serves a member of the ruling class in
Vietnam's good old days. © *Al Rockoff*

FINDING THE PAIN THRESHOLD

Accepting losses as high as ten-to-one and enduring horrible suffering made it possible for the North Vietnamese and the Vietcong to exact the steady toll that would sap the American public's will to go on. Vietcong left in agony in the rain after being interrogated by South Vietnamese. © *P. J. Griffiths/MAGNUM*

Air Force Maj. Chester L. Brown directed air and artillery fire for hours into the houses of the village of Ben Tre, destroying 85 percent of it in order to "save it" from the Vietcong. *P. J. Griffiths/MAGNUM*

American calculations on how to defeat their Vietnamese opponents did not account for the ability of an intensely nationalistic and ruthlessly totalitarian regime like North Vietnam's to withstand pain. Even napalm, defoliation, and massive bombing of civilian targets did not stop the war. The Vietcong had nowhere else to go. A woman tries to bring some relief to her child dying of napalm burns. © *P. J. Griffiths/ MAGNUM*

It is not entirely impossible for rural guerrilla warfare to work against a locally based government, but it does require that the target government be extraordinarily iniquitous, incompetent, and politically isolated, like Somoza's. Here, Sandinistas return from a victorious battle in the Nicaraguan mountains in 1979. © *Susan Meiselas/MAGNUM*

The primary urban guerrilla tactic is to drive target regimes into extreme repression; they are often successful, creating thoroughly nasty and repressive military governments dedicated to destroying them. *Frondezi/BLACK STAR*

Israel: all the motives that can drive a state to war. Guerrilla and counterinsurgency tactics and defensive war in the 1940s, alliance war for strategic objectives in the 1950s, war of conquest in 1967, defense against a surprise attack in 1973, politically motivated limited strikes in 1978, 1980, and 1982. Here, happy Israeli warriors show off a captured Egyptian jeep in 1973—the year they almost lost. © *Micha Bar-Am/MAGNUM*

Even cold war can be brutalizing. That both Soviets and Americans can contemplate immolating each other by the millions without a tremor says a great deal about the power of rhetoric and propoganda. This World War II poster exorts the defense of German motherhood against a slavering, non-Aryan enemy. *Courtesy of the Department of Rare Books and Special Collections of the McGill University Library, Montreal/Photo by Marilyn Aiken*

Although Israel has "won" all of its wars, it still lives in an atmosphere of constant military threat from its Arab neighbors. Wars are not as effective at settling things as they once were. *Remains of an Egyptian soldier in the Sinai desert, 1967; Leonard Freed/MAGNUM*

Deliriously happy (and probably surprised) Sandinistas celebrating the Somoza overthrow. The real constraint on local wars—from guerrilla to hypothetical nuclear—is that neither superpower will permit the other side's clients to triumph in any very satisfying way, lest the balance be upset. © *Susan Meiselas/MAGNUM*

8: Keeping the Old Game Alive

Because of their capacity for large-scale slaughter, [nuclear weapons] may be able to cause such sudden and startling reversals of military fortune as to increase the uncertainty and irrationality that are always so pervasive in conflict situations. If we employ them on the enemy, we invite retaliation, shock, horror, and a cycle of retaliation with an end that is most difficult to foresee. . . . We are flung into a straitjacket of rationality, which prevents us from lashing out at the enemy.

Warfare must be returned to its traditional place as politics pursued by other means. We may not be able to create the refined distinctions that characterized the politics of the seventeenth and eighteenth centuries . . . but we may at least be able to approach the relatively compartmentalized pattern of the nineteenth century, and that itself would be a significant gain. Whatever the nature of the situation, we will . . . want to ensure our ability to go on playing the game. . . ."

William Kaufmann, RAND analyst, 1955[1]

The peace-at-any-price party would leave an unarmed Europe a prey to Russia."

Karl Marx, 1867

The United States and the Soviet Union have no common border, no claims on each other's territory, no history of national animosity—they are not even serious rivals for trade or resources—but their postwar confrontation was perfectly predictable (and widely predicted) as soon as the probable outcome of World War II became clear around 1943.

Our gravest error, in the late twentieth century, is to overestimate our distance and our difference from the past. We believe that the present round of competition between the great powers is different from all the others in history, that it is invested with special significance because of its ideological dimension and because of the appalling consequences if it were to lead to war (as all such competitions have eventually done in the past). We also believe—or at least we are told—that this conflict need not end in war precisely because of the nuclear weapons that make it so perilous: deterrence "has kept the peace for forty years."

The peoples of the East and West also have their special, selective mythologies to explain how the victorious alliance of forty years ago split into the competing power blocs of the present. The West remembers the continued presence of huge numbers of Soviet troops in Eastern Europe after 1945, the installation of loyal Communist regimes throughout the region, the Berlin Blockade, the brutal suppression of the Hungarian revolt, and hundreds of other Soviet offenses down to the occupation of Afghanistan and the installation of SS-20 missiles in Europe. The Soviet regime recalls the U.S. attempt to use its nuclear monopoly as a means of controlling Soviet policy, the construction of overseas bomber bases that virtually encircled the USSR, the British and American military aid that helped suppress the left in the Greek civil war, the rearming of West Germany by NATO, the Suez invasion, the arrogant American overflights of Soviet territory right up to 1960, and hundreds of other American offenses down to the U.S. support for right-wing "contras" fighting to overthrow the Nicaraguan government and President Reagan's "Star Wars" plans. Both bills of indictment are true, and both are essentially irrelevent.

Each side has an ideologically watertight explanation for why the adversary behaves with such persistent wickedness and aggression, but none of the post-1945 developments would seem surprising to a seventeenth-century Spanish or Ottoman diplomat.

Neither Communism nor liberal democracy would mean anything to him, other than as a useful label for the players (and even then, players like Tito and Franco would cause some confusion), but he would have no trouble understanding why the victorious alliance so quickly fell apart. They almost always do after victory, because the winners are the biggest players left on the board—hence they automatically become the greatest potential threats to each other's power.

Once contemporary military technology had been explained to him, an experienced diplomat from three centuries ago would easily understand why the Soviet Union kept such large ground forces in Central Europe after 1945. The U.S. had a complete monopoly of nuclear weapons, and the only possible (though not very convincing) counterthreat available to the Soviet Union was the maintenance of a capability to overrun Western Europe quickly with nonnuclear forces. He would find nothing unusual in the fact that almost all the countries liberated by the Soviet forces ended up with Communist regimes, while all those freed by Western armies got Western-style political systems—the Catholics and Protestants followed just the same policy throughout Central Europe during the Thirty Years' War of his own time. Indeed, the diplomatic time-traveler would soon realize that the late twentieth-century conflict between rival ideologies was actually not so different from the struggle between rival religions three centuries before. Most of the participants generally believed in their particular religious or political creed in both cases, and since the boundaries of the faith tended to coincide with those of the state or alliance they belonged to, it was easy for those who actually acted in terms of the imperatives of power to convince themselves and their followers that the conflict they were engaged in had profound moral implications as well.

Shared political or religious beliefs certainly make it easier for great powers to cooperate when their particular strategies in the game of international power make an alliance desirable, but there is no question about which comes first, strategy or ideology. The Catholic kingdom of France had no hesitation in making an alliance with the Muslim Turks of the Ottoman Empire against its Christian rivals in Europe when French strategic interests dictated that move during the 1500s, nor do the United States and the People's Republic of China find opposing ideologies any impediment to their growing strategic relationship today. Common ideology, on the other hand, failed to hold the Chinese and Soviet governments together when their national interests diverged.

The threat of another world war does not come from the fact that the great powers cloak their thoroughly traditional behavior with a screen of ideological cant. (Indeed, the situation would be far more dangerous if the rulers of East and West were really ideological crusaders willing to die for their faiths.) The threat comes from the fact that simply behaving in the traditional ways has always resulted, in the end, in a world war.

We normally count only the two great wars of our own century as "world wars," but what this phrase means in practice is a war in which all the great powers of the time are involved. By that criterion, there have been six world wars in modern history: the Thirty Years' War of 1618–48, the War of the Spanish Succession in

1702–14, the Seven Years' War of 1756–63, the Revolutionary and Napoleonic wars of 1791–1814, and the two world wars of 1914–18 and 1939–45.[2]

This is not just a catalogue of random disasters. The list has an alarmingly cyclical character. Apart from the long nineteenth-century gap, the great powers have all gone to war with each other about every fifty years throughout modern history.

Even the "long peace" of the last century is deceptive. Right on schedule, between 1854 and 1870, practically every great power fought one or several others: Britain, France, and Turkey against Russia; France and Italy against Austria; Germany against Austria; and then Germany against France. On several occasions it looked probable that one of these more restricted wars might expand to embrace all the great powers, but fortunately none of them lasted long enough (generally speaking, the longer a war between any two great powers lasts, the likelier it is to drag in the others). Instead, this anomalous series of smaller wars seems to have relieved the pressures for change that were building up within the international system and postponed the next world war for a further half-century.[3]

So why do the great powers all go to war about every fifty years? It is almost certainly because the most important international facts in any interwar period are determined by the peace treaty that ended the last war. Each world war reshuffles the pack, and the situation is then more or less frozen by the peace settlement; that is what fixes all the sensitive, disputed frontiers and allocates the various great powers their positions in the international pecking order.

At the instant it is signed, the peace settlement is generally an exact description of the true power relationships in the world. It is easily enforceable, because the beneficiaries have just beaten the losers in war. But as the decades of peace pass, some powers grow rapidly in strength and others face relative decline, so that after half a century or so the real power relationships in the world are very different from those prescribed by the last peace settlement. And it is at that point that some frustrated power whose allotted role in the international system is too confining, or some frightened nation in decline that sees its power slipping away, kicks over the apple cart and initiates the next reshuffle of the deck.

There is no magic in the figure of fifty years. That just seems to be how long it usually takes for the realities of power to become seriously out of kilter with the relations prescribed by the last peace settlement. That World War II came only twenty years after World War I seriously distorts our perception of the normal historical rhythm (and gives us a quite unwarranted confidence that we are doing better than earlier generations at avoiding a major war). But the unusually brief interval of peace after World War I is probably due mainly to the fact that it was the first total war, with the accompanying demand for unconditional surrender by the losers, and so the Treaty of Versailles in 1919, with its extreme terms, was a less accurate description of the real power relationships in the world than are most peace settlements: "Tremendous victories make bad peaces," as Guglielmo Ferrero remarked.

World War II ended in an equally tremendous victory, but the peace settlement has already lasted twice as long. This may be partly due to the inhibiting effect of nuclear weapons, but it can also be ascribed to the success of the big winners of the last world war, the two superpowers, in maintaining the highly satisfactory status quo (for them) that emerged in 1945. Indeed, their present alliances in Europe closely correspond to the furthest points reached by their troops in 1945, and their power continues to dwarf that of any potential rivals.

This entire line of argument is offensive to many people on both sides of the present confrontation, because it diminishes the importance of particular beliefs and loyalties that they hold dear. But if we are trapped in a historical pattern, then it would be best to recognize it.

This is not to say that all political systems are the same, or equally desirable, nor to pretend that Eastern Europe is as pleased with its fate since 1945 as Western Europe. Neither were the methods employed by the victorious superpowers to ensure the loyalty of the zones of Europe they liberated comparable: the Prague Coup of 1948 was far more offensive than the systematic and well-funded campaigns to isolate the large Communist parties of France and Italy and exclude them from any share of power in the early postwar years.

But it *is* to say that the Western powers pursued their interests just as single-mindedly as the Soviet Union during the early postwar years, and bear a significant share of the blame for the bitter confrontation that resulted. It is also, and more importantly, to say that there is really no point in allocating blame because the confrontation was virtually inevitable. That is how the international system works.

There is no way of telling whether we should count ourselves lucky because this interval between world wars has lasted so long compared to the last one, or whether we are back on the traditional fifty-year cycle and simply have not come into the danger zone yet. A historical cycle is not a natural law, but merely a pattern with a high probability of recurring. But I personally believe that the world just hasn't changed enough yet to make another world war probable.

It is easy to list the key changes that would violate or undermine the 1945 settlement in dangerous ways: the reunification of Germany, the rearmament of Japan to a level commensurate with its economic strength, or the relative economic decline of the Soviet Union to the point where it could no longer credibly sustain its role as a superpower and a guardian of the status quo. (The emergence of China as a genuine great power, rather than just a giant cripple, could be another.) There are clearly political and economic trends in the contemporary world that point in the direction of some, if not all, of these changes, but none of them has actually come to pass yet, so the principal risk at present remains that of involuntary world war.

I do not mean "accidental" war in the technical sense ("I *told* you not to touch that button"), but rather the kind of confrontation that escalates rapidly and un-expectedly out of some sudden crisis in a relatively peripheral area, with events moving faster than the decision makers can keep up. In other words, the Middle East, in the present decade, is a likelier place than Germany for World War III to start.

The potential for involuntary war between the great powers has grown greatly in the twentieth century (1914 is the classic case), because advancing technology and the planning reflex of the various general staffs have conspired to create ever more complex and sensitive war plans, with ever shorter warning times before something must be done. This applies most particularly in the realm of nuclear weapons—yet the speed with which national leaders can think things through and make rational decisions is unchanged since the time of the pharaohs. The two closest approaches to a superpower nuclear conflict in the past quarter-century, in Cuba in 1962 and in the Middle East in 1973, were both examples of how the world might blunder into an involuntary war.

Those who build, command, and man the nuclear delivery systems are convinced that deterrence now makes war between the great powers virtually inconceivable. (They could hardly believe otherwise and still sleep at night.) It is very much an act of faith, however. We have absolutely no proof that deterrence has ever prevented nuclear war, for nobody can demonstrate that such a war would already have occurred without it. If we are actually back on a fifty-year cycle, then deterrence has not even been seriously tested yet.

All the great powers give lip service to deterrence, but they continue to act on the unspoken assumption that history has not yet come to a stop and that the cycle of world wars may still have another (and probably final) round. They fear that an unexpected crisis somewhere could tumble them into an involuntary war at any time, and they know too that the fundamental pillars of the present international distribution of power, like the division of Germany and Soviet hegemony over Eastern Europe, are unlikely to last forever (though they are terrified of what might happen if those fundamentals begin to change). So the great powers still prepare for war despite all their theories of deterrence—and if the rules of the old political game have not actually changed despite the advent of nuclear weapons, then they would be wise to revive the rules of the old military game as well. So they reinvented conventional war, just in case.

If the bombardment [of London by V-bombs] really becomes a serious nuisance and great rockets with far-reaching and devastating effect fall on many centers. . . . I may certainly have to ask you to support me in using poison gas. We could drench the cities of the Ruhr and many other cities in Germany in such a way that most of the population would be requiring constant medical attention.

Winston Churchill to the Chiefs of Staff Committee, July 1944

The President observed that the quicker the operation [of using atomic bombs against China] was launched, the less the danger of Soviet intervention.

National Security Council minutes, May 1953

We know that since 1945 nineteen nuclear strikes have been considered in Washington—four against the Soviet Union.

Marshal Oleg A. Losik, Malinovsky Armored Forces Academy, Moscow, 1982

President Eisenhower's willingness to use nuclear weapons, if necessary, to break the stalemate in the Korean truce talks in 1953, like Churchill's expressed willingness to use poison gas (and anthrax germ warfare bombs) on Germany in 1944, was almost natural in an era already inured to the idea of total war. The fact that neither Churchill nor Eisenhower had to fear retaliation in kind also made it much easier for them to think in such terms. The doctrine was eventually formalized under the title of "massive retaliation": if the Russians attacked in Europe, there would be no preliminary shilly-shallying with conventionally equipped armies. The bombers of U.S. Strategic Air Command would simply destroy the Soviet Union with nuclear weapons.

The theory was that as soon as the other side established beyond a doubt that they were invading, you then let loose the American strategic arm and blasted, incinerated, irradiated enough of the people on the other side to make them stop what they were doing, whatever it was. Well, that was the raving of a feverish child, but I lost a lot of friends by saying this, particularly among the airmen. . . .

Gen. Sir John Hackett, former commander, NATO Northern Army Group

Massive retaliation flourished in its purest form in 1945–49, when the United States had a complete monopoly of nuclear weapons, but it continued to be the foundation of Western strategy well into the 1950s, even after the Soviet Union had begun to acquire a few bombs of its own (but little ability to deliver them to North American targets). It was the simplest, surest, most satisfying strategy imaginable— for the West, that is. For the Russians, it was a nightmare of impotence and dread.

Yet massive retaliation could never be more than a transient strategic phase, because technology never remains a single nation's monopoly for long. The rapid growth of a Soviet nuclear capability roughly comparable to that of the United States brought an end to the period when Washington actively considered nuclear strikes as a usable military tool (there have been no instances since the early 1960s), and eventually led to the adoption of a strategy of mutual deterrence, once crudely summed up in the phrase "Don't do that, or I'll kill us both!".

*There is no issue at stake in our political relations with the Soviet Union—
no hope, no fear, nothing to which we aspire, nothing we would like to
avoid—which could conceivably be worth a nuclear war.*

George Kennan, former U.S. ambassador to Moscow

In strict logical terms, the probability of a war between the United States and
the Soviet Union should have diminished to zero by the mid-1960s, since it was
obvious that both countries would effectively be destroyed in such a war. The generation of American strategic thinkers most ably represented by Robert McNamara,
secretary of defense in 1961–68, accepted the rise of the Soviet Union to a position
of "nuclear parity"—not that they had any choice in the matter—and sanctified the
resulting strategic impasse with the doctrine of "Mutual Assured Destruction."

That each side could believe it was now logically impossible for the other side
to plan a deliberate attack had a great deal to do with the end of the Cold War and
the opening of the era of détente. In the period 1967–75 there were a number of
Soviet-American and multilateral treaties that sought to codify the existing military
and political dispensation: such things as the Anti Ballistic Missile treaty, which
banned attempts to undermine the strategic nuclear stalemate, and the Helsinki
Final Agreement, which effectively recognized all the post-1945 borders of Europe.
The proportion of the U.S. federal budget devoted to military purposes fell from 49
percent to 23 percent between 1960 and 1980, and though no reliable comparable
figures are available for Soviet spending, the CIA's Office of Soviet Analysis has
estimated that Soviet expenditure on military hardware was almost flat from 1976
to 1983.

Yet it was in precisely this period, after 1960, that the West in particular
began to give serious attention to its nonnuclear forces in Europe. Indeed, both
sides devoted great effort to modernizing their conventionally armed troops along
the "Central Front" (the East-West German border) and elaborated theories for how
they might be used in circumstances short of all-out nuclear war.

*There is no such thing as a preplanned escalation which necessarily must
follow in steps, so that it would be first a conventional war and then a
nuclear war. This would be very much against our philosophy of flexible
response. Flexible response means that the enemy faces a completely incalculable risk. It might even be that we use nuclear weapons from the
outset. If the political decision is made for that, the military is prepared to
do it.*

Gen. Ferdinand von Senger und Etterlin, commander-in-chief,
Allied Forces Central Europe, 1982

The attempt by NATO to insert at least a brief period of nonnuclear warfare
at the beginning of a major war in Europe coincided with (and was largely caused
by) the achievement of rough parity in strategic nuclear weapons by the Soviet Union.
Indeed, agitation for a more flexible range of responses to a Soviet military challenge

in Central Europe began in the American defense community in the late 1950s, when the Soviet Union was just starting to acquire the ability to deliver a major nuclear blow against the American homeland. Once the United States itself was at risk, "massive retaliation" was no longer an acceptable doctrine. And although the doctrine of "flexible response" still contains a rhetorical element that threatens to employ nuclear weapons against the first Soviet reconnaissance platoon that crosses the border, its whole purpose is to enable the rival alliances to refight World War II for a while, using only conventional weapons, before they are really forced into fighting World War III. The old game must be kept alive, because the new game is not worth the candle.

Flexible response was already NATO policy in Europe by 1962 in practice, though it was not officially proclaimed until 1967. It has never been formally adopted by the Warsaw Pact, but it has been the dominant policy in the Soviet forces too since the early 1970s at the latest. Each side retains the option of moving up to the use of "battlefield" nuclear weapons (and the virtual annihilation of Central Europe), and on to the employment of "strategic" nuclear weapons (and the devastation of the entire Northern Hemisphere), but there would theoretically be at least an initial period—time for reflection and second thoughts, so to speak—in which the fighting would be merely "conventional."

However, the presence of substantial conventional military forces in Central Europe, and the creation and regular exercising of elaborate plans for how they would be used in the conventional phase of a war on the Central Front, have had the unfortunate but inevitable side effect of spawning a whole new constellation of anxieties on each side about the intentions of the other.

> *I believe that the Soviet Union has no intention of attacking Europe, with the elderly leadership which has known the last war, but they have the capability—and intentions can change very quickly. You may remember [Prime Minister Chamberlain coming back from Munich] waving a slip of paper: "Peace in our century, peace in our time"—and it was about ten months before the last world war started. So we must take capabilities into account.*   —Dr. Joseph Luns, NATO secretary-general, 1971–84

The members of the rival alliances do not stand to benefit in any practical way, economic, strategic, or emotional, from acquiring territory on the far side of the boundary between them (with the possible exception of the two Germanies), so there is no rational reason for either side to launch an offensive against the other. Even if one side managed to conquer a great deal of territory without becoming involved in a nuclear war, the principal result would be the reunification of Germany, which would be almost as unacceptable to Western Europeans as it is to the Russians. (As François Mauriac once remarked: "I love Germany so. Every day I thank God that there are two of them.") More important, it is unimaginable that change on that scale could be achieved by military means without triggering the use of nuclear weapons by the losing side, and in that case the costs of the war would quickly grow to outweigh any possible benefits by a thousandfold.

It is impossible to believe that sane leaders on either side would plan and execute a deliberate attack against the other in Europe, using either conventional weapons or a combination of those and tactical nuclear weapons. There is nothing to be gained by it. And yet the presence of large conventional forces on either side of the border, and their natural propensity to practice for the war they hope to avoid, succeed in creating the impression in the minds of each side's soldiers and politicians that the other side might well attack if they thought they could get away with it. We are all familiar in the West with the NATO version of this obsession, in which an avalanche of Soviet tanks will one day head west, quite unprovoked, for some unstated reason. It is inadequately understood in the West that there is a comparable fear of NATO's conventional forces in the Soviet Union.

I suppose what could give some concern to the Soviets are our capabilities in aviation. We, of course, have achieved these capabilities for very different reasons, but they automatically have an offensive capability. . . .

All our exercises in Central Europe assume a Soviet attack. In Soviet staff colleges, do they really run exercises in which NATO is on the offensive from the start?

That's exactly what they do: their scenarios, their equivalents to ours, always start with a NATO offensive, then after twenty-four hours or so they sort of turn this around and they start plodding through to the Rhine very quickly to counter this.

       Adm. Robert Falls, chairman of the NATO military committee, 1980–83.

For every nation at war, the enemy is invariably in the wrong and is therefore the real aggressor, regardless of whether one's own side happens to be employing offensive or defensive tactics at any given moment. At every level from platoon drills to national command exercises, Soviet military doctrine always assumes that NATO is the "aggressor"—indeed, the word is used interchangeably with *enemy* in Soviet military literature—even though Soviet conventional forces are clearly structured and deployed so as to take the offensive in Europe early in a war.

Soviet military doctrine has a defensive character. It foresees retaliation. We don't intend to capture foreign territories, but our good will doesn't mean that we will only defend ourselves from an aggressor. If attacked, we will retaliate with a devastating strike. We will crush the aggressor by a resolute offensive.

       —Gen. Rair Simonyan, Soviet army

NATO's posture is more ambiguous. Its soldiers, like those of the Soviet armed forces, have a profound professional aversion to fighting a purely defensive battle (in which the only alternatives are stalemate or defeat), and it too assumes that the other side will be the aggressor. But NATO's subsequent transition to a victorious offensive strategy (presuming such a thing to be possible) would take considerably longer than that envisaged by the Warsaw Pact. It would have to await the arrival of substantial American military reinforcements in Europe, so there would inevitably be a period of four to six weeks during which its existing forces on the ground would have to try to contain a Soviet offensive somewhere on West German territory.

NATO would not, in the meantime, make use of battlefield nuclear weapons unless the other side did it first, or unless the Soviet forces were about to gain a decisive breakthrough in the conventional fighting. Although the Soviets are far more reticent about how long they would try to keep a European war conventional, their public commitment to "no first use" of nuclear weapons would probably not be broken unless they found themselves in a similarly desperate military situation or felt that NATO was on the brink of going nuclear. (There is no military logic in a losing side deciding to initiate the use of battlefield nuclear weapons, since its forces, locked into their defensive positions, would be more vulnerable to such weapons than the highly mobile units of a successful attacker. But that doesn't matter, because the real signal conveyed by the decision to escalate to nuclear weapons is that the losing side is willing to blow up the world rather than accept defeat.)

In terms of how the professional soldiers on each side confirm to themselves that the other side has dangerous intentions, NATO's task is relatively simple. The NATO analysts simply count up the tanks, guns, and tactical aircraft available to the Warsaw Pact, find them more numerous than their own, and conclude (ignoring all the historical and political reasons for this imbalance) that the Soviet bloc forces have an aggressive, as well as an offensive, military posture. Soviet military officers have to make a slightly subtler argument to convince themselves of a U.S. policy of aggression, but the NATO doctrine known as "forward defense" suits their purposes adequately.

> *My mission is to defend the central region of Allied Command Europe as far forward as possible. That means immediately at the inner German border or the German-Czech border. And we will do that immediately there.*
>
> Gen. Ferdinand von Senger und Etterlin, commander-in-chief,
> Allied Forces Central Europe, 1982

NATO's greatest political problem in attempting to wage a conventional war in Europe is that all the territory it would have to give up "temporarily" while waiting for reinforcements to arrive from the United States is inhabited by West German voters, who take a dim view of any strategy that would make them refugees even temporarily. Since West Germany is also the country that provides the bulk of the soldiers who would have to withstand the initial shock of an attack and is the host country for all the others, West German political opinion cannot be ignored.

Geographically, the Federal Republic of Germany is a quite narrow country in the east-west direction: one third of its population and half its industry are located within 150 miles of the East German border. Conventional military wisdom would recommend a defense in depth as the only possible way to contain a Soviet attack—but that could well involve the loss of a third or more of the country's territory before the attack was eventually slowed down, soaked up, and halted. Losing all that territory, including major cities like Kiel, Hamburg, Hannover, and Nuremberg, is totally unacceptable to West Germany's political leaders, so they have always successfully insisted that NATO follow the alternative strategy, forward defense.

The doctrine of forward defense envisages almost all of NATO's ground forces in West Germany, when deployed in a crisis, lining up in a narrow band of territory just behind the frontier. It is a politically motivated strategy that is militarily senseless. The immediate border area would contain quite dense formations of NATO troops, but that is not what is required for a successful defense. Any moderately competent attacker would choose his points of attack, concentrate his forces there in an overwhelming local superiority, and break through NATO's shallow linear defense into the open country behind it before the defenders had time to shift forces to deal with the attacks.

Forward defense is a formula guaranteed to produce Soviet breakthroughs in any war in which the Warsaw Pact takes the offensive. And once the Soviet tank divisions have penetrated NATO's narrow defended zone, the only thing that could slow them down would be the twenty million-car traffic jam (as all of West Germany's population become motorized refugees)—or NATO nuclear weapons.

This prospect deeply offends Western army officers, who generally detest nuclear weapons (since they tend to make the soldier's profession irrelevant), and they have made constant attempts to deepen the defended zone even if it means sacrificing a bit more West German territory in the early stage of a war. The British army in the north, for example, now regularly drops back several dozen miles from the border in exercises before it even starts to fight seriously. But forward defense remains politically indispensable to West Germany, despite its implications of Soviet breakthrough and early nuclear use. Unfortunately, the fundamental illogic of this position leads Warsaw Pact observers of NATO's strategy to quite different conclusions about Western intentions.

The idea of this forward defense is to deploy NATO forces as close as possible to the Soviet frontier, so that in the case of necessity, they could act on our territory. This concept, this doctrine, this strategy, whatever it's called, is defensive in name only.
                                                    —Gen. Rair Simonyan, Soviet army

The people in the Kremlin are not stupid. They're quite logical in their thinking on these matters. We say we have no plans to . . . invade East Germany, and I believe I can say with perfect confidence that there are no such plans; they'd be dynamite. We have no such plans. "Very well," the

Russian planners would say, "but what provision have you made for defending in depth [in West Germany]?"

And when they look at this, they say, "How are we to believe your assertion that you've made no preparations to take the only other alternative [to invade East Germany], when you have made no preparations for defense in depth?
                                                          —Gen. Sir John Hackett

Professional military dissatisfaction with the forward defense concept and the emergence of new weapons technologies have recently combined to produce a new NATO policy that will confirm all the darkest suspicions of Warsaw Pact strategists. In December 1984, NATO formally approved the doctrine of Follow-On Forces Attack (FOFA), which envisages deep strikes into Warsaw Pact territory at the beginning of a war. As a senior NATO official explained it, "FOFA will provide NATO with something it has never had, defense in depth. In this case the depth will be behind the enemy's lines, not NATO's."

Follow-on forces are the large Soviet reserve formations that NATO expects will move west from the homeland after fighting commences on the East-West German border. They would arrive earlier than American reinforcements coming across the Atlantic and are generally expected to overwhelm NATO's shallow forward defenses— that is, if they have withstood the initial onslaught by the twenty-one Soviet divisions in Germany plus East Germany's own six divisions. New technologies that make it possible to launch pinpoint strikes deep behind enemy lines are now becoming available, which would allow NATO to attack these reinforcements on their way across Poland and East Germany, and it has adopted a policy of seeking to destroy Soviet follow-on forces up to 120 miles behind the front. (A further extension of this zone to over 300 miles is being advocated.)

The cruise and Pershing II missiles recently emplaced in Western Europe are part of this strategy, but much more sophisticated technologies are to follow. Targets on the move would be detected by electro-optical sensors carried by small remotely piloted aircraft, or by JSTARS (Joint Surveillance and Target Attack Radar System), a sideways-looking airborne radar able to locate moving tanks and other vehicles at a range of up to a hundred miles. These targets would then be attacked by highly accurate missiles carrying new conventional warheads that can destroy a key railway bridge several hundred miles away or dispense hundreds of bomblets that will annihilate everything in an area the size of several football fields.

In itself, FOFA is no more than an ambitious technological solution to a military problem that NATO previously proposed to deal with less effectively by interdiction with conventional aircraft, perhaps using nuclear weapons to compensate for their inability to strike small targets very accurately. As such, it would be unexceptionable—but it is well known to everybody that the origin of the concept is a broader tactical doctrine, jointly elaborated in 1980–82 by the U.S. and West German armies, known as Airland Battle 2000.

When I mentioned this doctrine to a senior Soviet general in 1983, he fulminated about NATO's aggressive intentions in high dudgeon for at least fifteen minutes, and it is easy to understand why. The U.S. Army itself explained the purpose of Airland Battle in the following terms: "What we seek is the capacity for early initiation of offensive action by air and land forces to bring about the conclusion of the battle on our terms. . . . The purpose of military operations cannot be simply to avert defeat but rather it must be to win." Airland Battle, unlike its publicly acknowledged offspring FOFA, envisages that after pumping firepower deep into Eastern Europe, NATO would follow it up with rapid offensives deep into enemy territory.

NATO does not now possess the technology to do what Airland Battle proposes, and in any case it is hardly more than what Soviet doctrine has always proposed for its own attack into Western Europe. Moreover, the American doctrine, like all its Soviet equivalents, presumes that the other side has brought this crushing offensive (or rather, "counteroffensive") down on its head by having the temerity to attack first. Neither Soviet nor American officers ever think of themselves as aggressors, but once a war has begun they all have the professional soldier's natural preference for being on the offensive and structure their war plans accordingly. And, of course, they then read the intelligence reports of each other's plans and are confirmed in their view of the other side as a potential aggressor.

I must confess that I would have structured this argument quite differently if I were addressing a Soviet audience, for they need no convincing that NATO appears aggressive. The great difficulty then would be persuading them that their own military forces appear threatening to the West—a daunting task in view of the fact that all Russians see their country as the eternal victim of foreign invasions and find it almost impossible to believe that other people genuinely fear a Soviet attack. For a Soviet audience, one would have to go far more deeply into how the Soviet army's tactical doctrines can appear aggressive to foreigners, and try to explain that NATO is not intending aggression despite *its* tactical doctrines. But very few people in the Soviet Union are ever going to read this book, so we may as well go on dealing mostly with Western perceptions and myths.

The balance of power in Central Europe has remained static since the early days of the Cold War. The Soviet Union now owns almost half the tanks in the world, and ever since 1945 it has kept a very large number of them in Central Europe, pointing west, but there are two reasonably convincing reasons for that. One is that the Russians had just been through the worst land war in history, which began with an invasion from the West and destroyed the lives of many millions of their people, and so they were and are determined that if there should be another war, this time it will be fought on the other side's territory.

This is basically silly, since all the tanks in the world could not protect Soviet territory from being devastated by nuclear weapons, which are what really threatens it today. However, during the late forties and fifties, when the Russians already faced an American nuclear threat but had no credible way of making a comparable threat against U.S. territory, a crushing preponderance in conventional weapons and an ability to overrun Western Europe rapidly were the only available Soviet counter-weights to American nuclear superiority. Although Moscow's achievement of effective nuclear parity with Washington during the 1970s has now robbed this second justification of any meaning, the tanks are still there.

It would be equally instructive, however, to inquire why the NATO forces in Europe do not have as many tanks, aircraft, and the like. The NATO nations, after all, contain over 250 million more people than the Warsaw Pact countries, they have economies that are at least twice as rich in total, and they do not, like Moscow, have to worry about other major enemies like China. So how do the NATO forces come to find themselves outnumbered and outgunned on the Central Front in Europe?

There are a couple of obvious factors. Around 40 percent of NATO's population and resources lie on the far side of the Atlantic, in the United States and Canada, which makes it more difficult and expensive for them to deploy military power in Europe. Moreover, NATO planners habitually discount a certain proportion of Warsaw Pact forces as being committed to internal security duties in Eastern Europe. The Soviets have had to use massive military force repeatedly in the capitals of their allies in peacetime, and the diversion of Soviet forces to such tasks might be even greater at a time of impending war, whereas it is inconceivable that U.S. forces might ever be used in the streets of a Western European capital. But more important than all this is the fact that NATO, despite all the facts, still secretly believes in nuclear weapons.

That is to say that it once believed in " massive retaliation," which cheerfully left the expense and burden of supporting huge conventional armed forces to the Russians and relied on Western nuclear superiority to counterbalance it—and even now, when Soviet nuclear forces are fully comparable to those of NATO, that old Western willingness to depend on nuclear armaments and to accept a Soviet supe-riority in the number of conventional weapons has never vanished. There has been considerable growth in Western conventional armaments over the years, of course, and the disparities between East and West are by no means as alarming as some propaganda sources suggest, but there *is* a conventional imbalance.[4] What it rep-resents, however, is merely tradition and inertia: the old Soviet delusion that tanks can solve the problem, and the old Western delusion that nuclear weapons can.

> *I already know on Thursday evening if there is going to be a war at the weekend. It really doesn't bother me in the least that the soldiers go home on Friday.*
> —Gen. Wolfgang Altenburg, 1985

The fact that the West German armed forces commander rules out the pos-sibility of a Soviet surprise attack on a Saturday or Sunday, and regularly gives the majority of West Germany's half-million servicemen the weekend off, says more about the real military assessment of the danger of war in Central Europe than all the propaganda about force levels and "military build ups" purveyed by both sides. It is extremely doubtful that either side has ever seriously contemplated attacking the other in Central Europe for so much as a single day since 1945—nor even seriously believed that the other side was really going to attack. If they had, they would have invested a great deal more in increasing and rationalizing their conventional military capabilities there. As it is, West Germany, with twenty times Israel's population, feels impelled to own only the same number of tanks.

This is, in my view, a reasonably accurate reflection of the respective probabilities that the West German and Israeli governments assign to the likelihood of a war on their frontiers. I also believe that the West Germans are right; since we are not yet in the danger zone, there is no pressing reason for any of the major powers to risk a war at the moment. But the danger of an involuntary war arising out of some unexpected and mismanaged crisis elsewhere is always there, and European history has not come to a halt forever, so it is worth considering just what would happen if NATO and the Warsaw Pact stumbled into a conventional war in Europe.

Q. What is the difference between a Soviet dwarf and an American dwarf?

A. Soviet dwarfs are taller.
—*Czechoslovak joke*

When you utter the word conventional, *you utter the word* expensive.
George Schultz, U.S. secretary of state

The most striking fact about conventional military forces in the latter part of the twentieth century is that the armies have become small again. If war were to come to Europe tomorrow, the NATO commander on the Central Front, between the north German coast and Switzerland, would have approximately a million men and two thousand combat aircraft under his command, and his Soviet counterpart would have roughly comparable forces at his disposal. These are certainly larger mechanized armies than can be found anywhere else in the world—at least half the world's advanced conventional weaponry is concentrated on this small area—and the forces of both sides would receive substantial reinforcements in the first weeks of a war. But loss rates would be so high that neither side's front-line troops would be likely to exceed their initial numbers at any point in the proceedings. And though million-man armies are nothing to be sneered at, they do not remotely compare with the forces that the great powers deployed during either of the world wars of this century.

This drastic shrinkage in the scale of conventional military forces available for service in Europe has something to do with the fact that nuclear weapons have supplanted them as the ultimate arbiter of war, but the principal reason is simpler. Conventionally armed military forces have grown so expensive that most nations cannot justify maintaining very large forces in peacetime—and the production rates for modern military equipment are so slow that there is little chance that they would be able to expand significantly after a war had begun. On the contrary, both sides would immediately start losing their major weapons systems like tanks and aircraft at a rate they could not hope to replace.

It used to be you could send up hundreds of aircraft, and they weren't too successful in combat: nobody shot too many people down. Whereas now the lethal rate is very, very high, so consequently the war probably won't last very long. . . . You'll have to fight with what you have right now, and the war will go at such a pace that it will be difficult to use your industrial capacity to replace airplanes lost on the battlefield because the lead time to produce that airplane may be longer than the war lasts. It's a very difficult situation, in that you want a sophisticated airplane that will do a lot of roles, but you need quite a few of them because that's what you're going to fight with—and they come very expensive.

Jack Krings, flight operations head, McDonnell-Douglas Corp.

The F-15 Eagle, the U.S. Air Force's current first-line fighter, is a case in point. It takes about eighteen months to build an F-15, and it costs $42.5 million per copy, the cost being mainly a reflection of the tens of thousands of man-hours of highly skilled labor that go into building it. It is an extraordinarily impressive and lethal machine—but it is also very scarce.[5]

The increase in the cost of weapons over the past half-century has been staggering. The Spitfire, probably the best fighter in the world in 1939, cost £5,000 to build, or £98,000 at today's prices. Its current equivalent, the air defense version of the Tornado, which is just now entering service with the Royal Air Force, costs £17 million: it is 172 times more expensive *after* allowing for inflation. And since no country is 172 times richer than it was at the beginning of World War II, the result is that far fewer weapons can be built. Approximately the same amount of factory space is devoted to the construction of military aircraft in the United States today as was devoted to the same purpose in Germany during World War II. But whereas in 1944 Germany was building three thousand planes a month (and losing them at about the same rate), current American production is about fifty aircraft a month.

The present generation of fighters is, of course, enormously better than those of World War II. They can fly three times as fast and carry five or six times the weight of munitions; they can detect and attack an opponent at ten times the distance— and they are much more likely to destroy that opponent, because their weapons are far more accurate and lethal. But that simply makes the problem worse: not only can air forces afford fewer aircraft, but they are going to lose them at a faster rate.

This phenomenon is not confined to military aircraft, though they are the most extreme case. All military technology today, from tanks and warships to communications equipment and antiaircraft guns, has undergone the same transformation. It has become so expensive that the number of items bought must be severely curtailed, and at the same time the weapons have become so lethal that loss rates in battle are dramatically higher.

The consequence is that no nation today, not even the richest, can afford to equip mass armies in the old style with modern weapons, unless it mobilizes its entire economy for military production and keeps it that way for a long time. (Israel has accomplished that feat, but it has spent around 30 percent of its GNP on defense for a quarter-century, has received vast amounts of aid from outside as well, and is bankrupt in the bargain.) In the major industrialized nations of both power blocs— which are, after all, at peace—nothing of the sort has been attempted. NATO and the Warsaw Pact together, with a combined population of almost a billion people, have enough first-line conventional military weapons to equip fewer than ten million men: under 1 percent of their population.

Moreover, they have not been able to afford to build up "war stocks" of military equipment to allow for the extremely high consumption rates that will inevitably occur. For thirty years NATO has been striving unsuccessfully to increase its reserves of conventional ammunition—artillery shells, antitank missiles and the like—from a fifteen-day supply to a thirty-day supply. As for the large and vital elements of weaponry like tanks and aircraft, there is absolutely no way that production facilities could be expanded fast enough to keep up with losses in a European war, let alone to equip additional forces. It is entirely likely that the major combatants in a European conventional war today would lose as many tanks and combat aircraft each day as they can produce each month (if not more). The problem of attrition will be paramount.

We started out with eleven tanks . . . and we lost five in the space of thirty minutes.

Q. Is that normal?

A. It will be if they come at us. We had about three combat teams come at us then, that's about thirty or forty tanks, and that would be normal—half our force would be knocked out. . . . Normally we would be expected to last in a tank battle about two hours.

British tank commander, NATO exercises, West Germany

In the Middle East war of 1973, probably the closest equivalent in recent experience to a conventional war in Europe in style and scale (though most of the weaponry used there would now be one and a half generations out of date), both the Arabs and the Israelis lost close to half their total stock of tanks in less than three weeks of heavy fighting. Loss rates in all major items of weaponry in a European war in the 1980s would probably be even higher. It is not unreasonable to talk in terms of a thousand tanks and several hundred aircraft being destroyed in each day of heavy fighting—and in this case, unlike the Middle East, there would be no outside source of supply to which the combatants could turn for replacements. It would, as an American aircraft manufacturer remarked, be a "come as you are" war. The weapons that had already been built on the first day of the war would be the only ones available, and once they were destroyed, that would be it for the kind of conventional war everybody expects to fight.

What you might have, if there were a clash of conventional forces in Europe, is an extraordinarily short burst of mutual wiping out of first-line equipment, leaving the armies dependent on quite simple weapons—a return to an earlier phase of warfare. We had that in 1914: all the sides had gone to war with stocks quite inadequate for the scale of the fighting that took place, and there was then the famous "winter pause" which was partly to lick their wounds . . . and very much to gear up the shell factories. Because the inventory of weapons is so much larger in the 1980s it would be a pause for the replacement of almost everything: tanks, aircraft, missiles, missile launchers, armored vehicles of all sorts. . . .

John Keegan, Royal Military Academy, Sandhurst

It could just conceivably come to that, if we were very lucky: both sides running out of equipment more or less simultaneously, at around the third or fourth week of the war, and simply digging in while the factories geared up and the governments had a chance to consider whether they really wanted to go on with it. But it's about as likely as tossing a coin and having it land on its edge. Even if the commanders on both sides handled their forces equally well or equally poorly, so that neither army achieved a major strategic victory, the sheer diversity and complexity of the technologies in use would make it very probable that one side would run out of some key weapon before the other.

It is now over forty years since anybody has fought a big conventional war, and though numerous bits of the changing weapons technologies have been tried out in smaller wars like those between India and Pakistan, Iran and Iraq, or Britain and Argentina; nobody really knows what would happen if all these weapons were used in large numbers, in combination with each other, in a European environment. The generals are well aware (in private) that our assumptions about the course of a European conventional war are a house of cards; it's quite an elaborate house, but the cards that make it up are no more than a series of educated guesses as to how the technology would work out in practice.

What happens when you have an antitank missile which, if it strikes an enemy tank, has a 100 percent probability of disabling or destroying that tank, but in which the system for aiming and firing the missile is really only capable of being used by someone with an IQ of over 100—whereas most of the people in forward combat units in your army have an IQ of about 85 or 90, and the smart ones have a lot of other jobs to do?

Tom Tulenko, military analyst, Historical Evaluation and Research Organization, Washington, D.C.

There are imponderables all over the map. For example, at most times and in most places, relatively marginal differences in aircraft performance and pilot training have resulted in hugely disproportionate losses between the two sides in aerial combat: kill ratios of three-to-one, five-to-one, even ten-to-one are by no means unusual in air warfare. All recent evidence suggests that Western aircraft would enjoy at least some advantage over their Warsaw Pact opponents in individual combat, but what would be the position of Soviet ground forces if the kill ratio in the air turned out to be very heavily in the West's favor? And all this is not even to mention the more exotic forms of "conventional" weapons.

> *The U.S. Army has developed a weapons system that sweeps low-energy laser beams across a battlefield to blind enemy soldiers up to a mile away. It also neutralizes machine optical systems such as tank periscopes. . . . Colonel Edwin Beatrice, head of the Division of Ocular Hazards at the Army's Letterman Research Institute in San Francisco, said that when the laser hits the eye there is a "vitreal haemorrhage" and the eye is filled with blood. Blindness was irreversible.*
>
> London Times, *19 December 1983*

> *I think a battlefield would change very significantly with the use of chemicals. You would slow everything down tremendously. People can only work about a third as much in a day in their chemical protective suits as without them. That is one real reason for us having a retaliation capability. If we are the ones that are slowed down and the Soviets are not, you are going to imbalance the battlefield even further than it is today.*
>
> *Amoretta Hoeber, principal deputy and deputy assistant secretary for research, development and acquisition, U.S. Army, Washington, D.C.*

By the time things like nerve gas come into play (which could be quite early in the battle), it is questionable whether a European war could still be called conventional in any meaningful sense. It certainly wouldn't be for the civilians, who lack gas masks and protective clothing and could be expected to die in huge numbers if gas were widely used in populated areas (the Soviet stockpile of chemical agents is estimated at over 300,000 tons, and the U.S. stock at 270,000 tons). But even for the soldiers, encased in layers of clumsy protective clothing and mostly confined to their vehicles, the key question might become one of physical and psychological endurance.

Almost all the troops on both sides of the Central Front are now mounted in vehicles of one sort or another, and it is the machines that set the pace. The prevailing concept of "continuous operations" presumes the ability of human beings to go without sleep or rest, to wear extremely uncomfortable clothing, to tolerate tremendously high heat and noise levels inside their vehicles for very long periods, and to go on fighting day and night in extremely lethal conditions without breaking down. It seems unlikely that they would actually be able to continue fighting for more than a few days in such a situation before their general level of efficiency and alertness became gravely impaired—and that is even before nuclear weapons come into play.

Nobody has fought, ever, in a nuclear environment. . . . We think that in our prepared positions and in our armored vehicles, which maintain a nuclear, biological, and chemically free environment within them through filters, that we could do pretty well in a nuclear environment, but it's all conjecture from both sides.

Col. Roderick Jones, Queen's Royal Irish Hussars, British Army of the Rhine

It scarcely matters which strategies and which pieces of technology work more or less as planned, which succeed beyond expectation, and which unexpectedly fail to work at all. The essential point is that a conventional war in Europe would probably move very fast toward a crisis in which one side or the other was facing defeat or total military breakdown, though it is far from certain which side that would be. But once one side starts to lose badly, the next step is the introduction of tactical nuclear weapons into the battle.

In the last war we didn't use nuclear weapons, because we didn't have them. Now we do, and no side will accept defeat before it uses all the weapons it has. —Gen. Rair Simonyan, Soviet army

Much of the NATO war-fighting written material defines the sorts of levels of loss where we would be inclined to consider using nuclear weapons. The Soviets would tend to expect it at that point and would want to use theirs first.

Q. So if they're losing they'll nuke us, and if we lose we still get them used on us?

A. I believe that even if we lose [conventionally], we get them used on us. Perhaps even sooner if we were losing fast, because they expected a Western use at that point. —Francis Hoeber, member of the U.S. Arms Control General Advisory Committee, Washington, D.C.

We've turned Central Europe into a kind of game park where we're trying to preserve an endangered species—conventional war—because we're desperately trying to stave off the alternative: a return to total war. *Nuclear* total war, this time.

The problem is that this distinction we have created between conventional and nuclear war is, in the end, an artificial distinction, and probably a pretty flimsy one. If either side started to win a conventional war, the other would bring out its nuclear weapons. A stalemate would also bring strong pressures for escalation. Win, lose, or draw, conventional war in Europe leads toward nuclear war, probably in a matter of only a couple of weeks. At heart, the whole concept of "flexible response" that makes a conventional war possible at all is only a drawn-out version of the deadly old 1950s strategy of "massive retaliation." The only differences are that the conventional tripwire is now expected to go on resisting a Soviet attack for a little longer—and that the nuclear massive retaliation will travel in both directions.

The doctrine does attempt to interpose a phase of "theater nuclear war," restricted to the Central European region and to battlefield nuclear weapons, between the point at which conventional defense fails and the final escalation to strategic nuclear weapons fired at the homelands of all the great powers. About six thousand of the twenty-five thousand American nuclear weapons are relatively low-yield devices kept in Western Europe, and the Soviet Union keeps a somewhat smaller number of tactical nuclear warheads in Eastern Europe. Nor would they necessarily use all of these weapons at once.

If it were NATO that was losing, the Supreme Allied Commander Europe would probably begin by requesting political permission from NATO and the White House for the release of one or more "packages" of nuclear weapons for use on defined areas of the front where collapse was imminent or had already occurred. A typical package, as defined by U.S. Army Field Manual F 100-5, would consist of two atomic demolition land mines, thirty rounds of W48 warheads (plutonium fission, yield: under 1 kiloton) and W33 warheads (enriched uranium, variable yield up to 10 kilotons) for 155mm and 8-inch artillery shells, ten Lance or Pershing surface-to-surface missiles for deeper nuclear strikes, and five B-43 air-delivered bombs (yield: between 500 and 1,000 kilotons). A modest start: forty-seven nuclear explosions in the vicinity of the Fulda Gap, say, with a total yield of around 3,000 kilotons.[6] (The Hiroshima bomb, for purposes of comparison, was under 20 kilotons.)

There is no point in pursuing the military logic of a limited nuclear war in Central Europe any further. Whichever side initiated the use of tactical nuclear weapons, the other would immediately have to respond in kind or lose the war, and within a few days several thousand nuclear weapons would probably be exploded over Germany. This would almost certainly result in the virtual extermination of both armies and the decimation of the German nation—but it probably wouldn't stop there.

> *It has always frightened me to death, ever since I was to command a division in Germany in the late fifties and the nuclear weapon appeared for the first time as a cotton-wool cloud on the sand table. The assumption that you can control a nuclear war is pure fantasy. From the moment the nuclear weapon is released on the European battlefield, you open Pandora's box and you don't know what's coming out. But one thing you can count on is that there will be a very high probability of early and steep escalation into the strategic all-out exchange that nobody wants. So you mustn't use the things.*
> —Gen. Sir John Hackett

In Wintex '83, NATO's annual command and staff exercise conducted in early 1983, the Warsaw Pact forces crossed the border into West Germany on 3 March. On 8 March, NATO's commanders requested nuclear release, and the first nuclear strike against the Warsaw Pact was ordered on 9 March. The conventional war lasted six days.

NOTES

1. Kaufmann's 1955 essays were very influential in shaping the United States army's thinking on the possibility of restricting war in Europe to conventional weapons. Fred Kaplan, *The Wizards of Armageddon*, New York: Knopf, 1984, pp. 197–200.

2. Though all of these wars except the first have involved fighting in almost every continent, that has nothing to do with my description of them as "world wars." What makes them significant is the fact that they involved *all* the great powers, and had a climactic character about them.

    It is true that the War of the Spanish Succession and the Seven Years' War stand out less prominently from the other wars of their era than the other four "world wars" on my list, though they were certainly the largest wars of their respective periods. The late seventeenth and eighteenth centuries were a time when the dynasties of Europe engaged in almost perpetual limited wars among themselves, so the level of "background noise," so to speak, is much higher.

    Nevertheless, I believe that both these wars qualify for inclusion as "world wars" not only on the grounds of their all-embracing cast of participants, but also because they each represented the culmination and comprehensive settlement of a long and disparate list of preceding lesser wars and disputes between the great powers. They were, in a sense, about *everything*: the Seven Years' War, for example, decided not only the ownership of Silesia but also of Quebec and India. Most significantly, contemporary observers themselves regarded these wars as having "settled" things conclusively, and having defined the relative status of the great powers in the ensuing period of comparative peace—which is precisely the function of "world wars" in the present international system.

3. I am conscious of the danger of bending history to fit my hypothesis, but the mid-nineteenth century wars did bring about changes in the international distribution of power of a scope comparable to that generally accomplished by world wars. A united Italy and a powerful German empire emerged in the heart of Europe, while the relative decline of Austria was confirmed and France irrevocably lost its previous position as the greatest continental power.

    The great power system, having thus been adjusted to take account of the new realities of power which had been created by the preceding half-century of differential rates of population and industrial growth in various parts of Europe, then settled into a long period of peace. The Treaty of Frankfurt in 1871, like the Congress of Vienna in 1815, was followed by four decades in which no European great powers fought each other.

4. NATO's own figures for 1983 suggested that in the early phase of a European war the Warsaw Pact would have a 2-to-1 superiority in tanks and 1.5-to-1 in men (the latter narrowing to 1.3-to-1 on full reinforcement). *NATO and the Warsaw Pact: Force Comparisons*, Brussels: NATO Information Service, 1983.

5. Edward N. Luttwak, *The Pentagon and the Art of War*, New York: Institute of Contemporary Studies/Simon & Schuster, 1984, p. 175.

6. A recent World Health Organization study calculated that the use of twenty megatons (twenty thousand kilotons) of nuclear weapons on military targets in Central Europe would kill or seriously injure nine million people and cause less serious injuries to another nine million. Twenty megatons, however, is only a very small fraction of the total battlefield nuclear weapons available to the two sides in Central Europe. *Effects of Nuclear War on Health and Health Services*, Geneva: World Health Organization, 1984.

British soldiers blinded and permanently crippled by a 1915 gas attack. This kind of offensive weapon is only useful if you're sure the other side can't do it back. "Massive Retaliation," for example, became highly implausible once both sides had plentiful nuclear weapons. *Ullstein Bilderdienst*

Marshal Ivan Konev, Commander of the First Ukrainian Front in the final offensive against the Nazis. There is no disputed border and no history of national animosity or economic rivalry between the Soviet Union and the United States. Yet, the two largest powers involved in World War II emerged as rivals and "enemies" as soon as the probable outcome became clear, a situation any seventeenth-century diplomat could have predicted. *SOVFOTO*

The line further from the East German border
marks the minimum depth required to make
NATO defense effective. The closer line marks
actual NATO positions, their "forward defense"
policy. This impossibly shallow defended zone
makes perfect political sense to West Germans,
who do not wish their country to be used as the
battlefield for World War III, but it looks an awful
lot like offense from the other side. *Courtesy of
the National Film Board of Canada*

WHEN YOU SAY CONVENTIONAL, YOU SAY EXPENSIVE

The F-15 Eagle, the U.S. Air Force's current first-line fighter plane, takes eighteen months to build and costs $42 million. © *Herman Kokojan/MAGNUM*

The F-16, now being snapped up by Israel. Modern fighters are much more accurate and lethal than previous planes, and are therefore more likely to be destroyed. © *Steve Northrup/BLACK STAR*

The latest in U.S. armored personnel carriers, costing a half million dollars each, invading Grenada. Tanks run anywhere from $2 million to $3 million. © *P. J. Griffiths/ MAGNUM*

What happens when you have an anti-tank gun with a 100 percent kill probability if it strikes its target, but it has to be aimed and fired by someone with an IQ of over 100, and most of the men in the forward combat units have IQs of 85 or 90? In other words, when does the fancy equipment get beyond practical control? *Two soldiers with a "Tube- Launched Optically-Sighted Wire-Guided Anti-Tank Weapon;"* © *David Doody/BLACK STAR*

The use of nerve gas would kill civilians—who wouldn't have the masks and special outfits pictured here—by the millions. But even the soldiers' ability to withstand chemical attack encased in all this gear or in special vehicles is completely unpredictable. *Soldiers in chemical warfare gear;* © *Herman Kokojan/BLACK STAR*

The belief that nuclear-armed powers can fight a conventional war is a severe case of cultural lag, but that sort of thing is quite common. An illustration from a seventeenth-century manuscript purports to show how a mounted knight could still pick off an arquebusier with his lance before the latter's bullet could plug his horse. *From L'Art Militaire à Cheval by Johann Joacobi Wallhausen; Courtesy of the Royal Military College Library, Kingston, Ontario/Photo by Marilyn Aiken*

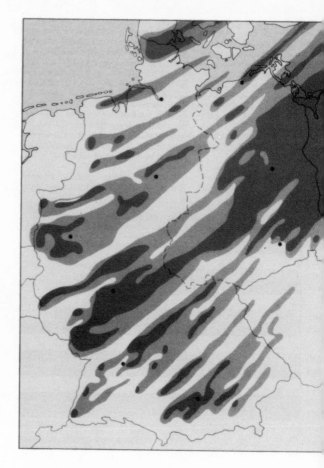

Pattern of radioactive fallout resulting from a hypothetical "limited" nuclear war confined to targets in East and West Germany, according to the wind and weather conditions of a typical June day in central Europe. The attacks here would amount to about 30,000 kilotons. The light-gray areas show between 200 and 600 rads, the dark areas more than 600 rads. Deaths from radiation sickness begin at less than 200 rads. The illustration is based on a study by William Arkin, Frank von Hippel, and Barbara G. Levi originally appearing in *Ambio*, a publication of the Royal Swedish Academy of Sciences. *Reprinted from "No First Use" of Nuclear Weapons by Kurt Gottfried, Henry W. Kendall and John M. Lee. Copyright © March 1984 by Scientific American, Inc. All rights reserved.*

9: Notes on Nuclear War I: Running on Empty

If one goes to strategic nuclear war, it is unlikely that there will continue to be a need for tactical operations by troops on the battlefield. There is, however, the concept of the so-called broken-back war, which can't be ignored. It is possible that the two sides could cause each other serious damage, almost impossible damage, and yet neither is willing to give in to the other. . . . The strategic exchange would use up all or most of the missiles that they have, and then somehow or other this broken-back war—which would probably be closer to wars of the Middle Ages than more modern war—could continue.   —Col. T. N. Dupuy, U.S. Army, ret'd.

$\mathbf{A}$s late as 1982, it was perfectly logical (if not entirely sensible) for strategic analysts to talk like that. Few of those who had experienced actual war took pleasure in such speculations, but they felt it was their duty to "think about the unthinkable," as one of them put it. Even though the amount of destructive power available to the industrialized countries had grown utterly disproportionate to any political ends they might seek, war remained a possibility, so somehow that destructive power had to be forced into the mold of traditional military thought. They did what they had to do, and we all reluctantly pretended that the results made some kind of sense—and we were all wrong.

We have, by slow and imperceptible steps, been constructing a Doomsday Machine. Until recently—and then, only by accident—no one even noticed. And we have distributed its triggers all over the Northern Hemisphere. Every American and Soviet leader since 1945 has made critical decisions regarding nuclear war in total ignorance of the climatic catastrophe.

Carl Sagan[1]

At the time of the Cuban missile crisis in 1962, President Kennedy controlled over six thousand nuclear weapons, many of them of even greater explosive power than those the United States deploys today; General Secretary Khrushchev probably had in the vicinity of eight hundred nuclear bombs and warheads under his command. For two weeks they hovered on the brink of nuclear war, acutely conscious that a single false step could condemn tens of millions of their countrymen to death. But they had absolutely no inkling that the use of those weapons might precipitate a global catastrophe resulting in the end of mankind. One wonders if they would have run quite the same risks if they had known the true potential consequences.

There is no point in rehearsing the familiar horrors of nuclear war. They have been dwelt on by the media over the years to the point where they induce only numb indifference in the mass of the population, and they are discounted in advance by governments as part of the price that may have to be paid for continuing to do business in the old ways. In any case there are not, to be crude, all that many ways to die, and apart from radiation sickness there are not many agonies that could befall the residents of a city hit by nuclear weapons that have not been experienced already by those who were caught in the Hamburg firestorm. The number of victims would be hundreds of times greater, but people have a very high tolerance for disasters that remain only potential.

Over the past few years, however, it has gradually been realized that for at least the past twenty-five years we have been living under the permanent threat of a "nuclear winter." We have added ICBMs and submarine-launched missiles to our bomber fleets, then MIRVed the missiles and added cruise missiles; we have gone from "tripwire and massive retaliation" to flexible response and Mutual Assured Destruction, and moved on to "limited nuclear war." The political leaders, the generals, the scientists, and the strategic theorists all swore that they knew what they were doing—and all the time they were ignorant of the fact that to use *any* of those weapons and *any* of those doctrines in the ways they envisaged would probably plunge the entire planet into an almost limitless ecological disaster.

The discovery of what a nuclear war would really do to our planet began in 1971, when a small group of planetologists who had gathered to analyze the results of the Mariner 9 observations of Mars found, to their intense frustration, that the entire planet was covered by an immense dust storm, which lasted three months. With nothing better to do, they set about calculating how such a long-lasting dust cloud would alter conditions on the Martian surface. They concluded that it would lower the ground temperature drastically.

Intrigued, they then examined meteorological records here on earth to see if the relatively small amounts of dust boosted into the upper atmosphere by exploding volcanoes produced similar effects. They found that every time a major volcano has gone off over the past few centuries, there has been a small but definite drop in the global temperature, lasting a year or more. They went on to examine the prehistoric climatic catastrophes that may have been caused by stray asteroids colliding with the earth and blasting vast quantities of dust into the atmosphere (such a collision is now suspected of having been responsible for the extinction of the dinosaurs sixty-five million years ago).[2]

In early 1982 the informal group of scientists saw an advance copy of a paper written by two scientists working at the Max Planck Institute for Chemistry in West Germany that calculated that massive forest fires ignited by nuclear blasts would inject several hundred million tons of smoke into the atmosphere in a nuclear war, and that the smoke "would strongly restrict the penetration of sunlight to the earth's surface." That paper had not even considered the smoke from burning cities and the dust from groundbursts, but the American group saw the significance at once. In 1983 they published their results.

A major nuclear exchange, they concluded, would cover at least the Northern Hemisphere, and perhaps the entire planet, with a pall of smoke and dust that would plunge the surface into virtual darkness for up to six months and cause a drop of up to 40 degrees centigrade (104 degrees Fahrenheit) in the continental interiors (which would be far below the freezing point in any season) for a similar period. And when enough of the dust and soot particles had drifted down out of the stratosphere to let the sun's light back in, the destruction of the ozone layer by thermonuclear fireballs would allow two or three times as much of the harmful portion of its ultraviolet spectrum to reach the surface. This could cause lethal sunburn in exposed human beings in less than half an hour and would cause blindness in a short time. However, added the scientists comfortingly, "we have tentatively concluded that a nuclear war is not likely to be followed by an ice age."[3]

We had grown almost inured to what we thought would be the consequences of a nuclear war: at least several hundred million dead in the NATO and Warsaw Pact countries, plus the destruction of most of the world's industry and the artistic, scientific, and architectural heritage of mankind. We were resigned to the fact that fallout and the disruption of the existing technological infrastructure would damage Northern Hemisphere agriculture to the point where hundreds of millions more would probably succumb to famine and disease in the aftermath. But even the most drastic estimates, like that made by the World Health Organization in 1984, assumed that an all-out nuclear war in which ten thousand megatons were exploded (90 percent in the Northern Hemisphere, the rest elsewhere) would only kill 1.1 billion people at once and seriously injure another 1.1 billion (most of whom would subsequently die for lack of medical care).[4]

It was hardly a pleasant prospect, but most of the victims would be those who had actively or passively collaborated in causing the disaster, and over half of humanity would survive. In the Southern Hemisphere, some societies would probably emerge from the ordeal badly scarred but basically intact, and perhaps the new great powers—India, South Africa, Brazil, Indonesia, and Australia—might find some way to avoid repeating the experience in another couple of generations. At any rate, history would not come to an end, though it would be small consolation to the few surviving Russians and Americans.

But it turns out that we may not get off so lightly after a nuclear war. The cold and the dark may persist worldwide for half a year, killing off entire species of animals and plants already gravely weakened by high doses of radioactivity. And when the gloom finally clears, ultraviolet radiation, starvation, and disease may account for many others. In April 1983, a symposium of forty distinguished biologists met to consider the effects of the predicted postnuclear climate changes on living things and came to the following conclusion:

> Species extinction could be expected for most tropical plants and animals, and for most terrestrial vertebrates of north temperate regions, a large number of plants, and numerous freshwater and some marine organisms. . . . Whether any people would be able to persist for long in the face of highly modified biological communities; novel climates; high levels of radiation; shattered agricultural, social, and economic systems; extraordinary psychological stresses; and a host of other difficulties is open to question. It is clear that the ecosystem effects alone resulting from a large-scale thermonuclear war could be enough to destroy the current civilization in at least the Northern Hemisphere. Coupled with the direct casualties of perhaps two billion people, the combined intermediate and long-term effects of nuclear war suggest that eventually there might be no human survivors in the Northern Hemisphere.

Furthermore, the scenario described here is by no means the most severe that could be imagined with present world nuclear arsenals and those contemplated for the near future. In almost any realistic case involving nuclear exchanges between the superpowers, global environmental changes sufficient to cause an extinction event equal to or more severe than that at the close of the Cretaceous when the dinosaurs and many other species died out are likely. In that event, the possibility of the extinction of Homo sapiens *cannot be excluded.*[5]

The basic physical processes that would produce these consequences are not in any question. Uncertainties about the nuclear winter phenomenon remain principally in only two areas: whether the veil of dust and smoke would spread rapidly and comprehensively to the Southern Hemisphere; and precisely how many nuclear weapons of what types, used in which ways, would be needed to trigger a nuclear winter.

There are presently no three-dimensional models of the working of the earth's atmosphere that will give a fully satisfactory answer to the first question (though much work is being done). However, a relatively crude simulation done by the computing center of the USSR Academy of Sciences predicted that forty days after a nuclear war the temperature would have fallen 15 to 40 degrees centigrade (59 to 104 degrees Fahrenheit) in countries as widely separated as Chad, Saudi Arabia, and Sri Lanka.[6]

As to how big a nuclear war would need to be to produce these effects, it seems fairly certain that the "base-line" case of a war in which five thousand megatons of nuclear weapons were exploded, 57 percent as groundbursts against "hard targets" like missile silos and 20 percent as airbursts over urban and industrial targets, would more than suffice. (The total stockpile of the superpowers is currently about thirteen thousand megatons.) But it is also possible that far smaller exchanges might be sufficient.)

Calculations are complicated by the fact that the overcast screening out the sun has two components: dust from soil particles vaporized in groundbursts, and soot from burning cities, forests, and grasslands ignited by airbursts. It takes considerably more dust than soot to produce the same screening effect: two thousand to three thousand high-yield groundbursts would probably be needed. This is precisely the range of detonations that would be required if one side were to make a successful first strike on the other's missile silos, with no attacks on cities and no retaliation; even if the aggressor got away with the attack, the nuclear winter would probably ensue.[7]

The millions of tons of soot given off by burning cities would be a far more efficient screening agent, especially if firestorms produced huge convection columns, which would draw most of the soot up into the stratosphere, where it would remain for many months. As little as one hundred megatons on one hundred NATO and Warsaw Pact cities could be too much.[8] Anybody who imagines that cities would be spared in a nuclear exchange is living in a dreamworld.

Would cities be struck? Almost certainly. The deterrent targets are embedded in them. Whatever the declarative policy of either country, the weapons that go after leadership, control, military capability, industrial capability, or economic recovery will hit cities. Whatever our rhetoric or theirs, in a general nuclear war cities will be struck, and they will burn.

Adm. Noel Gayler, USN, former head of the National Security Agency

In the face of such evidence, it is clear that the institution of war is running on empty. It is simply no longer possible for the major powers to achieve anything against each other by means of war. Indeed, even to try is to risk obliterating not only their own futures, but everyone else's too.

The United States and the Soviet Union bear a special responsibility at this point in history, but they deserve no special blame. They just happen to be the strongest powers in the world at the moment, and they are trying to ensure their security by bending new technological realities to fit the traditional ways of achieving that goal—the only ways they know. Other states are no wiser. When France and Britain have completed the re-equipping of their nuclear forces in the mid-1990s, they too will probably have enough nuclear weapons to end history all by themselves, and they will not be the last.

The problem we face is as simple as it was inevitable: war is deeply ingrained in our culture, but it is lethally incompatible with an advanced technological civilization. Four decades after Hiroshima we have a somewhat clearer grasp of the precise nature of our fate if we fail to solve the problem, but the essence of our dilemma was already obvious to Albert Einstein in 1945: "Everything has changed, except our way of thinking."

How would you feel if you ever had to do it for real?

Well, we're trained so highly in our recurrent training that we take every month in simulators like this, so that if we actually had to launch the missiles, it would be an almost automatic thing.

You wouldn't be thinking about it at the time?

There wouldn't be time for any reflection until after we turned the keys. . . .

Would there be reflection then, do you think?

I should think so, yes.

conversation with Minuteman ICBM crew commander, Whiteman Air Force Base

Even bomber pilots used to see the cities burning beneath them (though not the people), but the commander of a Minuteman launch capsule is separated from the targets of his missiles by six thousand miles. The pleasant young Air Force captain who would not have time for reflection until after he had turned the key that would send fifty nuclear warheads toward the Soviet Union was intellectually aware of the consequences, but they were so remote and hypothetical that imagination failed to make them real. His principal reason for volunteering for missile duty—like many of his colleagues—was that the uneventful twenty-four-hour watches in the capsule gave him ample time to work on a correspondence course for a master's degree in business administration.

He wore a neatly pressed uniform, an amber scarf with lightning bolts, and a label on his pocket that said, "combat crew," but he did not fit the traditional image of the warrior. The job more closely resembles that of the duty engineer at a hydroelectric power plant, and even launching the missiles—"going to war," as they quaintly put it—would involve less initiative and activity than the duty engineer would be expected to display if a turbine overheated: "We're taught to react, and we are not part of the decision-making process ourselves. We simply react to the orders we receive through the messages that come to us, and then reflect after we have taken our actions."

There are tens of thousands of clean-cut young men like him—Russians, Americans, French, Chinese, and British—who have their fingers on some sort of nuclear trigger. None of them seem very military, compared to your average infantryman, but that is quite appropriate, since nuclear war is not really a military enterprise in any recognizable sense. Nor can they fairly be said to bear any real responsibility for the existence of their job.

Between them, the five nuclear powers have over twenty-five hundred land-based ballistic missiles, well over a thousand submarine-launched missiles, and thousands of aircraft capable of carrying nuclear bombs, plus land-, sea- and air-launched cruise missiles and a panoply of battlefield nuclear weapons that ranges down to a fifty-eight-pound portable atomic explosive device intended to be carried behind enemy lines by commando teams. The large missiles can carry numerous separate warheads, and the sum of nuclear weapons in the world is now over fifty thousand. In recent years the United States alone has been building eight new nuclear warheads a day (though many are recycled from obsolete warheads).

By the targeting criteria of only twenty years ago, there are not nearly enough worthwhile targets in the NATO and Warsaw Pact countries to justify the existence of such a profusion of nuclear weapons. How did we end up in such an illogical and potentially lethal situation?

Basically, American nuclear policy has been a stated policy of war–fighting with nuclear weapons from the beginning.
        Robert McNamara, U.S. secretary of defense, 1961–68[9]

We don't want to fight a nuclear war, or a conventional one either, but we must be prepared to do so if such a battle is to be deterred, as we must also be prepared to carry the battle to our adversary's homeland. We must not fear war.
                            —James Wade, U.S. under secretary of defense, 1983[10]

Our present predicament certainly is not caused solely by the United States, but it is easiest to trace its development in that country because it was the first to acquire nuclear weapons and has always been far more open about the subject than any other nuclear power. There is a further reason for focusing on the United States, however: it has led the dance in nuclear strategy since 1945 and continues to do so today. Until the early 1970s the United States was always far ahead of the Soviet Union in the number and destructive power of its nuclear weapons. And at all times down to the present it has led in the deployment of significant new nuclear delivery systems: long-range bombers, intercontinental ballistic missiles, submarine-launched missiles, multiple warheads, cruise missiles. . . . And this is not merely a reflection of America's technological prowess.

In the Soviet-American confrontation that was the principal consequence of World War II, it has always been in the strategic interest of the United States (but not of the Soviet Union) to make nuclear weapons usable in war. The confrontation is centered in Europe, where geography would give the Soviet Union an overwhelming military advantage over its rival if there were no nuclear weapons in the world. From the beginning of that rivalry, the United States has therefore compensated for that Soviet advantage by a stated willingness to resort to the use of nuclear weapons against the Soviet homeland if necessary, and this has naturally driven American strategists to a perpetual search for ways to keep the threat to escalate to a nuclear war credible.

The consistent Soviet lag in nuclear weapons has nothing to do with higher morality or lesser strategic ambition. To some extent it is due to the Soviet system's lower capability for technological innovation and the relative scarcity of resources, but basically the Soviet Union *needs* fewer nuclear weapons than the United States. In strict logic, Moscow only needs enough nuclear weapons to deter Washington from initiating the use of its own in a war, and it would then enjoy effective military superiority in the most important strategic theater, Europe, whereas the United States needs enough nuclear superiority to make its threat to use them against the Soviet Union—even in response to a conventional attack—believable.

In the past twenty years, the sheer number of nuclear weapons available to both rivals has grown so large as to blur these distinctions substantially, and the Soviet Union has also begun to flirt with first-strike strategies against the other side's homeland. But the fundamental difference remains: the Soviet Union must achieve "strategic superiority" in nuclear weapons only if it plans to embark on a supreme gamble to overthrow the existing political and military boundaries that circumscribe its sphere of influence; the U.S. government has always instinctively felt that it must achieve and maintain a credible ability to fight and "win" a nuclear war against the Soviet Union merely to preserve those boundaries.

Public discussion of this basic calculation in American strategic thinking virtually ceased in the early 1960s, partly because it was politically embarrassing, but largely because the growth of Soviet nuclear retaliatory ability made the U.S. strategy increasingly incredible, and so it was best not to talk about it too much in public. That the Soviet Union did not proceed to exploit its preponderance in conventional military force to overrun Western Europe after it had achieved nuclear parity in the early 1970s suggests that Washington's estimate both of Moscow's strategic intentions and of its willingness to run risks may always have been excessive, but the fundamental conviction of the United States that its nuclear forces must be "usable" never died. It resurfaced quite unchanged at the end of the 1970s. Once again the United States has taken the lead in both doctrinal and technological innovations, with theories about the feasibility of "limited" strategic nuclear war and projects like "Star Wars" which seek to restore the lost credibility of the U.S. threat to initiate nuclear war as a counterweight to Soviet conventional military power.

It is a strategic imperative that drives the United States to take the lead in pursuing the impossible goal of usable nuclear weapons, rather than any distinctive and particular flaw in American society. Any other nation finding itself in the same strategic situation would almost certainly behave in the same way—and *any* nation possessing nuclear weapons is likely to use them if it actually gets into a major war. But the continuing American leadership in the development of nuclear weapons and strategies makes it the most useful example to examine (as well as the most accessible). And it was, after all, also an American who first realized that nuclear weapons were *not* usable.

The writer . . . is not for the moment concerned about who will win the next war in which atomic bombs are used. Thus far the chief purpose of our military establishment has been to win wars. From now on its chief purpose must be to avert them. It can have almost no other useful purpose.

Bernard Brodie, 1946[11]

Bernard Brodie was a promising young scholar who had just joined the Institute of International Studies at Yale University when the first atomic bomb fell on Hiroshima in August 1945. While the rest of the American academic community resounded with calls for world government as the only possible way of containing the awesome destructive power of the new weapon, Brodie and a small group of like-minded colleagues who recognized the realities of power and the impossibility of reaching such an objective in the short or medium term set about working out the ground rules for survival in a world of stubbornly independent nation-states armed with nuclear weapons. In two conferences in September and November 1945, and in innumerable private arguments, they created the theory of nuclear deterrence—complete, definitive, and incontestable.

It was Brodie who formulated the key concepts. "Everything about the atomic bomb is overshadowed by the fact that it exists and that its destructive power is fantastically great," he wrote, and that had changed the nature of war and the conditions of peace beyond recognition. There could be no effective defense against atomic weapons, since all defense in aerial warfare works by attrition, and only a relatively small number of nuclear weapons had to get through for the destruction to be utterly unacceptable. British defenses against V-1 missiles aimed at London had shot down 97 out of 101 on their single best day, letting only four V-1s get through, but, he pointed out, "if those four had been atomic bombs, London survivors would not have considered the record good."

Moreover, there were a limited number of targets in any country—mostly cities—that were worth using a nuclear weapon on, and the destruction of those targets would be effectively the same as the destruction of the society. Therefore, beyond a certain point the relative numbers of nuclear weapons each side had did not matter. The atomic bomb was an absolute weapon: "If 2,000 bombs in the hands of either party is enough to destroy entirely the economy of the other, the fact that one side has 6,000 and the other 2,000 will be of relatively small significance."[12]

The unavoidable conclusion flowing from these facts was that military victory in total war was no longer possible. The only possible military policy was the deterrence of war. The actual use of nuclear weapons to attack the enemy was pointless, since each side "must fear retaliation, [and] the fact that it destroys the opponent's cities some hours or even days before its own are destroyed may avail it little. . . ." The main goal of military preparations in peacetime would be simply to ensure that a country's ability to retaliate with its own nuclear weapons against an attack should survive the attack, which would be achieved by dispersing the weapons well away from cities and perhaps storing them underground.[13]

And there it was—there really was nothing important left to say. By February 1946, Bernard Brodie and his colleagues had given a complete description of the grim and precarious terms on which the peace might perhaps be kept in a nuclear-armed world until, someday, the international system that breeds war could itself somehow be changed. But at the time, nobody in power was listening to this little band of civilians who presumed to offer opinions on military affairs (and though they and their intellectual heirs would eventually come to have a great, even predominant, influence on American nuclear strategy, by that time they would have changed their tune).

_____

To be fair, there was no compelling reason for the U.S. government to accept the conclusions of Brodie and his friends in 1946, for it was not yet a nuclear-armed world. It was a conventionally armed world that contained one nuclear power, the United States, so deterrence was a one-way street. The first U.S. plan for a nuclear attack on the Soviet Union was drawn up in October 1945—not because the wartime alliance had begun to break down seriously, but simply as part of the contingency planning that all great powers reflexively indulge in against potential rivals. It envisaged delivering twenty atomic bombs on the largest Soviet cities. By late 1947, when the Soviet Union was clearly identified as the enemy, Emergency War Plan "Charioteer" called for the newly formed Strategic Air Command (SAC) to drop 133 atomic bombs on seventy Soviet cities in the event of war (though the actual U.S. arsenal at that date was less than 50 bombs, none of them assembled, and SAC only had thirty aircraft that had been modified to carry these primitive ten-thousand-pound monsters).[14]

In these early years, the confidence induced in the U.S. government by its monopoly of nuclear weapons was so great that its actual preparations for war verged on the lackadaisical. There was no sense of urgency in the production of more bombs and bombers, and nobody outside SAC gave any thought to the actual choice of targets in the Soviet Union. Even the creation of NATO in early 1949, which was essentially a device for strengthening the nerves of shaky Western European governments by underwriting their security with an American nuclear guarantee, was not accompanied by any major measures of conventional rearmament on either side of the Atlantic or by any acceleration in American nuclear programs. The U.S. nuclear monopoly was regarded as a magical and virtually effortless solution to the West's military security problems.

All that changed with the first Soviet nuclear test in 1949—which came as a shock to the United States, though it should have been obvious that the Russians would make any sacrifice necessary to break the American monopoly as soon as possible. The outbreak of the Korean War only a year later was generally interpreted by Western governments as a Soviet-sponsored initiative that grew directly out of Moscow's new nuclear-armed confidence, and that was specifically intended as a strategic feint to draw America's limited conventional forces into Asia prior to an all-out Soviet invasion of Western Europe. NATO's response was a massive program of rearmament (defense budgets doubled or tripled in most Western countries in 1950–52), and Washington plunged headlong into an expansion of its nuclear forces to preserve the "deterrent" that backed up NATO's troops on the ground.

In reality, this was the point where Brodie's rules for nuclear deterrence began to become relevant. Once an opponent had the ability to retaliate with its own nuclear weapons, any attempt to exert political or military leverage by threatening to drop atomic bombs would be both unconvincing and extremely dangerous. There were those in the U.S. government who recognized this. George Kennan, then director of policy planning at the State Department, who could scarcely be regarded as soft on the Soviet threat, wrote papers in 1950 warning against the danger of allowing nuclear weapons to become a central element of Western defense policy. Instead, they should be divorced from normal military calculations and reserved for what he called "deterrent-retaliatory purposes" (that is, solely to deter the Soviet Union from using its nuclear weapons on the United States). That way, everybody would be much safer, and only a few hundred bombs would be ample to devastate the Soviet Union and thus deter it from attacking America. Moreover, Kennan added (echoing Brodie), the number of U.S. nuclear weapons needed to provide that assurance could be determined quite independently of how many bombs the Russians had.

It was a brave but doomed attempt to apply rationality to strategic affairs. "Minimum deterrence," as it later became known, is the only logical policy for two hostile powers with an equal ability to hurt each other, but the United States and the Soviet Union were not yet in that position. Moscow was starting the nuclear arms race from far behind both in weapons and in delivery systems, and it could not hope to achieve the capability to devastate the United States in a retaliatory strike for some years. For the U.S. government to abandon its existing threat to respond to a Soviet conventional attack with a crushing nuclear strike against Soviet cities would involve the United States (and other NATO countries) in vast expenditures on their conventional forces, so Washington instead chose to embark on a frantic buildup of its nuclear forces to maintain its lead over the Russians. The number of U.S. nuclear weapons reached one thousand in 1953—it was about then that a nuclear winter first became possible, though nobody knew it at the time— and by 1960 it had grown to some six or seven thousand thermonuclear bombs, all of them dozens of times more powerful than the atomic bombs of 1953.[15]

At all times down to 1960 the United States maintained at least a ten-to-one lead over the Soviet Union in nuclear weapons, and its bomber bases ringing the Soviet borders and its far superior and more numerous bomber aircraft gave it an even wider margin of advantage in the amount of destruction it could wreak on its opponent's society. Confident that its nuclear superiority would permit the United States to go on threatening the Soviet Union with a devastating nuclear punishment for any unacceptable Soviet act, Secretary of State John Foster Dulles formally enshrined the policy of massive retaliation in a speech of January 1954, announcing that the United States would "depend primarily upon a great capacity to retaliate, instantly, by means and at places of our own choosing." A few weeks later, Vice President Richard Nixon stated the policy even more bluntly: "Rather than let the Communists nibble us to death all over the world in little wars we would rely in the future primarily on our massive mobile retaliatory power which we could use at our discretion against the major source of aggression at times and places that we could choose."[16]

_____

In practice, massive retaliation had already been tacit U.S. strategic policy for almost a decade (though it had not been invoked, interestingly enough, in the one major "little war" of that period, in Korea, which says much about how usable a strategy it really was even in circumstances of virtual U.S. nuclear monopoly). By the time Dulles codified it in 1954, however, massive retaliation was beginning to run out of time, for precisely the reason Brodie had pointed out at the beginning of the nuclear era: it simply wouldn't matter what numerical superiority the United States enjoyed in nuclear weapons once the Soviet Union achieved the ability to deliver a quite limited number of thermonuclear bombs on U.S. cities.

The response of the civilian defense analysts to this development they had long foreseen was not, however, to advocate the policy of minimum deterrence that Brodie had outlined in 1945 and Kennan had advocated in 1950. The defense intellectuals were by now well on the way to becoming a distinct profession in the United States—especially those gathered at the RAND (Research and Development Corporation) think tank in Santa Monica, California, which was founded and supported by the U.S. Air Force—but they were no longer contemplating the implications of nuclear weapons in a theoretical context. They were the citizens of a country involved in acute confrontation with a nuclear-armed opponent, and at least partly infected themselves by the anti-Soviet hysteria that reigned in America in those years, so they bent their efforts instead toward finding ways of keeping U.S. nuclear weapons usable.

As the Soviet Union began to approach a marginal capability to attack the United States directly, Albert Wohlstetter of RAND conducted a massive study of the vulnerability of SAC's bombers to a Soviet disarming surprise attack. In 1957, however, the Air Force was not interested. In response to Wohlstetter's elaborate charts and calculations showing how Soviet bombers might "Pearl Harbor" SAC on the ground, the Gaither Committee appointed by President Eisenhower to examine U.S. strategic security sent a delegation led by Robert Sprague to interview SAC commander Gen. Curtis LeMay. LeMay, however, simply replied that U.S. reconnaissance planes were flying secret missions over Soviet territory twenty-four hours a day.

> If I see the Russians are amassing their planes for an attack, I'm going to knock the shit out of them before they take off the ground. I don't care [if it's not national policy]. It's my policy. That's what I'm going to do.[17]
>
> Gen. Curtis LeMay

The U.S. Air Force's confidence in its ability to launch a preemptive nuclear attack on the Soviet Union left it equally uninterested in the theories of "limited nuclear war" that Bernard Brodie, now also at RAND, had begun to produce. As early as 1948 he had publicly suggested that there was "more strategic leverage to be gained in holding cities hostage than in making corpses," and by 1950 he was arguing that "the art or science [of war] comes in only in finding out, if you're interested, what *not* to hit."

Over the next seven or eight years, and especially after Brodie and some colleagues with similar concerns set up the Strategic Objectives Committee at RAND in 1952, they formulated theories both for limiting the use of nuclear weapons to the battlefield and, if the fighting escalated to an exchange of nuclear weapons between the homelands, for limiting it to "no-cities" strategies that would deliberately leave the enemy's urban targets untouched. This "counterforce" strategy, which used nuclear weapons to attack mainly military targets while leaving most of the enemy's population alive, would give the victor the ability to blackmail an opponent into surrender by subsequently threatening its cities, and had the equally important advantage of encouraging the Soviet Union to refrain from hitting American cities for fear of losing its own.[18]

If the requirement was to keep the U.S. superiority in nuclear weapons usable in a period when the Soviet Union was achieving a capacity to strike back at the United States, this was the only possible route to follow (though Soviet nuclear doctrine, as befitted the inferior power who would surely lose in a limited exchange, never wavered in asserting that no limitations would be observed once a war had escalated to the nuclear level). Eventually, Wohlstetter's concerns about vulnerability and Brodie's ideas on limited nuclear war would both be taken to heart by the U.S. forces and used as infallible arguments for more numerous and more sophisticated nuclear weapons, but in the 1950s they made no progress whatsoever against the strictly offensive, total-war tradition of strategic bombardment that dominated the U.S. Air Force.

Among themselves, the RAND analysts mocked this hidebound attitude. Brodie circulated an internal memorandum likening war plans and sex, in which his "no cities" restraint was coitus interruptus compared to the SAC war plan's blind terminal frenzy. His colleague Herman Kahn told SAC staff officers to their faces: "Gentlemen, you don't have a war plan, you have a war orgasm."[19] But it was all to no avail.

The civilian political authorities in Washington, too, were getting extremely anxious about the implications of U.S. strategy as the 1950s neared their end. In November 1957, when the Gaither Committee presented the results of its six-month investigation on the future resources required to maintain the strategy of massive retaliation and on the likely consequences of a nuclear war, President Eisenhower simply responded, "You can't have this kind of war. There just aren't enough bulldozers to scrape the bodies off the streets."[20] Exactly a year later, John Foster Dulles went to the Pentagon and formally told the Joint Chiefs of Staff that he was abandoning massive retaliation: "Dulles, in a most solemn manner, recalled that he had been the father of the massive retaliation doctrine—it had served the nation well, he said, deterring aggression for years. But he had reluctantly concluded that it was a wasting asset. With increasing Soviet nuclear forces, it would become less credible and the U.S. military should start preparing plans and weapons systems for alternative strategies."[21]

But Dulles revealed none of this to the public, of course, and down to its end the Eisenhower administration resisted any suggestion that it build up U.S. conventional forces to fight the wars that it no longer believed massive retaliation could deter. Eisenhower once told Army Chief of Staff Gen. Maxwell Taylor, who was urging an expansion of the ground forces, that larger conventional forces were not needed for overseas operations, but that "the Army will be truly vital to keeping order in the

United States . . . after the big war, the force that pulls the nation together again."[22] Yet he resisted with equal firmness Strategic Air Command's attempts to stampede the Department of Defense into greatly accelerating its programs for new bombers and missiles, which it supported by blatantly manipulating intelligence reports to produce a forthcoming "bomber gap" in the Soviet favor in 1955–57, and then an equally mythical "missile gap" in 1957–60.[23] The truth is probably that Eisenhower, a former career soldier wise in the ways of the services and equally experienced in discounting the more alarming interpretations of the international situation, saw no likely major war on the horizon and simply refused to embark on any kind of crash program to build up further a military establishment that was already terrifying enough to the Soviets for any practical purposes, whatever the theorists might say. "If it ain't broke, don't fix it."

Nevertheless, the time was coming when politicians concerned about the decay of massive retaliation would discover the emerging doctrines of limited nuclear war that were fermenting among the civilian defense intellectuals and impose them upon the military professionals in the hope of restoring the ability of the United States to coerce the Soviet Union with nuclear weapons. When the Kennedy administration came to office in 1961 (much helped electorally by the missile gap accusation against its predecessor), bringing hundreds of bright, youngish technocrats to Washington, including a whole group of analysts from RAND, the moment arrived. But first, for a brief moment, the question of minimum deterrence was raised at high levels for the first time since Kennan had advocated it in 1950.

In the late 1950s the U.S. Navy was developing its own strategic nuclear force: the Polaris missile, based in submarines. Its greatest virtue was its invulnerability to Soviet attack; its major defect was that it was insufficiently accurate to hit anything smaller than a city. So the Navy, seeking to advance the cause of its own weapons system against the Air Force's rival bombers and land-based missiles, which had precisely the opposite qualities, abandoned its earlier abhorrence for attacks on cities and adopted the policy of minimum deterrence wholeheartedly.

In a 1958 report, the Navy argued that the emerging counterforce strategic doctrines (which would obviously help to perpetuate the Air Force's strategic weapons), would lead only to an endless arms race without offering any real prospect that the United States could successfully fight a nuclear war. Instead, the United States should abandon any attempt to deal with nonnuclear problems by using nuclear weapons and "avoid the provocative overinflation of our strategic forces; their size should be set by an objective of generous *adequacy for deterrence alone* [i.e., for an ability to destroy major urban areas], not by the false goal of adequacy for 'winning.' " For that limited goal, the Navy's submarine-launched missiles alone would be quite sufficient, being both invulnerable and unstoppable. It was a return to Brodie's 1946 strategy of deterrence pure and simple, and if adopted it would mean the end of the Air Force's strategic nuclear role. As a senior naval officer boasted to his Air Force counterpart in 1958, "We've got something that's going to put you guys out of business."[24]

President Kennedy's defense secretary was Robert McNamara, a brilliant administrator imported from the business world who had neither expert knowledge nor any preconceptions in the field of nuclear strategy. Within a week of his arrival at the Pentagon, he had been captivated by the relative sanity of the Navy's minimum deterrence proposals (redefined as "finite deterrence" so as not to sound too skimpy), in which the threat of retaliation by a mere two hundred submarine-launched missiles would secure the United States against the threat of a Soviet nuclear attack. It would mean finding (expensive) non-nuclear means of securing the interests of the United States beyond its own borders and abandoning the pursuit of strategic superiority over the Soviet Union, but it would be as safe as any defense policy could be in a nuclear world.[25]

That was precisely the logic on which the British, French, and Chinese founded their own independent nuclear deterrent forces (all directed against the Soviet Union), which took approximately their present form in the course of the 1960s. None of these nations has the capability to place a nuclear weapon on every missile silo and small town in the Soviet Union, as the United States has, but they do not consider it necessary. The French speak in terms of the ability to "tear an arm off the Soviet bear." The British have an explicit "Moscow criterion" for their nuclear forces: so long as Britain has the ability to obliterate Moscow, they reason, the Russians would not be likely to initiate the use of nuclear weapons against United Kingdom targets even in a situation in which the United States was somehow neutralized. (Britain has just completed the extremely expensive Chevaline program to maintain the Moscow criterion by producing warheads capable of penetrating the limited antiballistic missile defenses around the Soviet capital.)

Neither Britain nor France is immune to the rage of numbers that goes on counting warheads even after the only task additional ones can achieve is to bounce the rubble. Each country has now embarked on a "modernization" (i.e., expansion) of its nuclear forces that will give it the ability to destroy close to a thousand targets in the Soviet Union by the mid-1990s. China, no doubt, will do the same as soon as it is able, and follow the British and French examples in sending its deterrent forces out to sea in submarines. But the policy of all these countries remains at least finite deterrence, if not quite minimum deterrence, because they are only seeking to deter an attack upon themselves.

The case of the United States is different and always has been. It is trying to defend other, more exposed positions (especially in Europe) with nuclear weapons, and that implicitly requires the ability to make a credible threat to use nuclear weapons first. McNamara's flirtation with minimum deterrence lasted scarcely a week.

When I was in the Pentagon, I suppose that 80 to 90 percent of the secrecy in the Navy was to keep the secrets from the Army and the Air Force.

Adm. Gene LaRocque, USN, ret'd.

This is as good a place as any to turn aside and examine the institutional factors that have increasingly come to drive the nuclear arms race in both super-powers. Most of the factors are similar to those that operate in other areas of every country's defense policy, but the extraordinary cost and enormous importance of nuclear weapons and delivery systems have tended to magnify the effects of these institutional motives. As always, the most important single factor is interservice rivalry: it is striking how many different branches of the armed forces in various countries have acquired long-range nuclear weapons and appropriate rationales to justify them. In the United States these are the submarine branch of the Navy, with its Poseidon and Trident missiles, and the Air Force's Strategic Air Command, with its long-range bombers and land-based missiles. Practically everybody else has some nuclear weapons too, of course—cruise missiles in the surface navy, aircraft-borne nuclear weapons in the carriers, nuclear artillery and short-range missiles in the Army, and nuclear bombs under the fighter-bombers of the Tactical Air Command—but the three very long-range systems, able to strike the Soviet homeland from many thousands of miles away, are collectively known as the Triad. The existence of this variety of systems is justified in theory by the proposition that if some technological or tactical surprise should make one system suddenly ineffective, the others would probably still be able to destroy the Soviet Union—but the real reason for their existence is a good deal less theoretical.

In the immediate postwar years the Army was developing rockets and the Air Force was focusing on aircraft, and so the Army got the jump on the Air Force. . . . After the invention of the hydrogen bomb it became evident to the Air Force that long-range rockets probably were the optimum way to deliver them, and so they immediately initiated long-range rocket programs of their own. It was a very difficult time for the higher management because there was an intense struggle between the principal people in the Air Force and the Army. The Navy also came to believe that the delivery of thermonuclear weapons was somehow the wave of the future, and so the Polaris submarine was invented and pushed as yet another way of accomplishing the same objective.   —Herbert York, director of Defense Research and Engineering,
                                              office of the secretary of defense, 1958–61

The Triad of the bombers, the missiles, and the missiles in the submarines has grown to such proportions that it has become the Holy Trinity. It's ridiculous, because it's just something that grew like Topsy. The Navy was going ahead with its submarines, the Air Force was going ahead with its bombers and its land-based missiles, and they got the happy idea, well there are three of us, so we'll call it a Triad. . . . Anyone who suggests cutting one out is [attacked as though] he's going to take one of the legs out of a stool. They resort to all sorts of paradigms to suggest that you can't touch any of our weapons systems.   —Adm. Gene LaRocque

If the Army had succeeded in keeping its own ballistic missiles, the Triad would presumably be known as the Rectangle [or the Quadruped]. And the same kind of rivalry exists between the different armed forces possessing strategic nuclear weapons in the Soviet Union, with comparable results, although the mix is different there. The army was always overwhelmingly the dominant armed service in Russia, and so in the Soviet Union it was the army that won the battle for control of the land-based missiles; the Strategic Rocket Forces, though now a nominally separate service, was initially populated mainly by artillery officers. The air force was not a serious rival, for in the Soviet Union it has never succeeded in becoming a single, powerful institution; Soviet military aviation is mostly divided up between various other branches of the armed forces. The navy has acquired ballistic-missile firing submarines, and its relative influence in the Soviet armed forces is rising, but it is still not comparable to that of the U.S. Navy.

There are no senior participants in the interservice struggles in the Soviet military bureaucracy who have spoken as frankly (or indeed, at all) about how decisions get made as their counterparts in the United States, but the same process is at work. The evidence is there in the structure of the Soviet "triad." Not only does the army own the land-based missiles, but they form a much larger proportion of total Soviet strategic forces than in the United States. The Soviet navy's share is proportionately smaller, and the Soviet bomber force, whose sponsor is the small Long-Range Aviation service, is a virtual orphan: it has never amounted to even a third of its American equivalent.

When I first came into the Navy in 1940, we made everything that we could possibly use, and we bought very little from commercial sources. Now, some forty years later, we make almost nothing. Everything is made by commercial enterprises.

They come to us now with a black box under their arm, to the Pentagon, and say, "Look, we've got a new black box which is better than your green box, and it'll only cost you $100,000 per box and it's marginally better than what you had."
—Adm. Gene LaRocque

Almost as important as interservice rivalry in driving the weapons acquisition process is the relationship between the armed forces and their civilian suppliers, which was christened the "military-industrial complex" by President Eisenhower in his famous farewell speech in 1961. Eisenhower had good reason to warn the republic about the unwarranted influence of this military-industrial complex, for his presidency was dogged by such extraordinary boondoggles as the "nuclear airplane," an Air Force project for a bomber that would be invulnerable to surprise attack because it could stay aloft virtually indefinitely without refueling. The principle was similar to that underlying the Polaris submarines, but in practical terms the weight of nuclear reactors and associated shielding was such that it would have been easier to make a coal-fired, steam-driven airplane fly. Nevertheless, the project proved almost impossible to kill.

> *There was a lot of pressure to continue. It came from people within the Air Force, and it came especially strongly from industrial organizations who were deeply involved in the development of the nuclear airplane, General Electric for one, and Pratt and Whitney for another. . . . There were also gross exaggerations from some of the elements on the periphery of the intelligence community; that is, the CIA was not a problem, but people who then got intelligence data, some of them making kind of free-wheeling interpretations of it, were insisting that the Soviets were about to fly a nuclear airplane. . . .*
>
> *And then there is . . . the "missile press," the magazines whose clientele is made up of people in the aerospace and missile business, and whose advertising revenue comes from the missile and aerospace industry—they were also very strongly supportive of the nuclear airplane, and in one case they ran articles purporting to show pictures of a Soviet nuclear airplane. . . . Just complete nonsense. There was no Soviet nuclear airplane.*
>
> Herbert York

In the end Eisenhower did manage to kill the nuclear airplane program, but many others got past him—and subsequent presidents, with no military background have been in weaker positions to oppose such excesses (if they even wanted to). The genesis of the Space Defense Initiative, from the first allegations about five years ago of similar developments in the Soviet Union, purveyed by peripheral members of the U.S. intelligence community and by the missile press, to today's growing alliance of military professionals, scientists, technologists, and commercial enterprises, has followed a distinctly familiar path.

Eisenhower, it is often forgotten, also gave a warning against an unwarranted influence on military affairs by a scientific and technological elite.

> *I had a number of opportunities to discuss it with [Eisenhower] afterwards, and what he had in mind were the hard-sell scientists and technologists who came in then, still come in today, with ideas which they insist are absolutely necessary if the republic is to survive for very many more months. That it's necessary to adopt these ideas, develop them, build weapons based on them, and deploy them, and so on.*   —Herbert York

While the scientists and the technologists provide the physics and the gadgetry of new weapons, it is the civilian defense analysts who furnish the strategic and tactical doctrines that ratify the whole process. Their relationship with the armed forces, their only customer, is symbiotic, and it does not require an undue amount of skepticism to suspect that those think-tanks that survive and flourish are not those that consistently report that new weapons are undesirable, new technology doubtful, and new roles and resources for the armed forces unnecessary.

> *When I was in the Pentagon I had as many as fifty contracts under my supervision to think tanks around Washington to give us advice on strategy and tactics and even how to deploy various weapons systems. . . .*
>
> *If they didn't answer the mail, in the sense of providing reasons for our weapons systems, I wouldn't renew the contract. . . . One day I met a young man from one of the most prestigious of the think tanks, and he said he was doing a study for the Navy on aircraft carriers. I said, "Why in the world are you doing a study for the Navy? The Navy is the world's expert on aircraft carriers." He said, "Well, I don't know, but we've got a $50,000 contract from the Navy, and all we did was to tell them that we thought we could show that the Navy needed eighteen carriers rather than fifteen."*
>
> *Adm. Gene LaRocque*

It is demonstrably true that a very large part of U.S. defense spending is due to an informal alliance between military officers in the Pentagon, whose prospects of promotion depend almost entirely on their success in defending their own service's interests and in acquiring new weapons, roles, and resources for it; ambitious scientists and technologists who provide ideas for new weapons; defense consultants who ratify their purposes; and private industry, which provides a large part of the political clout necessary to sell the package. The defense contractors have not only the influence conferred by the possession of large amounts of money but, probably more important, the direct political influence that comes from being the providers of a great many jobs. It is a formidable combination, and it usually gets its way.

One must not be too cynical. There is very little overt corruption in any of these relationships as a rule, and almost all the people involved usually believe that the projects they are promoting will genuinely serve the military interests of the United States. It just detracts somewhat from their credibility as impartial judges of what is needed that their convictions should coincide so closely with their career interests.

In the Soviet Union, of course, it is all very different—and Soviet citizens at every level do genuinely believe that it is capitalism, operating through this nexus of interests, that is the reason for arms races and wars. This belief is evident in the constantly repeated Soviet accusation that the imperialists "are seeking to unleash a world war" and are only deterred by the Soviet Union, the world's strongest force for peace. This is not simply shorthand for an accusation that the West wants to take over Ruritania, and that that might cause a war; it is an accusation that the capitalist countries seek war for its own sake, or at least a world permanently poised on the brink of war. Both Marxist analysis and simple observation tell the Soviet leaders that there are very powerful interests in the West whose career interests are directly linked to a continuing high level of preparedness for war.

Whereas the same analysis tells the Soviets that their own system is, by definition, "peaceful." All industry is owned by the state, so there can be no profit motive; all thinking on military doctrine is done by military officers, so it is based on an analysis of the real military situation, undistorted by outside considerations. Yet though the formal structure for decision making in defense is greatly different in the Soviet Union, the new weapons and doctrines are churned out there almost as fast. Given that the Soviet Union almost always lags behind the United States in the introduction of new weapons technology, there is a temptation to accept the Soviets' claim that they simply respond to the Americans' initiatives—but it is more significant (and more illustrative of the true nature of the Soviet military-industrial relationship) that Soviet defense spending remains at a high and fairly steady level regardless of the relatively large fluctuations of the U.S. defense budget as American fears wax and wane.

For all the power of the military-industrial-scientific-defense consultancy alliance in the United States, its ability to extract resources from the government depends to a large degree on the level of external threat perceived by the broad American public. Although the alliance can and does work (with the sincerest of conviction) to raise the public perception of threat—almost every spring the Pentagon releases "intelligence" about a new military danger just before Congress votes on defense appropriations—it must compete with many other sources of information in seeking to mold public opinion, and so U.S. defense budgets oscillate quite markedly. In the Soviet Union, by contrast, there is no independent public opinion, and the level of military expenditure is largely determined by the relative strength of various elements within the immense bureaucratic apparatus of the state. Since those relationships change very slowly, Soviet military spending is relatively stable and remarkably unresponsive to changes in the level of U.S. defense expenditure. In a sense, indeed, there is no arms race—just two bureaucracies independently pursuing their own institutional interests, and producing nuclear weapons as a by-product.

There is no military-industrial complex in the Soviet Union, but there is the "metal-eaters' alliance," so named by less privileged areas of the state apparatus, which unites the armed forces and certain high-technology industrial ministries, military factories, and defense research establishments in effectively the same way. If you are a colonel in the Pentagon or the Soviet Defense Ministry and you want to become a general, you need to show success in getting your service more resources and weapons. If you are a scientist in Soviet or American defense industry, you gain recognition by developing new weapons. And if you are an executive in a U.S. aerospace company or a bureaucrat in the Soviet Ministry of Heavy Machine Building, you get control over more resources and climb up the career ladder by success-fully bringing the scientists, the engineers, and the soldiers together.

There is no profit motive in the Soviet Union, but then the vast majority of those who make the system work in the United States are as much employees as their Soviet counterparts: in both cases it is largely people's desire to advance their careers that drives the system to create more and "better" weapons. There are no civilian defense analysts in the Soviet Union, and so Soviet military doctrine changes less radically and fewer truly bizarre weapons projects are undertaken than in the United States. But the "military-industrial complex" and the "metal-eaters' alliance" comprise mostly the same sorts of people doing the same kind of jobs (though the formal job descriptions differ greatly) and producing very similar results.

And yet, after full account is taken of all these distorting factors, which certainly account for a large proportion of the nuclear weapons and the doctrines governing their use, there remains a core of strategic logic grounded in the realities of each individual country's international situation. This was very evident in the great turning point in U.S. nuclear strategy, which occurred in 1961–63.

NOTES

1. Carl Sagan, "Nuclear War and Climatic Catastrophe: Some Policy Implications," *Foreign Affairs*, Winter 1983/84, p. 285.

2. Paul R. Ehrlich et al. *The Cold and the Dark: The World After Nuclear War*, London: Sidgwick and Jackson, 1985.

3. Richard B. Turco et al., "The Climatic Effects of Nuclear War," *Scientific American*, vol. 251, no. 2 (August 1984), pp. 33–43.

4. *Effects of Nuclear War on Health and Health Services: Report of the International Committee of Experts in Sciences and Public Health*, Geneva: World Health Organization, 1984.

5. Paul R. Ehrlich et al., "The Long-Term Biological Consequences of Nuclear War," *Science*, vol. 222, no. 4630 (December 1983), pp. 1293–1300.

6. Sagan, op. cit., p. 281.

7. Ibid., p. 276; Turco et al., op. cit., p. 38.

8. Turco, ibid.

9. Gregg Herken, *Counsels of War*, New York: Knopf, 1985, p. 306.

10. Peter Pringle and William Aikin, *S.I.O.P.: The Secret U.S. Plan for Nuclear War*, New York: Norton, 1983, pp. 243–44.

11. Bernard Brodie, ed., *The Absolute Weapon: Atomic Power and World Order*, New York: Harcourt Brace, 1946, p. 76.

12. Fred Kaplan, *The Wizards of Armageddon*, New York: Simon & Schuster, 1983, pp. 26–32.

13. Ibid.

14. Desmond Ball, "Targeting for Strategic Deterrence," *Adelphi Papers*, No. 185 (Summer 1983), London: International Institute for Strategic Studies, pp. 3, 5.

15. Ibid., p. 40.

16. Gerard H. Clarfield and William M. Wiecek, *Nuclear America*, New York: Harper & Row, 1984, p. 155.

17. Kaplan, op. cit., pp. 133–34.

18. Ibid., pp. 47, 79–80, 203–19; Herken, op. cit., pp. 79, 84–87.

19. Kaplan, op. cit., pp. 222–23.

20. Herken, op. cit., p. 116.

21. Gerard C. Smith, *Doubletalk: The Story of the First Strategic Arms Limitation Talks*, Garden City, N.Y.: Doubleday, 1980, pp. 10–11.

22. Maxwell D. Taylor, *The Uncertain Trumpet*, New York: Harper & Brothers, 1960, p. 123.

23. Kaplan, op. cit., pp. 155–72, 286–89.

24. Ibid., pp. 233, 235.

25. Ibid., pp. 149–50; 258–60.

There is now strong evidence that for the last forty years we have had no idea what we were fooling with. A hypothetical one-megaton nuclear explosion over New York showing the blast (1); shock waves and high winds (2); and a full-scale firestorm (4) and (5). The smoke and dust boosted into the upper atmosphere (6) would blot out the sun. A "nuclear winter" could follow the explosion of only 100 such bombs over cities. *From "The Climactic Effects of Nuclear War," by Richard P. Turco, Owen B. Toon, Thomas P. Ackerman, James B. Pollack, and Carl Sagan. Copyright © August 1984 by Scientific American, Inc. All rights reserved.*

War is deeply ingrained in our culture, but it is lethally incompatible with an advanced technological civilization. As Albert Einstein said in 1945, "Everything has changed, except the way we think." A young B-52 bomber crew stands in front of its nuclear-armed bomber. © *Herman Kokojan/BLACK STAR*

"There wouldn't be time for reflection until after we turned the keys." Tens of thousands of clean-cut young men—Russian, American, French, Chinese, and British—have their fingers on nuclear buttons. They practice regularly. *A Minuteman II launch facility;* © *Herman Kokojan/ BLACK STAR*

Bernard Brodie, the man who developed the theory of nuclear deterrence, and one of the first to realize that nuclear weapons were unusable. He later spent fifteen years trying to prove himself wrong by developing strategies for "limited nuclear war," only to return at the end to his original view. *Courtesy of the Yale University Library*

These dead Canadian soldiers—stripped of their boots by the North Koreans—were seen by the West as victims of a Soviet strategic feint in Asia prior to an all-out invasion of Western Europe. The Korean War plunged Washington headlong into a frantic expansion of its nuclear forces to preserve the "deterrent" of massive retaliation that backed NATO's troops on the ground. *W. H. Olson/DND/Public Archives of Canada (PA 140410)*

The "Holy Triad" of bombers, land-based missiles, and submarine missiles has only a symbolic rationale, but it does help to justify the continued participation of all the major institutional players in the nuclear game. *A Polaris missile being fired from a submarine;* © *F. W. Owen/BLACK STAR*

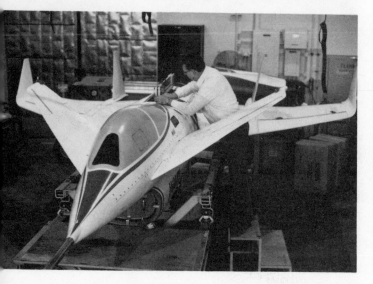

Non-military reasons for military weapons: the "military-industrial complex" claims to create jobs and boost the economy, but for many within it, the primary motive is the sheer intellectual delight of designing these elegant, expensive, and amazingly complicated machines. *Model by Lockheed for the S-3A Viking bomber,* © *Herman Kokojan/BLACK STAR*

10: Notes on Nuclear War II: The Deep, Dark Pit

I thought they were the most dangerous, depraved, essentially monstrous people. They really had constructed a doomsday machine.

Daniel Ellsberg, 1961

Soon after he was brought into McNamara's Defense Department at the beginning of the Kennedy administration, together with a number of other RAND analysts, Daniel Ellsberg was given a classified briefing on SAC's war plan. What he was shown was the first of the Single Integrated Operational Plans (SIOPs), a plan to coordinate the use of nuclear weapons by all the various branches of the U.S. armed forces, and he recoiled from it in horror. It contained only one option: the immediate launch of all U.S. nuclear delivery vehicles against every city and significant military target in the Soviet Union and China, and most of those in the Eastern European countries as well, at the very outbreak of a nuclear war. There was no provision for strategic reserves, no way of exempting China or Eastern Europe from the carnage even if they were not involved in the crisis—and SAC coolly calculated that the strike would kill between 360 and 425 million people.

He thought the plan plainly crazy, pointing out that the SIOP provided for the delivery of a total of 170 atomic and hydrogen bombs on Moscow: "Everybody who could put a weapon on Moscow did so. If you could somehow jury-rig a weapon so that your unit could have a weapon on Moscow, you did it." And Ellsberg also realized something that even the RAND analysts, not to mention the U.S. public, did not know: SAC, aware of America's overwhelming nuclear superiority over the Soviet Union, invariably assumed that the United States would use its nuclear weapons first in a war. The Air Force, in its quest to justify more bombers and missiles of its own, had manipulated intelligence reports to produce a more impressive Soviet nuclear force than actually existed. They had been so successful that the civilian authorities had begun to back away from the strategy of massive retaliation, considering it no longer feasible. But SAC itself knew better—the Soviets had only four operational ICBMs in 1961—and so massive retaliation lived on in the actual war plan.[1]

McNamara had the same SIOP briefing and was similarly appalled. He was thus primed to be seduced by the Navy's proposal for a "minimum deterrence" policy, which would have put an end to any thought of a first strike as well as to most or all of SAC's forces. But the Air Staff, which thought much more broadly than the closed fiefdom of SAC, had foreseen this challenge from the Navy's Polaris missiles, and all through 1960 a team of RAND analysts led by William Kaufmann had been working on a counterforce targeting strategy. As the Air Force chief of staff, Gen.

Tommy White, wrote to the SAC commander, a continuation of the Air Force's policy of indiscriminately targeting cities "would not only be used as further justification of Polaris but . . . would be used as a strong position (which is already emerging) to eliminate virtually any strategic requirement other than Polaris, i.e., SAC."[2]

The more politically sophisticated Air Force senior officers realized that a no-cities strategy, which offered the hope that a nuclear war could be fought (and won) without a holocaust, was bound to appeal to political leaders who wanted to retain the possibility of using U.S. nuclear weapons first, despite the inevitable growth of Soviet retaliatory capability. So, only a month after McNamara had become secretary of defense, the Air Force arranged for him to be briefed by William Kaufmann.

"Within a week he had reversed himself," Kaufmann later said about Mc-Namara's brief temptation to settle for minimum deterrence: "I talked him out of it."[3] The core of Kaufmann's briefing was to contrast three scenarios. The first envisaged a Soviet surprise (counterforce) attack aimed at destroying American strategic forces, followed by an all-out retaliation on Soviet cities by the surviving U.S. nuclear forces, and the destruction of American cities by the Soviet reserve forces—results: 150 million Americans and 40 million Soviets dead. The second, corresponding to the existing SIOP, saw a "max effort" U.S. nuclear attack on the Soviet Union in a crisis, followed by retaliation against U.S. cities by the surviving Soviet missiles and bombers—results: 110 million Americans and 75 million Soviets dead. (The higher number of American casualties is due in both cases to the greater urbanization in the United States in 1960.)

Kaufmann was presenting worst-case examples, based on the Air Force's grossly inflated intelligence estimates of Soviet missile strength. But it was perfectly obvious that the Soviet Union would eventually achieve the kind of retaliatory capability Kaufmann described, so his third scenario was still enormously attractive to McNamara. In it, the United States, unable to hold a Soviet attack in Western Europe with conventional forces, strikes at Soviet bomber fields, missile sites, and submarine pens with nuclear weapons but avoids hitting Soviet cities and holds part of its force in reserve. The Soviets, knowing that their own cities are hostages to the United States, strike back but avoid attacking U.S. cities. The United States wins the counterforce exchange and then tells the Soviets to surrender or it will pick off their cities one by one. Moscow surrenders, and the total cost of the war is "only" three million American lives and five million Soviet lives.[4]

McNamara bought the concept hook, line, and sinker and promptly issued instructions for the development of policies for counterforce strikes and a doctrine that "would permit controlled response and negotiating pauses" in the event of thermonuclear war. By the end of the year, the SIOP had been drastically revised, dividing the list of Soviet targets into five categories from which the United States could pick and choose in a nuclear war.

The options and suboptions contained in the revised U.S. strategic plan, SIOP-63, together with technical changes that enabled the U.S. military command to reprogram the targets of American missiles on short notice and fire them singly or in small numbers (rather than in minimum batches of fifty) made it theoretically possible for the United States to fight a "limited" nuclear war—if the Russians agreed.[5]

When McNamara went public with his new strategy in 1962, the Soviet response was uniformly negative. Marshal V. D. Sokolovskiy rejected McNamara's "rules for waging a nuclear war" and described his no-cities doctrine as a strategy for first strike, pure and simple: "A strategy which contemplates attaining victory through the destruction of the [Soviet] armed forces [by nuclear strikes] cannot stem from the idea of a 'retaliatory' blow; it stems from preemptive action and the achievement of surprise."[6] He neglected to mention, of course, that the official Soviet strategy was also first strike. "Mass nuclear missile strikes at the armed forces of the opponent and at his key economic and political objectives can determine the victory of one side and the defeat of the other at the very beginning of the war. Therefore, a correct estimate of the elements of supremacy over the opponent *and the ability to use them before the opponent does* [emphasis added] are the key to victory in such a war," said *Marxism-Leninism on War and Army.*[7]

McNamara's strategy for a limited and controlled nuclear war proved equally unpopular with America's NATO allies when he revealed it to them at a secret meeting of the alliance's defense ministers in Athens in the summer of 1962. McNamara told them that "the U.S. has come to the conclusion that to the extent feasible, military strategy in general nuclear war should be approached in much the same way that more conventional military operations have been regarded in the past." Most of the allies concluded in great alarm that the American nuclear deterrent that guaranteed their security by threatening (however implausibly) to blow up the world in their defense was becoming even more incredible.

There were two European great powers whose doubts about the reliability of the American nuclear guarantee were already so grave that they were building up their own nuclear deterrent forces, and they were simply confirmed in their determination to possess their own triggers for a general nuclear war. President Kennedy had told McNamara that he should "repeat to the point of boredom" at Athens that on the one hand the United States was not contemplating a first strike, and on the other hand, the Europeans should not believe they could gain the ability to drag the United States into a general nuclear war simply by being able to fire their own independently controlled nuclear weapons at Soviet cities. But it remained obvious to the French (who said so publicly) and to the British (who have always been more tactful) that they could do precisely that, which undermined the whole concept of limited nuclear war.

Public reaction was equally negative when McNamara gave an unclassified version of the Athens speech at the University of Michigan in June 1962. The new strategy was almost universally interpreted as making nuclear war more possible. But the most powerful factor in forcing McNamara to retreat from his no-cities strategy was the way the U.S. armed forces seized upon the counterforce doctrine as a justification for demanding huge numbers of new strategic weapons to hit the almost numberless new targets that now became militarily relevant. By late 1962, the U.S. Air Force was seeking a new strategic bomber, the B-70, and talking about an eventual total of *10,000* Minuteman missiles. In January 1963, McNamara told his staff to inform the military that it was no longer to use counterforce as a rationale for asking for new weapons.[8]

Overwhelmed by the insatiable demands of his armed forces for new nuclear weapons, McNamara resorted to the bureaucratic tactic of compromising on a level of forces far higher than he thought necessary, but much lower than they wanted— and then fortifying himself against further demands by devising a strategic doctrine that ratified that level of forces on arbitrarily chosen theoretical calculations of how much destructive power the United States needed for deterrence.[9] It was an extraordinarily high level, however. As one beleaguered assistant secretary at McNamara's Pentagon observed to Sir Solly Zuckerman, chief scientific adviser to the British Ministry of Defense:

> *First, we need enough Minutemen to be sure that we destroy all those Russian cities. Then we need Polaris missiles to follow in order to tear up the foundations to a depth of ten feet. . . . Then, when all Russia is silent, and when no air defenses are left, we want waves of aircraft to drop enough bombs to tear the whole place up down to a depth of forty feet to prevent the Martians recolonizing the country. And to hell with the fallout.*[10]

The doctrine McNamara adopted to satisfy his NATO allies, calm public opinion, and contain his own armed forces was known as Assured Destruction. Although it contained no explicit elements of first strike (though neither did it contain any formal pledge of no first use by the United States). It could be characterized as a kind of minimum deterrence but with a great many more weapons than were strictly necessary for that doctrine. As McNamara explained it to Congress in early 1965, "A vital objective, to be met in full by our nuclear strategic forces, is the capability for Assured Destruction. . . . It seems reasonable to assume the destruction of, say, one-quarter to one-third of its population and about two-thirds of its industrial capacity . . . would certainly represent intolerable punishment to any industrialized nation and this should serve as an effective deterrent."[11]

Assured Destruction, a purely retaliatory strategy that promised to deter a Soviet nuclear attack on the United States by guaranteeing that enough of the U.S. forces would survive to inflict an "unacceptable" level of damage on the Soviet Union, became the only publicly acknowledged U.S. nuclear doctrine. With the derisive addition in 1969 of the word *Mutual* (by Donald Brennan, a disgruntled campaigner for counterforce, so that he could ridicule the doctrine as "MAD"), Mutual Assured Destruction remained the official U.S. strategy until quite recently. It was never adequately explained how this could be compatible with NATO's policy of "flexible response" in Europe, which envisaged the possibility of a Western first use of nuclear weapons. But this contradiction existed only in public, for the actual target plan, SIOP-63—motivated by McNamara's original desire for "counterforce reception"— was not changed in any significant way for over a decade.

All public officials have learned to talk in public only about deterrence and city attacks. No war-fighting, no city-sparing. Too many critics can make too much trouble (no-cities talk weakens deterrence, the argument goes), so public officials have run for cover. That included me when I was one of them. But the targeting philosophy, the options and the order of choice remain unchanged from the McNamara speech [at the University of Michigan in 1962]."
— *private correspondence to Desmond Ball*[12]

What really happened in 1963 was a split between declaratory U.S. strategy and the real war plan. Assured Destruction was there to deter an attack on the United States (and, less credibly, on Western Europe) and to contain the appetites of the U.S. armed forces for new weapons. But if war actually came, it would probably be fought according to the rules and limitations laid down the previous year. At the political (though not necessarily the military) level, Assured Destruction did involve a renunciation of the idea of a disarming first strike against the Soviet Union. McNamara had never personally believed that a first strike could succeed and privately advised both President Kennedy and President Johnson that they should never decide on the first use of nuclear weapons against the Soviets under any circumstances. But the SIOP never abandoned the expectation that restraint and rationality could prevail even after nuclear weapons had begun to explode over the homelands.

Moscow, like the United States, persisted in its public declarations that nuclear war, if "imposed" on it by the "aggressor," would be waged without limitations, but nobody really knew what strategy the Russians would actually follow if a nuclear war happened. American strategists tended to assume that there was a similar split between declaratory strategy and the real war plan in the Soviet Union, on the grounds that all reasonable men would reach the same conclusion. This view received apparent confirmation when a Russian general revealed in 1966 that the Soviet targeting plan contained five categories of targets almost identical to the "options" in SIOP-63.[13]

Even as assumptions about the possibility of fighting a controlled and limited nuclear war were becoming entrenched in U.S. war plans, events had already demonstrated how far removed they were from reality. During the Berlin crisis of 1961, in which the West was at a hopeless disadvantage in conventional military forces at the point of confrontation, a special task force headed by Paul Nitze was created by President Kennedy to examine his options. It considered and almost instantly rejected the idea of a nuclear warning "shot across the bow," on the grounds that it could lead to a tit-for-tat exchange of symbolic nuclear shots that one side might suddenly escalate into something more serious to prove its determination. "When that happens then you know that you're in for keeps, and you've lost a hell of a lot," observed Nitze.

More seriously, some of the RAND experts on the task force looked into the possibility of a disarming first strike against the Soviet Union (avoiding cities as far as possible) and discovered that it was eminently feasible. American intelligence, depending on the newly available reconnaissance satellites, had discovered that Soviet nuclear forces were in truly dreadful shape: far weaker than Americans had assumed and in an extremely low state of readiness. So they designed a "clever first strike," which they estimated had a 90 percent chance of catching almost all the Soviet weapons on the ground—and found that nobody wanted anything to do with it. "It was amazing how people who had no mathematical background discovered distribution," William Kaufmann noted. "Very quickly they'd come to understand that . . . there was also a 10 percent chance it will all go haywire," and then "they'd lose interest in fifteen minutes."[14]

The Berlin crisis petered out when Khrushchev realized that the United States had discovered that his loudly advertised claims of growing Soviet nuclear striking power and, in particular, of a large intercontinental rocket force were mostly bluff adopted for diplomatic purposes, or at least extremely premature. But this discovery put him under great political pressure at home and internationally, and in the following year he took the great gamble of secretly deploying some shorter-range missiles in the territory of his newly acquired ally, Cuba, in order to put the United States within range of a substantial Soviet missile force and close the strategic gap that was symbolically opening against him. The U.S. discovered the missiles before they became operational, declared a blockade of Cuba, and forced Khrushchev to withdraw his missiles.

What was most significant about the Cuban missile crisis from the point of view of nuclear strategy, however, was that nobody paid the least attention to the idea of a limited nuclear war. Khrushchev may have been suffering from a symbolic strategic inferiority, but there was little doubt that at least a few of his bombers and missiles could get through to devastate American cities no matter what the United States did. By late 1962 the new SIOP was in existence, with all its options for selective and limited nuclear attacks, but in the face of a real crisis everybody fled back to the relative sanity of Brodie's original deterrent formula. On 22 October Kennedy declared that the United States would regard "any nuclear missile launched from Cuba against any nation in the Western Hemisphere as an attack by the Soviet Union on the United States *requiring a full retaliatory response upon the Soviet Union* [emphasize added]."[15]

There is a measure of reassurance to be had from these events. The penalties for miscalculation—or even for success—in nuclear war are so terrifyingly huge that theories of controllability carry little weight when political leaders face real decisions in a crisis. They became extremely cautious and conservative in their actions; people *do* recognize the difference between simulation and reality. Thinking up theories for how to fight a nuclear war does not mean people will be tempted to try them out, at least in any situation short of an utterly apocalyptic crisis.

There have been no such crises since 1945, but they can occur, even between rational governments. The danger then is that the notion of limited nuclear war would make it easier for the war to get started, as frightened and desperate leaders seize on the promise of controllability as drowning men clutch at straws. And in the meantime, the search for that grail serves as a justification for the creation of ever more sophisticated strategic systems, both offensive and defensive. This in turn results in more nuclear weapons and more complex and sensitive control systems, whose reliability and interactions in real war cannot, by the nature of things, be fully tested beforehand. It was the recognition of these consequences by some analysts, after long years of trying to rationalize nuclear war, that created the great split in the fraternity of U.S. defense intellectuals between the believers and those who had lost the faith.

The fastest growth industry is, of course, undertaking: the disposal of the dead. But the second fastest growth industry is strategic analysis. These military metaphysicians shy like the Devil from holy water at being introduced to a practitioner. They don't like generals mucking about, you know, they don't like talking to the people who have to do it, because sometimes their feet are invited back to earth, and that's a very uncomfortable posture for a military metaphysician.
—*Gen. Sir John Hackett*

A touch of the Mephistopheles adheres to anyone who works in the field of nuclear strategy, and particularly to the civilian intellectuals who have dominated the discussion in the United States. But they are only ordinary men and women, and most of them are more frightened of nuclear war than the majority of their fellow citizens, whose trades do not compel them to face the ultimate realities every day. They conceive of themselves as courageous realists who recognize the facts and have taken upon themselves the task of confining nuclear war to a scope commensurate with the stakes over which it is likely to be waged.

Their styles differ widely. Herman Kahn, who once admitted, "I don't understand people who aren't detached," deliberately cultivated a style of cold-blooded analysis that dealt in millions of deaths as others might deal in dozens of eggs. (On one occasion, when his coolness was criticized, he replied: "Would you prefer a nice warm mistake?"[16]) Others frankly admit to being both intellectually intrigued by the complexities of nuclear war planning and seduced by the sense of power and responsibility that comes with it. William Kaufmann has remarked that once he slipped into the deep, dark pit of nuclear strategy, "it was easy to become totally absorbed, living, eating, breathing the stuff every hour of every day"—but that once he had emerged from that realm and could see it from a distance, it all seemed crazy and unreal.[17] It is a monumental task that the nuclear strategists set for themselves. It takes a great deal of arrogance to undertake it at all, and it teaches a fair number of them humility in the end.

Everything we know about Soviet military thinking indicates rejection of those refinements of military thought that have now become commonplace in this country, concerning, for example, distinctions between limited war and general war, between "controlled" and "uncontrolled" strategic targeting, and between nuclear and non-nuclear tactical operations. . . . Violence between great opponents is inherently difficult to control, and cannot be controlled unilaterally. . . . Once hostilities begin, the level of violence has in modern times tended always to go up.

Bernard Brodie, 1963[18]

After fifteen years of wandering in the swamps of limited nuclear war, Brodie returned to his original conclusion that nuclear weapons had changed everything, that their only rational use was to deter war, not to fight it. A great many of the other people who have labored over this particular issue have eventually arrived at the same conclusion. Robert McNamara ultimately ceased to believe that nuclear war was controllable at all and did not even try to defend the war plan he had left behind in 1968 as his legacy: "If you never used the SIOP—or any one of the SIOPs—to initiate the use of nuclear weapons, then they weren't as inappropriate as they might have seemed. But if you were responding to a conventional force or movement by (escalating to the selective use of nuclear weapons) then it was totally inappropriate, because it would just bring suicide upon yourself."[19]

Henry Kissinger, who spent 1968–76 struggling to achieve the goal McNamara abandoned, ultimately admitted to him that he had also been unable to make U.S. nuclear strategy any more "appropriate" to the facts. In 1957, as an academic, he had written that the central problem in nuclear strategy was "how to establish a relationship between a policy of deterrence and a strategy for fighting a war in case deterrence fails"—but by 1974, after six years of experience in shaping the actual foreign policy of a nuclear power, he too had lost the faith: "What in the name of God is strategic superiority?" he asked. "What is the significance of it, politically, militarily, operationally, at these levels of numbers [of nuclear weapons]? What do you do with it?"[20]

Shortly before his death in 1978, Bernard Brodie told me he believed that most of the thinking on limited nuclear war by civilian strategists was, in effect, simple careerism. The theory of deterrence, the only one appropriate to nuclear weapons, had been worked out and was virtually complete within a year of the Hiroshima bomb; it was simple, robust, and not susceptible to fine tuning. But later entrants to the field of nuclear strategy had to establish their reputations by making some new contribution to the theory, which had led to a lot of "hypersensitive tinkering" with the basic assumptions. The best way for ambitious strategic analysts to advance their careers, he pointed out, was to identify some "flaw" in the existing deterrent theory and to provide some solution to it that enlisted the support of powerful interests in the military establishment and/or defense industry because it required new weapons.

But Brodie was being unfair to many of his colleagues (and to his earlier self) who had worked long and hard to make limited nuclear war credible. His bitterness was understandable, for he was virtually ostracized at RAND after his apostasy in the early 1960s, but most of the people who have tried to make nuclear war rational and controllable have been neither careerists nor monsters. They were and are people who believe, more or less explicitly, that it is practically impossible to change the international system quickly and radically enough to avoid another major war, in which nuclear weapons would certainly be used, and so have set themselves the equally impossible task of trying to limit the destructiveness of a nuclear war and ensure that most of their own nation, at least, will survive. Which of these impossibilities is less impossible is the most important debate of our time, and it does not help for either side to despise the other's motives.

A similar debate presumably goes on in the Soviet Union, though it certainly takes place in muted tones and with different assumptions about the nature of history and political power. At the risk of indulging in what Soviets would see as typically Western arrogance and condescension, it seems to me that the highly formalized character of Soviet political ideology places very serious constraints on people's thinking when they have to consider a world of absolute—but absolutely unusable—military power that the founders of that ideology never envisaged. On the other hand, the Marxist-Leninist tradition, with its brutal realism about the nature of power and conflict, has probably helped to preserve Soviet strategists from some of the excesses of sophistication that have afflicted Western thinking on strategy.

Civilians are rigidly excluded from questions of nuclear strategy in the Soviet Union, and both the Russian military tradition and Marxist methods of analysis push the doctrine in rather different directions from those it has taken in the United States. Limitations in warfare, once a war has begun, are almost incomprehensible to this intellectual tradition, and in any cases, until the early 1970s the Russians were so grossly inferior in nuclear forces that their only available strategy was massive retaliation—or a first strike, if they saw an American attack coming and had a chance to get their retaliation in first.

In the past decade Soviet strategists have undoubtedly been exposed to the same intellectual temptations to make nuclear war "rational" to which American strategic analysts long ago surrendered. Given the nature of Soviet political culture and the fact that all Soviet nuclear planners wear uniforms, however, it is highly improbable that Soviet strategy for fighting a nuclear war has even now been transformed into a mirror image of the American concept of a controlled nuclear war.

Soviet strategists are intelligent men confronted with the same set of unpalatable alternatives as their American counterparts, and they are well informed about American strategy. This gives U.S. planners enough hope that the Soviets might finally choose to fight a limited nuclear war, if it actually came down to it, that they have even set up a system called Selected Target for Attack Characterization (STAC) which would provide almost real-time information to the U.S. president on the targets of a Soviet attack on the United States. These doomed American targets are instantly divided into five categories roughly corresponding to the five categories of Soviet targets in the SIOP, so that the president could order retaliatory nuclear strikes against a similarly limited list of Soviet targets if he wished.[21] It is probably just whistling in the dark, though: the national traditions are too different.

> There are . . . fundamental sociological, institutional, and cultural forces at work in defining the differences between U.S. and Soviet approaches to this apocalyptic problem we've got—nuclear weapons. The United States is a commercial, legalistic, democratic society which tends to regard war in general and nuclear warfare in particular as an intrinsic absurdity, leading in turn to the judgment that somehow it can't happen. It comes very naturally to Americans that since this predicament is intrinsically absurd, and all rational beings, including the Russians, will likewise see it as absurd, then we can readily come to a deal that minimizes the probability of war in terms of a contract of shared vulnerability. That's what Mutual Assured Destruction is all about: it's the strategic equivalent of a price-fixing deal between two competitive firms.

> Soviet political culture puts completely different messages or lessons into Soviet strategy (from a Russian as well as "Soviet" vantage point). History is the product of forces gaining ascendancy over other forces. Somebody wins, somebody loses—Kto kovo ("who gets whom"), as Lenin said—and strategy has to be designed for an environment of fundamentally uncompromising conflict. It doesn't mean that compromises aren't necessary as a tactical expedient, or even as a long-term means of keeping under control certain problems one doesn't want to deal with. But in the end warfare, political struggle, the conflict of social forces that define the evolution of modern states, are, from a Soviet vantage point, very uncompromising; and therefore the notion of a contract of shared vulnerability, the notion of even stable strategic relationships, are quite unnatural to Soviet thinking.
>
> *Fritz Ermarth*

Fritz Ermarth, a second-generation RAND alumnus, is expressing the collective wisdom of most of the American strategists who lived through the era after McNamara "capped" American nuclear forces at about 2250 delivery vehicles and the Soviet Union caught up with and then somewhat surpassed that figure. No serious strategic analyst would argue that the arms control agreements concluded during this time "permitted" the Soviets to build their nuclear forces up to near parity with the United States—after all, how was the United States to have prevented that buildup even without the treaties?—but because the period of détente and arms control coincided with the loss of America's traditional strategic superiority in nuclear weapons, so a certain air of disillusionment is to be expected even in some who pride themselves on their lack of illusions.

Ermarth's description of the contrasts between the Soviet and American political systems is quite accurate so far as it goes, but it leaves quite a bit unsaid. To begin with, the United States has no intention of being the loser in the present strategic competition either, and its own historical experience, even before the twentieth century, has been that wars end with the unconditional surrender of the enemy. The doctrine of massive retaliation did not betray any reluctance on the part of the United States to exploit a military advantage, and there have been few holders of power in Washington since 1945 who did not believe that they lived in an "environment of fundamentally uncompromising conflict" with the Soviet Union.

The intellectual roots of the doctrine of Mutual Assured Destruction, it is true, lie in the commercial and legalistic traditions of the United States, but that doctrine has always been more declaratory than real. The search for a nuclear warfighting capability has never slackened for long in the United States. The Soviet Union's passionate attachment to massive nuclear firepower has been a consistent impediment in the various arms control negotiations, but certainly no greater an obstacle than the United States's repeated and mostly successful attempts to exclude from the negotiations whichever technological innovation it was currently counting on to restore its strategic superiority: MIRVs (multiple independently targetable reentry vehicles) from the SALT I treaty, [22] the MX and cruise missiles from the SALT II treaty, [23] and Star Wars from the present START talks.

The appropriate image for the Soviet-American strategic competition, therefore, is not that of a contest between a Soviet state whose ideology forces it to think solely in terms of struggle and victory, and an American opponent hampered by a legalistic rationalism and basically inclined toward compromise. It is rather of two military and political establishments with markedly different styles but equally ruthless in their determination not to lose a struggle that both regard as being of fundamental moral and practical importance.

Our national security planners have to take into account not only what is happening now, but what might happen ten years from now, because it takes ten years or more to respond to something, to build a totally new system for defense or offense. They do have to be prudent. But like any sensible approach it can be overdone and, I think, very often is: people imagine that the Soviets could do something down the road that they cannot do, and that the more reasonable person would know they couldn't. But these hypothetical, exaggerated possibilities do get ground into what is called worst-case analysis, and that leads to exaggerated responses from time to time.

It is a very fundamental problem, because presumably the Soviet planners also have to be prudent, and if there's justification for us in applying worst-case analysis, there's justification for them. That means that it's impossible for the two sides simultaneously to see a situation of parity as really being one of parity. By exaggerating, by taking the worst possible analysis of what the other side is doing—when each side does that simultaneously, it cannot do anything except lead to a sometimes frantic search for solutions to what might be on both sides.

Herbert York, director of Defense Research and Engineering,
office of the secretary of defense, 1958–61

The increasingly luxuriant proliferation of nuclear weapons is partly due to an atavistic tendency to count them as though they were spears and to believe that safety lies in having more and bigger ones (the Russians are particularly prone to this fantasy). The American fascination with theories of limited nuclear war has ironically led to much the same result, since it has given rise to demands for a wide variety of accurate nuclear weapons adapted to the various thrusts and parries envisaged by the strategic analysts. The most intractable element in the push for new weapons on both sides, however, is the fear of being left behind by technological change.

Even as the first full generation of American intercontinental ballistic missiles, the Minuteman I missiles, began to go into their silos in 1963, the next step in the game of technological leapfrog was underway. The Limited Nuclear Test Ban Treaty of that year had forced the cancellation of a U.S. Air Force test of how well those fortified silos could protect their missiles from a nuclear attack—the Air Force had planned to build a sample silo in Alaska and explode a nuclear weapon over it—and so the question of missile vulnerability seemed destined to remain permanently in doubt. The official Defense Department line was that it didn't matter, because there was no strategic advantage to be gained by using one Soviet missile to destroy one American missile. One physicist at RAND, Richard Latter, had a disturbing idea: what if a single missile carried numerous warheads, each able to strike a different target?

He told his idea to the Pentagon's director of Defense Research and Engineering, Harold Brown (later secretary of defense in the Carter administration), who agreed to put money into investigating it. But the potential Soviet threat of the future quickly turned into the American threat of the present: new guidance technology and a "space bus" developed by the civilian National Aeronautics and Space Administration (NASA) to dispense several satellites from a single rocket launcher were quickly married to provide a workable system for delivering multiple nuclear warheads to separate targets. In 1965 the defense secretary approved a program for equipping American ICBMs with MIRVs.

In secret memoranda, Defense Secretary McNamara admitted that this amounted to a counterforce system (designed to go after the enemy's missiles), but he was also using MIRV in the battles he was waging on the bureaucratic front.

Having restricted the Air Force to only one thousand Minuteman missiles, he was now able to offer it a compromise that more than doubled the number of nuclear warheads its missiles could deliver. And as growing Air Force concern about the potential vulnerability of its fixed land-based missiles to the as-yet-nonexistent Soviet MIRVs gave rise to demands for antiballistic missile (ABM) defenses to protect the missile fields, McNamara could counter by pointing out that MIRV technology could cheaply saturate any ABM defense system.[24]

> *I didn't see—and I don't think anyone else saw—the implications of MIRV for the strategic balance. . . . It gave us a good argument for why we didn't have to buy more forces.*
>
> Alain Enthoven, director, Office of Systems Analysis, 1961–68

The pattern that emerged in the late 1960s has been predominant in the arms race ever since—and from about this period the Soviet side has been sufficiently competent in the technology of strategic weaponry to be an active, if subordinate, partner in the process. Each new U.S. technological advance is heralded by claims that the Soviet Union either might do it or has already done it.

In the case of MIRVs, there was both the anxiety that Soviet multiple warheads might eventually pose a serious threat to America's land-based missiles, and the fact that the Soviets had already begun work on a primitive ABM defense that provided a strategic justification for American MIRVs capable of overwhelming it. For McNamara, however, MIRVs were a diplomatic lever for persuading the Soviets not to pursue the costly and ultimately futile path of ABM deployment: "We thought we could get by without deployment . . . that the Russians would come to their senses and stop deploying ABM—in which case we would not have deployed MIRV."[25] But as usual, the bargaining chip ultimately became a technological reality, and when the Soviet Union did finally follow the example of the United States and install MIRVs, the American defense establishment used that as a justification for the next large advance in missile technology.

> *I've long been an advocate of getting all the accuracy you possibly can in ballistic missiles. . . . If the evidence is overwhelming that you're about to get hit, the advantage of preempting under those conditions are very substantial. . . . I don't think there'll be an Armageddon war, but I'll put it this way. There has never been any weapon yet invented or perfected that hasn't been used.* —Gen. Bruce Holloway, commander-in-chief, SAC, 1968–72[26]

When General Holloway submitted SAC's first official request for a new, very large ICBM with a high degree of accuracy in 1971 (the missile that later became known as MX), the "undead" doctrine of limited nuclear war was already struggling out of its shallow grave. The various strategic options embodied in McNamara's SIOP-63 had never been revised, and President Nixon's national security adviser, Henry Kissinger, had already sponsored a study that advocated an American nuclear capability for early "war termination, avoiding cities, and selective response capabilities [that] might provide ways of limiting damage if deterrence fails." In early 1970 President Nixon, addressing Congress, asked, "Should a president, in the event of a nuclear attack, be left with the single option of ordering the mass destruction of enemy civilians, in the face of the certainty that it would be followed by the mass slaughter of Americans?"—and Mutual Assured Destruction, to the extent that it had ever been the real U.S. strategy, fell stone dead.[27]

Much of the thinking about U.S. nuclear strategy that went on during the next decade was considered too upsetting for the American public's delicate sensibilities, and even now, MAD is often rhetorically invoked as a proof of the U.S. government's devotion to a purely retaliatory nuclear strategy. But the Foster Panel, set up by the Department of Defense to review U.S. nuclear strategy in early 1972, recommended "a wide range of nuclear options which could be used . . . to control escalation." It envisaged a limited nuclear war in which the United States would achieve its political objectives and avoid mass destruction of its cities by adopting a strategy that would "(a) hold some vital enemy targets hostage to subsequent destruction by survivable nuclear forces, and (b) permit control over the timing and pace of attack execution, in order to provide the enemy opportunities to reconsider his options." Its recommendations were incorporated in National Security Decision Memorandum 242, signed by President Nixon in January 1974 after Secretary of Defense James Schlesinger had applied pressure by publicly disclosing that he was inaugurating a change in targeting strategy that would give the United States alternatives to "initiating a suicidal strike against the cities of the other side."[28]

The resulting revision of the U.S. nuclear target plan, SIOP-5, which remains the essential basis of U.S. strategy today, explicitly took Soviet residential areas off the target list and even contained provisions for reducing the effectiveness of nuclear strikes against Soviet military targets in some circumstances by changing the aiming points to reduce damage to heavily populated areas. At the same time, the plan made far more elaborate provisions for attacking all elements of the Soviet leadership—party, army, and technocrats—in order to ensure that "all three of those groups . . . would individually and personally and organizationally and culturally know that their part of the world was not going to survive," as Gen. Jasper Welch of the Foster Panel put it. Finally, SIOP-5 paid great attention to ensuring that at any level of nuclear exchange, the Soviet Union should not emerge as the more powerful economy in the postwar world.[29]

If we were to maintain continued communications with the Soviet leaders during the war, and if we were to describe precisely and meticulously the limited nature of our actions, including the desire to avoid attacking their urban industrial bases . . . in spite of what one [said previously] that every-thing must go all out, when the existential circumstances arise, political leaders on both sides will be under powerful pressure to continue to be sensible. . . . Those are the circumstances in which I believe that leaders will be rational and prudent. I hope I am not being too optimistic.

James Schlesinger to Congress, March 1974[30]

The possibility of a "splendid first strike" by the United States that would totally destroy Soviet ability to retaliate with nuclear weapons had vanished by the early 1960s, but the strategic requirement for usable U.S. nuclear weapons re-mained. U.S. strategists still felt the need for an ability to counter Soviet conven-tional attacks around the periphery of Eurasia, where the Soviet Union's geographical position would give it enormous logistical advantages, with a credible threat to escalate to the use of American nuclear weapons—against the Soviet homeland, if necessary. They therefore had to devise strategies for launching highly selective nuclear attacks against a strictly limited list of Soviet targets (not including cities), which would terrify Moscow into stopping its advance, without leading the Russians to believe that they were facing an all-out U.S. nuclear attack that would require a similar response.

James Schlesinger, yet another RAND product, was well suited by intellect and temperament to implement such a policy. He admitted that he did not share the "visceral repugnance" of Robert McNamara, his predecessor, to even the selective use of nuclear weapons. They could be extremely effective in influencing Soviet behavior in a crisis, he believed, and he was confident (or said he was) that the consequent nuclear exchange could be controlled. Of all the defense secretaries who had striven to keep American nuclear forces usable for purposes beyond that of deterring a direct nuclear attack on the United States, he was the most persuasive and sophisticated.

Schlesinger put no stock in simpleminded yearnings for a full counterforce strategy aimed at disarming the Soviets (he knew that Soviet missile-launching submarines, at the very least, would survive): "I was more interested in selectivity than in counterforce per se. Going after selected silos might be a way of delivering a message."[31] He was a paid-up member of that school of American strategic thinkers that believed that national leaders could remain "rational and prudent" even after nuclear warheads had exploded on their territory, and that it could be strategically sensible to bargain by "taking out" certain Soviet military or industrial installations as a demonstration of U.S. determination to prevail in a crisis.

Or perhaps Schlesinger did not really believe that and merely wanted the Soviets to think that he believed it. From quite an early stage, the RAND style of thinking on nuclear strategy has incorporated large elements of psychology. (Con-sider Thomas Schelling's classic formulation of how "preemptive" attacks could happen: "He thinks we think he'll attack; so he thinks we shall; so he will; so we must."[32]) Schlesinger was well aware of the role that prior declarations of strategic intentions by either side could play in influencing the calculations of decision makers in an actual crisis. "Occasionally the Russians should read in the press that a counterforce attack may not fall on silos that are empty," he once remarked. "Why give the Soviets that assurance?"[33] The same calculation, of course, applied to any other declaration of U.S. strategic intentions, such as Schlesinger's assertions of willingness to respond to some local Soviet military initiative with selective U.S. nuclear strikes. *Credible* is not necessarily the same as *true*.

However, the need for credibility impelled Schlesinger to approve the requests of the U.S. armed forces for new nuclear weapons—the Air Force's B-1 bombers and MX and cruise missiles, and an "improved accuracy program" for the Navy's missiles which would lead to the Trident II—all of which featured an increased ability to strike Soviet counterforce targets.

It was all tied up with the importance of perceptions: Schlesinger's estimate of what Soviet strategists would perceive as convincing evidence of U.S. strategic resolve. Thus, when it became clear that the Soviet Union would follow the United States's example in MIRVing its missiles, which were larger and could carry more and bigger warheads—thanks largely to the happenstance that the Soviets' lower technological capabilities had forced them to build bigger rockets in the 1960s— Schlesinger felt compelled to approve an equivalent large U.S. missile, the MX, in response. "I ordered MX to be designed in the summer of 1973," he said, "as a way of showing the Soviets that we meant to make up the gross disparity in throw weights between their missiles and ours. My purpose was to persuade the Soviets to get their throw weights down. MX was my bargaining chip."[34]

For those who genuinely believed in the feasibility of a disarming first strike, the appearance of MIRVed Soviet missiles that could carry many more warheads than existing U.S. land-based missiles was an alarming development. The large "throw weight" of Soviet missiles and their growing accuracy led these American strategists to imagine a Soviet counterforce first strike that would destroy almost all of America's land-based missiles in a surprise attack and thus force the United States to choose between strategic surrender and engaging in a hideous countercity war with its surviving, less accurate weapons. This hypothesis, which was to lead to the prediction of the notorious "window of vulnerability" that plagued the subsequent Carter administration, assumed a positively heroic Soviet faith in American rationality—since this sort of Soviet first strike would kill at least ten million Americans, and the United States would retain the ability to strike back at Soviet cities with its submarine-launched missiles and its surviving bombers. But it was much favored by those who supported the big, accurate MX missile as a means of acquiring an equivalent American capability.

Schlesinger rejected the possibility of a full counterforce first strike by either side, partly on an assessment of the degree of risk that any rational leadership would accept. For even in the most advantageous circumstances there was inevitably a substantial probability that the first strike would fail and lead to a war of mutual extermination. But he was also aware that assertions about the accuracy of American missiles were built on very shaky foundations. The predictions were based on the performance of missiles over the Western Test Range (from California to the South

Pacific), and the equivalent Soviet calculations were drawn from the accuracy of their missiles on another east-west test range, from western Siberia to the North Pacific.

In a real war, however, all the missiles would be going north-south across the pole, and the same calculations would not necessarily apply. Each missile flight path is subject to different gravitational and electromagnetic influences that affect its accuracy, and the only way to eliminate these inaccuracies is to test missiles repeatedly on the intended trajectory and compensate for the deviations by a process of trial and error. Yet nobody has ever test-flown an ICBM from the United States to the Soviet Union or vice versa (just as well, really), so all assertions about missile accuracy in a real war are highly suspect.[35] As Schlesinger told Congress in 1974:

> *I believe there is some misunderstanding about the degree of reliability and accuracy of missiles. . . . It's impossible for either side to achieve the degree of accuracy that would give them a high-confidence first strike [capability], because we will not know what the actual accuracy would be like in a real-world context. As you know, we have acquired from the Western Test Range a fairly precise accuracy, but in the real world we would have to fly from operational bases to targets in the Soviet Union. The parameters of the flight from the Western Test Range are not really very helpful in determining those accuracies to the Soviet Union. . . .*
>
> *The point I would like to make is that if you have any degradation in operational accuracy, American counter-force capability goes to the dogs very quickly. We know that, and the Soviets should know it, and that is one of the reasons that I can publicly state that neither side can acquire a high-confidence first-strike capability.[36]*

Yet knowing this (and knowing that the Russians must know it too), Schlesinger felt compelled to approve the MX missile, whose entire rationale rested on assumptions about accuracy, to prove to the Soviets and his domestic critics that he would counter every real, potential, or alleged Soviet advantage. He was not as much a victim of SAC manipulation as McNamara had been a decade before, but in practice he faced the same consequences: the adoption of an explicit nuclear war–fighting doctrine created the justification for an entire new generation of strategic weapons.

For a brief instant at the beginning of the Carter administration in 1977, the idea of abandoning the whole massive edifice of nuclear war–fighting technology and withdrawing to a strategy of minimum deterrence was raised once again at the highest level. President Carter, a former submariner who had had no direct contact with orthodox U.S. military thinking on nuclear war for two decades, was taken aback when he was shown the U.S. war plan at a preinaugural briefing and learned that the SIOP now listed forty thousand potential targets in the Soviet Union. The U.S. Joint Chiefs of Staff were even more shocked, however, when Carter responded by suggesting that a mere two hundred missiles, all kept in submarines, would be sufficient to deter a Soviet attack on the United States.[37]

But it was not necessary this time for the defenders of American strategic orthodoxy to resort to emergency measures to convert the heretic, as the Air Force had in bringing in William Kaufmann to seduce Robert McNamara with theories of limited nuclear war in 1961. Carter himself was swiftly drawn into the deep, dark pit, betrayed by his technocratic fascination with the elegance of the engineering and the theories that supported U.S. nuclear strategy. By the end of his term, all the developments implicit in the limited nuclear war theories of the early 1960s had become reality.

The most significant weapon acquisition of the Carter years, the MX missile, was designed entirely in accord with these theories. The event that triggered Carter's decision to deploy the MX was the Soviet tests in November 1977 of MIRVed SS-17 and SS-18 missiles, which demonstrated far greater accuracy in their multiple warheads than American intelligence had anticipated. This clearly revealed a Soviet intention to match the United States's ability to attack missile silos, and the larger size and greater number of Soviet ICBM warheads meant that they would stand a somewhat better chance (however small in reality) of eliminating the other side's ICBM silos in a surprise attack. This should not have impressed Carter, since the accuracy calculations for Soviet missiles were as suspect as those for their American counterparts, and in any case, as a minimum deterrence man he had wanted to scrap all the American land-based missiles and move the U.S. deterrent out to sea anyway. But as William Perry (under secretary of defense for Research, Engineering and Acquisition, 1977–81) put it: "Once we explained the significance of those data to the President, he accepted that the problem was real."[38]

The significance of Carter's announcement in September 1979 that he planned to deploy two hundred MX missiles with ten warheads each was obscured by the grotesquerie of his proposed basing plan. The missiles, to keep them safe from a Soviet surprise attack, would be shuttled around between approximately forty-six hundred shelters at random intervals in a bloated version of the old shell game. This plan attracted such ridicule that it was abandoned by the following administration, but it was a natural consequence of the tactics that the advocates of a new land-based missile had adopted to promote their project during the 1970s.

Their primary objective was to gain a convincing counterforce capability against Soviet missile silos, which sheltered over 85 percent of Soviet nuclear warheads at the time (over half of U.S. warheads are in submarines). Two thousand warheads on MX missiles—with a claimed average accuracy of four hundred feet—in addition to almost two thousand less accurate warheads on the older Minuteman missiles, would bring the United States within reach of this goal (assuming, as they did, that their accuracy calculations were correct). Their concern over the vulnerability of fixed U.S. missile silos to a Soviet first strike, and their consequent desire to make the new missile mobile, were genuine but secondary. For presentational purposes, however, they found it much more tactful to stress the vulnerability factor and downplay the disturbing implications of their counterforce ambitions—which got them into a lot of trouble.

All the possible ideas on how to make land-based missiles safe from surprise attack had been brainstormed by a special study team called Strat X long before, in 1967. Some were quite bizarre: move them around on trains, or on the Interstate Highway System in giant trucks, or around the southwestern deserts on ground-effect machines; make them "airmobile" by putting them in giant transport aircraft, or under blimps floating over the United States, or in amphibious aircraft ("sea-sitters"), "which would lurk off the coasts; put them on barges on the nation's major rivers, or in canisters anchored to the ocean bottom offshore, or run them back and forth in a long buried trench (a "zipper-ditch"); shuffle them around a multitude of shelters whose numbers would exceed the number of available Soviet warheads; dig them into the south-facing slopes of mountains where Soviet warheads skimming in at a shallow angle from the north could not reach them; bury them deep in abandoned mines and dig holes out to the surface with excavating machinery after the Soviet first strike was over.

The Red Team (a sort of institutional devil's advocate) kicked large holes in most of the ideas, on the grounds of expense, danger to the civil population, or sheer vulnerability to Soviet countertactics. There was, of course, an easy solution to vulnerability: put the missiles into submarines. But this would not provide the degree of accuracy that was required for a counterforce strategy (at least with late 1960s technology)—and more important, perhaps, missiles in submarines would not belong to the Air Force. The Strat X team dispersed, and its studies were filed away.[39]

Almost all these basing proposals crept back out into the light of day during the great MX debate of the late 1970s, to the alternating amusement and alarm of the public, but in the end, the vulnerability question was simply dismissed as relatively unimportant. The most likely use for a counterforce weapon, after all, is first strike, in which case vulnerability is irrelevant. In the end, the Reagan administration abandoned the whole attempt to protect the MX missiles and simply opted to put one hundred of them (a number subsequently cut to fifty by Congress) into existing Minuteman silos. As a member of the Scowcroft commission, which recommended deployment of the MX in the spring of 1983, put it:

> The mistake that the administration made with all its grandiose talk about the "window of vulnerability" and so forth was to put all the attention on silo vulnerability. That was not the main reason for deploying the MX. . . . One of the things we hoped to convey to the Soviets is our capacity to go after

their theoretically vulnerable land-based missile force. It is that which the acquisition of the MX provides to the United States. What one is indeed conveying to the Soviet Union is that here is a deployment that is fundamentally oriented toward reacting to an all-out Warsaw Pact invasion of Western Europe.[40]

The MX decision was certainly an implicit signal of United States's determination to fight a nuclear war in order to protect its interests and commitments overseas, but it was also a demonstration of the U.S. Air Force's determination to defend its right to stay in the missile business down to the last ditch. However, the accuracy argument will no longer favor land-based missiles so heavily in the later 1980s. The Navy's new Trident II missiles will also have ten warheads and much-improved accuracy, which in the words of a 1981 Pentagon briefing paper, "will allow us to use sea-launched missiles to attack any target in the Soviet Union, including their missile silos."[41] In the next decade, the Air Force may finally lose its long battle to keep its land-based ballistic missiles, as the United States's moves from the present Triad to a less vulnerable Diad of advanced aircraft-launched cruise missiles and submarine-launched ballistic missiles.

But that will not alter American strategy for fighting a nuclear war. This was finally made absolutely explicit by the Carter administration in Presidential Decision 59 of July 1980 and the accompanying revision of the targeting plan, SIOP-5D. One of the authors of that revision, Gen. Jasper Welch, explained that the purpose "was to make it perfectly clear that nuclear weapons have a very rightful place in a global conflict, not just in a spasm of tit-for-tat." Thus the SIOP had to provide a wide menu of selective and limited "nuclear options" permitting the use of nuclear weapons in an almost boundless and partly unforeseeable range of military contingencies: "Fighting may be taking place halfway between Kiev and Moscow, for all I know. Maybe it's taking place along the Siberian border—which is a fairly likely place for it—with Americans, Chinese and Russians. But for the planning and construction of the thing, it doesn't matter."[42]

The new strategic target plan, in addition to providing virtually limitless choices as to whether to hit Soviet strategic forces or conventional military forces or economic targets, laid great stress on attacks on the leadership—army, party, or both. (But it also contained target plans that would deliberately spare Moscow and the senior Soviet leadership, so that they would survive as negotiating partners.) It incorporated additional wrinkles such as selective attacks on Soviet food supplies, or on Soviet troops and military facilities in the Far East to make the Soviet Union more vulnerable to an attack by China, or a pattern of attack deliberately designed to facilitate regional insurrections against Moscow among the large Soviet minority populations in the intra- and postwar period.

Zbigniew Brzezinski, President Carter's national security adviser, claimed that the meaning of the new strategic policy was that "for the first time the United States deliberately sought for itself the capability to manage a protracted nuclear conflict." He also took personal credit for introducing a new distinction into the

SIOP, which gives the United States the option of choosing to kill ethnic Russians—the "real enemy"—while sparing other Soviet nationalities. (Brzezinski, after all, is of Polish descent.) But as Defense Secretary Harold Brown admitted, the Carter administration's changes were mainly a clarification and codification of existing U.S. strategic doctrine: "PD-59 . . . is not a radical departure from U.S. strategic policy over the past decade or so."[43]

His predecessor as defense secretary, James Schlesinger, disagreed, claiming that PD-59 represented a shift in emphasis "from selectivity and signaling to that of victory . . . in a way that was still barely plausible on paper, but in my guess is not plausible in the real world." After he left the Pentagon, Brown virtually conceded Schlesinger's accusation, explaining that the administration had been divided between those who believed in the possibility of winning a protracted nuclear war and those who did not. The argument revolved around what was necessary to deter the Soviet Union effectively, with many people arguing that the Soviets had to believe that if they started a war, the United States would win it. "We started down that path and got into that morass," said Brown. "And PD-59 was the result."[44]

The Reagan administration has taken the public blame for the alleged recent transformation of American nuclear strategy, but that is almost entirely due to its members' guileless habit of chattering publicly about the need to "prevail" in nuclear war, which tends to frighten the children. Defense Secretary Caspar Weinberger's Defense Guidance of 1982 talked frankly of the need for U.S. nuclear forces that could "prevail and be able to force the Soviet Union to seek earliest termination of hostilities on terms favorable to the United States . . . even under the conditions of a prolonged war." Still greater stress was put on attacking the Soviet leadership by the revised SIOP-6, and RAND veteran Andrew Marshall, who presided over that revision of the war plan, even talked of protracted nuclear wars in which the opponents might launch nuclear strikes at each other at intervals of as much as six months.[45] But these were mere refinements of a basic strategic policy that had long been in place. The only truly new departure of the Reagan administration has been Star Wars—and that was new only in technology, not in its basic intent.

People outside science and technology find it difficult to understand how someone like Oppenheimer, who was known to have been opposed to going ahead, could say that something as awful as the hydrogen bomb is technically so sweet that you had to go ahead with it. But it's a point of view that's common within science and technology. —Herbert York

Much of the research in the basic physics and ultrasophisticated technology involved in creating the high-energy lasers, particle beam weapons, electromagnetic cannons, and detection, data-processing, and aiming systems involved in President Reagan's Strategic Defense Initiative (SDI) exert an equally powerful fascination on the researchers in the field. But it is an exorbitantly expensive area, and the political and military leadership of the United States require better reasons for spending the money than the sheer sweetness of the concepts. Brodie's 1946 definition of the problem still holds true: all air (and space) defense operates on the principle of attrition, which means that some portion of the attacking weapons will always get through—and if they are nuclear weapons, even a very small fraction is far too many. Cities will not survive.

The more realistic supporters of SDI are well aware of this fact. As the Defense Science Board reported in 1981, "Offensive and defensive weapons always work together, and in this case adversaries, unwilling to live without an offensive capability, would undoubtedly plan to attack space lasers with anti-satellite systems, including other space lasers, so as to free their offensive weapons."[46] However, the Star Wars advocates have two powerful reasons for pursuing the goal of space-based defenses despite the fact that they can never be impenetrable. One is that the promise of an effective defense against nuclear attack someday in the future has a very useful political effect in calming popular anxieties about a national strategy that envisages fighting and winning a nuclear war. The other, and more important, reason is that to the extent that space-based defenses could eventually deal with a ragged retaliatory strike by an opponent who had been devastated by a largely successful first strike, they make that war-fighting strategy more credible and enhance its political utility.

> *The inescapable reality is that there is literally no hope that Star Wars can make nuclear weapons obsolete. . . . [But] as long as the American people believe that Star Wars offers real hope of reaching the President's asserted goal, it will have a level of political support unrelated to reality.*
>
> *McGeorge Bundy, George F. Kennan, Robert S. McNamara, and Gerard Smith[47]*

> *On the face of it, laymen may find it even attractive as the President speaks about what seem to be defensive measures. . . . In fact the strategic offensive forces of the United States will continue to be developed and upgraded at full tilt, and along a quite definite line at that, namely that of acquiring a first nuclear strike capability. Under these conditions the intention to secure itself the possibility of destroying with the help of antiballistic missile defenses the corresponding strategic systems of the other side, that is of rending it unable to deal a retaliatory strike, is a bid to disarm the Soviet Union in the face of the U.S. nuclear threat.* —President Yuri Andropov, 1983[48]

The superpowers rarely reveal their own real intentions, but they often tell the truth about those of the other side. As Roald Z. Sagdeyev, director of the Institute for Space Research of the Soviet Academy of Sciences, wrote in early 1985, "Although

[Star Wars] cannot be regarded as an effective means of defense against a massive first strike, it may create illusions about possible defense against a retaliatory strike."[49] Ideologically impeccable American authorities with long experience of nuclear strategy have reached the same conclusion about the purpose behind the Star Wars technology. "Such systems would be destabilizing if they provided a shield so you could use the sword," stated Richard Nixon,[50] and William Kaufmann simply described SDI as the latest manifestation of the search for the lost "nuclear Arcadia" of American nuclear superiority.[51]

To the extent that Star Wars is not mere political show business, its ultimate strategic intent is to provide a partial defense not for American cities (which is unattainable), but for the intrinsically more defensible missile fields and other strategic installations from which the United States would try to wage and win a limited nuclear war. The more closely the United States approaches that goal, however, the more it will reinforce the existing predisposition of its technologically inferior Soviet rival to trump any American resort to limited nuclear war by going straight to a massive all-out nuclear strike that would saturate American defenses and initiate the war of extermination.

In the broader context, it does not matter whether some of the technology of Star Wars can eventually be made to work as promised, for countertechnology will follow hard on its heels, and the scale of destructiveness that can be achieved with scientific weaponry will not diminish. Indeed, if the laws of physics were such that nuclear fission was not possible, we would still not be much better off at this stage of our history. Instead of nuclear weapons, we would have concentrated on developing alternative weapons of mass destruction, probably of various chemical and biological varieties, in order to produce much the same dilemma we presently find ourselves in. We would not be facing the final abyss of a nuclear winter, perhaps, but our prospects would still not be bright. At bottom, the problem of war is political, but modern scientific weaponry has turned it from a bearable affliction into a potentially terminal crisis. And science and technology have not yet ceased to advance; the day could come—if we last long enough—when we look back on the era of nuclear weapons with nostalgia.

For the achievement of victory in a present-day nuclear war, if it is unleashed by the imperialists, not only the enemy's armed forces, but also the sources of his military power, the important economic centers, [and] points of military and state control . . . will be subjected to simultaneous destruction.

Colonel M. Shirokov, Soviet Army[52]

Military force, either direct or indirect, must remain an available part of America's foreign policy. —*President Ronald Reagan, 1984*

Both superpowers—and all the other nuclear powers, to a lesser extent—are trapped in a seemingly insoluble dilemma: the need to assure their national security and safeguard their "vital interests" by military means that, if used, are very likely to result in the destruction of their nations, if not of all civilization.

The Soviets deal with this dilemma, at least in public, by incantatory declarations that History will not allow them to go under; nuclear war (which of course would be the other side's fault) will be terrible, but it can be won thanks to the superior moral qualities of socialist man. Soviet faith in the ability of human will to triumph over reality bridges the gap in this chain of logic. The school textbook *Basic Military Training*, printed by the millions and in use throughout the Soviet Union, instructs young soldiers that upon noticing the flash of a nuclear explosion they should lie down with their feet toward the explosion. "In addition," it tells them, "you should turn up your greatcoat collar and protect your hands under yourself. . . . Immediately after the shock wave passes, you must at once get up and continue to carry out your military mission."

Americans deal with the same dilemma in a more managerial style, asserting that even nuclear war can somehow be controlled in such a way that U.S. technological superiority will preserve the American state and deliver victory. In the light of their assumptions about the unchanging nature of the international system and the virtual inevitability of armed conflict, the attempts by American strategic theorists to devise some way of fighting a limited, survivable nuclear war are not utterly illogical, but their chances of success are forlorn. Not only declared Soviet strategic policy, but also everything we know about the vulnerability of command systems and about basic human psychology, argues that no war would stay limited in any way after the first dozen or so nuclear weapons fell on the homeland.

Millions of words are written each year on the strategy of nuclear war. In effect, the history of World War III is being written in advance (just as well, since it is unlikely to be written afterward). But all the theories and doctrines do not change the realities of weapons deployment and human psychology: the strategy of the superpowers, in response to any grave challenge to their "vital national interests," will be to blow up the world.

I don't think there can be any limited use of nuclear weaponry. If a nuclear war starts, after the first nuclear explosion, the war will escalate to a total nuclear war. That is the logic of modern war and the character of modern weaponry. —*Marshal Oleg A. Losik, Soviet army, 1983*

NOTES

1. Herken, *Counsels of War*, New York: Knopf, 1985, pp. 143–45; Desmond Ball, "Targeting for Strategic Deterrence," *Adelphi Papers*, No. 185 (Summer 1983), London: International Institute for Strategic Studies, p. 10.

2. Kaplan, *The Wizards of Armageddon*, New York: Simon & Schuster, 1983, pp. 235–45, 263–72.

3. Herken, op. cit., p. 51.

4. Kaplan, op. cit., pp. 242–43, Herken, op. cit., p. 145.

5. Ball, op. cit., pp. 10–11; Kaplan, op. cit., pp. 272–73, 278–80.

6. V. D. Sokolovskiy, "A Suicidal Strategy," *Red Star*, 19 July 1962; Lawrence Freedman, *The Evolution of Nuclear Strategy*, New York: St. Martins Press, 1981, p. 239.

7. *Marxism-Leninism on War and Army*, quoted in Joseph D. Douglass, Jr., and Amoretta M. Hoeber, *Soviet Strategy for Nuclear War*, Palo Alto: Hoover Institute, 1979, p. 36.

8. Kaplan, op. cit., pp. 283–85, 316–17; Ball, op. cit., pp. 11–13; Herken, op. cit., pp. 163–65, 168–69.

9. Herken, op. cit., pp. 317–19.

10. Sir Solly Zuckerman, *Nuclear Illusion and Reality*, New York: Vintage Books, 1983, pp. 46–47.

11. Senate Armed Services Committee, *Military Procurement Authorization, Fiscal Year 1966*, Introduction, note 1, p. 39.

12. Private correspondence to Desmond Ball from an assistant secretary of defense in the last years of the Johnson administration, quoted in Ball, op. cit., p. 15.

13. Col. Gen. N. A. Lomov, ed., *Scientific-Technical Progress and the Revolution in Military Affairs* (translated and published by the U.S. Air Force), Washington, D.C.: U.S. Government Printing Office, 1974, p. 147.

14. Herken, op. cit., pp. 157–60; Kaplan, op. cit., pp. 294–304.

15. Robert F. Kennedy, *Thirteen Days: A Memoir of the Cuban Missile Crisis*, New York: Norton, 1968, p. 156.

16. Herken, op. cit., p. 208.

17. Kaplan, op. cit., p. 373.

18. Kaplan, op. cit., p. 340.

19. Herken, op. cit., p. 267.

20. Ibid.; Henry Kissinger, *Nuclear Weapons and Foreign Policy*, New York: Harper & Row, 1957, p. 132; U.S. State Department *Bulletin*, 29 July 1974, p. 215.

21. Peter Pringle and William Aikin, *S.I.O.P.: The Secret U.S. Plan for Nuclear War*, New York: Norton, 1983, p. 99.

22. Gerald C. Smith, *Doubletalk: The Story of the First Strategic Arms Limitation Talks*, Garden City, New York: Doubleday, 1980, pp. 154–78, 479–80.

23. Zbigniew Brzezinski, *Power and Principle: Memoirs of the National Security Adviser, 1977–81*, Farrar, Straus & Giroux, 1983, p. 337; Strobe Talbott, *Endgame: The Inside Story of Salt II*, New York: Harper & Row, 1979, p. 35; Cyrus Vance, *Hard Choices*, New York: Simon & Schuster, 1982, p. 55.

24. Kaplan, op. cit., pp. 360–64; Michael Parfit, *The Boys Behind the Bombs*, Boston: Little, Brown & Co., 1983, pp. 38–40.

25. Herken, op. cit., p. 201.

26. Parfit, op. cit., pp. 251–54.

27. Kaplan, op. cit., pp. 366–67.

28. Ibid., pp. 368–73.

29. Herken, op. cit., pp. 261–62; Ball, op. cit., p. 20.

30. Aikin, op. cit., pp. 178–79.

31. Herken, op. cit., pp. 263–64.

32. Thomas Schelling, *The Strategy of Conflict*, London: Oxford University Press, 1963, p. 229.

33. Herken, op. cit., p. 264.

34. James Canan, *War in Space*, New York: Harper & Row, 1982, p. 120.

35. For a full explanation of the insurmountable obstacles to predicting ICBM accuracy on operational trajectories, see Thomas H. Etzold, *Defense or Delusion: America's Military in the 1980s*, New York: Harper & Row, 1982.

36. James Fallows, *National Defense*, New York: Vintage Books, 1982, pp. 155–56.

37. Aikin, op. cit., pp. 172–73; Thomas Powers, "Choosing a Strategy for World War Three," *Atlantic*, November 1982, pp. 82–109.

38. Parfit, op. cit., pp. 188–94.

39. Ibid., pp. 104–10.

40. Herken, op. cit., p. 334.

41. Canan, op. cit., p. 144.

42. Herken, op. cit., pp. 297–98.

43. Brzezinski, op. cit., pp. 455–56; Ball, op. cit., pp. 20–23.

44. Herken, op. cit., pp. 301–2.

45. Ibid., pp. 320–22; Kaplan, op. cit., p. 387.

46. Canan, op. cit., p. 162. The best sources on Star Wars are Sidney D. Drell, Philip J. Farley, and David Holloway, *The Reagan Strategic Defense Initiative: A Technical, Political and Arms Control Assessment*, Palo Alto: Stanford University Press, 1984; and a series of articles in the *New York Times* on 3–8 March 1985.

47. McGeorge Bundy, George F. Kennan, Robert S. McNamara and Gerard Smith, "The President's Choice: Star Wars or Arms Control," *Foreign Affairs* 63, no. 2 (Winter 1984–85), p. 265.

48. Ibid., p. 271.

49. Charles Mohr, "What Moscow Might Do," *New York Times*, 6 March 1985.

50. *Los Angeles Times*, 1 July 1984.

51. Herken, op. cit., p. 312.

52. Leon Goure and Michael J. Deane, "The Soviet Strategic View," *Strategic Review* VIII, no. 1 (Winter 1980), p. 81.

Behind all the theories of "limited nuclear war" lurks the yearning to believe that wars can still be fought and won in the good old-fashioned way. But these theories require the creation of more sophisticated nuclear weapons and more complex plans for delivering them. They also assume that the enemy will cooperate and not launch an all-out retaliation, something that hasn't happened in war so far. *Cover page of the article "Eat Death, Comrades!" by Henry Zeybel, from* Eagle *magazine, December 1984, p. 8*

EAT DEATH, COMRADES!

By Henry Zeybel

Today's SAC crews can get in under the radar, deliver twelve nuclear weapons and get out to do it again.

Pfzt! The lenses of these goggles contain 21 layers of lead-lanthanum zirconate-titanate ceramic. Sudden bright light causes the lenses to turn opaque so quickly that light beams never reach the wearer's eyeballs. Used in wartime by pilot and copilot, the pfztes prevent flash blindness whenever the flash curtains are down, such as during takeoff and air refueling.

Robert McNamara, a secretary of defense who privately advised both Kennedy and Johnson to never consider a nuclear first strike because of the almost total unpredictability of the outcome, ultimately ceased to believe that nuclear war was controllable at all. Subsequent secretaries did not share his "visceral repugnance" to the use of nuclear weapons. © *Cornell Capa/ MAGNUM*

The nightmare come true—the most intractable element in the push for new weapons is the terror on both sides of being technologically out-gunned. The Soviet Union's security blanket of massive nuclear firepower has been a constant impediment to various arms control negotiations, but no worse than U.S. efforts to exclude its current technological innovation from any control—the MIRVs in SALT I, the MX in SALT II, and Star Wars now. *The Polish cavalry on maneuvers just before the Blitzkrieg in 1939; UPI/Bettman Newsphotos*

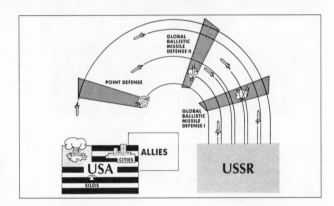

More sweet technology: high-energy lasers, particle-beam weapons, electromagnetic cannons, computerized detection and aiming systems, plus the idea, however chimerical, that maybe someday they could stop a nuclear attack, is politically very useful. In real life, the Star Wars concept helps out limited nuclear war strategy by increasing the options for a first strike. A diagram of how Star Wars might work. *Courtesy of Project High Frontier, Washington, D.C.*

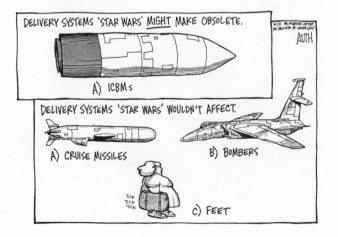

Star Wars can try to defend missile fields and other "hardened" military installations that would be the prime targets in a "limited" nuclear war, but an opponent who was losing such a war would almost certainly escalate to all-out nuclear strikes against cities— which cannot be protected. *Cartoon by Tony Auth, © Philadelphia Enquirer 1985/Washington Post Writers' Group, reprinted with permission*

11: Goodbye War

You can say more truly of the First World War than of the Second or of the Third that if the people had known what was going to happen, they wouldn't have done it. The Second World War—they knew more, and they accepted it. And the Third World War—alas, in a sense they know everything about it, they know what will happen, and they do nothing. I don't know the answer.

—A. J. P. Taylor

There is a terrifying automatism in the way we have marched straight toward scientific total war over the past few centuries, undeterred by the mounting cost and the dictates of reason and self-interest. We *do* know what is going to happen, and we are frightened, but we do none of the seemingly obvious things that might let us alter our course away from oblivion. We resemble a column of intelligent lemmings, holding earnest meetings to denounce the iniquity of cliffs during halts in the march. Everybody agrees that falling off cliffs is a bad idea, many have noticed that the cliff edge is getting steadily closer, and some have come to the heretical conclusion that the column's own line of march is causing this to happen. But nobody can leave the column, and at the end of each halt it sets off again in the same direction.

I do not mean this as a purely rhetorical analogy: there is a serious question as to whether civilization was a wise experiment. We were doing quite nicely without it, compared to other large land animal species, and seemed set for a successful run of some millions of years. Here we are, only ten thousand years into the experiment, facing a crisis of vast proportions which we can now see was inevitable once we took the civilized road. War and the state were centrally important elements in our strategy for gaining more control over our environment, but they have brought us inescapably to our present dilemma, which involves the potential extinction of the human species.

> *[The prospect of a nuclear winter] raises the stakes of nuclear war enormously . . . A nuclear war imperils all our descendants, for as long as there will be humans. Even if the population remains static . . . over a typical time period for the biological evolution of a successful species (roughly ten million years), we are talking about some 500 trillion people yet to come. By this criterion, the stakes are one million times greater for extinction than for the more modest nuclear wars that kill "only" hundreds of millions of people.*
> —Carl Sagan[1]

> *Nature has no principles; she furnishes us with no reason to believe that human life is to be respected—or any particular species either: just look what happened to the ammonites and pterodactyls.*
> —Victor Hugo

High intelligence, at least in the form represented by the human species, may prove not to be an evolutionary trait favorable to survival. The potentially fatal flaw is that our intelligence tends to produce technological and social change at a rate faster than our institutions and emotions can cope with—and this tendency becomes more pronounced the deeper we get into the experiment of civilization, because innovation is cumulative and the rate of change accelerates. We therefore find ourselves continually trying to accommodate new realities within inappropriate existing institutions, and trying to think about those new realities in traditional but sometimes dangerously irrelevant terms. Our treatment of nuclear war is a striking and perhaps terminal example of this behavior.

It is very probable that we began our career as a rising young species by exterminating our nearest relatives, the Neanderthals, and it is entirely possible we will end it by exterminating ourselves, but the universe is not in the business of dealing out poetic justice. Nor are we instinctively ferocious killers of our own kind. It is not some fatal flaw in our nature that now threatens our survival, but something much more prosaic: our political institutions, and the habits of thought which support them, are adapting too slowly to stay in control of the awesome powers of creation and destruction we are now acquiring. One might have wished for something grander, but if we go under as a species that will be our epitaph.

Yet I do not believe we could or should have refused to set out on our present course, whatever the dangers. Civilization has given us a capacity for knowledge and love we could not have had in any other way—and in any case, intelligence is our main competitive advantage as a species, so we were bound to experiment with developing its potential to the fullest. The fact that this strategy also turns us into very high rollers, in evolutionary terms, is just part of the bargain.

If we succeed, we get to dominate every other species, leave the planet, understand the workings of the universe, and even learn how to protect ourselves from natural catastrophes utterly beyond the comprehension, let alone control, of any other species. If we fail to control our powers, on the other hand, we will kill ourselves off very quickly. But, win or lose, being human is a lot more interesting than being a turtle.

We must get the modern national state before it gets us.

Dwight MacDonald, 1945[2]

Justice without force is a myth. —Blaise Pascal

The solution to the state of international anarchy which compels every state to arm itself for war was so obvious that it arose almost spontaneously in the aftermath of the first total war in 1918. The wars by which independent states had always settled their quarrels in the past had grown so monstrously destructive that some alternative system had to be devised, and that could only be a pooling of sovereignty, at least in matters concerning war and peace, by all the states of the world. So the victors of the World War I promptly created the League of Nations.

But the solution was as difficult in practice as it was simple in concept. Great nations with long traditions of absolute independence and deep-rooted suspicions of their neighbors do not easily abandon all their habits just because they have created some new institution that will allegedly take care of their security problems. The idea that all the nations of the world will band together to deter or punish aggression by some maverick country is fine in principle, but who defines the aggressor, and who pays the cost in money and lives that may be needed to make him stop?

More specifically, every member of the League of Nations was well aware that if the organization somehow acquired the ability to act in a concerted and effective fashion, it could end up being used against them. So no major government was willing to give the League of Nations any real power in practice—and therefore they got World War II instead.

That war was so bad—by the end the first nuclear weapons had been used on cities—that the victors made a second and much more serious attempt in 1945 to create an international organization that really could prevent war. The United Nations Charter was a great deal more realistic about the role of power in the world: it made the five victorious great powers permanent members of the Security Council and gave them the right to veto any U.N. action of which they disapproved. It also gave them the right to coerce any other government into submission by armed forces operating under the U.N. flag, if they could agree that its actions represented a danger to peace. These arrangements didn't work either, however, because the five great powers at once fell apart into two hostile military blocs—as victorious nations almost always do after a great war, simply because as the largest surviving military powers in the world, they automatically represent the greatest potential threats to each other's security.

> If the permanent members [of the Security Council] had stuck together as the wartime alliance in peacetime, they would have constituted, for better or worse, a very genuine, powerful authority in the world . . . but of course, there was never any chance of that. . . . I don't see very much sign of governments, in advance, relinquishing elements of national sovereignty to an international organization which they can't control.
>
> It's going to be a very long time before governments are prepared in fact to submit to limitations on their national policies by an international body. Of course, in theory they've all said they would do that in the Charter, and they're all for everybody else doing it—but when it gets to a particular

government having to do that, it's not so easy. Not least because you've got a tremendous domestic opposition to it, very often.

Brian Urquhart, under secretary-general, United Nations

It would be futile and depressing to catalogue the stages by which the United Nations rapidly declined after 1945 from its intended role as a genuine world authority able to prevent war to its present status as a largely powerless talking-shop. It would also be misleading, because the implication would be that this was an enterprise that might have succeeded from the start, and has instead failed irrevocably. On the contrary, it was bound to be a relative failure at the outset, and that is no cause for despair. Obviously, it was always going to be extremely hard to persuade sovereign governments whose institutions have served them and their predecessors well for ten thousand years to surrender any significant measure of power to an untried world authority which might then make decisions that were against their particular interests, and progress will necessarily be measured in small steps even over a period of decades.

In the words of the traditional Irish directions to a lost traveler: "If that's where you want to get to, sir, I wouldn't start from here." But here is where we must start from, for it is states that run the world. There is no point in yearning for some universal Gandhi who could change the human heart and release us from our bondage to considerations of national interest and power. We do not behave as we do for stupid or paltry reasons: those considerations really matter. We no longer can afford to settle our conflicts by war, but there is no simple solution to the problem of war which magically bypasses the existing structure of power in the world.

That structure exists to defend the many conflicting interests of the multitude of separate human communities in the world. It is true that the present nature of the international system, based on heavily armed and jealously independent states, often exaggerates the element of conflict in relations between these communities and sometimes even creates perceptions of conflict and threat where genuine interests are not at stake, but the system does reflect an underlying reality. Namely, we cannot all get all we want, and some method must exist to decide who gets what.

At the international level, that method traditionally has been a brutally simple test of strength through war. If we now must abandon that method of settling our disputes and devise an alternative, it only can be done with the full cooperation of the world's governments. That means it certainly will be a monumentally difficult and lengthy task, but it is the only relevant one. Because it is the absolute independence of national governments, and the consequent need to protect their interests with their own armed forces, that is the source of war in the first place.

As to how governments can be persuaded to do what is now required of them, that is a more difficult problem. Some are more responsive than others to the opinions of their citizens, but the main incentive for any of them to cooperate with the United Nations is a recognition that it is in their own broader self-interest—that of long-term survival—to do so. That is manifestly true, but politics is mainly the art of managing short-term problems.

The short-term disadvantages which might ensue from a surrender of sovereignty to the United Nations have deterred every national government from making any serious gesture in that direction. Mistrust reigns everywhere, and no nation will allow even the least of its interests to be decided upon by a collection of foreigners. Some existing regimes, by their very nature, would find it almost impossible to recognize the authority of any institution which did not profess their own ideological values: consider, for example, the Soviet Union or Iran. There are other governments—with major unsatisfied claims to "lost" territories which would almost certainly be frozen permanently by a genuine world authority in the interest of peace— that could not hope to survive domestically if they gave up the right to engage in war in pursuit of their national goals. Even the majority of states which are more or less satisfied with their borders and their status in the world would face great internal opposition from nationalistic elements if they were to consider even the most limited transfer of sovereignty to the United Nations.

Although nobody is thinking in terms of a "world government" that would collect the garbage and decide on local speed limits, the nationalists of all countries are quite right to worry about what a powerful United Nations might mean. The United Nations was created to end war—"not to bring mankind to Heaven, but to save it from Hell," in Dag Hammarskjold's words— and its founders were fully aware that in order to do that it had to be able to guarantee each country's safety from attack by its neighbors, and to make decisions on international disputes *and enforce them*. Neither order nor justice can be imposed without at least the threat of superior force, if not its actual use, so a United Nations that worked obviously would require powerful armed forces under its own command. (Indeed, the U.N. Charter makes provisions for member countries to contribute contingents to just such an armed force.)

That is why the United Nations has never worked as designed: a truly effective United Nations would have the ability to coerce national governments, so naturally they refuse to give it the powers it would need to do so. They all know what they must do to end international war, have known it since 1945 at the latest, but are not yet willing to do it. The possibility of their own interests being damaged somewhere down the line by the decisions of a United Nations grown too powerful to resist is so great a deterrent that they prefer to go on living with the risk of war. (That is, until the risk of some particular war involving them grows too great, or a war in which they are directly involved goes badly wrong. Then national governments are very glad to use the United Nations' fictitious authority to get themselves off the hook—and this applies especially to the superpowers, who have repeatedly used the United Nations in order to back away gracefully from dangerous confrontations.)

The United Nations as presently constituted is certainly no place for idealists, but they would feel even more uncomfortable in a United Nations that actually worked as was originally intended. It is, after all, an association of poachers turned gamekeepers, not an assembly of saints. Even if the organization eventually does gain some of the authority the member states have theoretically granted it, it is certain that the collective rights and interests of those states will be preserved, especially against their own citizens.

One of the implications of a powerful United Nations which is rarely discussed by its advocates (for obvious reasons) is that a world authority founded on the collaboration of national governments would inevitably attempt to freeze the existing political dispensation in the world in the interests of its members, or at least drastically slow down the rate of change. As a result, national and ethnic communities not already possessing legitimate states of their own would lose almost all possibility of gaining them in the future, simply because they didn't make it under the wire in time. If the established sovereign states of the world had created some equivalent of the United Nations with real power in the mid-eighteenth century—a mutual protection association that guaranteed their territories—the United States might never have won its independence from Britain. If they did it today, Lithuania, Tibet, and Zanzibar could abandon all hope of recovering their independent political existence, and Eritreans, Kurds, and Basques might as well forget their hopes of ever achieving it. (Not that any of them has much chance anyway.)

Even as presently constituted, the United Nations tends to place legitimacy above all other considerations. It still recognizes, for example, the Khmer Rouge as the legitimate government of Cambodia, despite its horrific record, because it was displaced by the illegitimate method of foreign invasion. Eventually some deal will be done, no doubt, and the new reality in Cambodia will be formally recognized. But the more power the United Nations is granted by its members, the more it will have to reciprocate by acting to defend their existing interests and possessions.

The consequences would be quite oppressive to many people and some would rebel. Guerrilla wars, terrorism, and other forms of armed protest against the existing distribution of power would not only continue, but might well increase. The most that could be expected, even from a United Nations with teeth, for a century or so, is an end to large-scale international war. Internal conflict, including the use of violence in pursuit of political objectives, would not vanish from the world even if all legitimate governments signed their armed forces over to the United Nations tomorrow.

There is a further, even more distasteful, implication to a United Nations with real power: it would not make its decisions according to some impartial standard of justice. There is no impartial concept of justice to which all of mankind would subscribe and, in any case, it is not "mankind" that makes decisions at the United Nations, but governments with their own national interests to protect. To envision how a functioning "world authority" might reach its decisions, at least in its first century or so, begin with the arrogant promotion of self-interest by the great powers that would continue to dominate U.N. decision-making and add in the crass expediency masked as principle which characterizes the shifting coalitions among the lesser powers in the present General Assembly. It would be an intensely *political* process. The decisions it produced would be kept within reasonable bounds only by the overriding shared recognition that the organization never must act in a way so damaging to the interest of any major member or group of members that it forced them into total defiance, and so destroyed the fundamental consensus that kept war at bay.

There is nothing shocking about this. National politics in every country op erates with the same combination: a little bit of principle, a lot of power, and a final constraint on the ruthless exercise of that power based mainly on the need to preserve the essential consensus on which the nation is founded and to avoid civil war. In an international organization whose members represent such radically different traditions, interests, and levels of development; the proportion of principle to power is bound to be even lower. But as a navy petty officer used to tell us many years ago whenever he gave us the latest piece of unavoidable bad news: "If you can't take a joke, you shouldn't have joined."

It's a pity there is no practical alternative to the United Nations, because otherwise nobody would dream of creating the kind of cumbersome and meddlesome monster that a powerful world authority will probably prove to be. Most of us already feel burdened by too much government within our own national states. Adding another layer of government above that— particularly one which would function on such a crudely pragmatic level and would have to take into consideration the views and interests of people whose traditions and priorities were radically different from our own—is a prospect that is frankly dismaying.

There is no need to panic, of course, because such a thing is not going to happen in our lifetimes. Perhaps it will be less dismaying to our descendants, who *will* have to live with it (if they live at all). But the political unification of the world, on some sort of extremely loose federal basis, is virtually a certainty in the long run; the tide has been running strongly in that direction for several centuries now. Indeed, the present political fragmentation of the world into more than 150 stubbornly independent territorial units is already an anachronism, for in every other context, from commerce, technology, and the mass media to fashions in ideology, music, and marriage, the outlines of a single global culture (with wide local variations) are visibly taking shape. National governments naturally resist the diminution of their powers that would occur if they too were to conform to this trend, but they have no good alternatives in the long run.

> *There are two possibilities, it seems to me. The first one is that we run into another global disaster, which doubtless, if there's anything left, will finally change people's minds about the benefits of unlimited national sovereignty. The second alternative is something much more gradual and slower, which is that we convince governments that, just as they have given up sovereignty in certain specialized fields—for example, radio frequencies or postal systems or something like that—that they have to do this also in the political field.*
> —Brian Urquhart

We consent to all the impositions and inconveniences of a distant and unwieldy government apparatus at the national level because, in the final analysis, its benefits outweigh its costs. For all its drawbacks, it provides us with civil peace, a measure of protection from the rival ambitions of other national communities, and a framework for large-scale cooperation in pursuing whatever goals we set ourselves as a national society. All the same arguments theoretically operate with equal strength in favor of an international authority—even more strongly, given the catastrophic consequences that await us if we do not manage to contain the military rivalries of our separate sovereign states within such an organization.

Yet it is not surprising there is no widespread popular support for the surrender of sovereignty to the United Nations in any major country in the world. Most people are reluctant to accept that war and national sovereignty are indissolubly linked, and that to be rid of one they must also relinquish much of the other. The instinctive belief in the need for complete national independence is so strong in most people that change will inevitably be very slow.

Curiously (or perhaps not so curiously), that belief tends to be less strong in governments than in the people they govern. The United Nations was not founded by popular demand. It was created by *governments* who were terrified by where the existing system was leading them, and could not afford to ignore the grim realities of the situation by taking refuge in the comforting myths about independence and national security that pass for truth in domestic political discourse. The people who actually have the responsibility for running foreign policy in most countries, and especially in the great powers, know that the present international system is in potentially terminal trouble, and many of them have drawn the necessary conclusion.

It goes against the grain to speak well of diplomats, but I suspect if they didn't have to worry about the enormous domestic political resistance to any surrender of sovereignty, the foreign policy professionals in almost every country (without regard to ideology) would immediately make the minimum concessions necessary to create a functioning world authority, because they understand the alternative. Many of the more reflective military professionals would concur for the same reason.

But it is politicians who are in charge of states, and even if they understand the realities of the situation themselves (which many of them do not, for their backgrounds and their primary concerns are usually in domestic issues, not international affairs), politicians cannot afford to get too far ahead of the people they lead. Nevertheless, progress has been made.

We are already some small distance (perhaps as far as anybody could reasonably expect) down the road we must travel if we are eventually to escape from the danger of wars that would threaten our survival. The enormous growth of international organizations since 1945, and especially the existence of the United Nations as a permanent forum where the states of the world talk about the avoidance of war (and occasionally do something about it) already has created a historically new situation. We are not moving fast enough, but there is no doubt we are beginning to adapt our institutions to the lethal new realities that were made brutally clear to us by World War II.

People often wonder why it is that one continues to batter away here in the U.N. In the first place, it's extremely interesting. If you want to watch the human tragicomedy unfold, this is a terrific front-row seat, and every now and then you can do something about it. You can stop somebody from being executed, you can prevent somewhere from being destroyed. It's a drop in the bucket, but . . . you can sometimes control a conflict—and the most important thing is to provide a place where the nuclear powers can get out of their confrontations. . . . As Hammarskjold once said, while none of us are ever going to see the world order we dream of appear in our lifetime, nonetheless the effort to build that order is the difference between anarchy and a tolerable degree of chaos.

—Brian Urquhart

A t best, we all will live out our lives amid this barely tolerable chaos, permanently poised on the brink of something infinitely worse, and the most that any of us can do is to try to push things some tiny distance in the direction they must eventually go if the race is to survive. In this effort, formal arms control agreements have a certain limited usefulness (more for their symbolic value as indications that both sides wish to avoid war, perhaps, than for any real decrease in the potential destructiveness of war they allegedly achieve). There is one disarmament measure that would have the highest practical value: an agreement to reduce the world's stockpile of nuclear weapons below the threshold (roughly 500 to 2000 warheads) at which an all-out war would be likely to trigger a nuclear winter. But because that would require the superpowers to cut their nuclear arsenals by more than 90 percent, it will be rather difficult to attain.[3]

In general, however, arms races are only responses to real or perceived strategic confrontations, and it is the attitudes which we and our governments bring to these confrontations that constitute the gravest danger to peace. In the long run institutions must change, but we would be a good deal safer in the meantime if the citizens and governments of the great powers could learn to believe in the fear of others, and stop demonizing the "enemy."

Our beliefs about the nature of fear have special relevance for the theory of nuclear deterrence, which is founded on some singularly unrealistic ideas about how human beings perceive and react to threats. It is readily observable in ordinary life that the greater an individual's own fear, the more difficulty he has believing his opponent is feeling similar fear. There is an overwhelming tendency to treat the source of our fear not as human beings like ourselves, but as a blind, malevolent force which only can be managed by threats.

Threats are the very essence of deterrence, but both sides habitually fall into the same logical trap. Any deterrent threats *we* make are justifiable and nonprovocative by definition, because our fear is real and unquestionable—but they should not produce fear in our opponent unless his intention is to attack us, because *we* know that our intentions are purely defensive. Thus when our opponent responds to our threats not with mere passivity (why doesn't he just take our word that our intentions are good?), but by making his own counterthreats, we are confirmed in our conviction of his evil intentions. Naturally, we reply by piling up yet more threats of our own—again perfectly justifiable, because *our* fear is real. Every time some proposal emerges for yet another weapon to "reinforce deterrence," we should ask: how would we react if an enemy whom we feared were to deploy this weapon against us?

As for the "peace movement" in particular, it is both a manifestation of some of those changes of attitude which may eventually enable us to escape from our present dilemma and a stimulus to further change. By and large, the peace movement in each country only can affect the behavior of its own government. Its most important long-term goal, therefore, should be creating a domestic climate of opinion which will not rebel in narrow nationalistic wrath when hard choices eventually have to be made and some elements of national sovereignty must be surrendered for the sake of survival.

If this priority is accepted, however, there are major implications for the strategy of peace movements. They should resist the naive temptation to reject all the existing structures of governmental power as corrupt and irrelevant, and recognize that they need allies at the heart of those structures. They already have some secret allies there, and what they, and others who might join them, most need is to be freed of the domestic constraint of primitive nationalism that shackles them to traditional policies.

To be effective as agents of (slow) change with a broad public appeal, peace movements must avoid a descent into sectarian dogmatism at all costs. Changing popular attitudes toward peace and war and, above all, sovereignty, is a long process that can only be accomplished one step at a time. It would be foolish to reject the support of those who are not ready to accept the ultimate objective if they are at least willing to support the next step. The peace movement needs all the allies it can get. And although the fear of nuclear weapons is its most effective means of mobilizing popular support, it should not allow itself to fall into the simplistic trap of blaming our peril on the weapons or, worse yet, the soldiers.

The military makes demands which few if any other callings do. And of course emotionally disturbed people talk about being trained to kill. . . . The whole essence of being a soldier is not to slay but to be slain. You offer yourself up to be slain, rather than setting yourself up as a slayer. Now one can get into very deep water here, but there's food for thought in it.

Gen. Sir John Hackett

Go, tell the Spartans, you who pass by,

That here, obedient to their laws, we lie.

Epitaph for Leonidas and the 300 who died
holding the pass at Thermopylae, Simonides 480 B.C.

Soldiers are not the enemies of peace. They are there to do our bidding, and to pay the price of our ambitions and our mistakes. They probably always will be there in one form or another, for conflict and the need to impose order are not likely to disappear from the human world no matter what kind of changes we make in our institutions. But the kinds of international wars we now ask them to prepare for and fight in are destructive far beyond any rational proportion between ends and means, and so *that* form of conflict must be changed and brought under control. Relatively few soldiers can see how this might be achieved in practice (knowing what they do about the roles of force and irrationality in the world), but the military profession probably has a clearer instinctive understanding of how much such a change would cost, if it could be achieved, than most civilians.

The rest of us, most of the time, still believe that we can have our cake and eat it too: we want both peace and independence, and we talk of international security and national sovereignty as though they were not mutually exclusive concepts. The ideas are all jumbled together in our minds, and sorting them out will be a lengthy and painful process.

The universe is so vast and so ageless that the life of one man can only be justified by the measure of his sacrifice.

By one of the miserable coincidences in which war abounds, those were the last words Pilot Officer V. A. Rosewarne wrote to his mother before he was shot down and killed, at the age of 24, in the battle of Britain. His mother sent his last letter to *The Times*, which published it on 18 June 1940. The words are now inscribed on the wall of the Royal Air Force Museum in north London.

Rosewarne probably did not say those words to himself as he fell out of the sky in his burning Spitfire, but he did mean them. Strip away all the rhetoric, and the core remains: we expect our young men to sacrifice their lives for us if war comes, and they are willing to be asked.

We cannot help believing that a sacrifice like Rosewarne's—one which hundreds of thousands of young men make every year—confers a kind of dignity on those who make it, and also on those for whom it is done. It is a deeply entrenched notion in any culture with a military tradition, and that is practically every culture on earth. However, in most wars of the past half-century the civilian dead have outnumbered the military casualties, and in a total war today there would be a hundred dead civilians for every soldier killed. The ancient compact between ourselves and our soldiers has become meaningless and we cannot go on pretending it still works.

But the essential idea of sacrifice does not become meaningless. It's just that we can no longer place that burden solely on our young men. Instead of asking them to die in war so the nation can get its way, we will all have to make the lesser sacrifices necessary to avoid war.

Lesser sacrifices, but not small ones. We will not avoid war of unimaginable destructiveness just by expressions of good will. We will have to stop trying to make ourselves invulnerable to others (not that it is possible nowadays anyway), and we will have to let all sorts of foreigners who think in strange ways have a say in what we do. It will hurt, and it will cost us dearly.

In short, we will have to give up our precious independence—not all of it, or all at once, but quite a lot of it over just a few generations. It may sound naive to talk of independent states ever relinquishing even the smallest fraction of their sovereignty, but they now have a very powerful incentive: the need to survive.

Our principal source of hope, in what is admittedly a quite desperate situation, is that the human race is not only intelligent but extremely malleable. To a large extent, we are our own invention: the values we now hold and the ways we now behave are often quite drastic modifications of those we started out with at the dawn of civilization. The changes were necessary in order for us to live in large groups within a civilized society, and we were able to make them. More changes are needed now, and we can make them, too, if we have the will and enough time. Indeed, the most fundamental change of attitude which must occur if we are to survive our present dilemma *is* already underway: large numbers of people, especially in the great industrialized states whose next war might destroy mankind's future, are gradually moving beyond "tribal" definitions of humanity.

There is a slow but quite perceptible revolution in human consciousness taking place: the last of the great redefinitions of humanity. At all times in our history we have run our affairs on the assumption that there is a special category of people (our lot) whom we regard as full human beings, having rights and duties approximately equal to our own, and whom we ought not to kill even when we quarrel. Over the past fifteen or twenty thousand years we have successively widened this category from the original hunting-and-gathering band of a couple of hundred people to encompass larger and larger groups. First it was the tribe of some thousands of people bound together by kinship and ritual ties; then the state, where we recognize our shared interests with millions of people whom we don't know and will never meet; and now, finally, the entire human race.

There was nothing in the least idealistic or sentimental in any of the previous redefinitions. They occurred because they were useful in advancing people's material interests and ensuring their survival. The same is self-evidently true for this final act of redefinition: we have reached a point where our moral imagination must expand again to embrace the whole of mankind, or else we will perish.

Both the necessary shift in cultural perspective and the creation of political institutions which will reflect the new perspective are clearly changes that must take a very long time. We already have been immersed in this process for most of a century, and it is hard to believe we are even halfway to our goal yet.

To the reasonable objection that not all cultures are changing at the same speed, and that it would be dangerous for us (virtuous us) to get too far ahead of the rest, one only can say there is certainly no imminent danger of that happening. Perhaps, in twenty or fifty years, there will come a time when some recalcitrant countries who are still wedded to absolute national independence backed by military force will become an obstacle that compels all the others to slow down their transfer of sovereignty to an international authority. But we'll have to cross that bridge when we come to it. At the moment, when *all* countries are recalcitrant, the risks involved in trying to change things just a little— the most that can be hoped for—are incomparably less than the risks of standing pat with the present system.

As for the argument that there will never be universal brotherhood among mankind, and so any attempt to move beyond the current system of national states is foredoomed: of course we aren't going to end up loving one another indiscriminately, but that isn't necessary. There is not universal love and brotherhood *within* national states either. What does exist, and what must now be extended beyond national borders, is a mutual recognition that everybody is better off if they respect each other's rights and accept arbitration by a higher authority rather than shooting each other when their rights come into conflict.

There is no irony in the fact that the period in which the concept of the national state is finally coming under challenge by a wider definition of humanity is also the period which has seen history's most catastrophic wars, for they provide the practical incentive that drives the process of change. There would be no possibility of change without the wars, but the transition to a different system is a risky business. The danger of another world war which would cut the whole process short and perhaps put a permanent end to civilization is small in any given year, but cumulatively, given how long the process of change will take, it is extreme. That is no reason not to keep trying.

> *However deficient in many ways the United Nations may be, I think it's an absolutely essential organization. There is no way in which this effort cannot be made—it has to be made—knowing perfectly well that you're pushing an enormous boulder up a very steep hill. There will be slips and it will come back on you from time to time, but you have to go on pushing. Because if you don't do that, you simply give in to the notion that you're going to go into a global war again at some point, this time with nuclear weapons.*
> —Brian Urquhart

If we should succeed over the next few generations in transforming the world of independent states in which we live into some sort of genuine international community, however quarrelsome, discontented, and full of injustice it probably will be, then we shall effectively have abolished the ancient institution of warfare as well—and teachers of the twenty-fifth century will bore students with tedious explanations of how the Era of the Sovereign State was inevitably accompanied by ten thousand years of war. The students will pay little attention, being caught up in whatever crises trouble civilization in their own time. If we should fail, however, there probably will be no teachers, no students, and no civilization.

Some generation of mankind was eventually bound to face the task of abolishing war, because civilization was bound to endow us sooner or later with the power to destroy ourselves. We happen to be that generation, though we did not ask for the honor and do not feel ready for it. There is nobody wiser who will take the responsibility and solve this problem for us. We have to do it ourselves.

NOTES

1. Carl Sagan, "Nuclear War and Climatic Catastrophe: Some Policy Implications," *Foreign Affairs*, Winter 1983–84, p. 275.

2. Dwight MacDonald, *Politics*, August 1945.

3. Sagan, op. cit., pp. 275–84.

Intelligent lemmings? German soldiers get a send-off from a delighted populace as they head for the last of the popular wars; Berlin, 1914. *Ullstein Bilderdienst*

The League of Nations and the U.N. were born of the states' fear of pushing one another into a single mass grave. The remains of Stalingrad in 1943, when, in World War II, about one million people were dying every month. *SOVIET LIFE from SOVFOTO*

The most basic change necessary to our collective survival is underway: the last redefinition of humanity—gradually extending from family to tribe to nation to the human
race. A wounded Canadian lights his wounded German enemy's cigarette in the mud
of Passchendaele, November 1917. *Public Archives of Canada (PA 3683)*

In every context except politics—
from commerce, technology and
the mass media to styles of ideology, music and marriage—the outlines of a single global culture are
taking shape. A small Russian enjoys a Moscow park in her Mickey
Mouse sweatshirt. *AP/WIDE
WORLD PHOTOS*

Good-bye war. Probably worth a try. *Courtesy the Imperial War Museum (Q 30505)*

Index

in Latin America, 166–67
in World War II, 162
rural, 162–64, 166, 167
urban, 166–67
Guevara, Ché, 166
Guicciardini, Luigi, 35
Gunpowder. *See also* Firearms
development of, 54
Gustavus Adolphus, King, 61–62

Hackett, Gen. Sir John, 140
Haig, Gen. Sir Douglas, 86
Hamburg, bombardment of, 93–94
Hammarskjold, Dag, 256
Harris, Gen. Sir Arthur, 92
Helsinki Final Agreement, 182
Hill, Gen. A. P., 77
Hiroshima, bombardment of, 96–97
Holloway, Gen. Bruce, 236–37
"Home front", 83–85
attack of, 84–85
Homer, 31
Hoplites, 36–37. *See also* Infantry
Horses, 23, 47–48
Hundred Years' War, 49–50
Huntington, Samuel, 146–47

Iliad (Homer), 25
Indians, warfare and, 9–10
Infantry, 38
firearms and, 55–56
revival of, 49–50
shift away from, 48–49
Iron Cross, Order of the, 71
Israel, 168–70
Egypt and, 169
1973 war and, 192
Issus, battle of, 38

Jackson, Stonewall, 77
Japan, bombardment of, 94–95
firearms and, 56–58
Jericho, 15–16
Jones, James, 141, 142

Kadesh, 23–24, 25
Kahn, Herman, 212, 230
Kaufmann, William, 224–25, 229, 230, 246
Kennan, George, 209–10
Kennedy administration, 213
Kennedy, John, 200, 226
Berlin crisis and, 228–29
Khe Sanh, siege of, 165
Khrushchev, Nikita, 200
Cuban missile crisis and, 229
Killing

basic training and, 125–28
during combat, 118–20
Kissinger, Henry, 231
Korea, invasion of, 57
Korean War, 166, 209, 210
use of nuclear weapons during, 181
Kriegsakademie, 148
Kursk, 90

Lagash, 20–21
Landships. *See* Tanks
Latter, Richard, 235
League of Nations, 254
LeMay, Gen. Curtis, 94, 211
Lepanto, 42
Limited Nuclear Test Ban Treaty, 235
Limited nuclear war, 211–12
London, air raids on, 84–85
Lord Cherwell, 91–92
Lord Takeda Shingen, 56–57
Louis XIV, 64
Lugalzagesi, King, 21

MacArthur, Gen. Douglas, 97
MAD. *See* Assured Destruction
Magdeburg, sack of, 60
Managerial approach, toward combat, 138–40
Manchester, William, 101–102
Manhattan Project, 95–96
Mantinea, battle of, 36
Marathon, battle of, 37
Marighella, Carlos, 167
Marlborough, 66
Marshall, Andrew, 244
Marshall, Col. S. L. A., 118–19, 120, 145, 146
Massive retaliation, 181, 189, 195, 210–11, 212, 234
flexible response and, 183
Mathy, Capt. Heinrich, 84
McNamara, Robert, 182, 214, 224–25, 226–27, 228, 231, 235–36
Megiddo, battle of, 22–24, 25–27
Mercenaries, 56
Mesopotamia, 20–22
"Metal-eaters' alliance", 219
Military. *See also* Armed forces, specific branches under
country
forces, conventional, 190
mind, 5, 146–47, 152
Military-industrial complex, 216–17
defense analysts (civilian) and, 218–20
Minimum deterrence, 210, 211, 213–14
Minuteman I missiles, 235–36

MIRV. *See* Multiple Independently Targetable Reentry Vehicles (MIRV)

Mobilization, 150

Mongols, 46, 47

Multiple Independently Targetable Reentry Vehicles (MIRV), 235–36, 239

Mumford, Lewis, 11

Mutual Assured Destruction. *See* Assured Destruction

MX missile, 236–37, 239–40, 241–43

Nagashino, battle of, 57

Napoleon, 69–71
   invasion of Russia and, 70–71

Napoleonic wars, 70–72

National Security Decision Memorandum 242, 237

NATO. *See* North Atlantic Treaty Organization (NATO)

Naupactus, battle of, 40–41

"Navalization" of combat, 136–40

Navies
   evolution of, 39–42
   fighting environment of, 137

Nerve gas, conventional war and, 194

Nicaragua, 158, 161

Nitze, Paul, 228

Nixon, Richard, 210, 237, 246

Nomads, 49
   history of, 45–47
   horses and, 47–48

North Atlantic Treaty Organization (NATO), 209
   Airland Battle 2000 and, 187–88
   flexible response and, 183
   Follow-On Forces Attack (FOFA) and, 187–88
   forward defense and, 185, 186–87
   use of nuclear weapons by, 185, 196
   war in Europe and, 182–90
   West Germany and, 185–86
   Wintex '83 and, 196

Nuclear parity, 182

Nuclear war
   attitudes toward, 247
   effects of, 201–204
   escalation from conventional war, 195
   limited, theory of, 211–12

Nuclear weapons, 171. *See also* Atomic bomb
   China and, 214
   France and, 214
   institutional factors and, 215–16
   Soviet Union and, 206–207
   stockpiles of, 205
   strategies for the use of, 209–14

United Kingdom and, 214
United States and, 206–07
use by NATO, 185, 196
use during Korean War, 181

Nuclear winter, 201–204

Oda Nobunaga, 57

Officers. *See also* Soldiers
   casualties during World War I, 141
   casualties during World War II, 141
   handling fear of soldiers, 142, 145–46
   military mind and, 146–47, 152
   officer/man distinction, 132
   "profession" of, 147–52
   self-respect and, 138

On War (von Clausewitz), 148

Ooley, Maj. Robert, 135

Ostrogoths, 44

Pakistan, 171

Parris Island, 109–11

Pastoral peoples. *See* Nomads

Peace movements, 261–62

Perry, William, 241

Pharaoh Narmer, 15

Pharaoh Tuthmose III, 23

Piegan Indians, warfare and, 9

Poison gas, use during World War II, 181

Polaris missile, 213

Pomerania, 67

Presidential Decision 59, 243–44

primitive societies, attitudes toward war, 6–11

Protestant Reformation, 59

Prussian army, 62
   conscription and, 71, 76
   general staff and, 148–49

Punic War
   Second, 38–39, 43
   Third, 31–32, 43

RAND. *See* Research and Development Corporation (RAND)

Reagan administration, 244

Red Team, 242

Religious wars, 59–60

Research and Development Corporation (RAND), 211–12, 213
   Strategic Objectives Committee and, 211–12

Roman army, 38–39, 44

Rome
   Carthage and, 42–44
   naval battles and, 41–42
   sacks of, 34–35, 45

Rosewarne, Pilot Officer V. A., 262

attitudes toward nuclear war, 247
Department of Defense, 213
Marine Corps, 108–22, 123–24, 125–28
military operations and, 160
Navy, 213–14, 243
nuclear weapons and, 206–207
USSR. *See* Soviet Union

Varus, 45
Vietnam War, 163–66
    collapse of morale during, 142
Virgil, 31
Visigoths, 34, 44
Vitelli, Gian Paolo, 58
Von Clausewitz, Karl, 75–76, 148, 149–50

Walbiri aborigines, 6
Warfare. *See* Combat
Warrior ethic, 14–15
Weapons, increase in cost of, 191–92
Weinberger, Caspar, 244
Welch, Gen. Jasper, 237, 243
Wellington, 64
West German army, 187–88
West Germany, NATO's war plans and,
    185–86
Westphalia, Treaty of, 60
White, Gen. Tommy, 224–25
Wintex '83, 196
Wohlstetter, Albert, 211, 212

Women
    as soldiers, 122–25
    attitudes toward in U.S. Marine Corps,
        123–24
World Health Organization, 202
World War I, 80–87, 160
    continuous front and, 80, 81–83
    economic warfare and, 83
    effects of, 86–87
    "home front" and, 83–85
    officer casualties during, 141
    use of tanks during, 87–88
World War II, 3, 160, 254
    aircraft production during, 191
    casualties during, 143–44
    civilian casualties during, 90
    consumption of resources during, 89
    fear during, 141–42
    guerrilla warfare in, 162
    killing during, 119–20
    mental breakdown of soldiers during,
        144
    officer casualties during, 141
    use of poison gas during, 181
    use of tanks during, 88–89
Wright, Quincy, 10

Ypres, Third Battle of, 82, 88

Zama, battle of, 38–39
Zuckerman, Sir Solly, 227